Risk, Governance and Society

Volume 18

More information about this series at http://www.springer.com/series/6643

Daniel P. Aldrich • Sothea Oum
Yasuyuki Sawada
Editors

Resilience and Recovery in Asian Disasters

Community Ties, Market Mechanisms, and Governance

Springer

Editors
Daniel P. Aldrich
Department of Political Science
Purdue University
West Lafayette, IN, USA

Sothea Oum
Economic Research Institute
for ASEAN and East Asia
Jakarta Pusat, Indonesia

Yasuyuki Sawada
Faculty of Economics
University of Tokyo
Bunkyo-ku, Tokyo, Japan

ISBN 978-4-431-55021-1 ISBN 978-4-431-55022-8 (eBook)
DOI 10.1007/978-4-431-55022-8
Springer Tokyo Heidelberg New York Dordrecht London

Library of Congress Control Number: 2014946349

Printed on acid-free paper

Springer is part of Springer Science+Business Media (www.springer.com)

Foreword

This book grew out of ERIA's research project entitled "Economic and Welfare Impacts of Disasters in East Asia and Policy Responses" in FY 2011–2012. We hope that it will improve the understanding of the impacts of disasters on production, demands, regional development, and welfare captured by income, poverty and health outcomes. It does so through in-depth analyses involving qualitative and quantitative methods at the community, regional, national, and international levels. The contents of all the chapters of this book were presented in two regional workshops held in Jakarta, Indonesia, and Bangkok, Thailand, in 2011 and 2012.

The book sets up a new, holistic framework for disaster recovery and mitigation, providing a multidisciplinary perspective on the field of risk management strategies and societal and communal resilience. This edited volume draws on the work of experts from around Asia to provide insights into disaster mitigation and response. Going beyond narrow approaches all too prevalent in the field, this book builds on an optimum combination of community-level networks, private market mechanisms, and state-based assistance strategies in handling disasters. Chapters show best practices in the field and illuminate cutting-edge research on recovery, highlighting the interaction between government, industry, and civil society. The book uses new data from a number of recent disasters across southeast and east Asia to understand the interaction between residents, the state, and catastrophe, drawing on events in Malaysia, Vietnam, Cambodia, Japan, China, and Thailand. Grounded in theories of risk mitigation and empirical research, the book provides practical guidance for decision makers along with future research directions for scholars.

This book and the project could not have been completed without the contribution from many individuals. First, ERIA would like to express deep appreciation and gratitude, first and foremost, to the members of the research project in FY 2011–2012 who have actively participated in the workshops and have made a scholarly contribution to the completion of the research project. Most of their papers appear in this book. Second, ERIA is indebted to Professor Fukunari Kimura, Chief Economist of ERIA, for his encouragement and support for the research project. Our thanks also go to the esteemed support staff of ERIA, especially Yunita Nababan and Fadriani Trianingsih, for their invaluable logistic assistance to ensure the successful completion of the project and for their excellent efforts in the preparation of the book manuscript.

Last but not least, ERIA would like to express our profound gratitude to Professor Yasuyuki Sawada for his intellectual leadership of the research project and to Professor Daniel P. Aldrich and Dr. Sothea Oum for their joint commitment and excellent editorial work, and to Springer Japan for the publication of the book.

Finally, ERIA is hopeful that this book will contribute to a better understanding of the disaster risks, their impacts on welfare, agriculture, food security, production networks, regional economies, and the role of community ties, market mechanisms, and governance in mitigating the risks in many East Asian economies and beyond.

Executive Director of ERIA Hidetoshi Nishimura
April 2014

Acknowledgments

Given recent disasters in East and Southeast Asia, including Typhoon Haiyan in the Philippines, we feel all the more strongly that research on disaster recovery in Asia remains a critical priority for residents, scholars, and decision makers alike. Our hope is that this book provides to all of these groups knowledge that can be acted upon.

We are indebted to the many respondents across the region who took their time to fill out surveys, respond to questions, speak with us in the field, and help us understand their experiences. Our book project could not have been completed without their help.

We gratefully acknowledge ERIA for its academic and financial support of our research. Specifically, thank you to ERIA Executive Director Hidetoshi Nishimura, Chief Economist Prof. Fukunari Kimura, and Senior Research Adviser to the Executive Director, Prof. Shujiro Urata. We thank the Risk, Governance, and Society Series editors Ortwin Renn and Jeryl Mumpower, and especially Professor Norio Okada of Kyoto University for his close reading of the entire manuscript and many suggestions for improving it.

Finally, we would like to thank our colleagues and students at Purdue University, Tokyo University, and the ERIA for their many constructive comments and support. Although Professor Yujiro Hayami is no longer with us, we were inspired by his thoughtful work which combined community, market, and governance mechanisms into a single theoretical framework. His lifetime of research pushed us to think more thoughtfully about these issues.

About the Editors

Daniel P. Aldrich is an associate professor and university scholar in the Department of Political Science at Purdue University. Aldrich was a Fulbright research fellow at the University of Tokyo's Economics Department for the academic year 2012–2013 and an American Association for the Advancement of Science fellow at USAID from 2011 to 2012. He has been a visiting Abe scholar at the University of Tokyo's Law Faculty in Japan, an advanced research fellow at Harvard University's Program on US–Japan Relations, a visiting researcher at Centre Américain, Sciences Po in Paris, France, and a visiting professor at the Tata Institute for Disaster Management in Mumbai, India. He is a board member of the journals *Asian Politics and Policy* and *Risk, Hazards and Crisis in Public Policy,* and is a Mansfield U.S. Japan Network for the Future alumnus. He is the section organizer for the American Political Science Association's Disasters and Crises Related Group. Aldrich received his Ph.D. and M.A. in political science from Harvard University, an M.A. from the University of California at Berkeley, and his B.A. from the University of North Carolina at Chapel Hill.

Sothea Oum is an economist at the Economic Research Institute for ASEAN and East Asia (ERIA) Jakarta, Indonesia. He joined ERIA in 2009 as an associate researcher after completing his Ph.D. in economics, specialized in computable general equilibrium (CGE) modeling, from Monash University, Australia, on full scholarships. At ERIA, he manages region-wide research projects on ASEAN and East Asian integration and community building process, small and medium enterprises (SMEs), social protection, disaster management, income distribution, and poverty. He also holds an M.A. in economics from Kobe University, Japan, and a B.A. from the National Economics University, Hanoi, Viet Nam, both on full scholarships from the governments of Japan and Vietnam, respectively.

Yasuyuki Sawada is a professor in the Faculty of Economics at the University of Tokyo. He also has been a visiting researcher of the JICA Research Institute of Japan International Cooperation Agency (JICA); faculty fellow of the Research Institute of Economy, Trade, and Industry (RIETI); and visiting fellow at the Asian Development Bank Institute (ADBI). He was a visiting professor at Stanford University in 2012 and a visiting fellow at the Bangladesh Institute of Development

Studies (2012–2013) and BRAC (2011–2012). His research interests include econometric investigations of individual, household, and firm behaviors under risks using micro-data from developing and developed countries such as China, India, Pakistan, the Philippines, Sri Lanka, Vietnam, and Japan. Sawada completed his M.A. in food research and a Ph.D. in economics from Stanford University in 1996 and 1999, respectively, and a B.A. from Keio University, Japan. He is also a recipient of the 2013 Nikkei Book Award; the 2011 Ishikawa Prize of the Japanese Economic Association; the 2010 Kiyoshi Kojima Prize of the Japanese International Economic Association; the 2009 Enjoji Jiro Prize; and the Masayoshi Ohira Memorial Prize. He is a co-editor of *The Japanese Economic Review*.

Contents

Contributors

Daniel P. Aldrich Purdue University, West Lafayette, IN, USA

Mitsuyo Ando Faculty of Business and Commerce, Keio University, Tokyo, Japan

Roehlano M. Briones Senior Research Fellow, Philippine Institute for Development Studies (PIDS), Manila, Philippines

Ngai Weng Chan Universiti Sains Malaysia, Pulau Pinang, Malaysia

Sommarat Chantarat Crawford School of Public Policy, The Australian National University, Canberra, Australia

Colas Chervier Senior Researcher, Council for Agricultural and Rural Development, Social Protection Coordination Unit, (CARD-SPCU), Phnom Penh, Cambodia

Ikumo Isono Institute of Developing Economies, Chiba, Japan

Danilo C. Israel Senior Research Fellow, Philippine Institute for Development Studies (PIDS), Manila, Philippines

Ju-Liang Jin Hefei University of Technology, Hefei, China

Ponhrith Kan Social Research Junior Assistant, Council for Agricultural and Rural Development, Social Protection Coordination Unit (CARD-SPCU), Phnom Penh, Cambodia

Satoru Kumagai Research Fellow Sent Abroad (Kuala Lumpur), Economic Integration Studies Group, Inter-disciplinary Studies Center, IDE-JETRO

Allen Yu-Hung Lai The Institute of Health Economics and Management, ESSEC Business School – Asia Pacific, Singapore, Singapore

Brent Layton Chairperson, The Electricity Authority, Wellington, New Zealand

Pitsom Meethom Thailand Development Research Institute, Bangkok, Thailand

Hiroyuki Nakata The University of Tokyo, Tokyo, Japan

Hidetoshi Nishimura Executive Director, Economic Research Institute for ASEAN and East Asia (ERIA), Jakarta, Indonesia

Ilan Noy Victoria University of Wellington, Wellington, New Zealand

Sothea Oum Economic Research Institute for ASEAN and East Asia, Jakarta, Indonesia

Krirk Pannangpetch Faculty of Agriculture, Khon Kaen University, Khon Kaen, Thailand

Kamphol Pantakua Thailand Development Research Institute, Bangkok, Thailand

Nipon Poaponsakorn Thailand Development Research Institute, Bangkok, Thailand

Nattapong Puttanapong Faculty of Economics, Thammasat University, Bangkok, Thailand

Preesan Rakwatin Geo-Informatics and Space Technology Development Agency, Ministry of Science and Technology, Bangkok, Thailand

Yasuyuki Sawada Faculty of Economics, University of Tokyo, Tokyo, Japan

Seck L. Tan Centre on Asia and Gloablization, Lee Kuan Yew School of Public Policy, National University of Singapore, Singapore, Singapore

Thanasin Tanompongphandh Faculty of Economics, Kasetsart University, Bangkok, Thailand

Le Dang Trung Executive Director, Real-Time Analytics, Ho Chi Minh, Vietnam

Sann Vathana Deputy Secretary General, Council of Ministers, Council for Agricultural and Rural Development, Social Protection Coordination Unit (CARD-SPCU), Phnom Penh, Cambodia

Qiong Wang National University of Singapore, Singapore, Singapore

Yi-Ming Wei Center for Energy and Environmental Policy Research, Beijing Institute of Technology, Beijing, China

Chapter 1
Community, Market, and Government Responses to Disaster

Daniel P. Aldrich, Yasuyuki Sawada, and Sothea Oum

1 Background

Natural disasters, whether in advanced or developing nations, regularly take lives, ruin livelihoods, force large-scale evacuations, and disrupt manufacturing chains. A series of recent disasters, including the 2013 Typhoon Haiyan (Yolanda) in the Philippines, the 3/11 compounded disasters in Tohoku, Japan in 2011, the 2008 Sichuan earthquake in China, and the massive floods in Thailand in 2011 underscored the high impact of catastrophes on people and economic development. Data from a variety of organizations indicate that the number of disasters and the amount of damage caused have both been increasing in recent years. No government policy or set of programs can prevent the occurrence of natural hazards, whether earthquakes, tsunami, or typhoons. However, higher levels of disaster preparation, investment in engineering and infrastructure resilience, and deeper community awareness can at least partially mitigate damage arising from disasters in terms of the number of casualties and economic impacts.

In East and Southeast Asia, leaders have noted and reiterated the need to enhance disaster management cooperation for the region at a number of recent high-level forums. For example, regional leaders participating in the special ASEAN-Japan Ministerial Meeting in April 2011 emphasized the need to strengthen such cooperation through sharing of exercises and lessons-learned as well as conducting

D.P. Aldrich (✉)
Purdue University, West Lafayette, IN, USA
e-mail: daniel.aldrich@gmail.com

Y. Sawada
Faculty of Economics, University of Tokyo, Tokyo, Japan
e-mail: sawada@e.u-tokyo.ac.jp

S. Oum
Economic Research Institute for ASEAN and East Asia, Jakarta, Indonesia
e-mail: sothea.oum@eria.org

D.P. Aldrich et al. (eds.), *Resilience and Recovery in Asian Disasters*, Risk, Governance and Society 18, DOI 10.1007/978-4-431-55022-8_1

training and capacity building programs for disaster preparedness, emergency response, relief, and reconstruction efforts. The Chair's statement at the 18th ASEAN Summit held in Jakarta, Indonesia in May 2011 noted the potential transboundary impact of accidents at nuclear plants in the aftermath of the Fukushima incident. Also, a series of East Asia Summit (EAS) meetings focused on enhancing disaster management beginning with the 4th EAS in Cha-am Hua Hin, Thailand in 2009 through the eighth EAS in Brunei in October 2013. In the chairman's statement of the 8th EAS, it has been reported that the leaders of participating countries exchanged views on regional and international issues such as disaster management as well as food and energy security and climate change. At such meetings, researchers also emphasized that the differentiated type of disaster or external shock—for example, the nuclear power plant meltdowns at Fukushima Dai-ichi or the flooding in Bangkok—should drive specialized responses from government and civil society.

In general, disasters can be classified into four major groups (Sawada 2007). Natural disasters comprise the first category which includes hydrological disasters (floods), meteorological disasters (storms or typhoons), climatological disasters (droughts), geophysical disasters (earthquakes, tsunamis and volcanic eruptions), and biological disasters (epidemics and insect infestations). The second type of disaster revolves around technological disasters, i.e., industrial accidents (chemical and oil spills, nuclear power plant meltdowns, industrial infrastructure collapse) and transport accidents (by air, rail, road or water transport). The final two disaster types involve manmade disasters which include economic crises (hyperinflation, banking crisis, and currency crisis) and violence-related disasters (terrorism, civil strife, riots, and civil and external wars).

The Center for Research on the Epidemiology of Disasters (CRED) in Belgium, collects and organizes detailed, long-term time series data on natural and technological disasters per country. Professors C. Reinhart of the University of Maryland and K. Rogoff of Harvard University similarly constructed cross-country panel data on economic crises and disasters resulting from the violence of war. Figure 1.1 brings these streams of data together to show the average occurrence of the four types of disaster per country per year. While natural and technological disasters have been rapidly increasing, financial crises and war have maintained stable patterns over time. These long-term trends indicate the importance of community, market, and government-based preparations and responses in reducing the damage arising from disasters.

Decision makers in Asia have recognized the vulnerability of the region to these shocks, especially due to natural disasters. According to the World Disasters Report (International Federation of Red Cross and Red Crescent Societies (2010)), Asia remains most the natural disaster prone continent as Table 1.1 displays below. On average between 2001 and 2010, Asia experienced more than 150 disasters per year (40 % of the world total), with more than 200 million people in the area (88 % of the total) affected every year, and more than US$ 41 billion in annual damage (38 %). Yet the availability of formal insurance mechanisms varies significantly even across developed countries in the region, not to mention in developing nations.

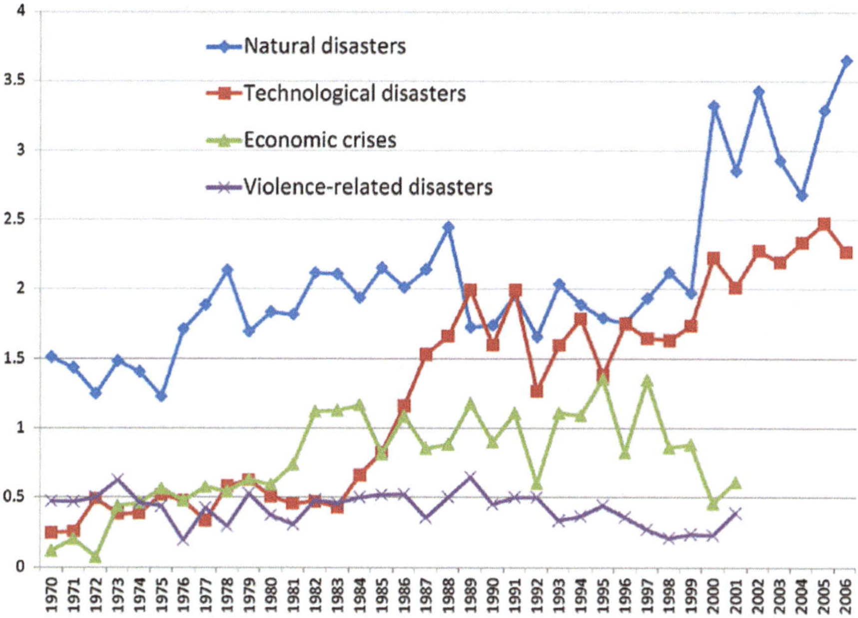

Fig. 1.1 Frequency of four types of major disasters in the world (Average per country). *Note*: Data from CRED (natural disaster and technological disaster) and Reinhart-Rogoff databases (economic crisis and war)

Table 1.1 Distribution of disasters by continent, number of disasters, number of victims, and damage (Annual average figures between 2001 and 2010)

Continent	Number of natural disasters	Number of victims (in millions)	Estimated damage (in billion USD)
Africa	65	14.91	1.1
Americas	92	8.27	50.27
Asia	153	207.92	41.61
Europe	58	0.74	13.4
Oceania	16	0.12	2.97
Total	384	231.95	109.35

Source: Guha-Sapir, Hoyois, and Below (2013)

For example, the Japanese Cabinet Office (2011) reported that the total property losses from the Tohoku compounded disaster in March 2011 could amount to more than US$250 billion. According to the private re-insurer Munich Re (2012)[1] and World Bank (2012),[2] private insurance covered only US$ 40 billion (16–20 %) of

[1] http://www.munichre.com/en/media_relations/press_releases/2012/2012_01_04_press_release.aspx.

[2] http://wbi.worldbank.org/wbi/Data/wbi/wbicms/files/drupal-acquia/wbi/drm_kn6-2.pdf.

the overall damage from the tsunami, earthquake, and nuclear meltdowns. In the case of the Great Hanshin-Awaji Earthquake of Japan in January 1995, the formal insurance coverage rate was even lower (Sawada and Shimizutani 2008). These figures can be compared with about US$13 billion of the US$16 billion in total property losses covered by private insurance in the case of the February 2011 earthquake in Christchurch, New Zealand.

Obviously, disasters pose threats to both short and long term development in an affected region by disrupting production and flows of goods and services, worsening the balance of payments and government budgets, and derailing programs and activities focused on economic growth, income distribution, and poverty reduction. Disasters also impose negative effects on social structures and the environment.

In response to the "wicked problem" of disasters and catastrophes, this book uses new data and a broad set of theoretical approaches to illuminate multi-level disaster mitigation and recovery tactics in East Asia. Importantly, this volume looks to a variety of types of disasters in the region along with and pre- and post-disaster mitigation and response mechanisms to lay out political, social, and economic policy implications for research. It forwards a number of policy recommendations for reforms at the national level and explores the prospects for a regional cooperation framework. We hope that results from the study provide policy approaches which improve the effectiveness of market and non-market disaster management systems within each country studied and assist in forging a framework for collaboration and joint research across Asia.

2 Community, Market, and Government

In preparation for or the aftermath of a disaster, a variety of market and non-market mechanisms are indispensable for people to maintain their livelihood. To illustrate such mechanisms, we have structured this book into three sections based on community, market, and government levels of research, extending a framework of community, market, and state in the economic system of Hayami (2009) as seen below in Fig. 1.2.

The first part of this volume focuses on local community and family level responses and policy programs while the second section looks at the market-based mechanisms focusing on production networks, urban management, and market insurance mechanisms. The third portion involves five chapters that investigate government-level disaster management, such as agricultural development, food securities, and environmental sustainability. While our framework implies divided risk management and coping strategies based on different market and non-market mechanisms, the roles for markets, the government, and community in disaster mitigation and response often overlap. The framework is also corroborated by the risk governance concept of International Risk Governance Council (IRGC) in which the governance of global, systemic risks requires cohesion

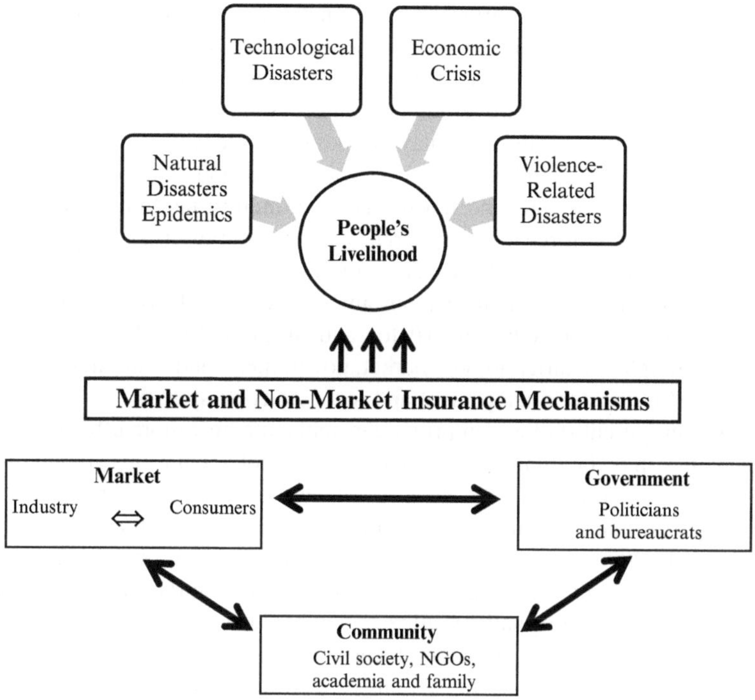

Fig. 1.2 Risk governance in the system of community, market, and government. *Source*: Authors' figure based on Hayami (2009)

between countries and the inclusion within the process of government, industry, academia and civil society.[3]

The market serves as the mechanism that coordinates profit-seeking individuals and firms through competition using price signals. Naturally, the market has an advantage in matching the demand and supply of private tradable goods. Potentially, risks can be traded in credit and insurance markets, but it is often difficult to trade risks of disasters which are characterized by rare and unforeseen events. Hence, insurance market mechanisms are incomplete at best in trading disaster risks. This is a typical case of market failure. When markets fail, the government works as the institution that forces people to adjust their resource allocations by regulation or fiat so that resource misallocation due to market failure can be corrected. Typically, the government plays an important role in supplying global or pure public goods that private forms may be reluctant to provide. A public insurance mechanism for disasters is an example of such public goods. Disaster risks can be diversified away through governmental tax and expenditure mechanisms as well as other intertemporal resource smoothing mechanisms through the government's budget. In sum, market and government mechanisms play mutually

[3] http://www.irgc.org/risk-governance/what-is-risk-governance/.

complementary roles when markets are not functioning well against disasters. Yet, the government may also fail due to misbehavior of selfish politicians and bureaucrats who maximize their own benefits. To fill the gap in resource misallocation arising from the market and government failures, community enforcement mechanisms based on social capital also play an indispensable role. A local community guides residents and members to work voluntarily and collectively based on historical social interactions and norms. The community facilitates the supply of local public goods, enforces informal transactions, and preserves reciprocal social safety nets.[4] In the aftermath of a disaster, community's mutual insurance as well as family's self-insurance mechanisms can amend the lack of effective market and government insurance mechanisms (Paton and McClure 2013; Paton et al. 2013). Hence, the complementarity among market, government, and community is the key for a successful disaster management and reconstruction system.

Previous empirical studies can provide insights into how more effective disaster management can be facilitated by strengthening complementarities among markets functioning using price signals, government enforcement mechanisms, and the community informal insurance mechanisms. In a study of the Chuetsu Earthquake, Ichimura et al. (2006) found that both earthquake insurance and public transfers had functioned quite well. According to Kahn (2005), natural disasters occur in advanced and developing nations alike, but when a nation is democratized and has better governance, the number of casualties is drastically reduced. This is because more democratic and transparently governed nations better communicate and share disaster risk information, develop early warning systems and infrastructure and undertake other risk management mechanisms to prevent or mitigate the impact of disasters. Because the global insurance market for natural disasters is far from complete, the government plays an important role in disaster management and rehabilitation. Also, a report by the World Bank and United Nations (2010) describes how Bangladesh, where frequent cyclones have affected several 100,000 people, has significantly reduced the number of casualties. It has done so by investing in emergency infrastructure such as improving its early warning system, which operates via radio, and building numerous cyclone shelters.

Having noted the importance of the government in complementing the lack of effective market-based mechanisms for disaster risks, Yang (2008) used data on the world's storms of the past 30-plus years to show that their economic damage has been enormous, finding that for poorer countries, hurricanes stimulated to significant increases in migrants' remittances, filling about four-fifths of estimated damages. This suggests the importance of community- or family-based informal insurance network against disasters. His research also informs us that we should balance emergency information systems and infrastructure that prevent injury to people with community- and market-based insurance systems that prevent economic damage, so as to prepare ourselves for natural disasters. The contributors to

[4] In doing so it can conserve, for example, common land along with other common pool resources such as local irrigation facilities (cf. Ostrom 1990).

this volume build on the qualitative and quantitative research done in the past to provide cutting edge assessments of disaster reduction and preparation in Asia.

3 Overview of the Book

Our edited volume begins with a recognition of the power of community and family ties. Residents of communities are the actors who face risks and hazards associated with disasters and pre-existing social cohesion and networks may assist them in mitigating the effects of these events. Such social infrastructure allows individuals to share resources and information, work as a group to overcome collective action problems, and also mitigate exit during crisis.

3.1 Family and Community Ties

In Chap. 2 Daniel Aldrich investigates the new mechanisms through which social capital and networks assist with disaster recovery, departing from traditional approaches which have focused primarily on factors external to disaster-affected communities. These new mechanisms include the choice between "exit" and "voice" in the sense of Hirschman (1970), elimination of barriers to collective action; and provisions of informal insurance and mutual aid. Through examples such as the 1923 Tokyo earthquake, the 1995 Kobe earthquake, the 2004 Indian Ocean tsunami, and the 2011 compound disaster in Tohoku, Japan, Aldrich seeks to underscore a potentially efficient and cost effective response to crises.

Aldrich suggests a new paradigm for thinking about disaster recovery and for designing emergency management responses. Moving beyond "bricks and mortar" approaches to recovery, his chapter stresses that the ties between residents may serve as a critical engine during what may be a long and difficult recovery process. Rather than merely responding to disasters as they occur in the future, visionary decision makers in these and other countries should move to embrace a social-capital based approach to policy making. Bringing residents to the forefront and increasing community involvement in planning will ensure a strong future for these important countries.

Sann Vathana, Sothea Oum, and Ponhrith Kan use Chap. 3 to focus on Cambodia, mapping the pattern of risks faced by the poor and vulnerable in rural areas where the consequences of natural disaster pose an increasing threat to their livelihoods. The damage caused by flood and drought is comparable, although the flood of 2011 was the most extensive of recent disasters. Chapter 3 presents the linking of social protection interventions to address the entitlement failure of poor and vulnerable people suffering from the negative impacts of flood and drought on welfare captured by household consumption.

Because the data analyses in this chapter show that ex post supports from the government or NGOs were ineffective, there is a strong need at the policy level to design social protection interventions to emphasize ex-ante instruments rather than the ex post response to natural disasters, focusing on emergency assistance and relief. Cash transfer programs provide direct assistance in the form of cash to the poor. Ex-ante cash transfer programs can play a crucial role in strengthening poor households' resilience by encouraging them to invest in business rather than spending on food. Microfinance schemes can also facilitate ex-ante income diversification that can bolster households against widespread natural disasters.

In Chap. 4, Le Dang Trung focuses on Vietnam which is located in one of the five cyclone centers on the planet and therefore is prone to many natural hazards. More than four storms and three floods hit Vietnam per year. Trung's chapter provides an evidence-based welfare assessment of natural disasters, and recommendations to policymakers, to help the country move toward effective disaster risk management. More specifically, the chapter examines the welfare impact of Typhoon Damrey which hit Vietnam in September 2004 using the propensity score matching method applied to micro-data from the Vietnam Household Living Standard Survey (VHLSS) 2006. Research finds that the storms greatly affect household welfare and livelihoods captured by rice production, household income, food expenditure, household expenditure and house repairs over the 12 months: While short-term aftermaths are tremendously high, the impact of natural disasters can also persist, bringing down living standards for some time.

Based on a review of existing studies, the chapter suggests an array of recommendations with the hope that they can make positive contributions to the policy-making process in Vietnam, enabling it to achieve its declared goals. The recommendations focus on measures and approaches relevant for national implementation of effective programs such as the National Target Program to Respond to Climate Change (NTP-RCC) as well as regional collaboration such as adaptation and mitigation framework for South Asia to cooperate in climate change and food security policies.

In Chap. 5, Nipon Poaponsakorn and Pitsom Meethom analyze the causes of Thailand's 2011 flood, its impact on agriculture and household expenditure and income, and the government's response. They find that highest recorded rainfall, including five tropical storms, unregulated land-use patterns, and flood mismanagement are the causes of the major flooding in Thailand in 2011. Using 2009 and 2011 Socio-Economic Survey data, the empirical results show that the flooding caused significant negative welfare impact, reducing total household expenditures by 5.7–14 %. These findings are consistent with the reported negative national GDP growth of 8.9 % in the fourth quarter of 2011. The study finds that the 2011 floods had a negative impact on the money and wage incomes of some middle income households in the flooded areas.

The chapter underscores several weaknesses in the current information for flood management. Despite the huge volume of information on the impact of flooding on output and damage to property, no government agency has paid attention to computerizing the flood data-base and information system and strengthening the capability of their information centers. As precautionary policy measures, important ideas need to be urgently implemented, notably construction of a digital elevation map, investment in satellite images, including updated land-use patterns, and the digitization of village boundaries. Moreover, the capability of statistical agencies and agencies responsible for flood management should be urgently strengthened in the following areas: data collection, data base development, data processing and reporting using IT, and human resource development. Secondly, these agencies should be encouraged to communicate and exchange information and ideas with other data users.

While residents, families, and communities face hazards first during disasters, other institutions can mitigate their risks and reduce their exposure. Markets connect consumers and households to insurance frameworks and share risks across societies. Individual firms and businesses may have their operations disrupted by disasters, but production networks can help mitigate such events and allow for the delivery of goods and services even following catastrophe. We also recognize that firms operating well beyond the direct effects of a disaster may have their ability to produce goods paralyzed by production network disruptions. Our book now turns to look at the role of markets and production networks during and after disaster.

3.2 Market and Production Networks

Mitsuyo Ando in Chap. 6 attempts to shed new light on domestic and international production networks in machinery industries, and examines how economic crises and natural disasters affected the networks, mainly from the viewpoint of Japan's exports. Ando finds that regardless of whether creating a demand or a supply shock, the economic or natural disasters revealed the stability and robustness of production networks in the machinery sectors. In order to respond to massive shocks, firms try to save costs by preserving existing transaction channels for parts and components. As a result, exports in machinery parts and components tend to be sustained and are likely to recover rapidly even if they are temporarily disrupted. These findings suggest that firms' production networks can function as an effective insurance mechanism in weathering negative consequences of natural and manmade disasters.

Even the behavior of firms involved in the production networks and suffering from the floods in Thailand also confirms the existence of strong "continuation" or "centripetal" forces, and the deployment of efforts to keep production networks in being, in consideration of the various transaction cost implications of discontinuing a network. Once production networks are moved away from the original locations, it is not easy to get them back. It is also important to deal with various concerns in the business environment, lest private firms utilize the crisis as a trigger for removing production blocks to other countries.

Brent Layton in Chap. 7 looks closely at the effect of the series of earthquakes which struck New Zealand between 2010 and 2012. While the economic impact of these disasters was possibly as high as $25 billion US, a number of institutions helped to mitigate the damage across the democratic, developed nation. However, Layton underscores that the insurance itself complicated the recovery process by creating large number of alternatives for individual business owners and home owners.

The availability of insurance—or the struggle to ensure that homeowners and building occupants feel fully compensated for their losses—has introduced an additional element of waiting into the recovery process in New Zealand. As a result of high mobility and government policies which have barred reconstruction in the worst affected areas of the downtown areas, businesses must make decisions in a period of high uncertainty. Layton concludes with policy recommendations to help reduce some of the challenges facing Christchurch in its rebuilding phase, including clearer guidelines for residents on which areas will be open in the future for rebuilding.

In Chap. 8, Ikumo Isono and Satoru Kumagai focus on the recent flooding in Thailand to underscore the ways that production networks respond to large scale crisis. Using spatial simulation based on economic modeling they seek to understand how flood-caused disruptions of manufacturing facilities and therefore the shipping of goods across countries can change GDP across the region. Interestingly, despite the severity of the flooding and widespread media coverage of the catastrophe, there are mixed results for provinces across Thailand because of the mobility of resident firms.

For some areas, such as Rayong and Chonburi, the authors predict in-migration due to firms relocating and therefore positive effects from the disaster. Moreover, across all of Thailand the overall effect of the flooding is predicted to be less than previously forecast. To ensure that actual results match these predictions, the authors urge a combination of government support for firms seeking to relocate to less flood-prone areas and the reduction of transactions costs for firms trading across boundaries.

Sommarat Chantarat and four co-authors explore, in Chap. 9, innovations in index-based risk transfer products (IBRTPs) in depth as means of addressing important insurance market imperfections. Such market failures have precluded the emergence and sustainability of formal insurance markets in developing countries, where uninsured natural disaster risk remains a leading impediment to economic development. The chapter provides an analytical framework for and empirical illustrations of the design of nationwide and scalable IBRTP contracts to analyze hedging effectiveness and welfare impacts at the micro level, and to explore cost-effective risk-financing options. Thai rice production is used in the analysis, with the goal of extending the methodology and its implications in enhancing the development of national and regional disaster risk management in Asia. Using household level data in estimating basis risk and so simulating contracts' hedging effectiveness, Chantarat et al. find that the optimal provincial contract, based on basis risk, minimizing the combination of moving dry spell and excessive rain spell indices, could result in up to a 25 % reduction in the variations of household income available for consumption. The return to scale in terms of cost effective portfolio pricing can be achieved as part of a nationwide, multi-seasonal coverage insurance program.

The transparency of these weather indices and control measures could in fact further promote the possibility of cost effective risk transfers in the international market. Numerical results on the potential impacts on household welfare, agricultural loan portfolios and government of this nationwide program under various market arrangements show that the purely market driven program was found to result in more than 50 % reductions in the probabilities of household consumption collapsing to zero, in means and variations of five-year accumulated debt and annual loan default rates. Properly layering insurable nationwide risk, they further found public financing of tailed risk beyond the 20–30 % capped to insurer's payout rates to result in substantial reduction in market premium rates. These in turn resulted in up to twice the impacts of the purely market-driven program, though with substantially smaller budget exposures for the government, relative to the current government program. There could thus be a strong case for public financing of tailed risk in enhancing development values and the market viability of Thailand's nationwide index insurance program.

In Chap. 10, Hiroyuki Nakata identifies the core issues for designing a possible regional insurance scheme or mechanism for East Asia. He seeks to develop a risk sharing mechanism for catastrophe risks to households in the region and provide a consistent explanation for apparent anomalies concerning the demand for catastrophe insurance within the subjective expected utility framework. The key finding is that the number of observations would inevitably be insufficient to warrant a robust probability estimate for a rare event. The inherent lack of such a robust probability estimate leads to diverse probability beliefs.

Nakata concludes that a desirable insurance scheme is the one such as an index-based insurance scheme which can eliminate the possible moral hazard issues inherent to indemnity insurance. Moreover, since voluntary subscriptions are likely to lead to insufficient levels of insurance, an insurance scheme with subscriptions by local governments, in conjunction with ex post payments/compensation to the affected households, would be more desirable. However, the underwriting costs for index insurance may well not be low, whether the index insurance will be supplied and priced by insurance suppliers or traded on the capital market.

Production networks and markets may amortize risks across networks of firms or concentrate them on businesses. However, empirical studies have shown that disaster-affected areas may have low subscription rates of insurance along with missing insurance market for some disaster events such as wildfires, radiation leaks, and terrorist attacks. These outcomes—along with others such as externalities, information asymmetry, monopolies, and increasing returns to scale - are known as market failures, and in such events government decision makers may intervene. The next section of our manuscript looks at the role of government policy and risk management during and after disasters.

3.3 Government Policy and Risk Management

Ilan Noy in discusses operational aspects in facilitating national and regional risk management capacities in Chap. 11. He first presents a typology of disaster impacts that distinguishes between direct and indirect damage. Noy discusses indirect costs in the aggregate by examining variables such as GDP, fiscal accounts, consumption, investment, and the balances of trade and payments, and distinguishes between the short- and long- run. He concludes by identifying necessary future policy changes, in particular the construction of better and more robust early-warning systems, and suggests that the best way to incentivize disaster risk reduction (DRR) policy is through a dedicated fund—a Global Fund for DRR—that will support this work.

Noy proposes that countries should be constantly evaluated for their DRR plans, and given "Seals of Approval." The evaluation process would allow a "grading" of DRR policy and the allocation of the contingent 'seal of approval' for these policies. The positive externality from such a fund, with its associated monitoring and evaluation functions, would enable countries who receive this DRR "seal of approval" to more easily insure themselves explicitly (with re-insurers) or implicitly by issuing Catastrophic Bonds (CAT bonds) and further enable multi-year insurance. All three developments (re-insurance, CAT bonds and multi-year insurance) will be made easier by having a "seal of approval", as that seal will alleviate investors/insurers concerns regarding the moral hazard generated by disaster-contingent financial support.

Ngai Chan reviews flood risk management in Malaysia in Chap. 12. While Malaysia lies in a geographically stable region and is relatively free from natural disasters, it is affected by flooding, landslides, haze and other man-made disasters. Annually, flood disasters account for significant losses, both tangible and intangible. He finds that disaster management in Malaysia is traditionally almost entirely based on a government-centric top-down approach. The National Security Council (NSC), under the Prime Minister's Office, is responsible for policies, and the National Disaster Management and Relief Committee (NDMRC) is responsible for coordinating all relief operations before, during and after a disaster. In terms of floods, the NDMRC would take the form of the National Flood Disaster Relief and Preparedness Committee (NFDRPC). The NFDRPC is activated via a National Flood Disaster Management Mechanism (NFDMM). The NFDMM is largely targeted towards handling monsoon flooding. Consequently, this mechanism is less than effective and should be re-modeled into something more pro-active.

At the operational level of flood management, the Drainage and Irrigation Department (DID) is the responsible agency. However, being an engineering-based organization, the DID's approach is largely focused on structural measures in controlling floods. It needs to embrace a more holistic approach towards flood management via a multi-disciplinary effort. Non-structural measures are easy to implement, less expensive and community-friendly, and need to be employed more widely. There is also a need for greater stakeholder participation, especially from NGOs, at all levels in the disaster cycle. Capacity building for NGOs, local communities and disaster victims is also necessary. The disaster management mechanism should also adopt more non-structural measures, bring in state-of-the-art technology and cooperate internationally with other countries for addressing trans-boundary disasters.

In Chap. 13, Danilo Israel and Roehlano Briones analyze the impacts of natural disasters (particularly typhoons, floods and droughts) on agriculture, food security and natural resources and the environment in the Philippines. In general, they found that typhoons, floods and droughts have an insignificant impact on overall agricultural production at the national level, yet typhoons may have a significant negative impact on paddy rice production at the provincial level. The chapter shows how typhoons such as Ondoy and Pepeng in 2009 have a significant negative impact on the food security of households in the affected areas and that households have varying consumption and non-consumption strategies to cope with the impacts of typhoons. Finally their research illuminates that the different impacts of typhoons, floods and droughts on the natural resources and environment have not been quantitatively assessed in detail, although available evidence suggests that these are also substantial.

Based on their results and findings, they recommend a number of policy changes. First, since typhoons may have significant negative impacts on rice production at the local level as opposed to the national level, assistance for rice farmers and the agriculture sector as a whole should be made more site-specific, zeroing in on the affected areas that actually need it. Second, those assisting affected households and areas in overcoming the resulting ill-effects of natural disasters should consider not only consumption strategies, such as the provision of emergency food aid, but also non-consumption strategies, such as the provision of post-disaster emergency employment. Third, while the available evidence suggests that the natural resources and environment sector is significantly affected by natural disasters, it is currently of less concern, as attention is presently focused on agriculture. It may now be high time to provide concrete assistance to this sector, in particular the provision of defensive investments and rehabilitation expenditures to cope with natural disasters.

Yi-Ming Wei, Ju Liang-Jin, and Qiong Wang focus on disaster risk management in China in Chap. 14. Due to its complicated climatic and geographic conditions and distinct spatial-temporal variations, China is one of the countries severely hit by various kinds of natural disasters with high frequency and wide distribution. This chapter analyzes the impacts of natural disasters on livelihood security of people, agriculture safety, and economic security in the past 30 years. Wei, Jin, and Wang find China's economic system highly vulnerable to natural disasters. Moreover, climate change will further exacerbate the vulnerability of the social-economic development system to natural disasters.

They conclude that in order to deal effectively with the high risk of natural disasters and build a low disaster risk society, there is an urgent need to implement a comprehensive strategy of disaster reduction for sustainable development. They advocate an integrated disaster risk management approach throughout the whole process of natural disaster management. China faces increasingly complex natural situations for disaster management but has insufficient experience both for creating appropriate institutions and for capacity building. Accordingly, capacity-building for comprehensive disaster prevention and reduction will have to be strengthened, and sustainable development coexisting with disaster risks need be realized, so as to reduce the vulnerability of the socio-economic development system to natural disasters.

Chapter 15 by Allen Lai and Seck Tan focuses on Singapore, which is potentially vulnerable to both natural and man-made disasters alongside its remarkable economic growth. They focus on lessons from Singapore's experience in fighting the 2003 SARS epidemic and discuss implications for future practice and research in disaster risk management. Singapore's experience with SARS strongly suggests that risk mitigating measures can be effective only when a range of partners and stakeholders such as government ministries, non-profit organizations, and grass-roots communities become adequately involved. This is also critical to disaster risk management. Whether all of these aspects are transferrable elsewhere needs to be assessed in future research. Nonetheless, this unique discipline has certainly helped Singapore come out of public health crises on a regular basis. Singapore's response to the outbreak of SARS offers valuable insights into the kinds of approaches needed to combat future pandemics, especially in Southeast Asia.

Having provided data on community and family ties, markets and production networks, and government policy and risk management, we now turn to broader lessons learned from these studies along with best practices in the field. In the final chapter, Chap. 16, Aldrich, Sawada, and Oum use the studies in the book to provide an overview of effective disaster risk coping strategies and tactics for creating regional cooperation on disaster management. They find that advanced nations can deal with major disasters by managing their own domestic financial resources. But developing nations, which carry diverse risks of major disasters, have weak fiscal groundwork and are less tolerant of such risks. In order to develop formal mechanisms to diversify aggregate disaster risks at national and regional levels, the chapter suggests the need to elaborate on multi-country risk pooling schemes, i.e., regional funds, to cover sovereign disaster risk. Against natural disasters, index insurance at the regional level, such as the Caribbean Catastrophe Risk Insurance Facility (CCRIF) and the Pacific Catastrophe Risk Assessment and Financing Initiative (PCRAFI) can function effectively to support the disaster-affected country with immediate liquidity in the aftermath of a catastrophic disaster.

Aldrich, Oum, and Sawada also discuss the roles of microcredit and micro-insurance schemes in enhancing the disaster-resilience of individual households and firms. In the case of manmade disasters, the Chiang Mai Initiative (CMI), for example, has been and will continue playing an important role in diversifying disaster risks. Moreover, further development of Asian bond markets will also be indispensable, because bond markets are composed of a large number of individual bond holders, enabling idiosyncratic risks to be diversified away effectively, and it is generally considered that bond markets provide effective risk-sharing mechanisms. To further improve national and regional risk management capabilities, a global system of pooling the risks of the four types of disasters would be effective for both developing and advanced nations to diversify the risks of disasters.

4 Policy Implications

The research presented in this volume sets up a number of concrete policy recommendations for decision makers, NGOs, and communities in East Asia and beyond. First, self-insurance by each individual or family and informal social safety net mechanisms based on community or local enforcement mechanisms should be strengthened and complemented through market and government involvement. The government plays an important role in bridging communities and linking them to the government. Also, market-based insurance arrangements such as microcredit and microinsurance programs should be promoted by government to facilitate consumption smoothing and livelihood sustainability among those affected by disasters.

Second, it is imperative to develop formal mechanisms to diversify aggregate disaster risks at national and regional levels. There may need to be increased multi-country risk pooling schemes, for example regional funds, to cover sovereign disaster risk. Against natural disasters, regional level index insurance schemes can be designed through public-private partnership (PPP) such as index type risk-transfer mechanisms sold by private insurer with extreme losses underwritten by contingent loan schemes of international financial institutions and aid donor agencies to complement the lack of re-insurance coverage.

Third, to further improve national and regional risk management capabilities, it is necessary to facilitate further development of global insurance mechanisms such as re-insurance arrangements and trades of CAT bonds. Moreover, a global system of pooling the risks of the different types of disasters, such as natural and technological disasters, economic crisis, and conflicts, should be designed and implemented for both developing and advanced nations wishing to diversify the risks of natural and manmade disasters. It is also worth pursuing reforms that undertake comprehensive preparations against the risks of a variety of disasters in Asia.

Fourth, complementarities among the market, the government, and the community will be the key. The market is a resource allocation mechanism using price signals, the government is the mechanism based on legal enforcement, and the community is a mechanism based on social norms. Overall safety nets against natural disasters should be provided by an optimal mix of these resource allocation mechanisms. For example, market-based microinsurance programs could be supported by community and government enforcement mechanisms, and regional disaster funds could utilize insurance market transactions. Overall, however, intra-regional government cooperation is indispensable for Asia.

Finally, with investments in human capital in the form of properly trained experts, investments in physical and social infrastructure are indispensable as an ex ante risk management policy in strengthening resilience of individuals, households, communities, and a country. These investments include dams for flood control, seawalls and tsunami barriers, cyclone shelters, a barrier to control soil erosion, irrigation systems for droughts, earthquake-resilient houses and buildings, disaster early-warning systems, and effective disaster drills guided by experts. Experiences of developed nations in the region such as Japan tell that investments in broader infrastructure dramatically reduced human and physical losses due to natural disasters. Multilateral and bilateral development partners can play an important role in filling the investment gap in these disaster-mitigation infrastructures in developing Asian countries.

References

Cabinet Office. (2011). *Monthly Economic Report (in Japanese, Getsurei Keizai Houkoku)*. Cabinet Office, the Government of Japan, March.

Guha-Sapir, D., Hoyois, Ph., & Below, R. (2013). *Annual Disaster Statistical Review 2012: The Numbers and Trends*. Brussels: CRED.

Hayami, Y. (2009). Social capital, human capital, and community mechanism: toward a consensus among economists'. *Journal of Development Studies, 45*(1), 96–123.

Hirschman, A. (1970). *Exit, voice, and loyalty: responses to decline in firms, organizations, and states*. Cambridge: Harvard University Press.

Ichimura, H., Sawada, Y., & Shimizutani, S. (2006). *Risk sharing against an earthquake: The case of Yamakoshi village*, Working paper. Faculty of Economics, University of Tokyo.

International Federation of Red Cross and Red Crescent Societies. (2010). *World disasters report: Focus on urban risk*. Lyon: IFRC.

Kahn, M. E. (2005). The death toll from natural disasters: the role of income, geography, and institutions. *Review of Economics and Statistics, 87*(2), 271–284.

Munich Re. (2012). *Review of Natural Catastrophes in 2011: Earthquakes Result in Record Loss Year*. Press release, 4 January 2012. http://www.munichre.com/en/media_relations/press_releases/2012/2012_01_04_press_release.aspx

Ostrom, Elinor. (1990). Governing the Commons: The Evolution of Institutions for Collective Action. New York: Cambridge University Press.

Paton, D., & McClure, J. (2013). *Preparing for disaster: Building household and community capacity*. Springfield: Charles C. Thomas.

Paton, D., Okada, N., & Sagala, S. (2013). Understanding preparedness for natural hazards: A cross cultural comparison. *Journal of Integrated Disaster Risk Management, 3*, 18–35.

Sawada, Y. (2007). The impact of natural and manmade disasters on household welfare. *Agricultural Economics, 37*(s1), 59–73.

Sawada, Y., & Shimizutani, S. (2008). How do people cope with natural disasters? Evidence from the Great Hanshin-Awaji (Kobe) earthquake in 1995. *Journal of Money Credit and Banking, 40* (2–3), 463–488.

World Bank. (2012). *Knowledge note 6-2 cluster 6: The economics of disaster risk, risk management, and risk financing, earthquake risk insurance*. Washington, D. C.: GFDRR and The World Bank.

World Bank and United Nations. (2010). *Natural hazards, unnatural disasters*. Washington, D. C.: World Bank.

Yang, D. (2008). Coping with disaster: The impact of hurricanes on international financial flows, 1970–2002. *B. E. Journal of Economic Analysis & Policy, 8*(1), 1–45 (Advances), Article 13.

Part I
Family and Community Ties

Chapter 2
Social Capital in Post Disaster Recovery: Strong Networks and Communities Create a Resilient East Asian Community

Daniel P. Aldrich

After any major disaster, survivors must decide if they want to return to a destroyed home in a wrecked town with no viable infrastructure and few fellow residents. In the town of Rikuzentakata, Japan where 10 % of the population was killed and 80 % of the businesses were washed away by the Tohoku tsunami in March 2011, one resident—a baker named Masayuki Kimura—has been willing to return to the destroyed area to bake sweets, breads, and snacks for his community. He returned, cognizant of the fact that turning a profit was unlikely and that his start up costs would be high. Rather than returning because of his love for business or because he had no other options, he moved back to his hometown because of his personal ties to the area. Kimura had saved his own life, and that of his mother, by evacuating to higher ground soon after the 8.9 magnitude earthquake struck off Japan's northeastern shore at 2:46 p.m. on the 11th of March. From a hilltop nearby they watched as their home and bakery shop was destroyed; the tsunami, as high as 46 ft in some places, swallowed much of coastal Rikuzentakata.

The US$370,000 worth of business loans which Kimura had taken on before the disaster remained, though, and he considered leaving the area to start afresh elsewhere. Had he left, he would have been among many making similar choices; more than 1,200 people had left the city to move elsewhere by the end of 2011 (Barta et al. 2011). But the baking business was started by his grandfather in 1926 and he had specifically brought Kimura's father into the family to keep the enterprise going. Even while sitting in temporary housing following their evacuation, Kimura's mother soon began telling reporters that she wanted to rebuild and begin making sweets for the community again. Pushed by her words, Kimura found second hand baking gear and moved into a temporary location, discovering that many of his suppliers of equipment and foodstuffs refused to take his money when they found out where he was living. While distributing supplies at evacuation

D.P. Aldrich (✉)
Purdue University, West Lafayette, IN, USA
e-mail: daniel.aldrich@gmail.com

D.P. Aldrich et al. (eds.), *Resilience and Recovery in Asian Disasters*, Risk, Governance and Society 18, DOI 10.1007/978-4-431-55022-8_2

centers, he heard from many people discussing their nostalgia for the flavors of normal life: "People are longing for our local taste." Recognizing his personal connections to his community and the ways in which his sweets can help others rebuild their lives, Kimura has committed to rebuild whatever the costs (Wakabayashi 2011).

The story of Masayuki Kimura provides us with critical insights into the role of social capital and social networks in the process of disaster recovery. As the tsunami approached, many people survived the wave because of the actions of others; among them was Kimura's mother, who was saved by her son. For the elderly and infirm, the only hope of living through the event came from the assistance of caregivers, neighbors, and family. These connections were able to assist the bedridden into cars and vans and then out of the plain in which many homes were located. Once the waters had receded, Kimura, like other survivors, had to decide whether or not to return to his damaged home and community.

His personal ties to the town helped him to move back to the wasteland that was Rikuzentakata even though he understood the process would be costly and slow. In the process of rebuilding his business, aid from and ties to colleagues and acquaintances proved critical; financial and emotional support from network members cemented his desire to move forward. His story matches that of many other survivors and towns around the world who have displayed resilience in their recoveries. Individuals and localities bounced back from tragedy and hardship not solely through wealth, government aid, or top-down leadership, but through their neighbors, connections and social networks.

The 3/11 Tohoku compound disaster sits as one in a dizzying list of high profile disasters, including the Indian Ocean tsunami in 2004, Hurricane Katrina in 2005, and the 2010 Haiti earthquake. The last two decades of disasters have seen a clear trend of increasing casualties and higher amounts of damage (Guha-Sapir et al. 2011). Because of wide scale migration towards vulnerable coastal locations and increasing urbanization around the world, floods and water-related disasters have contributed to the increasing toll on human life. With anthropogenic global warming speeding up the rise of ocean levels and increasing the frequency of extreme weather events, disasters will continue to be part of the human condition. Under these conditions, scholars and policy makers alike should recognize the importance of providing usable knowledge about disaster recovery.

Much folk wisdom about disaster recovery remains focused on variables assumed to influence the efficiency and effectiveness of the process. Standard variables include damage from the disaster, quality of governance, the socioeconomic status of the individuals and communities affected, and the amount of aid provided by national governments and aid organizations. However, a great deal of research has shown that in a variety of important policy fields such as health, civic engagement, and livelihood searches, social networks strongly influence behavior and outcomes. One randomized experiment using five trials over 7 weeks which engaged more than 700 participants demonstrated that individuals were heavily influenced by the behavior of actors similar to them to take on new behaviors. Hence early adopters of diet diaries which recorded what foods each subject had eaten soon passed on their behaviors to fellow network members (Centola 2011). Other research has demonstrated that if our friends and acquaintances start going to the gym, we are likely to follow suit (Christakis and Fowler 2009). Social science has known since the 1970s that "weak ties"—the people whom we meet through our friends and acquaintances—are the ones who help us find new jobs (Granovetter 1973). This chapter draws on research from a variety of scholars and disciplines to emphasize the role played by social capital and networks in disaster mitigation and recovery. It begins with a review of the standard literature on recovery, moves into a discussion of the mechanisms by which social capital influence rebuilding, and then brings evidence from a variety of studies to back up its approach. I end with a discussion of broader lessons from these studies and conclude with a focus on future research agendas and directions for scholarship.

1 Standard Literature on Disaster Recovery

Typical approaches to disaster recovery focus on the role of standard variables such as damage, governance, socioeconomic status, and aid. The concept that the level of damage from the crisis would influence the path of recovery is intuitive and was highlighted by Douglas Dacy and Howard Kunreuther's pioneering work on the process of recovery and the role of the federal government in hazard mitigation following the 1964 Alaskan earthquake. In their book they argued that "it just seems reasonable to assume that the speed of recovery following a disaster will be determined primarily by the magnitude of the physical damage" (1969, p. 72). Given the tremendous damage from Hurricane Katrina, for example, which flooded roughly 80 % of New Orleans, many observers believe that the road to recovery will be a long one. This would be in contrast to smaller scale disasters in North America, such as tornadoes, which may touch down and strike only a few homes; in such cases, it may be a matter of weeks or months before lives of residents return to normalcy.

Other scholars and journalists have argued instead that the quality of governance matters, as they envision local mayors, governors, and even national decision makers speeding up or impeding the broader recovery process. Political scientists have called the rush to judgment after disasters the "blame game" and it can be found in developing and developed nations alike. After the 1995 Kobe earthquake, many blamed the Japanese national government for not bringing in the Self Defense Forces quickly enough to assist with fire fighting, search, and rescue. After Hurricane Katrina in the summer of 2005 many openly blamed Mayor Ray Nagin, Governor Kathleen Blanco, and President George Bush for failing to put sufficient disaster preparation and mitigation in place despite the widespread knowledge of the weakness of New Orleans' levee system. Similarly, after the Tohoku disaster in March 2011, observers were quick to argue that ties between Tokyo Electric Power Company (TEPCO) executives and the long ruling Liberal Democratic Party (LDP) in Japan resulted in less than sufficient safety standards at nuclear power plants (with one critic tweeting "amakudari kills" in reference to the practice of regulators descending from heaven into paid positions in the industries they have regulated while in government).

Sociologists and economists have focused on the socioeconomic status of victims and have tried to link their recovery processes to their wealth and private resources. In studies of recovery from the early twentieth century earthquake and fires in San Francisco, California, for example, researchers argued that lower class individuals had to move multiple times in their search for post-quake shelter. Such actions made it more difficult for them to effectively restart their lives. Other studies have underscored that many of the victims of Hurricane Katrina in New Orleans were individuals with low incomes and little education, and that their livelihoods suffered more than survivors of higher status. Many of the communities struck hardest by the 2011 Tohoku earthquake and tsunami were older, retired residents with little savings and no home or earthquake insurance. Government officials in Japan worry whether these residents will be able to carry out effective recoveries given their limited reserves of financial capital.

Finally, many researchers and policy makers have argued that the amount of aid provided from outside institutions, whether national governments, NGOs, or international organizations such as the United Nations or the United States Agency for International Development (USAID). After the eruption of Mount St. Helens in the state of Washington, the governor was asked what she needed. In her response, she spelled out the word "money." International observers have worried when autocratic regimes have refused to accept international aid offers, such as the government of Myanmar following its typhoon. Their core concern has been that a lack of aid for survivors will result in slower recovery overall.

2 A New Approach: Social Capital

Traditional approaches have focused primarily on factors external to disaster-affected communities, and have paid little attention to the ways in which social relationships within the community may drive or inhibit the process of rebuilding. New research on the role of social capital—the ties that bind us together and provide useless data and information on trustworthiness—has illuminated three mechanisms through which networks and relationships can influence the process of disaster recovery.

The first—illustrated well by the vignette about the baker in the town of Rikuzentaka—is known by economists as the choice between "exit" and "voice" (Hirschman 1970). Exit refers to the process of uprooting from one's initial community and starting life over again in a new one. Survivors of disaster may exercise exit early on—when they realize that their homes are damaged or destroyed—or later in the recovery process, when they see that their community is not recovering effectively. Following the Diaspora from New Orleans after Hurricane Katrina, many survivors decided to start their lives over again in communities in Houston, Dallas, Memphis, and so on. They did so because they believed that their new communities provided better livelihoods, or because they feared that their own recoveries in New Orleans might be stalled. Alternatively, survivors may choose to return to wrecked houses and rebuild their lives no matter how much damage has been done to them. When residents return and begin to work collectively, letting authorities in the area know their preferences and working to make themselves heard in the planning process, economists call this "voice." Research on the process of return has underscored that individuals with more ties to their old communities—whether through family, friends, a sense of belonging or place, or jobs—are more likely to return and exercise voice. Those who feel less connected to their neighbors, or who feel that their networks are not returning, will be more likely to select exit.

The second mechanism by which social capital can assist following disaster is with the overcoming of barriers to collective action. Around the world, people often have strong beliefs and deeply rooted ideals, but they may not actually work to see these put into practice. This may be because they lack the time, energy, or ability, but it can also because they assume that someone else will do the "heavy lifting" involved. Social scientists call this phenomenon free-riding, and because of it many are content to remain in their homes or offices while others go out and march, vote, sign petitions, blockade doors, and actually mobilize. Post-disaster situations often have collective action problems that require maximum participation. To deter looting, for example, everyone in the neighborhood has to chip in and give up us some of their sleep or free time to walk on patrol. If people opt out or decide to shirk their responsibilities, they may open up the area to potential thieves. To ensure that authorities will turn power back on to damaged areas, everyone has to ensure that they sign up through online or paper forms indicating their return.

Some communities, such as Village de L'est in northeastern New Orleans overcame their collective action problems (they convinced the local utility to restart their power) while other areas, such as the condominium owners in Kobe did not (they were unable to fully take advantage of an offer from the city government to remove debris if all owners signed onto the plan) (Aldrich 2012a). Areas with higher levels of trust and social capital can better overcome the barriers to collective action and mobilize their residents to participate; communities where people lack trust and believe that others will not come to their aid will find themselves mobilizing only a small fraction of the returnees.

The final mechanism by which social capital assists post-disaster is through the provision of mutual aid and informal insurance. An example may help illustrate the ways in which social capital provides information, fellowship, and support during times of crisis. After the Tohoku tsunami struck the town of Shichigahama (literally "Seven beaches") in Miyagi Prefecture and destroyed roughly 1,000 homes there, a knitting club named *Keito Iki-Iki* (Yarn Alive) has emerged to provide social support for its 20 or so mostly elderly neighbors. "It cheers me up so much that I don't even feel lonely at night, I just feel like knitting some more," reported one member whose home and store were washed away by the tsunami. Later, when the same resident missed a club meeting to attend an athletic event, her fellow knitters called to check up on her (Ono 2012). Informal insurance means that network members provide necessary resources at a time when standard suppliers of those resources—such as the government, private sector companies, and so forth—are unable to do so. Similarly, after Hurricane Katrina suppliers such as Wal-Mart, gas stations, and hotels were closed, so neighbors borrowed power tools, gasoline, and places to stay in order to work on their damaged homes.

3 Review of Literature on Social Capital

Research on social capital's role in post-disaster recovery has been building up gradually into a strong component of the broader field of disaster research. One of the earliest works on this topic came from sociologists who recognized that people in need of resources go to formal service providers, such as government welfare agencies, only as a last resort. Instead, many people prefer to use their friends, family, and network connections for support during crises. Using data on survivors of Hurricane Andrew in 1992, one team of scholars established the importance of network ties in the recovery process. At a time when normal sources of support were closed due to the damage wrought by the hurricane, survivors sought support from network members through formal and informal channels (Beggs et al. 1996).

Through a separate investigation of how three rural communities in Manitoba, Canada handled the 1997 Red River Flood, researchers soon confirmed the role of stronger social capital in the recovery process (Buckland and Rahman 1999). In their focus on how the communities prepared for and then handled the disaster, they found that the social ties among residents profoundly influenced the trajectory of disaster response. In the communities of Roseau River, Rosenort, and St Jean Baptiste, Rosenort had the highest levels of civic engagement as measured through both the number of organizations and the number of meetings. "Rosenort in particular demonstrated a vigorous response to the flood, which was made possible through intense social capital formation, reflecting the community's unique historic, cultural and religious background" (Buckland and Rahman 1999, p. 188).

Data from the Gujarat and Kobe earthquakes in India and Japan, respectively, further demonstrated the importance of bonding, bridging, and linking social capital in furthering recovery and rehabilitation efforts (Nakagawa and Shaw 2004). This comparative study used both qualitative and quantitative methods to better understand the factors responsible for speedier and more efficient recoveries. While the two areas struck by earthquakes had very different cultures and levels of socioeconomic development, "At every stage of the disaster cycle (rescue, relief and rehabilitation), the communities played the most important roles among other concerned stakeholders" (Nakagawa and Shaw 2004, p. 27). Further, individuals in more civically active and engaged communities expressed higher levels of satisfaction with the process of planning and recovery than survivors from more fragmented and less involved areas.

A number of recent studies have underscored the role of social networks in broader processes of adaptation and resilience. One highly-cited study in *Science* magazine argued that local institutions and social networks provided the basis for both local and international action in response to increasing vulnerability. The article brought examples from the 2004 Indian Ocean tsunami and the 2004 Hurricane Ivan to show how well-connected communities learned from previous hazards and used social connections to strengthen their resilience. The authors emphasized that "Networks and institutions that promote resilience to present-day hazards also buffer against future risks, such as those associated with climate change" (Adger et al. 2005).

One researcher set up in-depth, process-tracing case studies of how two communities in Nagata ward of Kobe, Japan handled the 1995 earthquake which devastated the city's urban center and killed more than 6,400 people (Yasui 2007). "Both communities were characterized by population decline, aging population, fragile old wooden housing, high building density, narrow streets and mixed residential and industrial land uses located near to each other" (Yasui 2007, p. 15). Despite these similarities, Mano has been known since the early post-War II days as a well-organized community with high levels of civic engagement and participation. Beginning with greening and anti-pollution movements, the community has been a locus for activism and involvement with strong, interconnected networks. It further demonstrated its ability to overcome collective action problems when handling the fires that broke out after the 1995 earthquake. As one local leader recalled, "when fire erupted after the earthquake, people started lining up and handing buckets full of water to the next person to put out the fire because the water pressure was too low to use the fire hydrant properly" (Yasui 2007, p. 186).

In contrast, Mikura has little history of past activism, and residents were hard pressed to remember community development activities in the past. When fires broke out following the quake, "the residents of Mikura community passively watched as their homes burnt to ashes" (Yasui 2007, p. 227). While Mikura developed its capacity post-disaster, many of its residents did not return, and much of the work done in the area was carried out through outsiders.

Another study of the 1995 Kobe earthquake recovery process looked less at communities and neighborhoods and more at the recoveries of individual survivors (Tatsuki 2007). Through four waves of surveys with roughly 1,000 respondents, the Hyogo Life Recovery Survey Project designed a life recovery scale based on 14 different factors. The author then categorized responses into fields of self governance and solidarity, and found that there were statistically significant differences in the same respondents before and after the quake.[1] Many survivors moved from more self-focused approaches to communitarian approaches, shifting their field of focus from themselves and their families onto the broader neighborhood and society. Individuals who reported higher levels of solidarity and civic-mindedness

[1] Supporting these findings, Cassar et al. (2012) provide experimental evidence that victims of disaster are more trusting of others and simultaneously moderately more trustworthy.

tended to have stronger recoveries than more isolated individuals. Through focus groups and interviews Tatsuki showed how social ties helped survivors to rebuild communities and then to retell the story of the disaster as one of recovery and engagement as opposed to one based solely on loss.

After the 2005 Hurricane Katrina which resulted in the collapse of the levees in New Orleans, Louisiana, a scholar showed how local community ties and the accompanying narratives of recovery strongly predicted levels of community recovery (Chamlee-Wright 2010). Chamlee-Wright saw post-disaster situations as ones in which many people have strong disincentives from expending time and energy on recovery, preferring to free ride on the efforts of others. Given that communities provide the associational worlds which govern norms and behavior, she "recognizes a reciprocal relationship between the institutional rules of the game and cultural processes" (Chamlee-Wright 2010, p. 16). Using this focus on social capital and community ties as a start, she used interviews and case studies to document the different levels of recovery across four neighborhoods in the city: Lower Ninth Ward, Mary Queen of Vietnam, Broadmoor, and St. Bernard Parish. Her approach showed how important the cultural tool kits and levels of solidarity are in the process of recovering after crisis.

Similarly, scholars researched the ways in which different types of social capital created different capacities in two neighborhoods devastated by Hurricane Katrina (Elliott et al. 2010). One neighborhood, the Lower Ninth Ward, was made up primarily of African-Americans who lived below the poverty line, while the other, Lakeview, was a neighborhood made up primarily of affluent whites. Interviewing 100 residents from each of the neighborhoods, the authors sought to understand how networks—especially bonding and linking social capital—played a role in recovery after the storm. Overall, it took more than twice as long for residents of the Lower Ninth Ward to return to their homes as their counterparts in Lakeview, and they also were about one-seventh as likely to contact a neighbor. In the Lower Ninth Ward, individuals were less likely to connect to their geographically proximal neighbors and friends and also less likely to be able to call on the help of outsiders who lived beyond the ruined area. "As a result, relative declines in translocal assistance dovetailed with a relative inability to re-establish local residential networks to undercut the reconstitution of local sources of social support for Lower Ninth Ward residents" (Elliott et al. 2010, p. 643).[2]

One final book drives home the power of social networks in rebuilding after crisis and hints at the potential for positive interaction between social networks and the state. Rieko Kage used the wide variation in reconstruction rates among Japan's 47 prefectures after World War II to reject explanations for post-crisis recovery based on economic or state-centric hypotheses which posit that higher levels of economic resources or the presence of a cohesive and autonomous state are sufficient conditions for better recovery (Kage 2011, p. 143). Through side-by-side

[2] The researchers are referring to the ability of individuals living outside the affected area—hence the term "translocal"—to provide resources at a critical moment.

process tracing of YMCAs in Kobe and Sapporo along with cases of judo clubs in Fukuoka and Yokohama, Kage showed how some areas in pre-war Japan had greater citizen enthusiasm for and involvement in voluntary activities while others withered, especially as war time conditions deteriorated and top-down, government coercion intensified.

4 Additional Evidence of Social Capital's Role

To further illustrate the role of social capital in post-disaster recovery, three "megacatastrophes" over the past century show how networks strongly influenced the trajectories of rehabilitation across time and space. The three disasters under review are the 1923 Tokyo earthquake, the 2004 Indian Ocean tsunami, and the 2005 Hurricane Katrina All resulted in the deaths of more than 1,000 people and caused tremendous amounts of property damage.

On 1 September 1923 at approximately noon a tremendous earthquake struck the capital of Japan, collapsing buildings and setting off fires which raged for several days. When the smoke cleared, the earthquake had caused more than 140,000 deaths and leveled roughly 40 % of Tokyo. Roughly two-thirds of the population became homeless and more than 345,000 homes were lost to fire and shaking. Residents began seeking to rebuild within days, constructing "barrack" type temporary housing units using debris and scrap metal in whatever land they could claim. Images from the town show popular parks filled with ramshackle cabin-like structures, often with carts filled with materials parked just outside.[3] However, even though the drive to rebuild was strong, some neighborhoods seemed to display more resilience than others, drawing back in old residents and attracting new immigrants, while other communities seemed to lose population. To better understand why some areas revitalized at the same time that similar communities became ghost towns, I used detailed police records from the 1920s and the 1930s to understand the conditions of recovery (Aldrich 2012b).

The Tokyo Metropolitan police operated out of neighborhood police boxes called *kōban*, and their records of daily life in their communities were extensive and well maintained. From their surveys, I extracted neighborhood level measures of population density (measured as individuals per kilometer), the number of factory workers per capita (who, on the whole, were uneducated migrants from the countryside) along with the number of commercial cars per capita in the neighborhood. I also collected information on the number of trucks and cars, the per capita cost of crime in the area, and the percentage of local residents killed in the earthquake. To understand the financial resources available to local residents, I included observations of per capita pawnbroker lending rates; pawnshops were seen

[3] The Reynolds collection (http://library.brown.edu/cds/kanto/about.html) has over 100 photographs taken in Japan immediately following the earthquake.

as such important sources of credit that the Tokyo municipal government itself sought to rebuild pawnshops to replace those that had been destroyed in the earthquake. To measure the ability of local residents to overcome collective action problems and to work cooperatively, I recorded the number of demonstrations per year (in each neighborhood) along with voter turnout in municipal elections (for which universal male suffrage had just been granted).

To check to see which of these potential factors—economic capital, population density, damage from the earthquake, and so on—had the strongest impact on the process of population recovery, I ran three different types of analyses. I first used a simple bivariate analysis, dividing the neighborhoods into those with high levels of social capital (above average levels of voter turnout and demonstrations) and those with lower levels of social capital (average or below average levels of these activities), and looked at their average population growth rates. The chi-squared value for a tab test of below-average/above-average social capital with below-average/above-average growth rates was 0.001, indicating a statistically significant difference between these two types of communities. Then, I used a method called propensity score matching to try to build a dataset which mirrors the "twin studies" often carried out by medical scientists looking to establish a causal relationship.

This approach creates a dataset of observations which are quite similar, in which all of the observations had a similar propensity to receive the treatment (in this case, high or low levels of social capital) but only some did. In doing so we can better create causal inference about our variables of interest. Using this method, I found that neighborhoods with higher-than-average numbers of political demonstrations had a 2 % higher level of population return than very similar neighborhoods (in terms of earthquake damage, economic and human capital, area, and so forth), with lower-than-average numbers of rallies, marches, and protests.

My final analysis of the data from Tokyo used time-series, cross-sectional, panel-corrected models to hold all of the control variables (damage from the earthquake, pawn broker lending, population density, and so on) at their means while allowing voter turnout to vary. Using the simulation program known as "Clarify" I generated predictions for the population growth rate along with 95 % confidence intervals around this prediction. The result showed a very strong, positive relationship between voter turnout and population growth, holding constant the values of the other factors. Communities in which the people turned out to vote had a far higher population growth rate than areas in which people voted in smaller proportion. Even a century ago, the impact of social capital on post disaster recovery is measurable and statistically significant. Some 100 years later, though, social capital proved equally important.

A great deal of work on the 2004 Indian Ocean tsunami has shown the power of social networks in the process of recovery. On the 26 December 2004 a "megathrust" earthquake of at least a 9.0 magnitude struck off the west coast of Sumatra, Indonesia and set off tsunami as tall as 100 ft in some areas. The tsunami devastated coastlines in India, Sri Lanka, and Indonesia, killing close to 200,000 people across these areas, with 35,000 killed in Sri Lanka. Seventy thousand (70,000) houses in Sri Lanka were destroyed completely with another 30,000 damaged. Many of the villages struck by the tsunami were coastal fishing villages with homes and livelihood locations directly next to the ocean. Recovery across villages has varied; some have recovered population and put their fisher people back to work, while others languished for months, if not years.

Minamoto (2010) carried out surveys of 187 households in eastern Sri Lanka located in areas which had suffered damage from the tsunami. To measure levels of social capital, the author looked at "(1) the social norms, people's behaviors and attitudes during reconstruction; (2) changes in networks during reconstruction; and (3) characteristics of the community-based organizations to which our respondents belonged" (Minamoto 2010, p. 551). The results of the quantitative analysis showed that linking social capital—that is, connections between survivors and national and international nongovernmental organizations (NGOs) proved critical at helping to secure necessities such as food, shelter, water, and education. Trust among the members of community-based organizations along with formal community networks had strong, positive relationships with livelihood recovery, while more bonding social capital—focused on the family and kin—occasionally contributed to negative perceptions of recovery.

The recognition of the role of social capital in Sri Lankan recovery pushed international aid organizations, such as UN HABITAT to help affected communities to rebuild not only their homes but their social networks as well (see details on the intervention at http://www.fukuoka.unhabitat.org/projects/sri_lanka/detail10_en.html). In their study of five affected districts in Sri Lanka, DeSilva and Yamao (2007) argued that "poor social capital status makes communities more vulnerable and highly dependent on donors" (DeSilva and Yamao 2007, p. 45) while "high levels of social capital facilitate the entrepreneurial ventures among farmers" (DeSilva and Yamao 2007, p. 46). The higher levels of trust and coordination among well integrated communities provided them with opportunities for risk-taking and entrepreneurial ventures which could, over the long term, secure their livelihoods and increase their income. In contrast, communities with lower levels of trust who were unable to coordinate their activities found themselves most dependent on the generosity and activities of the international aid community.

Another example came 1 year after the Boxing Day Tsunami—in late August, less than a year later, Hurricane Katrina arrived on the Gulf Coast of North America. The collapse of the levees after the landfall of Hurricane Katrina on 29 August 2005 submerged some 80 % of New Orleans; it was almost 2 months before the water was pumped out of some neighborhoods. While many neighborhoods in the city remain under populated and filled with debris and weeds, others quickly rebounded from the flooding and began renovating their homes and businesses. Observers suggested a number of potential explanations for the variation in recovery speeds. Some argued that economic resources held by survivors best predicted who would return and begin rebuilding, and who would stay away. Others argued that race—long a divisive issue in the city—would influence the recovery process. But one scholar has focused on the ways in which communities create their own narratives and norms of independence, hard work, and collective responsibility.

Emily Chamlee-Wright's book on the recovery process focused on the cultural toolkits held by residents of neighborhoods across the city. One area has stood out as a paradigm of independence, solidarity, and rapid rebuilding: the primarily Vietnamese and Vietnamese-American community centered around Mary Queen of Viet Nam (MQVN) church. "By spring 2007 over 90 % of the Vietnamese American residents but fewer than 50 % of the African Americans had returned to Village de L'Est" (Leong et al. 2007). Located in the northeastern, Village de L'Est area of the city, the community returned within months of the flooding and demonstrated its ability to influence broader public policy when it successfully shut down the Chef Menteur Landfill which had been reopened to accept storm debris. MQVN's residents comprise both older residents who came over from Vietnam at the height of its war in the mid 1970s along with a younger generation which has grown up with the norms and teachings of the community.

Interviews with local residents underscored their norms of collective responsibility and a belief in the value of hard work. One resident, when asked about concerns that the city was not up and running when they returned, argued that "it didn't really matter that we didn't have [municipal] services up" (quoted in Chamlee-Wright 2010, p. 69). Rather than waiting for the city to provide social services, or local businesses to restart and sell necessary materials for rebuilding, the community self-organized before returning, dividing up responsibilities and ensuring that they would be self sufficient upon their return. Further, because of their historical experiences and insular culture, the community saw the widespread damage from the storm as a relatively minor nuisance compared with their previous struggles during the Vietnam war. As one interviewee pointed out, "thirty years ago [we came] with empty hands…thirty years later we already have the tools for everything, strategies, [and] the understanding [that] we can rebuild that" (quoted in Chamlee-Wright 2010, p. 70)

The bonding, bridging, and linking social capital in the area allowed residents to not only coordinate their rebuilding processes internally but to ensure that their voices were heard by the city government and other relevant institutions. "In Village de L'Est, under the leadership of the Mary Queen of Vietnam Church and its new Community Development Corporation, residents have rebuilt most of the community's single-family homes; an unsafe landfill has been shut down; new senior housing and urban farms are under development; businesses have returned to the two main commercial districts; and a new health center and charter school are being planned" (Brand and Seidman n.d.). Few other neighborhoods in the city of New Orleans have been able to replicate the success demonstrated by MQVN after Katrina.

5 Discussion

In this chapter I have tried to underscore the ways in which social capital serves as a critical part of disaster recovery by bringing evidence from a variety of disasters and catastrophes in different nations and time periods. I believe that the growing body of evidence on social capital suggests three broader lessons. First, it hints at the importance of thoughtful and sustained interaction between government and local social networks. Next, some standard recovery strategies may in fact harm the social infrastructure so critical for the processes of rebuilding and hence should be planned carefully. Planners should be careful to think through and avoid these potential barriers to effective recovery. Finally, should these studies indeed capture the essence of social capital's role, the findings suggest next steps for both governments and NGOs which seek to improve the recovery process after crisis.

This chapter has shown how social capital—the ties that bind neighbors, friends, and acquaintances together, deepening their trust and making their collective action more likely—works in ways often guided by geography and distance. As local-level networks and community based organizations can coordinate group actions and deepen trust, governments should recognize their role in broader emergency management and disaster recovery planning. Kage (2011) showed how local civil society organizations interacted with government resources to further the process of recovery after World War II in Japan. National and regional governments have deep resources but can easily direct them to useless or damaging projects.

Through strong coordination with local social networks and community groups, valuable resources from the state can be used more effectively and efficiently. For example, while national planners may envision a bridge or road as critical, local residents may understand that restarting a school or local church will form a critical "anchor" in the recovery process. Governments able to tap into the local knowledge and mobilization potential of well-connected neighborhoods could use social capital as a "force multiplier" and extend the scope of their programs. Future quantitative and qualitative research should look closely at the ways that local social networks interact with government mitigation and recovery policies.

In a related way, standard recovery plans may actually harm reservoirs of social capital. For example, after large-scale disasters government agencies usually seek to rush survivors out of temporary emergency dwellings into long term shelters. This strategy, carried out in good faith, can easily harm existing networks by placing vulnerable individuals, such as the elderly and infirm, in areas far from their friends, family, and networks. Following the 1995 Kobe earthquake, for example, many older survivors were rushed into long term housing, but the tragedy that followed was unexpected: more than 240 survivors died "lonely deaths" in their new apartments. Without friends, family, and networks, these survivors had little to live for. New recovery plans should build instead on bottom up strategies which integrate a deep knowledge of the needs of the community with its own voice.

One example of a program to activate and sustain local community involvement in recovery efforts comes from the Tohoku disaster. The Hobo Nikkan Itoi Shimbun has documented the stories of a number of local residents whose homes and livelihoods were disrupted by the tsunami (http://www.1101.com/yamamotocho/english/2011-10-20.html). In telling the story of their activities - cleaning up debris, sorting out the relief supplies and sharing them among themselves—at the early stage in their life as evacuees, these narratives underscore the power of the group in both accomplishing measurable outcomes (e.g. making a mud-filled home livable again) and in creating a new identity. Through their group activities in the community, residents move from victims to active agents with dignity.

Finally, should these studies capture the reality of recovery, the next stage of work should be pursuit of research on increasing levels of social capital in vulnerable areas through public policy. Several studies have shown that tactics such as community focus groups (Brune and Bossert 2009; Pronyk et al. 2008) and community currency or "scrip" (Doteuchi 2002; Richey 2007) can deepen trust among participants and increase their civic engagement. Governments around the world should consider investing fewer funds in often misused or underutilized physical infrastructure and consider the ways that deepening their social infrastructure can improve recovery outcomes. Social capital-focused programs may not only be cheaper than interventions focused on physical infrastructure, but their impact will be felt for a longer period of time as well.

6 Conclusion

This chapter has suggested a new paradigm for thinking about disaster recovery and for designing emergency management responses. Moving beyond "brick and mortar" approaches to recovery, it has stressed that the ties between residents may serve as a critical engine during what may be a long and difficult recovery process. Ongoing research in related fields continues to support this approach. Coppock et al. (2011), for example, demonstrated that the establishment of collective action groups in rural Ethiopia, along with the creation of social safety nets, had led to measurable improvements in quality of life and to reduction in hunger. Working with more than 2,300 women in 59 collective-action groups on the Borana Plateau, researchers demonstrated that low cost (US$1 per month per person over 3 years), peer networking and participatory education programs improved lives and strengthened human development. These sorts of new public policies suggest a new wave of government and NGO action which move beyond the traditional sorts of interventions that have been the norm since the 1950s.

East Asia has suffered from a number of disasters over the past decades, and as nations like China, India, Indonesia, and Vietnam modernize and urbanize, their populations will be increasingly vulnerable to natural and man-made crises. Rather than merely responding to disasters as they occur in the future, visionary decision makers in these and other countries should move to embrace a social-capital based approach to policy making. Bringing residents to the forefront and increasing community based planning will ensure a strong future for these important countries.

References

Adger, W. N., Hughes, T. P., Folke, C., Carpenter, S. R., & Rockstrom, J. (2005). Social-ecological resilience to coastal disasters. *Science, 309*(5737), 1036–1039.

Aldrich, D. P. (2012a). *Building resilience: Social capital in post-disaster recovery*. Chicago: University of Chicago Press.

Aldrich, D. P. (2012b). Social, not physical, infrastructure: The critical role of civil society after the 1923 Tokyo earthquake. *Disasters, 36*(3), 398–419.

Barta, P., Wakabayashi, D., & Fairclough, G. (2011). After Tsunami, a Mayor Plants Seeds of renewal. *Wall Street Journal*, 10 December.

Beggs, J., Haines, V., & Hurlbert, J. (1996). Situational contingencies surrounding the receipt of informal support. *Social Forces, 75*(1), 201–222.

Brand, A. L., & Seidman, K. (n.d.). *Assessing post-Katrina recovery in New Orleans, community Innovators Lab Department of Urban Studies and Planning*. Massachusetts: Massachusetts Institute of Technology.

Brune, N., & Bossert, T. (2009). Building social capital in post-conflict communities: Evidence from Nicaragua. *Social Science and Medicine, 68*, 885–893.

Buckland, J., & Rahman, M. (1999). Community based disaster management during the 1997 Red River Flood in Canada. *Disasters, 23*(2), 174–191.

Cassar, A., Healy, A., & von Kessler, C. (2012). *Trust, risk, and time preferences after a natural disaster: experimental evidence from Thailand*, Working paper. San Francisco: University of San Francisco.

Centola, D. (2011). An experimental study of Homophily in the adoption of health behavior. *Science, 334*, 1269–1272.

Chamlee-Wright, E. (2010). *The cultural and political economy of recovery: social learning in a post-disaster environment*. New York: Routledge.

Christakis, N., & Fowler, J. (2009). *Connected: The surprising power of our social networks and how they shape our lives*. New York: Little, Brown and Company.

Coppock, D. L., Desta, S., Tezera, S., & Gebru, G. (2011). Capacity building helps pastoral women transform impoverished communities in Ethiopia. *Science, 334*, 1394–1398.

Dacy D, Kunreuther H (1969) The economics of natural disasters: implications for federal policy. Free Press, New York

DeSilva, D. A. M., & Yamao, M. (2007). Developing social capital to replace forgingdonors: A case of Sri Lanka. In M. Yamao (Ed.), *Developing social capital to replace foregoing donors: A study on the changes in the structure and functioning of coastal communities of Sri Lanka, Thailand and Indonesia in post-tsunami period* (pp. 22–61). Hiroshima: Hiroshima University. http://home.hiroshima-u.ac.jp/cbrmcm/tunami/tunami2.pdf.

Doteuchi, A. (2002). *Community currency and NPOs—A model for solving social issues in the 21st century*, NLI Research Paper No. 163. Tokyo: NLI Research.

Elliott, J. R., Haney, T. J., & Sams-Abiodun, P. (2010). Limits to social capital: Comparing network assistance in two New Orleans neighborhoods devastated by Hurricane Katrina. *Sociological Quarterly, 51*(4), 624–648.

Granovetter, M. (1973). The strength of weak ties. *American Journal of Sociology, 78*(6), 1360–1380.

Guha-Sapir, D., Femke, V., Below, R., & Ponserre, S. (2011). *Annual disaster statistical review 2010: The numbers and trends*. Brussels: Centre for Research on the Epidemiology of Disasters (CRED).

Hirschman, A. (1970). *Exit, voice, and loyalty: Responses to decline in firms, organizations, and states*. Cambridge: Harvard University Press.

Kage, R. (2011). *Civic engagement in Postwar Japan: The revival of a defeated society*. New York/London: Cambridge University Press.

Leong, K. J., Airriess, C. A., Li, W., Chia-Chen, A., & Keith, V. M. (2007). Resilient history and the rebuilding of a community: The Vietnamese American community in New Orleans East. *Journal of American History, 94*, 770–779.

Minamoto, Y. (2010). Social capital and livelihood recovery: Post-tsunami Sri Lanka as a case'. *Disaster Prevention and Management, 19*(5), 548–564.

Nakagawa, Y., & Shaw, R. (2004). Social capital: A missing link to disaster recovery. *International Journal of Mass Emergencies and Disasters, 22*(1), 5–34.

Ono, Y. (2012). Japanese elderly knit a safety net. *Wall Street Journal*, 5 March.

Pronyk, P. M., Harpham, T., Busza, J., Phetla, G., Morison, L. A., Hargreaves, J. R., et al. (2008). Can social capital be intentionally generated? A randomized trial from Rural South Africa. *Social Science and Medicine, 67*, 1559–1570.

Richey, S. (2007). Manufacturing trust: Community currencies and the creation of social capital. *Political Behavior, 29*, 69–88.

Tatsuki, S. (2007). Long-term life recovery processes among survivors of the 1995 Kobe Earthquake: 1999, 2001, 2003, and 2005 life recovery social survey results. *Journal of Disaster Research, 2*(6), 448–501.

Wakabayashi, D. (2011). Making home sweet again: After Tsunami, a Baker finds purpose. *Wall Street Journal*, 11 November 2011.

Yasui, E. (2007). *Community vulnerability and capacity in post disaster recovery: The Cases of Mano and Mikura neighborhoods in the wake of the1995 Kobe Earthquake*. Ph.D. University of British Columbia.

Chapter 3
The Role of Community Social Protection in Natural Disaster Risk Management in Cambodia

Sann Vathana, Sothea Oum, Ponhrith Kan, and Colas Chervier

1 Introduction

The pattern of risks faced by poor and vulnerable people in rural areas, particularly those involved in agriculture and other ecosystem-dependent livelihoods, serves as a major cause of chronic poverty. Dependency on subsistence agriculture, in particular for the rural poor in Cambodia, magnifies the impact of stresses and shocks (such as droughts or floods). This has profound implications for livelihood security and for welfare. Such stresses and shocks, on the other hand, will not necessarily always lead to negative impacts, as risks and uncertainties that are often associated with seasonality are embedded in the practice of agriculture. Further, people have considerable experience with coping and risk management strategies in this sector. However, in the face of climate change, the magnitude and frequency of stresses and shocks are changing and approaches such as social protection, disaster risk management and climate change adaptation will be needed to bolster local resilience and supplement people's experience.

The most common nature disaster impacts in Cambodia are relatively moderate flood and drought events combined with a high level of vulnerability. Additionally, rural people face major limitations in their ability to cope with the impact of these events on their livelihoods. Cambodia does not face flood risks of the magnitude and intensity of Bangladesh, nor does it face droughts of the magnitude and intensity of countries in the African Sahel. Yet the more moderate droughts and floods in Cambodia threaten livelihoods and cause widespread suffering among rural people. As natural disasters have a huge impact on social and economic

S. Vathana (✉) • P. Kan • C. Chervier
Council for Agricultural and Rural Development, Social Protection Coordination Unit (CARD-SPCU), Phnom Penh, Cambodia
e-mail: vathana20@yahoo.com

S. Oum
Economic Research Institute for ASEAN and East-Asia, Jakarta, Indonesia

D.P. Aldrich et al. (eds.), *Resilience and Recovery in Asian Disasters*, Risk, Governance and Society 18, DOI 10.1007/978-4-431-55022-8_3

welfare, policies to manage them need to be integrated and well-grounded to the specificities of natural hazards as well as local capacities in terms of fiscal, administrative and economic capabilities.

In Cambodia as well as in many other countries, social protection responses to natural disaster have been ad-hoc mechanisms. As discussed elsewhere in this volume (Aldrich Chap. 2), social cohesion and community connections provide informal insurance against hazards for members. However, social protection, including support payments and insurance against risk, does not reduce disaster risk in itself. Nor does social cohesion serve as an alternative to development investments in public infrastructure and services. There are compelling reasons why social protection should be part of strategic disaster risk management. This chapter, therefore, understands shocks as endogenous and seeks to integrate natural hazards into the design and implementation process of social protection as an ex-ante intervention.

This chapter makes the case for social protection being an important tool for managing the risk of natural hazards. Social safety nets and other components of community-level social protection prevent and mitigate the impact of natural disaster ex-ante and allow residents to cope with the impacts of natural shocks ex-post. We present a case study of the impact of the 2011 flood on Cambodia's rural poor, who require this comprehensive linkage between social protection and disaster management. This chapter conducts ex-post and ex-ante analysis of the past and potential socioeconomic impacts of disasters on the livelihoods of the rural poor in Cambodia, assesses risk-coping strategies of households, and highlights disaster management system.

The rest of the chapter is organized as follows. Section 2 briefly presents definitions of disasters and our research methodologies. Sections following deal with climate-related vulnerability in Cambodia, particularly the series of floods and droughts resulting from the unique hydrologic regime and agrarian system, and their impacts on people's livelihoods. Subsequently, the chapter presents the role of social protection for natural disaster management along with mechanisms to address the entitlement failures resulting from the impact of flood and drought, before concluding the chapter.

2 Research Methodologies

2.1 *Definition of Disasters and Disaster Risk Management*

Following Sawada (2007), we classify disasters into three major groups. The first type is the natural disaster, which includes hydrological disaster (flood), a meteorological disaster (storm or typhoon), a climatologically disaster (drought), a geophysical disaster (earthquake, tsunami and volcanic eruptions), or biological disaster (epidemic and insect infestation). The second type of disaster comprises technological disasters, i.e., industrial accidents (chemical spills, collapses of industrial infrastructures) and transport accidents (by air, rail, road or water). The final group of disasters is manmade, and includes economic crises (hyperinflation, banking or currency crisis) and violence (terrorism, civil strife, riots, and war).

Disaster risk management (DRM) describes the sets of policies, strategies and practices that reduce vulnerabilities, hazards and unfolding disaster impacts throughout a society. Disasters can have a huge impact on livelihood opportunities and on people's ability to cope with further stresses. Impacts such as loss of assets can lead to increased vulnerability of poor people and a "downward spiral of deepening poverty and increasing risk" (Davies et al. 2008). DRM aims to make livelihoods more resilient to the impacts of disasters, hazards and shocks before the event. Programs include early warning systems, infrastructure investment, social protection measures, risk awareness and assessment, education and training, and environmental management.

In the Cambodian context, disaster risk management should emphasize social protection measures to help people cope with major sources of poverty and vulnerability and promote human development. DRM consists of a broad set of arrangements and instruments designed to protect individuals, households and communities against the financial, economic and social consequences of various risks, shocks and impoverishing situations, and to bring them out of poverty. Social protection interventions include, at a minimum, informal social insurance, labor market policies, social safety nets and social welfare services. Community ties, norms, and trust serve to reduce the vulnerability of members to shocks such as droughts and natural disasters.

2.2 Methodologies and Data Sources

The chapter utilizes existing socioeconomic survey data from 2004 to 2009 and a unique questionnaire survey in 2012 for empirical analyses. The field research, carried out during February to April 2012, took place in 7 provinces (22 communes of 15 districts) which were selected to represent the major and sub-components of Cambodia's agrarian landscape. These 7 provinces were later categorized into 5 clusters of research areas based on an agro-ecological typology.

Cluster 1: Areas with inundated plains, prone to secondary river flooding and prolonged drought (Preah Net Preah and Serei Sophorn District of Banteay Meanchey Province and Banteay Srey District of Siem Reap Province). The majority of crops are large scale cash crops (cassava and maize).

Cluster 2: Areas with undulated plains, prone to flooding from Great Lake during the rainy season (Tonle Sap) but reliant on the delayed recession of floodwater during the dry season (Siem Reap and Chikreng District of Siem Reap Province and Kampong Svay and Baray District of Kampong Thom Province). Receding rice and occasionally floating rice are the major crops.

Cluster 3: Areas of riverbank, prone to Upper Mekong flooding during the rainy season but reliant on the fast recession of floodwater during the dry season (Cheung Prey and Batheay District of Kampong Cham Province). Diversified vegetables and cash crops can be found.

Cluster 4: Areas with extreme undulated plains, prone to Lower Mekong flooding and vulnerable to the speed of flooding and prolonged drought (Prey Veng and Svay Antor District of Prey Veng Province). The area is used mainly for rain-fed rice production.

Cluster 5: Areas of riverbank with secondary swamp lakes, prone to Lower Mekong flooding during the rainy season but reliant on the fast recession of floodwater during the dry season (Muk Kampoul and Khsach Kandal District of Kandal Province and Russey Keo District of Phnom Penh). The area is used mainly for vegetable production.

In total, we interviewed 239 households randomly selected with the help of Village Chiefs. Based on the proxy mean test procedure of the ID-Poor Database[1] (MoP (Ministry of Planning) 2011) including characteristics of housing, household properties, land sizes etc. interviewed households were divided into three categories, namely the poor, near-poor, and non-poor. We use these five clusters to identify areas and locations of household in the sample of the Cambodian Socio-Economic Survey in 2004 and 2009[2] to analyze the impact of droughts and floods on household welfare. Households were also categorized based the size of land ownership into small (0–0.5 ha), medium (0.5–3 ha), and large (more than 3 ha).

3 Vulnerability to Climate in Cambodia

Cambodia's unique hydrological regime and low coverage of water control infrastructure makes it vulnerable to climatic and natural disasters (Fig. 3.1). Most rural households rely heavily on subsistence agriculture for their livelihoods, especially rice cultivation, which accounts for 90 % of the country's total cultivated area and 80 % of agricultural labor input (World Bank 2006a). Agricultural production (and thus households' food security) is heavily dependent on weather conditions and can fluctuate significantly from year to year.

Accordingly, the growth rate of the crop sub-sector varies widely, reflecting high reliance on adequate rainfall and susceptibility to the weather (CDRI (Cambodia Development Resource Institute) 2008). Livelihoods and sources of income for the

[1] ID-Poor Database, an almost nationwide database of the "Identification of Poor Household Program" which divided the livelihood of people into three categories (very poor or ID-Poor I, poor or ID-Poor II, and non-poor) based on a set of proxy mean tests of household properties.

[2] CSES (Cambodian Socio-Economic Survey), last conducted in 2009, is a nationwide representative sample of 12,000 households focusing on livelihood and socio-economic characteristic at household level.

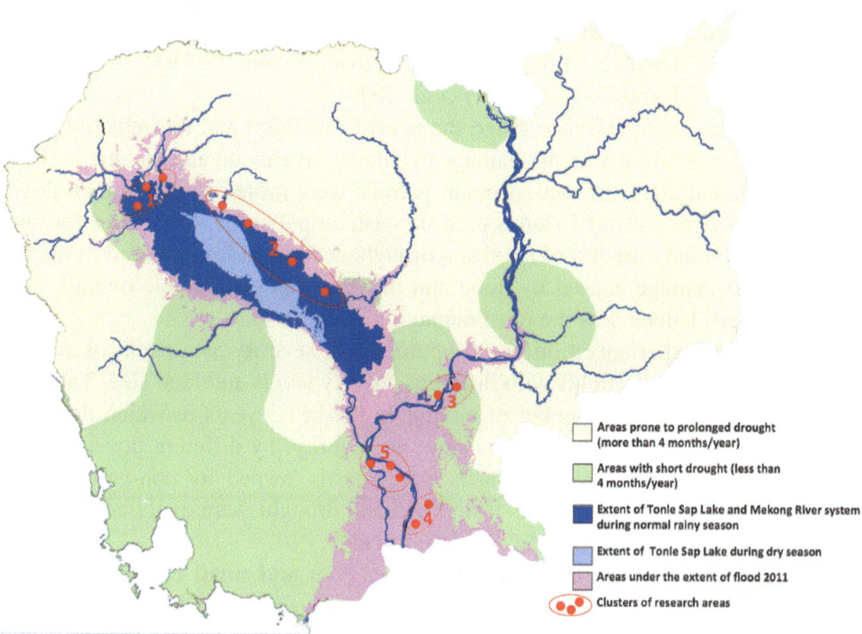

Fig. 3.1 Detailed extension of actual size of great lake (during dry season), expanded size (during rainy season), and the areas flooded in 2011

rural population may therefore be compromised, leaving them reliant on social protection from the state and development partners—in particular in the case of natural disasters.

Poor households also rely on natural resources such as water and forests to generate income. Access to common property provides an important safety net for the rural poor in bad harvest years. The 2006 Poverty Assessment found that one-quarter of the poor depended only on fishery and forest products for over half their income in 2004 and, on average, fishery and forest products accounted for 25 % of household income among the poor (World Bank 2006b). However, access to this common property is becoming increasingly limited. As captured in the qualitative Participatory Poverty Assessment (Ballard et al. 2007), many of the extractive activities in the forest do not comply with rules and regulations. Rising population numbers have also contributed to overexploitation and a decline in resource availability. In addition, leasing of water bodies to business interests and increasing restrictions on free access to fisheries are already evident in places where the poorest depend on hunting and gathering for their livelihoods.

Rural households' vulnerability to climate and economic shocks is exacerbated by the low productivity and low diversification of their income-generating activities. Most rural households rely heavily on subsistence agriculture for their livelihoods: an estimated 72 % of Cambodians are dependent on fishing and agriculture (CNCDM (Cambodia National Committee for Disaster Management) 2010).

In addition, household-level agricultural productivity remains low: rice yields, for instance, remain among the lowest in the region, owing to limited and poor use of improved seed, fertilizer, tillage and water management (CARD (Council for Agricultural and Rural Development) et al. 2009).

Interviewees were asked to range the severity of flood and drought from "no-impact at all =0" to "significant damage to harvest, livelihood and income = 10" in 2009, 2010, and 2011. In total, drought periods were more prolonged than floods especially in Area Cluster 1 (lands used for cash crops) and 4 (lands used for rain-fed rice). The total duration of flood and drought accounted for one third of the last 3 years. The damage caused by flood and drought was comparable overall, even though the 2011 flood was the most damaging event.

Households experienced different typologies of severity as a result of drought and flood among households with different poverty levels and land size. Table 3.1 below presents the total number of months in the last 3 years in which flood and drought were experienced, and the degree of severity, by different poverty levels and land sizes. Large-scale farmlands were mostly owned by non-poor in both figures. However, severe impacts from flood and drought were experienced extensively in large, medium and small-scale farmlands.

The severity of drought was quite diverse. Poor and small farm-land holders mostly faced lower levels of severity whereas as near-poor and medium farm-land holders were concentrated in the high severity zone, and the non-poor and large-scale holders experienced medium severity. In contrast to the degree of drought severity, the severity of flooding was more concentrated. Poor and small farmlands and near-poor and medium farmlands were located in the lower zone of severity whereas the non-poor and large farmlands were concentrated in the higher division of severity. The results presented in Table 3.1 indicated the extensive impact of drought on small and medium-scale farmlands and the high level of damage from flood (mostly sudden and prolonged) to the large-scale farmlands.

On the other hand, the non-diversification of household economies exacerbates the vulnerability of rural Cambodians. Most rural households rely heavily on subsistence agriculture for their livelihoods, with rice cultivation accounting for 90 % of total cultivated area and 80 % of agricultural labor input. Rice yields remain among the lowest in the region due to limited and poor use of improved seed, fertilizer, tillage, and water management. Because productive off-farm opportunities are limited, rural households lack alternatives that would allow them to maintain stable incomes or cope in times of poor harvest (CARD (Council for Agricultural and Rural Development) 2010).

Table 3.1 The total number of months in the last 3 years in which flood and drought were experienced, and the degree of severity by different poverty levels and land sizes

		Total number of months		Total level of severity		
Poverty	Land size	Flood	Drought	Flood	Drought	Flood 2011 severity
Poor	Small	5.28	6.6	13.28	8.8	7.44
	Medium	5.55	6.51	13.38	13.02	7.45
	Large	5.33	6.67	14.08	11.67	7.58
	Total	5.44	6.56	13.45	11.57	7.46
Near-poor	Small	5.93	6.62	14.89	12.82	7.71
	Medium	5.79	5.84	13.72	11.36	9.09
	Large	5.72	5.89	13.83	14.83	6.33
	Total	5.83	6.14	14.17	12.42	8.17
Non-poor	Small	5.5	7.75	18	12.75	8
	Medium	4.79	7.21	15.71	11.14	8.43
	Large	4.63	8	13.63	11.63	8.25
	Total	5	7.59	16.03	11.82	8.24
Total	Small	5.67	6.78	14.85	11.59	7.67
	Medium	5.58	6.27	13.82	11.99	8.36
	Large	5.37	6.58	13.87	13.16	7.13
	Total	5.58	6.49	14.18	12.04	7.93

Source: Authors' calculation from the surveyed data

4 The Impacts of Natural Disasters

4.1 The Socio-economic Impacts of Natural Disasters

In Cambodia, extreme floods and droughts are among the most damaging shocks afflicting rural households, and climate change will heighten their severity. In the past decade, unusual floods and droughts have severely affected large parts of the countryside, resulting in 3 years of negative agricultural growth. In 2009, for example, Typhoon Ketsana left 43 people dead and 67 severely injured and destroyed the homes and livelihoods of some 49,000 families or 180,000 people directly or indirectly (equivalent to 1.4 % of the population). Most of the affected districts were among the poorest in the country. The widespread damage to property and public infrastructure will have a long-term impact on these communities' livelihoods (CNCDM (Cambodia National Committee for Disaster Management) 2010). Looking ahead, although many regions in Cambodia are shielded geographically from climate hazards, almost all provinces are considered vulnerable to the impact of climate change, owing to their low adaptive capacity resulting from financial, technological, infrastructural and institutional constraints (UNDP (United Nations Development Program) 2009).

Poor households are less able to cope than the non-poor, even though empirical studies showed that households are partially able to smooth consumption after a natural disaster (Vakis et al. 2004). The poor are more vulnerable as they are typically more exposed to risks and have access to fewer coping mechanisms that can permit them to deal with the natural disasters. Many households use sub-optimal or even harmful coping options such as reducing consumption expenditures on food, health and education services, and trying to increase incomes by sending children to work. In addition, as the poor are more likely to reside in hazardous locations and in substandard housing, they are more susceptible to natural disasters. Finally, exposure to natural hazards (and to that extent to natural disasters) affects income-generating decisions, which can have long-term implications in the form of lower future income streams, longer recovery periods and poverty traps.

We looked at the impact of the 2011 flood at the macro level on livelihoods, rice production, and physical infrastructure in several provinces including Kampong Thom and Siem Reap (Area Cluster 2), Kampong Cham (Area Cluster 3), and Prey Veng (Area Cluster 4). While the impact of the flooding in 2011 was extremely high at the household level (affected households and resettlement), the damage to rice and agricultural activities, together with the effect on physical infrastructure (roads and schools) will have a long-term impact.

4.2 *Impact of Natural Disasters on Household Welfare*

In assessing the impact of natural disasters on household welfare in Cambodia, we follow the framework of "entitlement failures" proposed by Sen (1981) and elaborated by Devereux (2007). In rain-fed agricultural systems as Cambodia, erratic rainfall can have comprehensive and devastating impact on affected livelihoods and local economies. Addressing the sequence of entitlement failures caused by droughts or floods can prevent them from evolving into a food crisis, and can keep people out of poverty.

According to Devereux (2007), entitlement failures can occur sequentially. Production failure first leads to labor market failure, then commodity market (trade-based entitlements), and finally transfer failures. Table 3.2 illustrates that droughts and floods cause not only crop failures but a sequence of knock-on shocks to local economies and societies, where effective intervention, or lack of it, could mitigate or exacerbate the shock. Some of these policy responses will be discussed later in the context of the risk management system.

Using our household data from socioeconomic survey data collected in 2004 and 2009, the chapter tests whether droughts or floods can lead to one of the entitlement failures: production, labor markets, commodity markets (trade-based entitlements), or transfer failures. However, due to the limitation of the data, the specific failure cannot be identified. Only the consequence of these failures, i.e. low income or consumption is available in the data set. We use statistical regression to investigate how our dependent variables of income or consumption) at the household level are

Table 3.2 Entitlement failure as the result of natural disasters

Entitlement category	Impacts of drought and flood	Policy response
Production based	– Harvest failure	– Productivity-enhancing safety nets' (Starter Packs)
Labor based	– Employment opportunities decline	– Public work program
	– Real wage rates fall	
Trade based	– Market failure	– Open market operations
	– 'Failure of exchange entitlements' (terms of trade decline)	– Food price subsidies
		– Pricing policies
Transfer based	– Failure of informal safety nets	– Food aid
	– Food aid failure	– Cash transfers
	– "Priority regimes"	– Weather insurance

Source: Adapted from Devereux (2007)

a function of a set of explanatory variables that captures household characteristics and concerned variables (drought or flood-prone areas). Controlling for other household characteristics, we expect that households in the drought or flood-prone areas will have lower consumption than otherwise. Our study uses socioeconomic survey data collected in 2004 and 2009 corresponding to some sites in the 7 provinces and 5 clusters of the surveyed areas in April 2012. A total of 160 households were identified living in the same commune out of which 120 households resided in the affected villages. Age, gender, marital status, literacy of household head, household size, and irrigated land area are used as control variables.

We conduct a simple regression and check the impacts of the drought or floods on households' welfare, measured by their consumption. Results from the regression show that household consumption is dependent on literacy, size, and irrigated land area at the 1 % level of statistical significance. More importantly, the consumption level of households in drought or flood-prone areas is significantly lower than otherwise, confirming the negative impact of natural disasters on their livelihood. The negative sign of the coefficient of irrigated land area suggest that drought or flood compounds the impact on those households with larger holdings of cultivated land dependent on irrigation.

Using our unique survey data from 2012, we compiled information on the impacts of the aftermath of the flood in 2011 on households' consumption, crops, livestock, houses, and health. Table 3.3 summarizes the data on households who reported severe impacts from the flood in terms of damage to crops, livestock and houses, and health problems, differentiated by whether or not they reported a reduction in their consumption. The empirical results of our regression analyses suggest that the larger the size of household reporting severe flooding, resulting in house damage, the greater the likelihood of a reduction in their consumption in the aftermath of the flood in 2011, at the 1–5 % level of statistical significance.

Table 3.3 Summary of household characteristics

	Reported reduction in consumption			Reported no change in consumption		
Variables	N	Mean	S.D.	N	Mean	S.D.
Dummy of household status (poor)	48	0.583	0.498	191	0.524	0.501
Logarithm size of household	48	1.704	0.314	190	1.556	0.428
Severity of flood	48	2.091	0.291	190	1.926	0.509
Dummy for crop damage	48	0.688	0.468	191	0.565	0.497
Dummy for livestock damage	48	0.667	0.476	191	0.482	0.501
Dummy for house damage	48	0.500	0.505	191	0.319	0.467
Dummy for sickness	48	0.646	0.483	191	0.508	0.501

Source: Authors' computed from survey data 2012

5 Household Risk-Coping Strategies and Role of Social Protection in Natural Disaster Risk Management

5.1 *Household Risk-Coping Strategies*

Natural disasters can fit within the Social Risk Management (SRM) framework. The SRM provides instruments that allow the poor (but also the non-poor) to minimize the impact of exposure to risk and to change their behavior in a way that helps them exit poverty and reduce vulnerability (Vakis 2006; Holzmann and Jorgensen 2000; Holzmann 2001).

SRM instruments can be used at different moments in the risk cycle: there are ex-ante and ex-post coping strategies. Ex-ante measures aim to prevent the risk from occurring (risk prevention), or to reduce its impact (risk mitigation). Prevention strategies include measures designed to reduce risks in the labor market (the risk of unemployment), health care (the risk of preventable diseases) and standards (the risk of building collapse in areas prone to earthquakes). Mitigation strategies help individuals reduce the impact of a future risky event. For example, households may pool uncorrelated risks through informal or formal insurance mechanisms. Rotating credit associations, information exchange, and other approaches can assist disaster-affected communities during crises. Ex-post coping strategies are designed to relieve the impact of the risk once it has occurred. Some examples of coping are drawing from individual savings or borrowing. Similarly, the government may also provide ex-post support in cases of catastrophic events or in the aftermath of an economic shock. In general, household risk-coping mechanisms include: reduction in consumption expenditure while maintaining total caloric intakes, borrowing (credit), accumulation of financial and physical assets, and receiving assistance or remittances (Sawada 2007).

We conducted simple regressions to see how the affected households utilize each of these risk-coping mechanisms. The results suggest that poor households suffering from crop damage would heavily rely on changing crops, using (dis)saving, and tend not to receive support from the government or NGOs. Those who suffer damage affecting livestock, houses, and health would borrow more money from either relatives or micro-financing institutions. Moreover, poor sick households seem not to be able to change crops but do receive some assistance from the government or NGOs.

5.2 Household Risk-Taking Behavior and Subjective Probability of Loss from Disasters

In this current study, to assess the attitude toward risks, interviewees were asked to bet in three coin-flipping games ranging from the very secure behavior to riskier betting options. In our experiments, refraining from betting brings USD60. If the participant chose to bet, he/she would lose 60 for an unlucky toss with 120 for option 1 and 240 for option 2. In the lhe last game, the riskiest, if they chose not to bet they lose USD60, and when betting, the interviewee would either keep their money if lucky or lose USD120 otherwise.

As shown in Fig. 3.2, most households in all three groups were willing to bet in the second game where they might lose USD 60 or gain USD 240. This game sought to show the willingness of households to invest in measures designed to reduce risks (for example, innovative technology). To assess the relationship between risk-taking behavior and the subjective probability of loss, we conduct a simple ordered logit regression to capture the willingness of household taking riskier bets against their subjective probability of loss from natural disasters.

The empirical results from confirm the risk-averse behavior of the poor households, and also that households will only be take higher risks when they believe that the likelihood of disaster occurrence is higher. Subjective probability beliefs and a high degree of risk-averse behavior among the poor would make the demand for catastrophe insurance a potential option.

5.3 Role of Social Protection in Disaster Risk Management

In the absence of an integrated risk management system, it is important to incorporate community-level social protection into the "natural" disaster management system to address the entitlement failures discussed above. Understandably, social protection, including support payments and insurance against risk, does not reduce disaster risk in itself. Nor is it an alternative to development investments in public infrastructure and services, but there are three compelling reasons why social protection can be part of strategic DRM (Vakis 2006).

First, social protection instruments should be considered as part of a larger set of risk management arrangements, to complement and strengthen existing

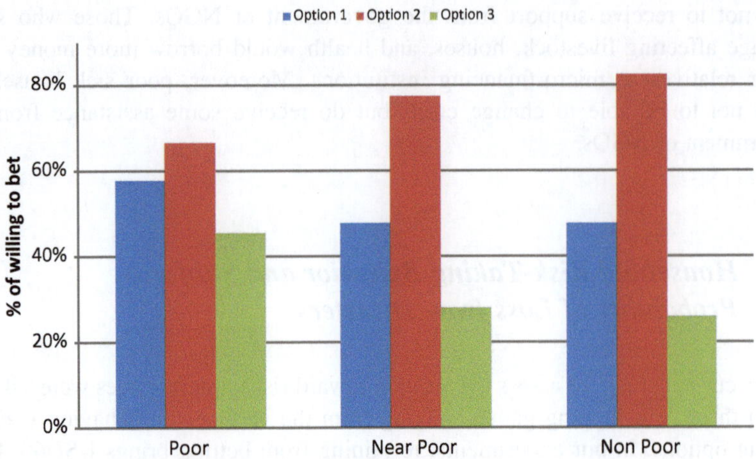

Fig. 3.2 Attitude toward risk as indicated by willingness to bet for different options. *Source*: Authors' calculation from the surveyed data

mechanisms and systems (cf. Aldrich 2012). They should not crowd out other risk management arrangements (informal, market-based or public) but instead be evaluated with other options, based on existing capacities, resources and the potential benefits of each arrangement.

Second, an emphasis on ex-ante instruments (risk mitigation or risk prevention aspects) is more crucial than ex-post, focusing on emergency aid and relief. Taking into consideration a country's limited resources, capacities and other short-term development priorities, the long term costs (and forgone benefits) from an emphasis on ex-ante instruments are large. Finally, an effective natural disaster system requires certain pre-requisites, such as flexibility to adjust and scale up easily, appropriate capacity and effective coordination efforts among government, non-government, private sector and other actors.

Existing schemes draw from informal arrangements, public support from the government and development partners, and civil society and non-governmental organizations (CSOs and NGOs). All these play an important role by complementing one another. It remains clear, however, that even together they do not manage to adequately protect the most poor and vulnerable. A strong case remains for expanding social protection coverage for the poor. A number of initiatives such as cash and food transfer, public works, service fee waiver programs, and microfinance are discussed below by Vakis (2006).

Cash transfers programs provide direct assistance in the form of cash to the poor with low cost of operating and inherent flexibility to scale up during emergencies. This kind of program seeks to address both short-term structural poverty objectives via the income support and also to break intergenerational transmission of poverty through the long-term accumulation of human capital. In the context of natural disasters, cash transfers can provide households with the highest flexibility in terms of how to deal with their problems. In the case of conditional cash transfers, they

Table 3.4 Primary purposes of using cash transferred at different levels

		Amount of cash transferred ($)		
		10	20	30
Poverty	Purposes	If transferred before the Flood 2011		
Poor	Domestic	57.32	53.66	41.46
	Business	36.59	42.68	51.22
	Health	2.44	1.22	2.44
	Other	3.66	2.44	4.88
Near-poor	Domestic	71.43	52.1	34.45
	Business	20.17	38.66	52.94
	Health	5.04	3.36	5.04
	Other	3.36	5.88	7.56
Non-poor	Domestic	50	47.37	44.74
	Business	28.95	36.84	39.47
	Health	10.53	10.53	10.53
	Other	10.53	5.26	5.26
Poor	Domestic	58.54	57.32	47.56
	Business	23.17	39.02	46.34
	Health	14.63	3.66	3.66
	Other	3.66	0	2.44
Near-poor	Domestic	68.91	64.71	48.74
	Business	17.65	32.77	41.18
	Health	10.08	1.68	6.72
	Other	3.36	0.84	3.36
Non-poor	Domestic	57.89	55.26	52.63
	Business	26.32	34.21	39.47
	Health	7.89	7.89	5.26
	Other	7.89	2.63	2.63

Source: Authors' calculation from the surveyed data

can deter the use of harmful coping strategies that often occurs after shocks like natural disasters, for example increases in the incidence of child labor, or reductions in food consumption (de Janvry et al. 2006).

Table 3.4 presents the purpose for which cash transfers of USD 10, 20, and 30 would be used by households at different poverty levels. In the cases of transfers both before and after a flood, the poor and near-poor households would allocate the first USD 10 and 20 of any transfer for domestic use. The allocations of USD 10 and 20 for domestic use rather than for business can be observed more clearly after a flood. However, the allocation for business purpose is higher when the transfer is USD 30.

Public works programs are an important counter-cyclical instrument in a country's programmatic portfolio, as they typically provide unskilled manual workers with short-term employment on projects such as road and irrigation infrastructure construction and maintenance, reforestation, and soil conservation.

After natural disasters, public works programs can provide direct income transfers to affected households, which can allow households to meet consumption shortfalls and other immediate needs.

A number of additional social protection instruments can also be used to address natural disasters. For example, service fee waivers, which allow poor households to access a variety of health, sanitation and education services, can be used to reduce the costs of health care and education for affected areas. Food transfer related programs can also address natural disasters. They can take a variety of delivery forms such as direct food relief, food vouchers or food for work (Del Ninno and Dorosh 2003).

Particular attention should be paid to vulnerable groups in the context of natural disasters such as disabled people. Assisting people with disabilities in the aftermath of natural disasters may require additional efforts and complications. Any new construction to replace buildings including a country's health infrastructure needs to take advantage of the opportunity to introduce cost-effective, accessible designs, both for the new contingent of disabled people and for the pre-existing disabled population.

Government should promote and strengthen microfinance schemes to help households diversify their incomes, which can mitigate against widespread natural disasters and can promote participation in civic and political organizations to invest in preventive measures such as drainage, emergency warning systems, and food storage.

6 Conclusion and Recommendation

The patterns of risk and vulnerability faced by poor and vulnerable people in rural areas, particularly those involved in agriculture and other ecosystem-dependent livelihoods, are becoming major causes of chronic poverty. Dependency on subsistence agriculture, in particular for the rural poor in Cambodia, magnifies the impact of stresses and shocks (such as droughts or floods). Cambodia's unique hydrological regime and low coverage of water control infrastructure makes it vulnerable to climatic and natural disasters. Over the past 3 years flooding and prolonged drought have accounted for almost one third of the elapsed time. The levels of flood and drought damage were comparable, even though the severe flood of 2011 was the most extensive disaster.

The above theoretical and field study provides evidence for policy decisions on linking the mechanism of disaster management to social risk management and social protection instruments that best fit the context of the series of flood and drought disasters in Cambodia. Households perceive social risk management instruments differently. Preventive strategies to reduce the probability of the risk occurring are not well understood by poor households.

There is a strong need at the policy level to design social protection interventions to emphasize ex-ante instruments rather than focus the response to natural disasters as ex-post actions, concentrating on emergency measures and relief. Cash transfer programs provide direct assistance in the form of cash to the poor. Ex-ante cash transfer programs can play a crucial role in encouraging poor households to invest in business rather than spending on food. Microfinance schemes can also help ex-ante income diversification to help households cope with a wide range of natural disasters. Finally, community cohesion, trust, and informal insurance can provide residents with additional mitigation for shocks and crises.

References

Aldrich, D. P. (2012). *Building resilience: Social capital in disaster recovery*. Chicago: University of Chicago Press.

Ballard, B., Sloth, C., Wharton, D., Fitzgerald, I., Murshid, K. A. S., Hansen, K., et al. (2007). *We are living with worry all the time: A participatory poverty assessment of Tonle Sap*. Phnom Penh: CDRI.

CARD (Council for Agricultural and Rural Development). (2010). *Towards a social protection strategy for the poor and vulnerable: Outcomes of the consultation process*. Phnom Penh: CARD.

CARD (Council for Agricultural and Rural Development), WFP (World Food Programme), & World Bank. (2009). *Safety nets in Cambodia. Concept note and inventory*. June 30.

CDRI (Cambodia Development Resource Institute). (2008). *Impact of high food prices in Cambodia*. Phnom Penh: CDRI.

CNCDM (Cambodia National Committee for Disaster Management). (2010). *Cambodia Post-Ketsana disaster needs assessment*. Phnom Penh: CNCDM.

Davies, M., Guenther, B., Leavy, J., Mitchell, T., & Tanner, T. (2008). *Climate change adaptation, disaster risk reduction and social protection: Complementary roles in agriculture and rural growth?* London: Institute of Development Studies.

De Janvry, A., Finan, F., Sadoulet, E., & Vakis, R. (2006). Can conditional cash transfers serve as safety nets in keeping children at school and from working when exposed to shocks? *Journal of Development Economics, 79*, 349–373.

Del Ninno, C., & Dorosh, P. A. (2003). Impacts of In-kind transfers on household food consumption: Evidence from targeted food programmes in Bangladesh. *Journal of Development Studies, 40*(1), 48–78.

Devereux, S. (2007). The impact of droughts and floods on food security and policy options to alleviate negative effects. *Agricultural Economics, 37*(Supplement s1), 47–58.

Holzmann, R. (2001). *Risk and Vulnerability: The Forward Looking Role of Social Protection in a Globalizing World*, Social Protection Discussion Paper 0109. Washington D. C.: The World Bank.

Holzmann, R., & Jorgensen, S. (2000). *Social Risk Management: A New Conceptual Framework for Social Protection, and Beyond*, Social Protection Discussion Paper 0006. Washington D. C.: The World Bank.

MoP (Ministry of Planning). (2011). *Reports from database of poor households. Identification of poor households programme*. Phnom Penh: Ministry of Planning.

Sawada, Y. (2007). The impact of natural and manmade disasters on household welfare. *Agricultural Economics, 37*(1), 59–73.

Sen, A. (1981). *Poverty and famines*. Oxford: Clarendon.

UNDP (United Nations Development Program). (2009). *Cambodia's first national Forum on climate change*. Press Release, 21 October 2009.

Vakis, R. (2006). *Complementing Natural Disaster Management: The Role of Social Protection*, Social Protection Discussion Paper 0543. Washington, D. C.: World Bank.
Vakis, R., Kruger, D., & Mason, D. A. (2004). *Shocks and Coffee: Lessons from Nicaragua*, Social Protection Discussion Paper 0415. Washington, D. C.: World Bank.
World Bank. (2006a). *Managing risk and vulnerability in Cambodia: An assessment and strategy for social protection*. Phnom Penh: World Bank.
World Bank. (2006b). *Halving poverty by 2015? Poverty assessment 2006*. Phnom Penh: World Bank.

Chapter 4
Economic and Welfare Impacts of Disasters in East Asia and Policy Responses: The Case of Vietnamese Communities

Le Dang Trung

1 Introduction

Although Vietnam has seen remarkable economic achievements over the last 25 years, it is still among the poorest countries in the world. Vietnam's economic growth rate had been nearly 8 % per annum for the period from 1990 to 2008 but it started to slow down since 2009. The GDP annual growth rate was 5.3, 6.8 and 5.9 % in 2009, 2010 and 2011, respectively. The global financial and economic crises and domestic macro-economic policies are cited as the main sources of the economic growth decrease. Currently, GDP per capita of Vietnam is reported at USD 722.8 at 2000 constant prices. It is estimated that more than 13 million people are living with less than USD1.25 per day.

The economy is heavily dependent on agriculture with 70 % of the population living in rural areas. The share of rural population has been shrinking due to a rapid urbanization process in recent years at a steady and low rate. The share of rural population was 69.83 % in 2010, down from 72.9 % in 2005. The contribution of agriculture to GDP has been decreasing rapidly over the last two decades. In 1990, agriculture contributed 39 % to total GDP, but by 2000, the share of agriculture was down to 20.5 %.

The World Bank has recently confirmed that Vietnam stands at the top in the list of countries most vulnerable to climate change in the world (Dasgupta et al. 2009). Vietnam is ranked number 2 by the percentage increase in storm surge zones when compared to current surge zones. By absolute impacts of sea level rise and intensified storm surges, Vietnam is number 3 on the list after Indonesia and China. At the city level, Vietnam is also dominant in the list of cities at risk from storm surges.

While the risk of climate change is potentially dangerous, natural disasters have always been disastrous and deadly. Vietnam is located in one of the five storm

L.D. Trung (✉)
Executive Director, Real-Time Analytics, Ho Chi Minh, Vietnam
e-mail: trungle@rta.vn

D.P. Aldrich et al. (eds.), *Resilience and Recovery in Asian Disasters*, Risk, Governance and Society 18, DOI 10.1007/978-4-431-55022-8_4

centers on the planet; the country is hit by on average 4.3 storms per year. Vietnam is also prone to floods and other natural disasters. The government's official data show that between 1990 and 2010 Vietnam experienced 74 catastrophic floods. Storms and floods almost always come with severe aftermaths. For instance, Typhoon Damrey, whose impact will be assessed in Sect. 2.2, caused 68 human deaths, devastated 118,000 houses and destroyed 244,000 ha of rice. The aftermath statistics might, moreover, just reflect the shot-term impacts of such disasters. Natural catastrophes can cause long-term and persistent impacts on households and the economy if, for instance, they destroy investment and lock people into a poverty trap and chronic poverty.

This chapter has several goals. Its first aim is to provide a thorough review of the circumstances of natural disasters in Vietnam by bringing together the existing research literature and utilizing the best data available to date. Its second goal is to conduct a scientific assessment of the impact of a natural catastrophe in order to help understand the multidimensional costs of disasters and draw lessons on how the impacts of natural disasters can be properly assessed. The third goal of this chapter is to present an overview of the management of natural disasters and climate change in Vietnam, to see how the policy system has been working to deal with the risk of natural disasters and climate change, and identify possible options for Vietnam to move forward to an effective disaster risk management system. Section 3 is dedicated to this third goal. Based on the analyses of the previous sections, together with lessons learnt from other countries, Sect. 4 is written for the purpose of providing recommendations, at the national level as well as in the context of regional collaboration, for Vietnam to move forward. Section 5 concludes the chapter.

2 Impact of Disasters on Households and Poverty Reduction in Vietnam

2.1 *Overview of Natural Disasters in Vietnam*

Vietnam's terrain is flat in coastal areas but relatively elevated in the midland and the mountainous regions of the Central Highlands, North East and North West. Vietnam can also be recognized as having an S-shape on maps, with narrow parts in the middle and wide parts in the two tails, in particular the upper tail of the land. Its climate is characterized by monsoon winds, blowing northeast and carrying considerable moisture. The climate is, however, diversified across regions. Based on climatic characteristics, Vietnamese meteorologists classify the country into seven regions, namely: Red River Delta, Northern Uplands, North Central Coast, South Central Coast, Central Highlands, South East and Mekong River Delta.

Located in the center of the South China Sea, one of the Earth's five typhoon centers, Vietnam is prone to natural disasters (Shaw 2006). Utilizing a unique comprehensive database on natural disasters occurring since 1989 as well as complete storm archive since 1951 I will describe the situation of natural disasters in Vietnam in the rest of this section. The comprehensive database has been maintained by the Central Committee for Flood and Storm Control (CCFSC) of the Government of Vietnam for the last two decades. It collects a wide range of information on the identification of disasters and their aftermaths and impacts at the provincial level. Further, Japan Meteorological Agency maintains information on every storm that occurred since 1951. I use these data sources in the analysis.

2.1.1 Tropical Storms and Typhoons

Tropical storms are the most frequent and disastrous natural disaster in Vietnam. I examine the yearly frequency of storms that made landfall in the boundary of Vietnam for the period from 1951 to 2009 and find that during the period Vietnam was hit by at least one storm every year. There are several years in which the number of storms exceeded ten, making almost a storm per month. On average, Vietnam was hit by 4.3 storms annually.

A number of research papers suggest that climate change may result in an increase in the frequency of storms in Vietnam (Hoang Tri et al. 1998; Pham and Furukawa 2007). Fortunately, our analysis indicates that the increase has not yet taken place in Vietnam. Strikingly, a regression of the number of storms on the time trend for the period from 1980 to present produces a coefficient of −0.016 which is statistically significant at 10 %, meaning that the frequency is even lower since 1980, although the size of decrease is marginally significant.

There is, however, enormous heterogeneity in terms of storm frequencies and exposure across regions of Vietnam. As clearly shown in Fig. 4.1, which presents the distribution of storms in three regions of Vietnam, the Centre is more frequently

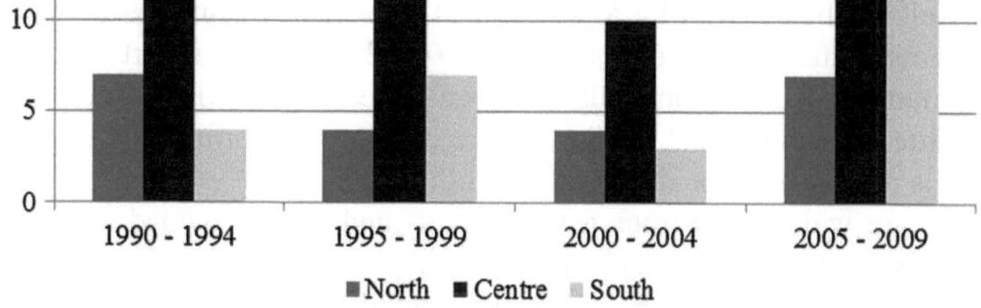

Fig. 4.1 Typhoon frequencies across regions of Vietnam. *Source:* Author's own calculation using CCSFC's disaster database

hit by storms in all the four periods. In the first period, the northern part appeared to be hit more frequently than the south but in the last period, the comparison has been reversed although both the two regions were hit more frequently than in the previous period.

The aftermaths of tropical storms in Vietnam are enormous, both in terms of human losses and economic impacts. I highlight the losses due to tropical storms in Vietnam for the period from 1990 to 2010 using the data from the CCFSC database. In two decades, storms killed more than 5,700 people and caused an additional 7,000 people injured. Moreover, many households have become homeless due to storms. The period from 1995 to 1999 is remarkable in terms of losses. This single period accounts for nearly 65 % of human lives lost, 36 % of houses destroyed and 55 % of bridges damaged. It is worth noting that in this period, the frequency of storms seems lower than the previous and the latest period. It indicates that the intensity of storms in the 1995–1999 period must have been considerable.

The frequency of being hit by storms alters the expectations and awareness of the local people. Exposure to very few disasters causes people to have low expectations about being hit by disasters. Consequently, this behavior lowers the awareness and preparedness required for dealing with disasters, both in terms of formal and self-insurance. Wang et al. (2012) point out that the level of risk closely relates to the acceptance of insurance against disasters. Awareness and preparedness also affect how well people mitigate the effects once disasters happen and thus affect the aftermaths of disasters. As an example, storms are very rare in the Mekong River Delta region of Vietnam. Local residents have almost no expectation of having a storm in this region. Unfortunately, in early November 1997, a storm, named Linda, swept through the farthest south communes causing historical losses, both in terms of human lives and asset losses, although Linda was not an extremely powerful storm in relative terms.

2.1.2 Rainfall and Runoff Floods

Vietnam is also prone to rainfall and river-runoff floods as well as flash floods. The CCFSC's data reveal that, over the last two decades, Vietnam has experienced more than 70 floods. Figure 4.2 visualizes the annual distribution of flooding and the trend of change overtime. The figure clearly indicates a five-year cyclical peak and it may well be aligned with La Niña effects. On average, Vietnam experienced 3.4 flood events annually in the period from 1990 to 2009. More importantly, it seems that the number of floods annually has been increasing overtime. The positively-sloping fitted line in Fig. 4.2 implies an increasing trend. Fortunately, the marginal increase is neither big, nor statistically significant.

Floods are widely disastrous natural events and ranked second to storms and typhoons in Vietnam. Over the same period, there were 5,024 people killed by floods, and an additional 1,641 people reported missing. Floods destroyed or damaged more than 220,000 houses. There is a clear separation in terms of losses between the 1990–1999 and 2000–2009 periods. Human losses tripled in the later

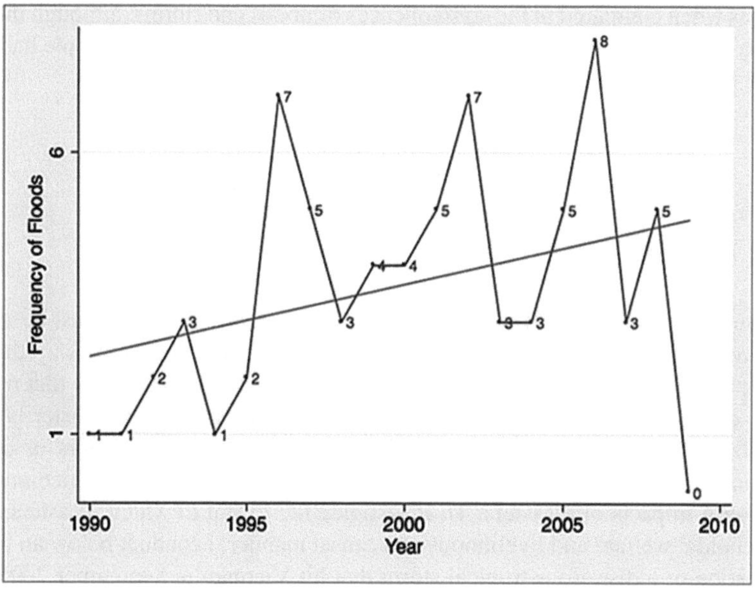

Fig. 4.2 Flood frequencies in Vietnam. *Source:* Author's own calculation using CCSFC's disaster database

period and house losses doubled. The increase in the magnitude of losses may be due to increases in the intensity of floods as well as the number of the floods.

Although regional distribution of floods is more even than that of storms and typhoons, the determinants of floods are still associated with regional characteristics. In the Mekong River Delta, floods are generally caused by runoff water along the Mekong River. Since this delta area is relatively flat and low-lying, runoff floods tend to stay for a very long time. In the central region, however, floods happen more often in the form of flash floods, resulting from intense rainfall, short and steep watersheds, and relatively little water storage capacity. In the Red River Delta, floods are characterized by intense rains, exacerbated by tidal effects (Pilarczyk and Nuoi 2005).

2.1.3 Other Hazards

In addition to storms and floods, Vietnam faces several other types of natural disasters. The CCFSC's disaster database has documented five other disasters, namely drought, cold wave, land collapse, flood-tide and tornado/hailstorm. Of these disasters, drought is also an awful natural event that several provinces, particularly in the southern part of Vietnam, have experienced. Fortunately, the frequency and intensity of the disasters mentioned above are not as substantial as those of storms and floods. Accordingly, the consequences of these disaster types are less when compared to the consequences of floods and storms, although they are clearly visible. Over the 20-year period from 1990 to 2009, 2,253 people had been killed by cold wave, land collapse, flood-tide and tornado/hailstorm.

2.2 *Impact of Disasters on Households and Poverty Reduction in Vietnam*

The analysis using the CCFSC data is informative and useful but it must be subject to several caveats. First, measurement errors can be huge due to the way the data collection system was organized. Secondly, there is a likely possibility that respondents or victims might exaggerate the impact and aftermath of a disaster because they have learnt that they might be given more support from donors or charity organizations. Thirdly, the aftermath statistics might not reflect the medium- and long-term impacts of disasters. To investigate the extent to which disasters affect households' welfare and livelihoods in a causal manner, I conduct below an impact evaluation of a disastrous tropical storm that hit Vietnam in September 2005. The typhoon was named Damrey by the World Meteorological Organization.

2.2.1 Typhoon Damrey

Damrey was the international name of tropical storm number 7 in 2005 in Vietnam. Damrey was born from Tropical Depression 17W (named by the Joint Typhoon Warning Center) on September 20, 2005. At 0:00 on that day, Damrey's eye was centered at latitude 18.7N and longitude 122.2E with a maximum wind speed of 34 knots. It became stronger in the following days and made landfall at Wanning, in the Hainan province of China at 4:00 am on September 26 local time, with a sustained maximum wind speed of 75 knots. Damrey kept moving west towards Vietnam with somewhat lower intensity. In the early morning of September 27th, Damrey made landfall in coastal areas of Thai Binh, Nam Dinh, Thanh Hoa and Hai Phong provinces with a wind speed of 60 knots. After about 15 hours devastating a large area of Vietnam, Damrey attenuated and disappeared in Laos on the following day.

According to meteorological specialists, Typhoon Damrey was the most powerful storm in Vietnam over the period 1996–2005. CCFSC statistics on the aftermath of Damrey, summarized in Table 4.1, reveals horrific human and asset losses. In less than a day of its life, Damrey killed 68 people and caused 28 others injured. To mitigate the aftermath of Damrey, more than 38,000 households, or more than 150,000 people, had to evacuate. In addition, Typhoon Damrey completely destroyed or badly damaged a wide range of physical assets and investments, such as agricultural crops, irrigation dykes, schools and hospitals. Although the aftermath statistics might be subject to measurement errors, the losses are undeniably huge.

Table 4.1 Summary of aftermath of Typhoon Damrey

Loss	Unit	Number
Human deaths	Person	68
Human injured	Person	28
Households evacuated	Household	38,317
Houses collapsed or swept away	House	4,746
Houses damaged	House	113,523
Schools collapsed, swept away or damaged	School	4,080
Hospital collapsed or swept away	Hospital	197
Paddy areas submerged or damaged	Hectare	244,619
Vegetable areas submerged or damaged	Hectare	62,507
Trees collapsed	Tree	1,106,263
Dykes collapsed, swept away or damaged	Meter	88,950
Length of roads damaged	Kilometer	267

Source: CCFSC Disaster Database

2.2.2 Evaluation Methodology

Although responsible organizations in Vietnam made detailed records in the aftermath of the typhoon, the statistics provided do not necessarily show the true impact of the typhoon, for a number of reasons. First, the data might be subject to enormous measurement errors. The responsible organizations acquire the aftermath statistics via a reporting system, starting from commune to district and finally to the province's level of authority. In addition, victims of the disasters, or relief agencies, have a tendency to exaggerate the effects of disasters in order to get more aid and support (Taylor 1979; Pelling 2003; Guha-Sapir et al. 2004). Secondly, the statistics may only reflect the short-term aftermath of disaster, while the disasters can cause long-term negative impacts on livelihood and poverty. In the worst cases, disasters can trap people into persistent poverty (Carter et al. 2007).

Evaluating the impact of such an event as Typhoon Damrey is very challenging. The first challenge is to identify the affected areas. One solution might be to rely on the media or storm tracking agencies. As storms are deadly and highly frequent disasters, a number of meteorological agencies have been paying attention to capturing, tracking and archiving the data for both forecasting and analysis purposes. The tracking data are very good in terms of providing the maximum wind speed and the path of the eye. Nevertheless, they do not identify affected localities precisely enough to link with micro data such as household surveys.

Another way to identify affected areas is through interviews with respondents in a household survey. This technique has long been employed to evaluate the impact of natural disasters (Morris et al. 2002; Alvi and Dendir 2011; Patt and Schröter 2008). Unfortunately, this approach is not always feasible because it is very expensive to conduct household surveys with adequate sampling characteristics and observations to capture the information. In addition, such an identification strategy can be subjectively biased by respondents due to forgetting and a tendency to self-interest.

The second challenge we have to face when evaluating the impact of storms is that natural disasters are surprisingly not random events. As we have seen in the review above, storm frequencies are very much different from place to place, which lead to differences in the likelihood of being hit by a storm, expectations of storms and awareness and preparedness for dealing with them. All of these factors accumulate overtime to cause the economic background of the places to alter. In other words, there is selection endogeneity in the types of intervention made in storm-affected areas.

Our method of evaluating the impact of Typhoon Damrey aims at overcoming both these two challenges. For the first challenge, which is to identify the areas affected by Damrey, I have successfully developed a method that allows us to objectively identify communes (the smallest administrative division in Vietnam) hit by Typhoon Damrey with the minimum wind speed of 35 knots. The core activity is to construct a trail following the path of the Typhoon's eye in which the wind speed is no less than 35 knots. An attempt to do this was made at the Division of Early Warning and Assessment of the United Nations Environment Program (Mouton and Nordbeck 2005). This work utilizes the wind prediction model suggested by Holland (1980) but improves it further by taking into account the asymmetric nature of storm winds. Holland's model allows us to estimate the distance from the eye of a cyclone given a level wind speed. This model, however, assumes that the wind profile is symmetric, which is never the case (Australia Government Bureau of Meteorology. (n.d.)). In really, in the Northern Hemisphere, wind speed on the right side of the eye is higher than wind speed on the left side. In the Southern Hemisphere, this relationship is reversed (Mouton and Nordbeck 2005).

I follow the routine described in Mouton and Nordbeck (2005) with special concentration on preparing the data from storm archives for the best identification of the trail. The output of this routine is a geo-referenced shape-file that can be overlaid with a commune shape-file to identify affected communes. It is worth noting that the process has been done for every severe storm that hit Vietnam between 1955 and 2010, rather than just for Typhoon Damrey. This is necessary because I need to obtain a measure of the long-term likelihood of being hit by storms to address potential selection biases.

In addition, to eliminate the potential selection biases, I employ a "matched-sample regression" strategy when estimating the impact of Damrey. This method involves two steps. First, I construct a better sample by selecting the most comparable households in the unaffected households using a propensity score matching, as pioneered by Rosenbaum and Rubin (1985). Secondly, once the most relevant control group has been identified, I employ the following specification to estimate the impact of Damrey:

$$Y_{ci} = \alpha + \beta D_c + \gamma PS_c + \delta X_{ci} + \varepsilon_{ci} \tag{4.1}$$

where:

- Y_{ci} is an outcome indicator of household i in commune c. Outcome indicators include food expenditure, total expenditure, total income, house repair expenses, and rice production.
- D_c is a dummy variable which takes a value of unity of commune c was hit by Typhoon Damrey and zero otherwise.
- PS_c is the propensity score used to construct the matched sample.
- X_{ci} is a set of control variables of household i in commune c, including demographic variables, education and employment variables.

The coefficient β captures the impact of Damrey. Since I will be fitting the model with the matched sample as well as controlling for the propensity score to being hit by Damrey, I am strongly convinced that biases will be eliminated to make β an unbiased estimate of the impact of Damrey.

2.2.3 Data and Empirical Results

Data used to fit the model above come from the Vietnam Household Living Standard Survey (VHLSS) 2006. The VHLSSs have been conducted by the General Statistics Office (GSO) of Vietnam since 2002 with technical and financial supports from the World Bank. The survey's questionnaire follows the structure employed by the Living Standards Measurement Study (LSMS) advocated by the World Bank since the early 1990s, and been conducted in a number of developing economies. The VHLSSs have been considered one of the highest quality surveys and are used in several research papers (Katsushi et al. 2011; Nguyen Viet 2011; Nguyen and Winters 2011; Sepehri et al. 2011; Mergenthaler et al. 2009).

The VHLSS 2006, like the other VHLSSs, collected information on various aspects of households such as demographics, education, health, expenditure, economic activities and income sources. The VHLSS 2006 interviewed 9,189 households in 3,063 communes, which account for approximately one third of all the communes in Vietnam. The survey covered both rural and urban communities. The ratio of rural communes to urban communes is 2294/769, unsurprisingly close to the corresponding population ratio. In this chapter I focus on the rural household sample. The rural households are much more vulnerable to natural disasters, both in terms of self-defense capacity and in terms of livelihood. The main livelihood of the rural households is agricultural activity, which is substantially fragile to storms. The rural sample comprises 6,882 households in 2,294 communes.

This sample is then merged with the commune-level data set containing a measure of Damrey and the long-term likelihood of being hit by a storm in a one-year period described earlier. It is not possible to match all of the communes in the two data sets, however, although most of them can be perfectly matched. Out of the 6,882 households in the rural sample, I can merge up to 6,831 households in 2,277 communes. This is the sample I will be working on.

There are 816 households in the sample, from 272 communes hit by Typhoon Damrey. The remaining 6,015 households were unaffected by Typhoon Damrey.[1] The 6,015 unaffected households were located in 2,005 communes. The sample of 275 Damrey communes and 2,005 non-Damrey communes form the sample (hereafter referred to as the Damrey dataset) that I will rely on to identify a "matched sample", used to measure the effects of Damrey at the commune level. I employ the propensity score method pioneered by Rosenbaum and Rubin (1985) and later adopted and developed further by many researchers (Rubin and Thomas 1996; Smith and Todd 2001; Becker and Ichino 2002; Jalan and Ravallion 2003).

The variable "Probability of being hit by storm" measures the long-term likelihood that the commune is hit a storm with wind speeds at least 34 knots. It is constructed using the following formula:

$$Pstorm = 1 - e^{-\lambda} \tag{4.2}$$

where λ is the expected number of storms that hit the commune annually.

The parameter λ is the mean of yearly storms calculated over the last 30-year period. In fact, it is the key variable, and I am convinced that once I control for it is possible to eliminate most (if not all) of the potential biases. This is because this variable actually captures a many factors affecting storm exposure. For instance, coastal areas are subject to many more storms than inland areas, since storms will quickly lose their strength once they make landfall; the "long-term probability of being hit by a storm" variable also reflects very well the north/south regional divide since, as we have seen earlier, storms do not happen frequently in the southern part of Vietnam.

I estimate the propensity score of impact by Damrey using the "pscore" routine in Stata. Basically, the score is the series of fitted values of the following logistic model:

$$Damrey_c = \alpha_0 + \alpha_1 Pstorm_c + \alpha_2 X_c + \varepsilon_c \tag{4.3}$$

where:

- $Damrey_c$ is a dummy variable which takes a value of unity if commune c was hit by Damrey and zero otherwise.
- $Pstorm_c$ is the long-term likelihood of being hit by a storm in a one-year period of commune c, estimated using the data on all storms in the last 30 years.
- X_c is a set of control variables for commune c.
- ε_c is the error term.

I have estimated Model (**4.3**) with several sets of control variables, such as distance to coast, and elevation, so as to seek for the specification that gives us the

[1] Unaffected households are households in communes in which wind speeds due to Damrey were lower than 35 knots.

Table 4.2 Mean comparison of Damrey versus Non-Damrey communes

	Pscore	Pstorm	Distance to coast	Elevation
Unmatched sample				
Non-Damrey communes	0.102	0.251	86,596.528	149.723
Damrey communes	0.249	0.420	28,498.465	37.999
All communes	*0.120*	*0.271*	*79,627.892*	*136.322*
Matched sample				
Non-Damrey communes	0.229	0.408	69,863.744	79.899
Damrey communes	0.249	0.420	28,498.465	37.999
All communes	*0.234*	*0.411*	*59,254.205*	*69.152*

Source: Author's own calculations

best matching result. The model is then determined to include no control X. This result does not surprise us, however. In fact, as discussed above, the *Pstorm* variable has already captured the information of elevation and distance to the coast, and it captures the information in a better way. Other infrastructure measures play insignificant roles because most of the communes have the infrastructure. In the end, 6 is the optimal number of blocks of the propensity score, so that the balancing property is satisfied (within each block).

Table 4.2 shows a summary of the two samples: the unmatched sample (Damrey sample) and the matched sample. The matched sampling proves to be highly significant in terms of finding a more comparable control group. The gaps in *Pscore* and *Pstorm* between Damrey communes and non-Damrey communes in the unmatched sample are very high. As expected, Damrey communes have much higher scores for both two variables because Damrey communes are located in storm-prone areas. The matched sampling has narrowed down the gaps significantly. The average *Pscore* in Damrey communes is 0.249 and 0.229 in the non-Damrey communes in the matched sample.

The matched sample contains 3,123 households in 1,041 communes, of which 801 households in 267 communes were hit by Damrey. I will estimate the impact of Damrey on 6 outcome measures, namely (i) household expenditure measured in log, (ii) household food expenditure measured in log, (iii) household total income measured in log, (iv) percentage of house repair expenses in total household expenditure and (v) the quantity of rice harvested in the summer-autumn season. It is worth noting that the number of observations for house repair expenses and rice production variables are smaller because those households who did not repair houses or did not grow rice were not included in the summary.[2] Table 4.3 summarizes the results of the mean-difference tests of the key variables between Damrey-affected hosueholds and Damrey-unaffected households in the matched sample.

A conventional approach to estimating the impacts of Typhoon Damrey using the matched sample is to simply compare the mean of the affected households with that of the unaffected households. However, one can make use of the propensity

[2] Actually, these household should have a value of zero for the variables.

Table 4.3 Comparison of control variables

Control variable	Non Damrey	Damrey
Log head's age	3.848***	3.880***
Head's gender	0.793**	0.828**
Minority ethnicity	0.152***	0.102***
Head's education is college	0.202	0.186
Head worked for firms	0.086	0.076
Household size	4.117**	3.973**
% of children	0.214	0.210
% of elderly	0.142	0.154
% of members with college degree	0.179***	0.151***
% of members working for wages	0.206	0.197

Source: Author's calculations; Asterisks for mean-difference test: * significant at 10 %; ** significant at 5 %; *** significant at 1 %

score as a regressor in regressions that estimate the impacts (Imbens 2004). This way of exploiting the propensity score is relevant for our case since Damrey is identified in the same way to all the households in a commune and is exogenous to all household characteristics. In other words, household characteristics are still useful in explaining the outcome indicators of interest and thus should be controlled for.

I present results of the regressions that estimate the impacts of Damrey on rice household expenditure and house repairs in Tables 4.4 and 4.5, respectively. In these tables, the first column shows the estimate of β with no controls. It can be considered the treatment effects estimated by the conventional matching method. In the subsequent columns, I gradually add more controls to see how robust the estimates of β are to the controls included.

Impact of Damrey on Rice Production

Typhoon Damrey was active during the last days of September 2005. This period overlapped with the Summer-Autumn rice season in Vietnam. The CCFSC data shows that 244,619 ha of rice were damaged due to Damrey. Our analysis allows us to quantify the impact of Damrey in terms of the quantity of rice loss which is a much more precise measure of the aftermath. I ran a Tobit version of Model (**4.1**) as for those households who do not grow Summer-Autumn rice the dependent variable will have a value of zero. This means that the variable is left-censored at zero. The coefficient of Damrey is highly significant and robust. Its sign is negative suggesting that Damrey negatively affected rice production. Specifically, Damrey caused a loss of about 1.5 ton of rice for the affected households. This amount of rice loss is 60 % of the average Summer-Autumn rice harvested by Summer–Autumn rice farmers.

Table 4.4 Dependent variable: log household expenditure

Variables	(1)	(2)	(3)	(4)
Damrey	−0.147***	−0.134***	−0.117***	−0.074***
	(0.025)	(0.022)	(0.020)	(0.022)
Pscore		0.600***	0.560***	0.244**
		(0.105)	(0.096)	(0.118)
Log head's age		−0.107***	−0.079*	−0.064
		(0.035)	(0.045)	(0.044)
Head's gender		0.094***	0.130***	0.132***
		(0.025)	(0.022)	(0.022)
Head's education is college or above		−0.243***	−0.228***	−0.213***
		(0.033)	(0.031)	(0.039)
Head works for firms		0.262***	−0.030	−0.022
		(0.024)	(0.026)	(0.026)
Household size		0.238***	0.169***	0.172***
		(0.034)	(0.033)	(0.033)
Head's ethnicity is minority		0.181***	0.168***	0.170***
		(0.009)	(0.009)	(0.009)
% of children			−0.300***	−0.285***
			(0.053)	(0.052)
% of elderly			−0.369***	−0.383***
			(0.043)	(0.042)
% with college or higher degree			0.692***	0.680***
			(0.053)	(0.052)
% wage workers			0.004	−0.035
			(0.041)	(0.041)
Region fixed-effects	N	N	N	Y
Constant	9.647***	9.057***	9.033***	9.099***
	(0.015)	(0.143)	(0.176)	(0.175)
Observations	3,099	3,099	3,099	3,099
R-squared	0.014	0.358	0.460	0.476

Note: Robust standard errors in parentheses, clustered at commune level Meaning of asterisks: *** $p<0.01$, ** $p<0.05$, * $p<0.1$

Impact of Damrey on Total Household Income

Damrey caused impacts on household income via rice losses and through other channels. I investigate the impact by fitting Model (**4.1**) with the OLS procedure since the dependent variable is uncensored. The regression result showed that the coefficient of Damrey is negative and strongly significant in all the specifications of the regression. In terms of the order of magnitude, the coefficient ranges from 0.05 to 0.16, meaning that Damrey-affected households experienced from 5 to 17 % reduction in income compared with unaffected households.

Table 4.5 Dependent variable: house repairs (% in total expenditure)

Variables	(1)	(2)	(3)	(4)
Damrey	0.13***	0.13***	0.13***	0.13***
	(0.042)	(0.042)	(0.042)	(0.045)
Pscore		0.08	0.06	−0.09
		(0.206)	(0.206)	(0.233)
Log head's age		0.05	−0.09	−0.10
		(0.072)	(0.099)	(0.098)
Head's gender		0.06	0.06	0.06
		(0.053)	(0.055)	(0.054)
Head's education is college or above		−0.07	−0.06	−0.04
		(0.059)	(0.059)	(0.072)
Head works for firms		0.06	0.02	0.02
		(0.050)	(0.062)	(0.062)
Household size		0.01	−0.05	−0.05
		(0.061)	(0.063)	(0.063)
Head's ethnicity is minority		0.01	0.02*	0.02*
		(0.012)	(0.014)	(0.015)
% of children			−0.24**	−0.24**
			(0.112)	(0.112)
% of elderly			0.09	0.10
			(0.102)	(0.102)
% with college or higher degree			0.13	0.12
			(0.119)	(0.120)
% wage workers			0.21**	0.21**
			(0.084)	(0.085)
Region fixed-effects	N	N	N	Y
Constant	−0.75***	−1.06***	−0.58	−0.49
	(0.087)	(0.328)	(0.397)	(0.394)
Observations	3,123	3,123	3,123	3,123
Pseudo R-squared	0.00438	0.00734	0.0137	0.0147

Note: Robust standard errors in parentheses, clustered at commune level
Meaning of asterisks: *** $p < 0.01$, ** $p < 0.05$, * $p < 0.1$

Impact of Damrey on Food Expenditure

I also rely on the OLS procedure to estimate the impact of Damrey on the food expenditure of the households (measured in log). In all the specifications, the coefficient of Damrey is always strongly significant and negative, suggesting a negative impact of Damrey on food expenditure. The size of the coefficient ranges from 0.038 to 0.104 showing that food expenditure in the affected households was 3.9–11 % lower than in the unaffected households.

Impact of Damrey on Total Expenditure

According to Table 4.4, which summarizes the results of regressions used to investigate the impact of Damrey on total expenditure, Typhoon Damrey caused significant welfare losses to the affected households. The impact coefficient ranges from −0.0147 to −0.074 suggesting that, due to Damrey, the affected households expenditure levels lower than unaffected ones by 7.4–15.8 %.

Impact of Damrey on House Repair Expenses

The aftermath in the form of shelter damage is particularly interesting to look at. Although households in storm-prone areas have a tendency to invest in more durable shelters, huge damage can easily occur during severe storms. To investigate whether this was the case with Damrey, I estimate Model (**4.1**) with the dependent variable being the expense incurred in house repairs. Since there are households who happened to have no spending on house repair over the last 12 months, the variable is left-censored at zero. Therefore, I will employ the Tobit procedure to estimate the coefficients.

As we have seen, the impacts of Damrey on income and consumption are very significant and robust (Table 4.5). I therefore expected Damrey to have a strong impact on houses as well. As it turns out, the coefficient of Damrey in all the specifications is strongly significant and the sizes are very robust. The coefficient's sign is positive, suggesting that households affected by Damrey had to raise their spending on house repairs. Specifically, due to Damrey, they had to spend from 12 to 14 % of total expenditure on repairing their houses. These expenses contribute to the reasons why households had to reduce food and other consumption.

3 Disaster Risk Management in Vietnam

3.1 Policy Responses

The Government of Vietnam has considered the dangers of climate change and natural disasters to be a national threat, and established a specialized agency to control and coordinate the whole system. In Vietnam, several ministries take part in the national system, including the Ministry of Natural Resources and Environment (MONRE), the Ministry of Agricultural and Rural Development (MARD), the Ministry of Transport (MOT), the Ministry of Health (MOH), the Ministry of Construction (MOC), the Ministry of Industry and Trade (MOIT), the Ministry of Investment and Planning, the Ministry of Finance (MOF) and the Ministry of Education and Training (MOET).

3.1.1 National Targeted Program to Respond to Climate Change (NTPRCC)

The NTPRCC was initiated in 2008, after a decade of preparation and gradually increasing international cooperation. The Program has specified 8 national objectives, including:

1. Assessing the extent and impacts of climate change in Vietnam in the context of global climate change;
2. Identifying measures to respond to climate change;
3. Enhancing research activities to develop scientific and practical foundations for measures to respond to climate change;
4. Enhancing and strengthening institutional, organizational policies and capacities on climate change issues;
5. Raising awareness and a sense of responsibility of the population and strengthening human resources;
6. Enhancing international cooperation and promoting low-emission development
7. Integrating climate change issues into socio-economic, sectoral and local development strategies, plans and planning; and
8. Developing and implementing the action plans of ministries, sectors and localities in responding to climate change.

The NTRPC has so far been operational for more than 4 years, with encouraging achievements. Five years ago, policies on climate change were vague and overlapped across ministries and sectors. As of today, according to Mr. Naoki Mori of the Japan International Cooperation Agency (JICA), efforts in responding to climate change have resulted in achievements in "designing and developing policies and legal frameworks; promoting policy discussions; strengthening coordination; identifying financing sources for climate change projects and mobilizing various resources" (MONRE 2012).

The Program has identified a 3-Year Policy Matrix that specifies clear objectives of responding policies and implementing agencies, focusing on three pillars, namely, coping, mitigating, and the legal framework and cross-sectoral coordination. The Matrix has been approved by the Prime Minister and in the process of implementation. To achieve an effective system for natural disaster risk management, one cannot separate disaster management and environment management. Tran and Shaw (2007) have pointed out that there is a big gap between policies and actions on disaster and environment management in Thua Thien – Hue province of Vietnam. They argue that most recent projects focus on addressing the hazard risk by building durable infrastructure to mitigate the impact of disasters, rather than looking at a broader picture having both hazard risk and environment dynamic elements.

3.2 Towards an Effective Disaster Risk Management System in Vietnam

3.2.1 Review of Disaster Risk Management Approaches

The literature has accumulated long chapters on disaster risk management approaches. de Guzman (2003) has briefly summarized the most important approaches that have been discussed in the field of risk management so far. To draw focus I discuss further several approaches that are potentially relevant for Vietnam.

The "all-hazards" approach proposes to tackle many disasters in one risk management framework. The all-hazards approach has certain strengths, such as the capacity to provide similar emergency responses in response to a wide range of disasters (Cornall 2005) and the ability to avoid the artificial divide between a physical and a social emphasis (Berkes 2007). Nevertheless, disasters are far from homogeneous in any aspect, from consequences to responses needed, and thus require specific actions to deal with them. The approach "cannot be stretched to every potential crisis situation" as argued in McConnell and Drennan (2006).

The integrated approach involves the participation of all the stakeholders, namely government, private sectors, public and community organizations and households, into the disaster risk management system. Thus, many responses such as mitigation, preparedness, and warning can be efficiently coordinated and carried out before disasters take place (Moe and Pathranarakul 2006).

The "vulnerability reduction" approach functions by interfering with and managing the risk exposure and coping capability components of the disaster risk. This approach seemingly assumes that the third component of the risk, namely the hazard potential or the possibility of being hit by disasters is out of human control. For instance, one can possibly argue that nobody has the ability to control when or where a typhoon will appear.

3.2.2 Total Disaster Risk Management (TDRM) Approach

This approach to disaster risk management is thoroughly documented in de Guzman 2003. The TDRM Approach originated in the Asian Disaster Reduction Center and UN Office for the Coordination of Humanitarian Affairs (OCHA) Asian Disaster Reduction Unit. de Guzman (2003) outlines the core of the TDRM approach as the following:

- The foundation of this approach is based on the integration of existing knowledge and techniques on disaster reduction and response, and risk management.
- It necessarily focuses on the underlying causes of disasters, the conditions of disaster risks and the vulnerability of the community. It also emphasizes multilevel, multidimensional and multidisciplinary cooperation and collaboration, in achieving effective disaster reduction and response. This approach

intends to integrate, complement, and enhance existing disaster reduction and response strategies.

- The approach promotes effective integration of stakeholders' action through multilevel, multidimensional and multidisciplinary coordination and collaboration, a critical strategy toward improving disaster reduction and response. Also, it facilitates broad-based participation in policy and program development in disaster reduction and response as they relate with other development concerns, such as poverty reduction, land use planning, environmental protection, and food security.
- However, in adopting the TDRM Approach, accurate and reliable hazard, vulnerability and disaster risk information is vital. The approach attaches great importance to hazard mapping and vulnerability assessment as a fundamental tool for good decision-making and efficient sharing of disaster risk information.

With the outlined foundation, the TDRM approach aims at achieving three objects:

1. To address holistically and comprehensively the various concerns and gaps in the different phases of the disaster management cycle by considering the underlying causes of disasters (i.e. the conditions of disaster risks) and the broader set of issues and contexts associated with disaster risk and its management;
2. To prevent, mitigate, prepare for, and respond effectively to the occurrence of disasters through the enhancement of local capacity and capability, especially in disaster risk management (i.e. recognizing, managing and reducing disaster risks, and ensuring good decision-making in disaster reduction and response based on reliable disaster risk information); and
3. To promote multilevel, multidimensional and multidisciplinary coordination and collaboration among stakeholders in disaster reduction and response as they ensure the participation of the community, the integration of stakeholders' action, and the best use of limited resources.

de Guzman (2003) proposes five implementation steps to achieve the three objectives as follows:

1. Achieving effective disaster reduction and response through multilevel, multidimensional and multidisciplinary cooperation and collaboration.
2. Making decisions based on reliable disaster risk information from hazard mapping and vulnerability assessment.
3. Enhancing coordination and integration of stakeholders' action through good communication and efficient exchange of relevant and reliable information
4. Ensuring that appropriate enabling mechanisms are in place, including policy, structure, capacity building, and resources.
5. Implementing the disaster risk management process from the national level to the community level.

A number of countries have adopted the TDRM approach and contributed good practices for other countries to draw lessons learnt. Among those countries are

Armenia, India, Indonesia, Japan, Myanmar, Nepal, Singapore, Sri Lanka, and Thailand. I strongly believe that adopting the TDRM approach could be a way towards effective disaster risk management for Vietnam.

4 Policy Recommendations

4.1 National Level

Recommendation 1: Concentrate on Implementing the NTPRCC
The Government of Vietnam has been very active in the fight against climate change and natural disasters. It has put these two areas among the top priorities such as poverty reduction and healthcare. The National Target Program to Respond to Climate Change (NTP-RCC) was approved by the Prime Minister in December 2008. In March 2012, the Government launched the National Strategy on Climate Change (NSCC). Issues, objectives, methods and tools have been identified; the Government now has to focus of the implementation of the NTP-RCC and the NSCC.

Recommendation 2: Stay Open-Minded and Make Necessary Changes Along the Way
Over a relatively short period of time, from 2007 to 2011, the Government has achieved much in terms of identifying climate change and natural disasters issues; setting objectives and goals; and setting legal frameworks for measures to be implemented. Policies have been designed and stated clearly in the NTP-RCC's documents and the NSCC. However, it is likely that the context will change in the years to come, and new issues as well as challenges will emerge. The Government thus needs to stay alert, open-minded to make necessary changes on time.

Recommendation 3: Achieve Objectives by Taking all Possible Opportunities
Issues of climate change and natural disasters can be addressed by direct measures such as raising awareness, conducting research and applying research outcomes and preventing deforestation. However, the Government should not restrict itself to direct measures. The ultimate and intermediate goals of the work in relation to climate change and natural disasters can also be achieved via indirect measures. For instance, deforestation is mainly due to human activities which are driven by economic pressures. In most cases, poor people are 'forced' to go to forests and cut down trees because they have no livelihood alternatives. Thus, to prevent deforestation, the Government can instead focus on job creation programs (together with others) rather than just stressing forest-policing work. Measures like this are called indirect measures and, in many cases, indirect measures help address the issues from their root-causes.

4.2 *Regional Cooperation*

As a matter of fact, Vietnam is part of a global chain when dealing with natural disasters and climate change. While Vietnam has to be proactive in dealing with natural disasters and climate change issues, it can shorten the road with cooperation and assistance from other countries. This section presents recommendations that can be relevant for Vietnam in the context of regional cooperation.

Recommendation 1: Utilize the Advantages of Being a Developing Country
Although Vietnam has achieved remarkable successes in economic growth and poverty reduction over the last few decades, it is still one of the poorest countries in the world. It is fair to say that a large part of recent success is due to external support. Vietnam can become a middle-income country in the near future, but until then, Vietnam should be active in approaching the donor community to seek both technical and financial support. However, the most important thing is that Vietnam has to utilize any support in the most responsible and effective way.

Recommendation 2: Promote Capacity Building
Capacity building is a useful measure to achieve stated goals, because how successful the implementation of a policy will be depends on people's awareness and cooperation. The government should intensify its capacity building activities to date (for example, community-based risk management projects) and set up channels for new activities. Strengthening local communities in Vietnam can create deeper levels of trust and more widely shared norms; as a result communities may overcome collective action problems more efficiently (Chap. 2 in this volume). Another reason to promote capacity building is that it is a good selling point in seeking financial support from the donor community.

Recommendation 3: Highlight Clean Energy and Low-Emission Development
A development strategy that developing countries like Vietnam are tempted to adopt is "cheap development", focusing on current and short-term economic growth and accepting a negative impact on environmental protection goals. Vietnam has already experienced the way in which such a strategy brings about increasing environmental problems (Agusa et al. 2006; Jacobs 1995; O'Rourke 2004). It is about time for Vietnam to reconsider and make necessary changes in its development strategy. A wise choice would be to highlight and stress the use of clean energy and to target a low-emission development strategy. Doing so, Vietnam can not only ensure engines to sustain economic growth, but also could appear more "friendly" to the donor community and is more likely to receive support.

Recommendation 4: Be Active in Regional Coordination
Vietnam should play a major role in the South East Asia region in the fight against climate change and natural disasters. In a recent publication, Aggarwal and Sivakumar (2011) discuss an adaptation and mitigation framework for South Asia to cooperate in climate change and food security policies and highlight the following key areas:

- Assisting Farmers in Coping with Current Climatic Risks
- Intensifying Food Production Systems
- Improving Land, Water, and Forest Management
- Enabling Policies and Regional Cooperation
- Strengthening Research for Enhancing Adaptive Capacity

The key areas are not only what Vietnam should focus on, but some of them are areas in which Vietnam can play a leading role, such as food production systems and land, water, and forest management.

Recommendation 5: Seek for More Bilateral Cooperation
Besides regional cooperation, Vietnam should also intensify existing bilateral partnerships and expand to new relationships. Bilateral collaborations such as the Norwegian-Vietnamese Scientific Cooperation on Climate Change should be expanded to take opportunities from developed countries.

5 Conclusion

After two decades achieving high and steady economic growth, in the midst of global financial and economic crises, the economy of Vietnam has started to slow down significantly. Vietnam's economic structure is still heavily dependent on agriculture with nearly three quarters of the population currently living in rural areas. The country is therefore very vulnerable to natural disasters and climate change. Unfortunately, natural disasters are real threats to the country. Storm and flood are deadly disasters that occur very frequently, killing many people and devastating huge amounts of assets every year. Vietnam is also considerably vulnerable to climate change. Under the scenario that the sea level rises by 100 cm, nearly one quarter of Ho Chi Minh city, Vietnam's largest city and its major economic driving force, will be submerged and 13 % of the Mekong River Delta, the major rice producing region, will be under the water.

The Government of Vietnam has been actively engaged in the fight against natural disasters and climate change. It has set climate change at the top of its priorities. At the same time, the Government is also very active in regional and international cooperation related to climate change. Nevertheless, the country has much to do to prepare for challenges in the years to come and help its people adequately mitigate and cope with natural disasters and climate change.

This chapter attempts to provide an evidence-based assessment of natural disasters and recommendations to policies makers to help the country move toward effective disaster risk management. It finds that storms greatly affect household welfare and livelihoods. The finding suggests that while short-term aftermaths are tremendously high, the impact of natural disasters can persist, bringing down living standards for some time. Based on a review of existing studies, the chapter suggests an array of recommendations with the hope that they can make positive contributions to the policy making process in Vietnam, so as to achieve its declared goals. The recommendations focus on measures and approaches relevant for national implementation as well as regional collaboration.

References

Aggarwal, P., & Sivakumar, M. V. K. (2011). Global climate change and food security in South Asia: An adaptation and mitigation framework. In R. Lal, M. V. K. Sivakumar, S. M. A. Faiz, M. Rahman & K. R. Islam (Eds.), *Climate change and food security in South Asia* (pp. 253–275) Springer.

Agusa, T., Kunito, T., Fujihara, J., Kubota, R., Minh, T. B., Kim Trang, P. T., et al. (2006). Contamination by arsenic and other trace elements in tube-well water and its risk assessment to humans in Hanoi, Vietnam. *Environmental Pollution, 139*(1), 95–106.

Alvi, E., & Dendir, S. (2011). Weathering the storms: Credit receipt and child labor in the aftermath of the great floods (1998) in Bangladesh. *World Development, 39*(8), 1398–1409.

Australia Government Bureau of Meteorology. (n.d.). *Tropical cyclones frequently asked questions*. Australia Government Bureau of Meteorology. http://www.bom.gov.au/cyclone/faq/. Accessed 22 April 2012.

Becker, S. O., & Ichino, A. (2002). Estimation of average treatment effects based on propensity scores. *Stata Journal, 2*(4), 358–377.

Berkes, F. (2007). Understanding uncertainty and reducing vulnerability: Lessons from resilience thinking. *Natural Hazards, 41*(2), 283–295.

Carter, M. R., Little, P. D., Mogues, T., & Negatu, W. (2007). Poverty traps and natural disasters in Ethiopia and Honduras. *World Development, 35*(5), 835–856.

Cornall, R. (2005). New levels of government responsiveness for 'All-Hazards': The management of natural disasters and emergencies. *Australian Journal of Public Administration, 64*(2), 27–30.

Dasgupta, S., Laplante, B., Murray, S., & Wheeler, D. (2009). *Sea-level rise and storm surges: A comparative analysis of impacts in developing countries*. Washington D.C: The World Bank.

de Guzman, E. M. (2003). *Towards total disaster risk management approach, Asian disaster reduction center and United Nations office for the coordination of humanitarian affairs – Asian disaster response unit*. Bangladesh: Nirapad.

Guha-Sapir, D., Hargitt, D., Hoyois, P., Below, R., & Brechet, D. (2004). *Thirty years of natural disasters 1974–2003: The numbers*. Brussels: University of Louvain Presses.

Hoang Tri, N., Adger, W. N., & Kelly, P. M. (1998). Natural resource management in mitigating climate impacts: The example of Mangrove restoration in Vietnam. *Global Environmental Change, 8*(1), 49–61.

Holland, G. J. (1980). An analytic model of the wind and pressure profiles in Hurricanes. *Monthly Weather Review, 108*(8), 1212–1218.

Imbens, G. W. (2004). Nonparametric estimation of average treatment effects under exogeneity: A review. *Review of Economics and Statistics, 86*(1), 4–29.

Jacobs, J. W. (1995). Mekong committee history and lessons for River Basin development. *Geographical Journal, 161*(2), 135–148.

Jalan, J., & Ravallion, M. (2003). Estimating the benefit incidence of an antipoverty program by propensity-score matching. *Journal of Business & Economic Statistics, 21*(1), 19–30.

Katsushi, I., Raghav, G., & Woojin, K. (2011). Vulnerability and poverty dynamics in Vietnam. *Applied Economics, 43*(25), 3603–3618.

McConnell, A., & Drennan, L. (2006). Mission impossible? Planning and preparing for crisis. *Journal of Contingencies and Crisis Management, 14*(2), 59–70.

Mergenthaler, M., Weinberger, K., & Qaim, M. (2009). The food system transformation in developing countries: A disaggregate demand analysis for fruits and vegetables in Vietnam. *Food Policy, 34*(5), 426–436.
Moe, T. L., & Pathranarakul, P. (2006). An integrated approach to natural disaster management: Public project management and its critical success factors'. *Disaster Prevention and Management, 15*(3), 396–413.
MONRE. (2012). Chính sách biến đổi khí hậu đã có nhiều thay đổi tích cực (in Vietnamesse). Hanoi: NTPRCC. http://ntprcc.gov.vn/index.php?option=com_content&view=article&id=231. Accessed 5 May 2012.
Morris, S. S., Neidecker-Gonzales, O., Carletto, C., Munguıa, M., Medina, J. M., & Wodon, Q. (2002). Hurricane Mitch and the livelihoods of the rural poor in Honduras. *World Development, 30*(1), 49–60.
Mouton, F., & Nordbeck, O. (2005). *Cyclone database manager–A tool for converting point data from cyclone observations into tracks and wind speed profiles in a GIS, (GRIDG Division of Early Warning and Assessment (DEWA), Trans.).* Geneva: United Nations Environment Programme (UNEP).
Nguyen Viet, C. (2011). Poverty projection using a small area estimation method: Evidence from Vietnam. *Journal of Comparative Economics, 39*(3), 368–382.
Nguyen, M. C., & Winters, P. (2011). The impact of migration on food consumption patterns: The case of Vietnam. *Food Policy, 36*(1), 71–87.
O'Rourke, D. (2004). *Community-driven regulation: Balancing development and the environment in Vietnam.* Cambridge: MIT.
Patt, A. G., & Schröter, D. (2008). Perceptions of climate risk in Mozambique: Implications for the success of adaptation strategies. *Global Environmental Change, 18*(3), 458–467.
Pelling, M. (2003). *The vulnerability of cities: Natural disasters and social resilience.* Sterling: Earthscan Publications.
Pham, H. T. T., & Furukawa, M. (2007). Impact of sea level rise on coastal zone of Vietnam. *Bulletin of the College of Science, University of the Ryukyus, 84*, 45–59.
Pilarczyk, K. W., & Nuoi, N. S. (2005). Experience and practices on flood control in Vietnam. *Water International, 30*(1), 114–122.
Rosenbaum, P. R., & Rubin, D. B. (1985). Constructing a control group using multivariate matched sampling methods that incorporate the propensity score. *The American Statistician, 39*(1), 33–38.
Rubin, D. B., & Thomas, N. (1996). Matching using estimated propensity scores: Relating theory to practice. *Biometrics, 52*(1), 249–264.
Sepehri, A., Sarma, S., & Oguzoglu, U. (2011). Does the financial protection of health insurance vary across providers? Vietnam's experience. *Social Science & Medicine, 73*(4), 559–567.
Shaw, R. (2006). Community-based climate change adaptation in Vietnam: Inter-linkages of environment, disaster, and human security. In S. Sonak (Ed.), *Multiple dimension of global environmental changes* (pp. 521–547). New Delhi: TERI Publication.
Smith, J. A., & Todd, P. E. (2001). Reconciling conflicting evidence on the performance of propensity-score matching methods. *The American Economic Review, 91*(2), 112–118.
Taylor, A. J. (1979). Assessment of victim needs. *Disasters, 3*(1), 24–31.
Tran, P., & Shaw, R. (2007). Towards an integrated approach of disaster and environment management: A case study of Thua Thien Hue Province, Central VietNam. *Environmental Hazards, 7*(4), 271–282.
Wang, M., Liao, C., Yang, S., Zhao, W., Liu, M., & Shi, P. (2012). Are people willing to buy natural disaster insurance in China? Risk awareness, insurance acceptance, and willingness to pay. In M. R. Greenberg (Ed.) *Risk Analysis, 32*(7), 1717–1740.

Chapter 5
The Impact of the 2011 Floods, and Flood Management on Thai Households

Nipon Poaponsakorn, Pitsom Meethom, and Kamphol Pantakua

The 2011 flood was the worst flood in modern Thai history, inundating 9.1 % of the total land area of the country, affecting more than 13 million people, with 680 deaths, causing total damage and loss of USD 46.5 billion, and paralyzing Bangkok and its vicinity for 2 months, which seriously affected investors' confidence. Damaged areas were dispersed in 69 provinces in every region of the country, with most damage and loss concentrated in the industrial estates and residential areas located in Bangkok, the adjacent provinces to the north and west of Bangkok, and the farm areas in some provinces in the Lower Northern region and Central Plains.

1 Rationale and Objectives

The government had been under political pressure to allocate 119.5 billion baht (or USD 3.85 billion) as assistance, restoration and compensation to the flood affected communities and victims. However, the compensation depends heavily upon self-report by the victims, which tend to be exaggerated. The responsible bureaucrats have neither adequate resources (capability) nor incentive to assess the claims. More important, since the estimate of output loss caused by the floods in the national income account is partly based on the loss and damage reported by the government agencies, it is useful to carry out an independent assessment of the impact of the flood on household expenditure, income and loss in agricultural output, based on scientific evidence. This chapter seeks to understand the actual output loss from the event along with the accuracy of the compensation claims.

N. Poaponsakorn (✉) • P. Meethom • K. Pantakua
Thailand Development Research Institute, Bangkok, Thailand
e-mail: nipon@tdri.or.th

D.P. Aldrich et al. (eds.), *Resilience and Recovery in Asian Disasters*, Risk, Governance and Society 18, DOI 10.1007/978-4-431-55022-8_5

This chapter also attempts to revise the World Bank's estimates of agricultural output loss in November 2011 for several reasons. First, the WB estimates were done when the flood was yet to recede. Secondly, the flooded area was the only parameter determining the agricultural loss and damage at the provincial level, regardless of the duration of the flooding, let alone its severity. Thirdly, despite the availability of primary data on the impact of the flooding collected by some government agencies, particularly the satellite images secured by the Geo-informatics and Space Development Agency (GISTDA) and the Socio-economic Survey, there has been no attempt to utilize such data.

This study has four objectives. It will first describe briefly the causes of the 2011 flood and the policy response of the government. The second objective is to revise the World Bank's estimates of agricultural loss. Thirdly the study will estimate the impact of the flood on the expenditures and incomes of households in 26 flooded provinces in comparison with those of households in the non-flooded areas. Finally, it draws policy implications for decision makers and communities alike.

2 The 2011 Thailand Flood: Causes and Policy Response

The 2011 flood affected 69 provinces with the total flood inundation area of 41,381.8 km^2 (GISTDA 2011). Of these, 19 provinces were most severely inundated, located in the Chao Phraya and Tha-Jeen River basin, including Bangkok and surrounding provinces. Flooding began around late July 2011, and receded in mid-December 2011.

Given the higher altitudes of the Northern provinces, the surface water from the Northern provinces flows south to the sea through a few major rivers in the three major river basins in the Lower North and the Central Plains, i.e., the Chao Phraya River, the Tha-Jeen River and the Pasak River basins. Once the floods flowed over the river banks in the Central Plains, they moved only very slowly, i.e., 2–3 km/day, thanks to the "flat" land. Farmers who live along the rivers or in the flooding areas near the rivers have been used to and well adapted to the annual flood. Thus, unlike in a flash flood, losses were greater than damage to property and life, because people had plenty of time to prepare and evacuate. In addition, since Bangkok's sewage and canal systems are designed for the drainage of rain water and not for flood discharge, most flood water had to be diverted either to the east or the west of Bangkok. The 2011 flood affected 12.8 million people, caused 728 deaths, and damaged 10.417 million rais (16,668.55 km^2) of agricultural area (Department of Agricultural Extension 2012) and 9,859 factories. It also affected 660,000 jobs as of 25 November 2011.

Overall, the total damage and loss amounted to THB1.43 trillion (USD 46.5 billion), with losses accounting for 56 % of the total. The World Bank estimates that recovery and reconstruction would cost THB1.49 trillion (USD 50 billion) over the next 6 months and beyond.

2.1 *Factors Causing the 2011 Floods: From Mother Nature to Man-Made Mistakes*

There were four major factors causing the 2011 floods (Suppaisarn 2011). These were (1) the highest recorded rainfall together with five consecutive tropical storms in the mid rainy seasons, which in turn, caused (2) water runoff from the major rivers, (3) unsuitable land use in the flood plains, and (4) flood mismanagement.

Factor 1: The average rainfall of 1,781 mm between January and October 2011 was the highest on record, and was 35 % higher than the 50-year average. Moreover, five tropical storms, which happened consecutively between the end of June and the beginning of October, contributed to heavy rain in the mountains to the North and in the Central regions. "The total rain for July to September was 1,156 mm—the highest amount of rain recorded since record keeping began in 1901. The probability of such a rain event has been estimated at 1 in 250 years" (World Bank 2012, p. 77). The storms also caused flash floods in several Northern and Northeastern provinces in the early rainy season and raised the water levels in the major dams to their maximum capacity (Suppaisarn 2011). The high density of rain between July and September generated an unprecedented flood peak in the Chao Phraya River at the tide station in Nakorn Sawan province (C2) of 4,686 m^3/s (cms) against the maximum channel capacity of 3,500 cm.

Factor 2: Water runoff from major rivers exceeded the capacity of the rivers. Both heavy rainfalls in the North and the Northeast and water discharged from major dams exceeded the capacity of the rivers, overflowed the riverbanks, and inundated vast flood plains. The World Bank (2012, p. 78) argued that "The main cause of the flooding was the low flow capacity of the river, which resulted in river dykes overtopping and breaching in many river arms. Also the river's capacity decreased downstream, which implies that spillage from the river channel gradually occurs in the upstream areas when a large-scale flood occurs." Though some questions were raised regarding the operation of the major reservoirs (more below), the Bank argued that "there was simply much more water upstream than the downstream channel was able (to) manage."

It should be noted that water runoff in the Lower North and the Central Plains did not exceed the channel capacity (3,500 m^3/s (cms) at Nakorn Sawan tide station (C2), and 2,500 cm in Chainart) until September. One reason is that water outflows from the two Northern dams, i.e., the Bhumibol and the Sirikit dams, were much less than the water inflows into the dams between June and September. This controversial issue of flood mismanagement will be discussed below.

Floods in Bangkok and surrounding provinces, therefore, were caused by a combination of four factors, i.e., high discharges from the upstream Chao Phraya River, releases from the mainstream reservoirs, high sea levels in the Gulf of Thailand and high intensity rainy in the city, exceeding the drainage network (World Bank 2012).

Factor 3: Rapid (and unplanned) urbanization and unsuitable land use in the flood plain areas is probably one of the most important factors worsening the floods. For example, industrial and housing estates were located in the areas which were supposed to be the flood plains, thanks to the mistake of industrial promotion policy in the 1980s and other reasons discussed below; and many infrastructural facilities also block the canals and rivers, etc.

Except in Bangkok, there has been no implementation of land use zoning in most provinces. In Ayuthaya province, several industrial estates and housing developments were allowed to locate in the flood prone areas, just because the land prices were the lowest.[1] Since the estates blocked the flood ways, it is not surprising that they were severely inundated for months. In Bangkok where there has been land use zoning, the zoning law has been changed by politicians to serve the interests of business and property developers. The most obvious example is the lobby to convert the eastern areas of Bangkok, which were designated as flood ways, to residential areas. To make things worse, the government is also the main culprit as it decided to build the new Suvarnabhumi airport in the flood plains of eastern Bangkok. Flood plains and canals were also blocked by both public and private infrastructure and urban sprawl. Many public canals simply disappeared because of illegal encroachment. Such changes in land use took away the ability to drain water from the northern part of Bangkok into the canals and drainage systems, and then to the drainage stations by the sea coast of the city.

Factor 4: The floods were worsened by man-made mistakes, particularly political intervention and mismanagement. Flood mismanagement includes (a) the weakness of existing operations of major reservoirs, (b) political intervention in dam operation and irrigation management, (c) ageing structures and deferred essential maintenance of the irrigation and flood protection infrastructure, which was the primary reason for structural failure and breaches of the flood protection embankment along the Chao Phraya River,[2] (d) the emergency mismanagement, e.g., slow response to repair damage irrigation facilities, failure to handle conflicts between groups of flood victims, and flood relief mismanagement, and (e) lack of effective flood forecasting and early warning system. We will discuss only the first four problems.

(a) *The weakness of the existing operations of major reservoirs.* This involves the validity of current estimates for extreme floods together with the ambiguous instructions for the operation of the spillway crest gates at major dams.

[1] Since the flood-prone areas can grow only low yield floating rice, the land price is low. Other reasons why the estates are located in Ayuthaya, which is 76 kilometers from Bangkok, are policy distortions, i.e., the factories there were entitled to higher tax "holidays" and lower minimum wages than those in Bangkok. The policy distortions to promote industrial development in Ayutthaya were necessary because of the delay of the Eastern Seaboard Development and construction of new Suvarnabhumi airport in the east of Bangkok.

[2] At least there were ten major dyke breaches and damage to the flood control infrastructure in the Chao Phraya River basin between 14 September and 3 October 2011 (Royal Irrigation Department (RID). 2011).

For example, the inflexible and probably out of date "Rule Curve"[3] results from lack of information on seasonal weather forecasts, out-dated flood hydrology evaluations and routing (or a process of selecting paths) of the probable maximum flood (PMF), and a one-in-10,000 year flood (World Bank 2012, p. A-36), and inadequate information on changes in cropping patterns which affect the detailed gate operation schedule. In addition, the small height difference between normal water level and maximum water level (narrow Rule curves) at several major dams means that there is little time for the dam operators to deliberate and seek approval from higher authority when they need to quickly change the schedule of gate opening in response to an emergency.

It is claimed that there were political pressures on the dam operators to delay opening the gates, in order to avoid flooding downstream and to conserve maximum water for the dry season crops, as well as financial incentives for the Electricity Generating Authority of Thailand (EGAT) to deliberately keep stock water in Bhumibol and Sirikit Dams at high levels since the second quarter of 2011 in order to gain higher revenue from the lower cost of electricity generation. In response, EGAT stated that their measures of water management, including discharging water from the dams, were taken in accordance with the Rule Curves of the dams. It also declared that EGAT could not profit from return on investment (ROI) by retaining more water in dams, given the method of fuel tariff (FT) charges.

In spite of the exceptionally high water inflow into the Bhumibol Dam between July and September 2011, which was higher than the average water inflow between 1984 and 2010, the rate of water outflow was lower than the inflow. From mid-September until November, the stock of water in Bhumibol Dam surged rapidly due to the effects of the Nok Ten, Haitang, Nesard and Nalgae storms. The water level quickly reached the dam's limit (see Fig. A.1). The exceptionally high rate of water outflow therefore had to be drained through the Ping River. Sirikit Dam's water inflow and outflow showed a similar trend. Water discharged from these two dams significantly increased the water level in the Ping and Nan rivers, which then flowed downstream to the Central Region, aggravating the flood there.

There are three main causes that may have contributed to the flood mismanagement. First, the dependence on rigid and out-of-dated Rule Curves may have caused the water discharge measure to be unfit for the extreme weather conditions, particularly in the case of the 2011 flood, according to some engineers. In addition to the bureaucrats' inadequate attention to the weather conditions and the exceptionally high water inflows in the major dams, the government does not yet have adequate capability in seasonal

[3] Rule curve is the optimum operation rules for reservoir systems with multiple purposes. The rules involve non-linear and complex mathematical relations among hydropower plant's efficiency, flow rate, reservoir water level, and storage.

weather forecasting (i.e., the weather forecast for 3–4 months), and does not yet have catchment-based flow forecasting systems. Next, EGAT argued that the water outflows from the two major dams were not the major factor contributing to the flood in the Central Plains since they accounted for only 16–17 % of total surface water flowing from the dams, and other Northern rivers, (which do not have large reservoirs, i.e., the Wang and Yom rivers) that flowed through Nakorn Sawan province. But this may lead to the conclusion that when EGAT made decisions to discharge water from the dams, they ought seriously to have taken into account the volumes of rain water that would have overflowed from all four Northern rivers between August and September. Finally, although EGAT cannot charge a higher tariff for its electricity, the lower cost of electricity generation when the water stock in the dams is at peak level will result in higher net revenue for EGAT and, hence, higher bonuses for its employees.

(b) *Political influences*. There were reports in the media of several political interventions during the flood crisis, for example Tobunmee (2012), Komchadluek (2012), and Bangkok Biznews (2011). The followings are some of the interventions. When the water from the four Northern rivers, reaches Nakorn Sawan, a Lower Northern province where the four rivers merge and form the Chao Phraya river, it can be diverted by the Chainart barrage into five major natural or artificial channels, three on the west bank (i.e., Makhamtao-Uthong canal, the Supan and Noi rivers), and two on the east bank (Chainart-Ayuthaya and Chainart-Pasak Canals). There is a criterion that all the sluice gates will open on August 15. But there was one newspaper report that some politicians might have influenced the decision to control the sluice gates, and to delay the water discharge into the western province for 15 days, to allow the farmers in their constituency to harvest their rice crop.

Water in Nakorn Sawan started to rise above its capacity in mid-September. It also shows that the Phothipraya sluice gate started to open to its maximum capacity at the same time, and remained open at a very high level until November.

Yet, the three sluice gates in the western side of the Chao Phraya river were not open to their maximum capacity until the beginning of October. Compared to the Phothipraya sluice gate in the east, the Pollathep, and Baromathad sluice gates in the west were only opened at their maximum capacity when it was too late, during October and November (see Fig. A.2). Water was not allowed to flow through the Makhamtao gate at maximum capacity for a week in September so that farmers in Supanburi had time to harvest their paddy. Most water, therefore, had to flow down the Chao Phraya river or was diverted to the east. If the sluice gates had been opened wider and earlier, water could have flowed to Derm-Bang Nangboach, Sri Prajan, Donjadee and Muang districts in Suphanburi Province, which have at least 500,000 rais of flood plain area to retain water. The result of these sluice gates' water mis-management, together with the deferred essential maintenance of the sluice gate at Bang Chomsri was that water inundated 402,164 rais of agricultural land in Lopburi, particularly in Ban Mi and Tha Wung districts, and other districts in Chainart and Sing Buri (Bangkok biznews 2011).

One reason the floods in Ayuthaya and Bangkok were more serious than they should be is that water was blocked from flowing into the Raphibhat canal for 3 weeks, according to water experts. The canal is the key channel to divert excess water to the east of Bangkok where there are flood way, canal network and large pumping capacity to bring water to the sea.

(c) *Ageing structures and deferred maintenance of flood protection and irrigation facilities.* There were at least 13 sluice gates that were damaged in the 2011 flood. Three of them collapsed causing major flooding in some areas. The damage was not only caused by the major flood but also by the lack of proper maintenance of the flood protection infrastructure.

(d) *Emergency mismanagement.* Here are some reported cases of emergency mismanagement of the 2011 flood.

- The slow response to the Bang Chom Sri sluice gate's collapse caused too much water to flow into Lopburi province, which then flowed back to Ayuthaya district via the Lopburi river. Not only was there a slow response, but the repair of the Bang Chom Sri sluice gate was left to the resource-poor local government instead of being undertaken by professional central authorities.
- There was a claim that the authorities in charge made a grave mistake by diverting a large flow of water to the west of Bangkok and then to the Tha-Jeen river, which does not have the facilities to manage the water runoffs. This measure had never been taken in the past and proved to be ineffective since the Tha-Jeen river is winding and not suitable to divert water to (Tobunmee 2012). There were several instances where local politics overrode the central government (FROC) authority in flood management and flood relief activities. On the other hand, there were also conflicts between people in communities that were outside the flood barriers which were used to protect people in another province. For instance, the locals of Chainart protested against the Minister of Agriculture and Cooperatives, and accused him of favoring Supanburi by blocking the flood water from entering into Supanburi, thus inundating Chainart. Ultimately, they, by force, removed three levels of sandbags that were placed across the Pollathep waterway to let water flow to Supanburi (Thairath 2011).
- There were serious coordination problems between the central government and the local government administration, especially Bangkok Metropolitan Authority (Komchadluek 2011), thanks to the fact that they belong to different political parties.

2.2 *How did Thailand Handle the Flood?*

(a) **Flood Management during the Crisis**

The Thai Government established a Flood Relief Operation Center (FROC) in October, 2011. FROC's central office was located in Don Muang district of Bangkok. It served as the migrant center and shelter for flood victims. It also functioned with assistance from the military to repair irrigation facilities, evacuated flood victims from flooded areas, delivered survivor kits, etc. About USD 17.89 million were spent for flood relief activities. Unfortunately, the FROC office in Don Muang district was later heavily flooded, and was forced to relocate.

(b) **Flood Management Master Plan**

Right after the flood, the government set up two committees to draft a flood management master plan, which was finished in a few months. The plan has three objectives: (1) to prevent, mitigate and reduce the damage caused by flooding, (2) to improve the efficiency of the flood prevention and the emergency flood management systems, (3) to build public confidence and security, to increase national income and to manage natural resources on a sustainable basis. The master plan (the Strategic Committee for Water Resource Management or SCWRM 2012) is based upon two approaches, i.e., the structural (or physical infrastructural) measures and non-structural measures based upon the Royal Initiative (which was first publicly disseminated in 1983).

The structural approach to flood management includes measures to "store and divert" water. One clear option is to increase the number and capacities of water reservoirs. At present Thailand has about 1,000 m^3 of water storage capacity per inhabitant compared to the US, which has over 5,000 m^3 (World Bank 2012, p. 81). Another flood protection structure is the construction of floodways to divert water. The government will rely upon a Japan International Cooperation Agency (JICA) study which will make recommendations on infrastructural investment and flood management for both short-term and long-term solutions.

The non-structural Royal Initiative is to create "room for the river", which would allow for increased areas for floods to spread. Reforestation is also part of the Initiative to prevent rapid flooding in the upstream river basins. The concept of "room for the river" consists of the large flood retention areas and Monkey Cheek reservoirs (the so-called *"Gamling"*). A study of the potential flood retention areas in Bang Ban sub-district in province finds that the Bang Ban area has the potential to be developed into a reservoir for the following reasons (Suppaisarn 2008).

The "Monkey Cheek" concept is also useful, as His Majesty the King Bhumibol Adulyadej stated in 2003 that, "...Monkey Cheek reservoirs are needed in order to retain water when the sea water rises and water excess cannot be drained. During the flooding season between September and November, the seawater will push water in rivers until it reaches Ayuthaya province, which will make it impossible to drain excessive rain water into the sea. As a result, the areas along the Chao Phraya river in the lower Central Plains will remain flooded. Therefore, we need Monkey Cheek reservoirs" to receive water excess during the flooding season" (Suppaisarn 2011).

(c) **Flood Action Plan and Budget**
The action plan budget consists of an immediate flood compensation budget and a budget for the flood action plans (SCWRM 2012).

(1) *Assistance, restoration, and compensation budget:* The government allocated USD 3,917 million of the central budget (~USD 1,534 in FY 2011, and ~USD 2,383 in FY 2012) to provide assistance, restoration, and compensation to flood victims.
From October 2011 to May 2012, state agencies have already spent 79,750 million baht (or USD 2,602.98 million at the exchange rate of 30.38 baht per USD) from these budgets through related projects/work plans.
(2) *Flood action plan,* including two related action Plans: an action plan for water management for the emergency period and an action plan for integrated and sustainable flood mitigation in the Chao Phraya river basin:

2.1 Action plan for water management for the emergency period. Its key principle is to reduce losses and damage due to flooding, and to minimize its economic and social impacts. There are six main work plans with a total budget of 18,110 million baht (see details in the Flood Management Master Plan 2012)
2.2 Integrated and sustainable flood management action plan. This comprises eight work plans (including restoration and conservation of forests, information warehouse and forecasting, and stakeholder participation plans) with a budget of 300,000 million baht.

2.3 What Is the Weakness of the Master Plan?

Though the master plan nominally consists of both the master plan for infrastructural investment, rehabilitation and maintenance, and the non-infrastructural management plan, the government does not give much attention to the latter. No concrete policy nor any measures have been proposed, e.g., (a) no concrete proposal on how to compensate farmers in the flood retention areas, (b) too little attention to the issue of drought, given the increasing incidence of extreme weather, and (c) inadequate attention to the complex long-term issues of fragmented water management and required institutional changes in integrated water management to cope with extreme weather conditions, plus the appropriate combination of a single command authority and decentralization. The most challenging issues are how to create effective coordination of more than 40 government agencies with overlapping responsibilities, and what is the appropriate combination of single command authority and decentralization of power.

There are also some crucial policies that are still missing, i.e., a policy to facilitate farmers' adaptation in the flood retention areas, and a water management institution. The plan is also silent on adaptation to climate change, which includes drought management. There are, therefore, research needs in the areas of adaptation strategies, water management institutions, and compensation measures. It is also important to bring attention to the enforcement of work plans and consistency in carrying them out, because practical strategies can only be effective when they are enforced in a consistent manner.

3 Impact of the 2011 Flood on Agricultural Output

This part of the discussion will first compare the farm areas damaged by floods as reported by the Department of Agricultural Extension (2012) in the Ministry of Agriculture and Cooperatives and Department of Disaster Prevention and Mitigation (DDPM 2011) with information obtained from satellite images. Then it will update the World Bank's estimate of loss of agricultural output caused by the 2011 flood. The update will employ a new set of secondary data from GISTDA radar satellite images which were taken weekly between May and December 2011, with 50 × 50 m resolution. Finally, it will compare the estimated agricultural loss and damage with the reported compensation paid by the MOAC and the DDPM.

In estimating the land areas that were damaged by floods, the researchers will use the Thai government's definition of 2-week flood duration as the criterion for payment of compensation to farmers whose farms were damaged by floods. Therefore the weekly satellite images that were taken between May and December 2011 are overlaid and the districts/sub-districts that were inundated for at least two consecutive weeks are identified. At the same time the land-use pattern is also overlaid so that the inundated farm lands by broad types of agricultural product can be identified. Then, the farm lands that were inundated for at least 2 weeks will, in turn, be used as the new proxy for damaged farm land in the estimate of agricultural output loss.

The first outcome to understand is the effect of flood on agricultural land. GISTDA only has information on the duration of flooding, classified by land use. It still does not have a digitized elevation map (DEP). The land use pattern is obtained from the Department of Land Development which carried out a survey during the period 2006–2009.

We compared the flooded agricultural areas estimated from the satellite images with the agricultural areas "damaged by flood" as reported by the farmers to the Department of Agricultural Extension (DOAE 2012) and the Department of Disaster Prevention and Protection (DDPM 2011). One striking observation is that the flooded areas in all Central provinces are larger than the damaged farm areas. There are two explanations. First, the estimates of agricultural land from the satellite images are based on the land-use survey by the Department of Land Development

(DLD 2010) in 2006–2009. The latest estimates of agricultural land (from farmer registration) by the DOAE are smaller than that of DLD, particularly in some rapidly developing provinces such as Ayuthaya, Lopburi, Saraburi, Supanburi, Nakorn Pathom, Pathum Thani, and Chachoengsao where large areas of farm land have been converted into areas of non-agricultural use. Secondly, since the flood travelled slowly, there was adequate time for the farmers in the lower part of the Central Plains to harvest their paddy, provided that their crop was ready for harvest. This is what happened in Supanburi where sluice gates were kept closed for more than a week so that farmers had time to harvest most of their paddy. It explains why the reported damaged farm areas in the Central Plains were very small, i.e., 1.69 million ha, compared with 6.31 million ha of flooded farm land estimated from the satellite images and DLD survey.

Therefore, the flooded farm areas from GISTDA (2011) need to be revised by subtracting the difference between farm land estimated by DLD and that by DOAE from the flooded agricultural lands estimated from satellite images. A second method of performing this estimation is to re-estimate the land area that were flooded for two consecutive weeks, and calculate the ratio of farm lands that were flooded for at least 2 weeks to total farm land in each district. This ratio is then used to estimate the loss of agricultural output. One observation is there are more districts and provinces that have higher ratios of flooded farm land in the GISTDA data set than those in the DOAE and DDPM data sets. But the DDPM reports seven districts where damaged areas were larger than their total agricultural land.

The World Bank's estimates of agricultural loss and damage were based on only one important parameter, i.e. the flooded areas reported by MOAC. This study will use the satellite images of farm lands that were flooded for at least two consecutive weeks to estimate the loss of agricultural output. Most, if not all, plants and permanent trees die after 2 weeks of immersion. The number of sub-districts (tambons) that were flooded for at least 2 weeks is smaller than the number of sub-districts that were flooded for at least 1 day. Moreover, floods were more serious in a few provinces in the Central Plains as most or all sub-districts (tambons) in the province were flooded for more than 2 weeks, e.g., Ayuddhaya, Ang Thong, Singburi and Patum Thani. So using the one-day flood duration, as in the World Bank study, will bias upward the agricultural loss and damage estimate. Moreover if plants are submerged under water for a few days, they will not die. Unfortunately, GISTDA does not yet have any DEM (digital elevation map) data. In addition to such information, the satellite images should be regularly confirmed by a systematic process of calibrating the satellite images with reality on the ground (known as a "ground-truthing" survey). Again the Thai government does not adequately invest in these activities.

We compared the World Bank estimates of agricultural loss and damage with estimates from two different sources of data. The first estimates were based on the flooded farm lands that were reported by the DOAE, while the second estimates use GISTDA's data on the "ratio" of farm lands that were flooded for at least two weeks. The World Bank estimates of crop loss and damage (USD 909 million) are higher than those based on information from both DOAE (USD 580.3 million) and GISTDA (USD 423 million). (Detailed estimated can be provided upon request). This is because the World Bank estimates were done when the flood had not yet receded and several bold assumptions had to be made. On the other hand, the World Bank estimates of loss and damage for livestock and fishery (USD 165.57 million) are lower than the new estimates (USD 193.28 million). This is because the new estimates of fishery loss are based on more complete (and thus higher) estimates of the cost of losses in fresh water fish production. The new estimates of livestock losses are also based on the latest survey information by the Ministry of Agriculture (Department of Livestock Development). One important observation is that the estimates which are based on the ratio of farm lands that were flooded for at least 2 weeks are lower than both those of the World Bank and the estimates based on the damaged farm lands reported by the DOAE.

As the government paid large amounts of compensation to the farmers for part of their loss and damage, it is interesting to compare the compensation with our estimates of loss and damage. Total farm compensation was USD 557.5 million, plus USD 348 million for farm (and house) property damage to be paid by the DDPM. Total compensation is 17% - 47% higher than our estimates of total farm loss and damage (USD 616 - 774.56 million). It is possible that there may be moral hazard in the farmers' claim for compensation. One reason is that the compensation payment structure may have distorted the farmers' reports of actual loss and damage. Although the compensation for each type of crop is fixed at an amount based on some percentage of production costs, there is no limit to the amount of crop lands for which claims for flood damage could be made. But there are limits on the number of livestock and the amounts of fish production for which claims could be made. This is why the compensation for livestock and fishery losses is relatively low.

Finally, our estimate of livestock loss and damage (USD 154.77 million) is several times higher than the compensation payment (USD 7.4 million), while our fishery damage and loss estimate (USD 38.51 million) is closed to actual compensation (USD 35.58 million).

4 Impact on Household Income and Expenditure

This section will estimate the impact of the 2011 flood on household income and expenditure. It will first compare the incomes and expenditures of households in the flooded sub-districts in quarters 1–3 (the non-flooding period) with their incomes and expenditures in the fourth quarter (the flooding period) of 2011. The incomes and expenditures of the flooded households will also be compared with those of non-flooded households for both periods. Secondly it will compare household income and expenditure in the fourth quarter of 2011 (the flooding year) with those in 2009. Thirdly, it will develop a "difference in difference" approach to measure the impact of flooding, using the quantile regression technique.

4.1 Method of Estimation of the Flood Impact

The "difference-in-difference" approach to measure the impact of the flood can be described by the following equations.

(1)
$$Y_{ist} = \alpha + \mathcal{T} D_{Ds} \times D_t + \beta D_s + \delta D_t + \mathcal{E}_{st} + \mu_{ist}$$

(2)
$$\bar{y}_{11} = \bar{y} + \mathcal{T} + \beta + \delta + \mathcal{E}_{11} \quad \text{where } \alpha = \bar{y}$$

(3)
$$\bar{y}_{10} = \bar{y} + \beta + \mathcal{E}_{10}$$

(4)
$$\bar{y}_{01} = \bar{y} + \delta + \mathcal{E}_{01}$$

(5)
$$\bar{y}_{00} = \bar{y} + \mathcal{E}_{00}$$

(6)
$$\bar{y}_{11} - \bar{y}_{10} = \mathcal{T} + \delta + \mathcal{E}_{11} - \mathcal{E}_{10}$$

(7)
$$\bar{y}_{01} - \bar{y}_{00} = \delta + \mathcal{E}_{01} - \mathcal{E}_{00}$$

(8)
$$\bar{y}_{11} - \bar{y}_{10}) - (\bar{y}_{01} -(\bar{y}_{00}) = \mathcal{T} + (\mathcal{E}_{11} - \mathcal{E}_{10}) - (\mathcal{E}_{01} - \mathcal{E}_{00})$$

(9)
$$\begin{aligned} E[(\bar{y}_{11} - \bar{y}_{10}) - (\bar{y}_{01} - \bar{y}_{00})] &= \mathcal{T} + E[(\mathcal{E}_{11} - \mathcal{E}_{10}) - (\mathcal{E}_{01} - \mathcal{E}_{00})] \\ &= \mathcal{T} \end{aligned}$$

where

Y_{ist} = income of household i, living in area "s" in the "t" period

$s = 0$ if non flood areas
$= 1$ if flooded areas (19 or 26 provinces)

$t = 0$ if non – flooded months (January – September)
$= 1$ if flooded months (October – December)

D_s = Area dummy
D_t = Monthly dummy
$(\bar{y}_{01} - \bar{y}_{00})$ = Change in income between 2 periods in non-flooded areas (control)
$(\bar{y}_{11} - \bar{y}_{10}$ = Change in income between 2 periods in flooded areas (treatment)
$(\bar{y}_{11} - \bar{y}_{10}) - (\bar{y}_{01} - \bar{y}_{00})$ = direct effect of flood

To estimate the effect of flood on income and expenditure, Eq. (1) is estimated using the quantile regression technique (Firpo et al. 2009). A quantile regression evaluates the impact of changes in the distribution of the explanatory variables on quantiles of the unconditional (marginal) distribution of an outcome variable. The method consists of running a regression of the (re-centered) influence function (RIF) of the unconditional quantiles on the explanatory variables.

4.2 Data Sources

This chapter used the NSO, 2009 and 2011 Socio-Economic Survey (which did not ask any question about the 2011 flood) along with satellite image data from on a list of flooded *tambons* (sub-districts). Because the Socio-economic Survey contains data on the address of the households, especially the names of village and tambons, this allows the researchers to identify the tambons that were flooded when the information from SES is matched with the satellite images. As a result, we can identify the households that were affected by floods in 19 provinces in the Lower North and Central Plains and seven Northeastern provinces. The period of flooding was between May and December 2011.[4] Note that all households in Bangkok were treated as flooded households, despite the fact that some districts in Bangkok were not flooded, because the satellite images do not allow us to identify flooded structures in highly dense cities.

4.3 Tabulation of Impact on Expenditures

In general, the 2011 floods had negative effects on expenditure and income of flooded households in the flooding period. The expenditures of households in the non-flooded areas were also affected but to a smaller extent (Table 5.1). One possible explanation of the indirect effect on those who live outside the flooded areas is that the flood in the most important business and industrial areas might have had a spill-over effect throughout the whole economy. The impact works through three channels of the supply chain effect, i.e., (a) a shortage of raw materials, parts and components for industrial plants outside the flooded area; (b) the loss of jobs or reduction of income as a result of the closure of industrial plants and firms; and (c) disruption of logistics.

The flood impact on household expenditures in 19 provinces was larger than that in 26 provinces because the flood was more severe in 19 provinces in the Lower North and Central Plains than the other 7 provinces in the Northeast. Households

[4] Although the Socio-economic Survey allows us to identify the villages in which the households live, the researchers cannot identify the village boundary from the satellite images due to the lack of official digitalized data on village boundaries.

Table 5.1 Effect of flood by type of expenditure (Baht per month)

Expenditure	Flooded 19 Provinces				Flooded 26 Provinces			
	Before flood	During and after flood	Total	%	Before flood	During and after flood	Total	%
A1.Housing and household operation	3,968.9	3,444.5	3,834.9	−13.2	3,698.6	3,389.7	3,621.3	−8.4
A2.Service workers in household	59.3	96.0	68.7	61.9	50.8	75.2	57.0	48.0
A3.Cloth-clothing material	574.4	408.2	531.9	−28.9	512.0	373.2	477.3	−27.1
A4.Personal care	662.7	599.9	646.6	−9.5	633.5	591.7	623.1	−6.6
A5.Medical and health care	297.8	259.1	287.9	−13.0	274.5	260.5	271.0	−5.1
A6.Transportation and communication	1,952.6	1,595.7	1,861.4	−18.3	1,779.0	1,535.6	1,718.1	−13.7
A7.Toys, pets, trees, sport and admissions	302.1	272.7	294.6	−9.7	272.4	270.7	272.0	−0.6
A8.Food	5,985.2	5,858.7	5,952.9	−2.1	5,868.6	5,939.3	5,886.3	1.2
A9.Alcoholic and non-alcoholic beverages	383.8	356.5	376.9	−7.1	366.0	351.4	362.3	−4.0
A10.Prepared food consumed at home, and	1,188.6	1,122.8	1,171.8	−5.5	1,162.4	1,124.6	1,152.9	−3.2
A11. . . .consumed away from home	815.0	741.8	796.3	−9.0	781.1	752.2	773.8	−3.7

Note: Baht 30.637 equal one USD
Source: NSO and Socio-economic Survey (2011)

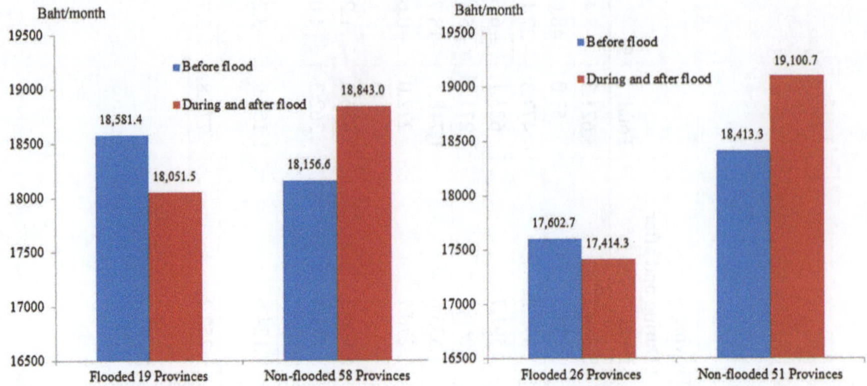

Fig. 5.1 Impact of flood on all money income. *Note*: Baht 30.637 equal one USD. *Source*: NSO and Socio-economic Survey (2011)

did not reduce expenditures across the board. Instead, they incurred higher expenditures on hiring household services. The expenses that were reduced by the largest percentage were clothing, transportation, housing, medical expenses, personal care, toys and sport activities, and eating out, respectively.

4.4 Tabulation of Impact on Income

The 2011 floods had a negative impact on the money income of households in the flooded areas, while those in the non-flooded areas still enjoyed an increase in total money income (Fig. 5.1 and Table 5.2). Yet, the flood had a negative impact on the wages and salary income of households in both the flooded and non-flooded areas (Table 5.2) implying that there was a negative spillover effect on wage employment throughout the country.

Despite the fact that most farm income occurs in October and December, it is surprising to find that there was no negative impact of flooding on farm income and profit from business. Thus, the appropriate way to measure the impact of flooding on farm income is to compare farm income in Q4/2011 with that in Q4/2009 (because there was no income survey in 2010). For business income, the result can be reconciled by the fact that household business might be able to make more net profit due to increased prices of consumer goods and services caused by the disruption of supplies. However, the price effect dominated the income effect of the flood, which resulted in lower household expenditures.

Table 5.2 Impact of flood by types of income and flooded areas

Province	Income	Flood months			
		Before flood	During and after flood	Total	%
Flooded 19 Provinces	All money income	18,581.4	18,051.5	18,446.0	−2.9
	Wage and salaries	11,538.7	9,911.5	11,123.0	−14.1
	Net profit from business	3,831.9	4,731.7	4,061.8	23.5
	Net profit from farming	694.9	812.2	724.9	16.9
Non-flooded 58 Provinces	All money income	18,156.6	18,843.0	18,321.2	3.8
	Wage and salaries	8,690.1	8,074.5	8,542.5	−7.1
	Net profit from business	4,385.6	4,466.1	4,404.9	1.8
	Net profit from farming	2,521.8	3,408.5	2,734.4	35.2
Flooded 26 Provinces	All money income	17,602.7	17,414.3	17,555.6	−1.1
	Wage and salaries	10,640.1	9,551.8	10,367.7	−10.2
	Net profit from business	3,661.7	4,379.2	3,841.2	19.6
	Net profit from farming	996.5	1,007.3	999.2	1.1
Non-flooded 51 Provinces	All money income	18,413.3	19,100.7	18,578.4	3.7
	Wage and salaries	8,738.1	8,050.4	8,572.9	−7.9
	Net profit from business	4,478.1	4,556.5	4,497.0	1.7
	Net profit from farming	2,572.2	3,540.3	2,804.7	37.6

Source: NSO and Socio-economic Survey (2011)

4.5 Tabulation of Impact by Areas

The income of urban households was more seriously affected than that of rural households, except for wages and salaries. While urban households suffered a decline in all types of income, their rural counterparts suffered only the reduction in wages and salaries.

4.6 Tabulation of Impact by Months

Monthly expenditures declined during the flooding months but there is no clear trend in the impact of the floods on monthly income.

Table 5.3 Regressions of flood effect on household's expenditure

Variables	lexpend_all	rif5	rif10	rif15	rif20	rif25	rif30	rif35	rif40	rif45
headsch	0.063***	0.043***	0.048***	0.046***	0.045***	0.045***	0.046***	0.048***	0.051***	0.053
	(0.001)	(0.002)	(0.001)	(0.001)	(0.001)	(0.001)	(0.001)	(0.001)	(0.001)	(0.001
malehead	−0.049***	−0.065**	−0.041**	−0.034**	−0.028**	−0.038***	−0.044***	−0.048***	−0.051***	−0.05
	(0.009)	(0.026)	(0.020)	(0.017)	(0.014)	(0.013)	(0.012)	(0.012)	(0.012)	(0.01
headmarried	0.074***	0.307***	0.242***	0.198***	0.163***	0.140***	0.123***	0.106***	0.094***	0.082
	(0.009)	(0.028)	(0.022)	(0.018)	(0.015)	(0.014)	(0.013)	(0.012)	(0.012)	(0.01
adultmale	0.222***	0.186***	0.218***	0.210***	0.195***	0.202***	0.209***	0.212***	0.216***	0.218
	(0.006)	(0.011)	(0.010)	(0.008)	(0.008)	(0.007)	(0.007)	(0.007)	(0.007)	(0.00
adultfem	0.289***	0.239***	0.269***	0.267***	0.264***	0.265***	0.270***	0.275***	0.278***	0.286
	(0.006)	(0.012)	(0.010)	(0.008)	(0.007)	(0.007)	(0.007)	(0.007)	(0.007)	(0.00
children03	0.043***	0.040***	0.058***	0.075***	0.066***	0.074***	0.070***	0.072***	0.067***	0.069
	(0.010)	(0.013)	(0.014)	(0.013)	(0.012)	(0.012)	(0.012)	(0.012)	(0.013)	(0.01
children415	0.090***	0.128***	0.145***	0.135***	0.124***	0.119***	0.115***	0.111***	0.110***	0.104
	(0.005)	(0.009)	(0.008)	(0.007)	(0.006)	(0.006)	(0.006)	(0.006)	(0.006)	(0.00
adult60	0.223***	0.084***	0.096***	0.106***	0.123***	0.133***	0.149***	0.162***	0.179***	0.193
	(0.006)	(0.013)	(0.011)	(0.010)	(0.008)	(0.008)	(0.008)	(0.007)	(0.007)	(0.00
t	−0.001	−0.001	0.018	0.031*	0.004	0.009	0.024*	0.023*	0.011	0.017
	(0.010)	(0.029)	(0.022)	(0.018)	(0.015)	(0.014)	(0.014)	(0.013)	(0.014)	(0.01
flodareal	0.105***	0.104***	0.129***	0.124***	0.122***	0.114***	0.119***	0.116***	0.129***	0.127
	(0.009)	(0.021)	(0.018)	(0.015)	(0.013)	(0.012)	(0.012)	(0.012)	(0.012)	(0.01
c.t#c. flodareal	−0.067***	0.04	−0.007	−0.031	0.01	−0.013	−0.057**	−0.095***	−0.088***	−0.1
	(0.020)	(0.048)	(0.040)	(0.033)	(0.029)	(0.029)	(0.029)	(0.029)	(0.029)	(0.02
Constant	8.153***	7.315***	7.441***	7.631***	7.785***	7.887***	7.952***	8.021***	8.069***	8.122
	(0.013)	(0.046)	(0.035)	(0.026)	(0.021)	(0.018)	(0.016)	(0.015)	(0.014)	(0.01
Observations	31,390	31,390	31,390	31,390	31,390	31,390	31,390	31,390	31,390	31,39
R−squared	0.463	0.112	0.173	0.22	0.248	0.268	0.281	0.291	0.298	0.301

Note: (1) Dependent variable is the log of household monthly expenditure. (2) Quantile regressions for every 5th
Source: Calculated from NSO, Socio-economic Survey (2011)

rif50	rif55	rif60	rif65	rif70	rif75	rif80	rif85	rif90	rif95
0.056***	0.060***	0.064***	0.066***	0.069***	0.074***	0.078***	0.083***	0.089***	0.104***
(0.001)	(0.001)	(0.001)	(0.001)	(0.001)	(0.001)	(0.002)	(0.002)	(0.002)	(0.004)
−0.055***	−0.051***	−0.052***	−0.053***	−0.055***	−0.066***	−0.066***	−0.058***	−0.045**	−0.018
(0.012)	(0.012)	(0.012)	(0.012)	(0.013)	(0.014)	(0.015)	(0.017)	(0.020)	(0.029)
0.066***	0.051***	0.031**	0.014	−0.003	−0.01	−0.034**	−0.064***	−0.095***	−0.113***
(0.012)	(0.012)	(0.012)	(0.012)	(0.013)	(0.014)	(0.015)	(0.017)	(0.020)	(0.030)
0.221***	0.220***	0.220***	0.219***	0.222***	0.237***	0.237***	0.240***	0.247***	0.254***
(0.007)	(0.008)	(0.008)	(0.008)	(0.008)	(0.009)	(0.010)	(0.012)	(0.015)	(0.023)
0.292***	0.302***	0.307***	0.301***	0.299***	0.309***	0.307***	0.306***	0.308***	0.323***
(0.007)	(0.008)	(0.008)	(0.008)	(0.008)	(0.009)	(0.010)	(0.012)	(0.015)	(0.024)
0.063***	0.058***	0.060***	0.046***	0.056***	0.043**	0.034*	0.03	0.002	−0.074**
(0.014)	(0.015)	(0.015)	(0.015)	(0.016)	(0.017)	(0.018)	(0.020)	(0.024)	(0.030)
0.099***	0.094***	0.087***	0.079***	0.069***	0.065***	0.066***	0.043***	0.036***	0.015
(0.007)	(0.007)	(0.007)	(0.007)	(0.007)	(0.008)	(0.009)	(0.010)	(0.011)	(0.016)
0.206***	0.220***	0.234***	0.247***	0.266***	0.284***	0.301***	0.326***	0.364***	0.442***
(0.007)	(0.007)	(0.008)	(0.008)	(0.008)	(0.009)	(0.009)	(0.011)	(0.014)	(0.023)
0.016	0.002	0.001	−0.001	−0.017	−0.029*	−0.030*	−0.026	−0.015	−0.011
(0.014)	(0.014)	(0.014)	(0.014)	(0.014)	(0.015)	(0.017)	(0.018)	(0.022)	(0.030)
0.121***	0.120***	0.113***	0.102***	0.105***	0.098***	0.090***	0.068***	0.057**	0.04
(0.013)	(0.013)	(0.014)	(0.014)	(0.015)	(0.016)	(0.017)	(0.020)	(0.023)	(0.032)
−0.108***	−0.102***	−0.088***	−0.090***	−0.076**	−0.064*	−0.106***	−0.106***	−0.118***	−0.141**
(0.029)	(0.030)	(0.030)	(0.030)	(0.030)	(0.033)	(0.034)	(0.037)	(0.043)	(0.057)
8.172***	8.216***	8.278***	8.362***	8.431***	8.470***	8.565***	8.670***	8.786***	8.893***
(0.013)	(0.014)	(0.014)	(0.013)	(0.013)	(0.015)	(0.017)	(0.020)	(0.027)	(0.044)
31,390	31,390	31,390	31,390	31,390	31,390	31,390	31,390	31,390	31,390
0.304	0.301	0.299	0.294	0.289	0.274	0.253	0.224	0.182	0.126

percentile. (3) Robust standard errors in parentheses *** p<0.01, ** p<0.05, * p<0.1

4.7 Results from Quantile Regressions on Household Expenditures

Based on Eq.(1) in section 4.1, we ran two sets of regressions, i.e., one OLS regression and 20 quantile regressions to measure the impact of flooding on household expenditures and income. The households that were in the sub-districts that were flooded for at least 1 day during May and December 2011 are identified by matching the list of flooded sub-districts in the satellite images with that in the Socio-economic Survey in 2011. The dependent variables are the household expenditures (in log form) and income (in level), while the independent variables include a dummy variable representing area that was flooded for at least 2 weeks (flodarea1), the flooding month dummy (t), an interaction between flooded area dummy and flooding month dummy (c.t#c.flodarea), and control variables, e.g., socio-economic and demographic characteristics. They are as follows: (1) years of education of household head, 'headsch'; (2) male household head dummy, 'malehead'; (3) married household head, 'headmarried'; (4) number of adult male family members, 'adultmale'; (5) number of adult female family members, 'adultfem'; (6) number of children aged 0–3 years, 'children03'; (7) number of children aged 4–15, 'children415'; and (8) number of older household members (aged 60 years and older), 'adult60'.

All control variables are statistically significant. The flooded area dummy is significant in both the OLS and quantile regressions. But the flooding month dummy is statistically significant only in some quantile regressions. The interaction of the flooding month dummy and the flooding area dummy is statistically significant in the OLS and most of the quantile regressions, except for a few lowest percentiles see estimated results in Table 5.3.

The expenditure distribution of households living in the flooded areas and non-flooded areas are compared in two periods, i.e., before and after the flood. Before the flood, the households in the flooded areas spent slightly more than those in the 56 non-flooded provinces, (with a higher value of mode). But after the flood, the former apparently reduced their spending.

The upper part of Fig. 5.2 plots the flood impact on the percentage change of household expenditures, by percentiles. The 95 % levels of change are also depicted. Floods caused the household expenditures to decline by 5.7 to 14.1 %, with an average of 6.7 %. Flooding had a statistically significant impact on the expenditure of the households in the 30th and higher percentile income classes. It is surprising that the poor households in the flooded areas did not spend statistically significantly less during the flooding months (Fig. 5.2).

Our results shows that the 2011 flood had more impact on the spending of middle income families than on households at both tails of the income distribution. The changes in food expenditures show a similar pattern.

Political economy: The estimates confirm that the 2011 flood seriously affected the middle class, who constitute the largest voting constituency. This explains why the government hurriedly allocated 350 billion baht for the flood management plan,

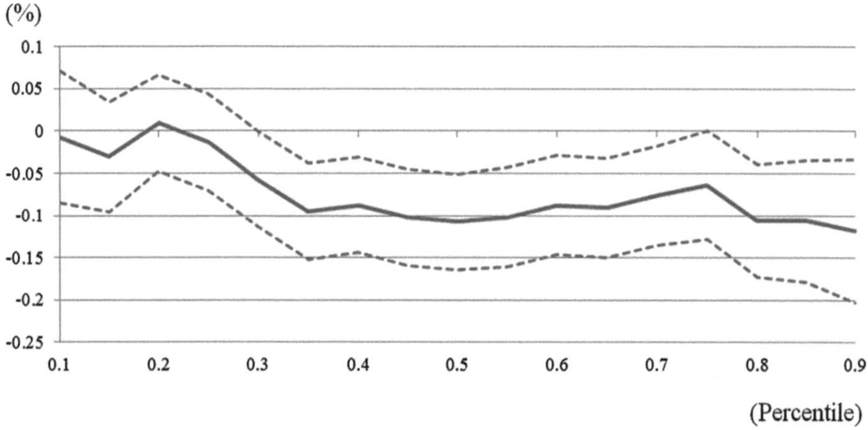

Fig. 5.2 Flood effect on total household expenditure. *Source*: Calculated from NSO and *Socio-economic Survey* (2011)

300 billion baht of which came from an emergency law which empowers the government to borrow the money. The food expenditures of most income quintiles declined by 6–12 %. Most coefficients are statistically significant. Again the percentage decline in food expenditure for the middle income class is the highest.

Since some households do not have every type of income, the dependent variable is total income level. But we also ran a subset of households who have at least one member who is a wage employee, using the log of monthly wage as a dependent variable.

We ran one OLS and 20 quantile regressions, i.e., every five percentiles. In general, the results of income regressions are mixed and not satisfactory, i.e., some key variables are not statistically significant with unexpected signs, e.g., the flooded area dummy and the interaction dummy which measure the impact of flooding.

In the OLS specification, the flooded area dummy is significant in four out of five equations of different types of income, but with positive sign in two wage regressions. The interaction dummy is not statistically significant in all OLS regressions, with negative sign in three regressions.

With regards to the quantile regressions on total money income in Table 5.4 and Fig. 5.3, the interaction dummy (t*s) is significant for the 30th, 35th, 40th … to 60th, and 75th to 95th quintuple regressions. This means that the 2011 flood had relatively more negative impact on the middle class and very severe impact on the upper middle-income class.

Most of the impact comes from the reduction in wages and salaries of the upper middle-income households, i.e., the 50th, 80th, 85th and 90th quintuple regressions.

The interaction term is not statistically significant in any business profit regressions. It is significant with negative coefficients in four regressions on farm income, i.e., 15th, 35th, 55th and 70th.

Table 5.4 Regressions of flood effect on household's money income

Variables	money_income	rif5	rif10	rif15	rif20	rif25	rif30	rif35	rif40	rif45
headsch	2,601.033***	166.356***	301.776***	438.830***	514.759***	610.272***	717.788***	832.265***	918.687***	1,075.344***
	(178.214)	(11.559)	(12.029)	(12.904)	(12.918)	(13.150)	(14.004)	(15.048)	(15.963)	(18.018)
malehead	−1,612.022**	−782.757***	−1,123.457***	−1,083.902***	−855.585***	−693.414***	−778.925***	−687.462***	−904.655***	−865.735***
	(691.253)	(134.219)	(161.962)	(177.764)	(178.525)	(179.074)	(185.630)	(197.865)	(209.070)	(233.177)
headmarried	516.068	−955.773***	247.901	411.742**	395.638**	423.185**	662.083***	830.994***	1,087.738***	1,159.963***
	(659.303)	(133.914)	(163.174)	(180.907)	(181.480)	(183.447)	(191.314)	(204.384)	(214.914)	(237.500)
adultmale	7,771.800***	104.387	579.785***	1,344.052***	1,664.146***	2,033.532***	2,426.419***	2,810.832***	3,182.181***	3,731.362***
	(782.590)	(77.649)	(87.586)	(94.290)	(96.801)	(100.388)	(105.611)	(114.632)	(122.389)	(137.997)
adultfem	8,059.988***	73.458	793.094***	1,494.909***	1,987.480***	2,415.860***	2,825.218***	3,297.497***	3,603.764***	4,148.529***
	(1,204.819)	(81.885)	(89.940)	(95.141)	(95.889)	(97.507)	(104.157)	(112.645)	(120.405)	(142.422)
children03	−3,033.535***	245.43	472.173***	399.381**	304.084*	129.776	229.139	−107.69	−295.551	−530.932**
	(833.362)	(154.907)	(147.183)	(170.317)	(175.191)	(189.951)	(200.661)	(218.026)	(232.727)	(259.271)
children415	28.415	19.229	443.243***	611.162***	706.615***	655.038***	513.782***	399.944***	300.968***	331.725***
	(578.616)	(80.798)	(80.829)	(87.927)	(89.360)	(94.109)	(100.157)	(107.568)	(114.239)	(126.993)
adult60	8,453.124***	1,145.138***	246.431**	289.293***	171.38	511.696***	746.378***	934.594***	1,258.387***	1,928.995***
	(1,060.894)	(82.507)	(98.227)	(106.581)	(108.302)	(109.575)	(114.241)	(122.221)	(128.387)	(141.028)
t	1,437.459*	583.203***	165.23	86.083	271.086	231.477	234.663	161.908	337.492	419.924
	(823.782)	(143.087)	(189.101)	(202.503)	(199.684)	(203.473)	(211.106)	(224.620)	(236.053)	(260.750)
flodareal	−1,386.252*	−420.332**	−235.079	238.55	565.897***	834.800***	1,063.760***	1,092.097***	1,098.681***	1,329.123***
	(743.595)	(178.859)	(185.506)	(188.058)	(186.189)	(186.349)	(193.852)	(207.254)	(219.054)	(244.042)
c.t#c. flodareal	−1,486.32	−1,192.548***	−541.024	−439.785	−636.432	−632.242	−835.623*	−934.094**	−1,239.794**	−1,448.258***
	(1,493.568)	(398.423)	(413.571)	(422.056)	(414.864)	(417.850)	(438.694)	(466.742)	(490.255)	(541.734)
Constant	−17,079.454***	−472.240***	−1,757.952***	−3,087.183***	−3,425.234***	−3,954.030***	−4,611.570***	−5,204.522***	−5,481.906***	−6,897.172***
	(2,634.886)	(179.527)	(241.024)	(256.094)	(251.720)	(246.883)	(247.229)	(253.484)	(258.708)	(276.704)
Observations	31,390	31,390	31,390	31,390	31,390	31,390	31,390	31,390	31,390	31,390
R-squared	0.068	0.027	0.042	0.092	0.133	0.168	0.2	0.223	0.235	0.248

Note: (1) Dependent variable is the household monthly income. (2) Quantile regressions for every 5th percentile.
Source: Calculated from NSO, Socio-economic Survey (2011)

rif50	rif55	rif60	rif65	rif70	rif75	rif80	rif85	rif90	rif95
1,239.309 ***	1,447.310 ***	1,578.924 ***	1,842.871 ***	2,162.554 ***	2,644.234 ***	3,267.548 ***	3,901.613 ***	5,649.895 ***	6,492.830 ***
(20.010)	(22.454)	(24.408)	(28.716)	(34.736)	(44.879)	(63.662)	(87.796)	(159.521)	(283.708)
−866.840 ***	−979.689 ***	−1,103.551 ***	−1,142.558 ***	−1,315.425 ***	−1,392.318 ***	−1,389.151**	−2,528.684 ***	−2,482.790*	−2,124.51
(257.990)	(282.290)	(299.672)	(338.716)	(391.073)	(479.019)	(625.349)	(802.755)	(1,311.969)	(2,039.063)
1,328.472 ***	1,312.204 ***	1,478.042 ***	1,286.974 ***	1,046.471 ***	565.458	226.79	351.409	−284.98	−909.92
(261.580)	(286.149)	(303.385)	(343.333)	(397.384)	(482.294)	(623.103)	(790.008)	(1,314.006)	(2,064.575)
4,185.651 ***	4,781.948 ***	4,825.763 ***	5,559.824 ***	5,894.378 ***	7,118.293 ***	8,551.235 ***	10,122.190 ***	14,146.749 ***	16,858.681 ***
(153.634)	(171.622)	(184.338)	(211.631)	(246.094)	(306.507)	(407.982)	(553.226)	(962.238)	(1,732.754)
4,710.407 ***	5,465.782 ***	5,592.435 ***	6,441.616 ***	7,254.604 ***	8,431.478 ***	10,123.128 ***	12,038.263 ***	16,502.679 ***	18,846.971 ***
(157.240)	(175.709)	(197.367)	(225.291)	(263.311)	(326.906)	(430.141)	(562.309)	(961.173)	(1,641.400)
−891.642 ***	−981.100 ***	−788.448**	−1,033.251 ***	−1,184.752 ***	−1,068.487*	−1,557.306**	−1,997.503**	−5,360.250 ***	−10,132.886 ***
(286.983)	(320.202)	(344.749)	(393.064)	(450.368)	(561.252)	(721.587)	(931.232)	(1,494.938)	(2,156.605)
288.290**	219.941	111.274	1.884	158.635	367.649	571.445	−533.522	−1,013.91	−2,794.150**
(139.968)	(154.254)	(163.826)	(184.486)	(214.599)	(266.108)	(349.585)	(444.304)	(730.745)	(1,107.649)
2,295.111 ***	3,106.959 ***	3,613.271 ***	4,545.651 ***	5,792.090 ***	7,392.913 ***	9,561.745 ***	12,478.319 ***	19,059.324 ***	22,763.541 ***
(154.829)	(170.767)	(181.777)	(206.759)	(239.523)	(294.656)	(394.758)	(524.571)	(916.932)	(1,579.068)
375.093	232.836	232.752	317.111	99.087	174.34	899.027	1,368.03	3,453.967**	7,347.375 ***
(286.791)	(314.978)	(337.128)	(385.522)	(440.992)	(545.510)	(707.782)	(928.997)	(1,570.266)	(2,596.823)
1,422.754 ***	1,425.263 ***	1,319.974 ***	1,082.470 ***	463.698	−537.652	−1,066.46	−1,553.171*	−3,302.300**	−5,636.062 ***
(271.273)	(304.137)	(322.971)	(370.529)	(429.922)	(526.729)	(675.388)	(860.884)	(1,365.175)	(2,055.344)
−1,144.186*	−1,374.835**	−1,753.561**	−1,300.02	−803.27	−1,849.092*	−3,786.939 ***	−3,740.769**	−7,293.960 ***	−8,113.003*
(598.106)	(667.063)	(708.107)	(816.989)	(940.066)	(1,085.930)	(1,336.315)	(1,720.657)	(2,728.850)	(4,402.806)
−7,701.619 ***	−9,182.793 ***	−8,538.819 ***	−10,334.700 ***	−11,534.327 ***	−14,717.278 ***	−18,934.794 ***	−21,453.673 ***	−34,279.352 ***	−25,731.404 ***
(294.794)	(313.514)	(339.690)	(376.459)	(437.207)	(539.865)	(716.871)	(971.079)	(1,756.762)	(3,114.636)
31,390	31,390	31,390	31,390	31,390	31,390	31,390	31,390	31,390	31,390
0.258	0.269	0.264	0.267	0.259	0.25	0.229	0.203	0.164	0.098

(3) Robust standard errors in parentheses *** p<0.01, ** p<0.05, * p<0.1

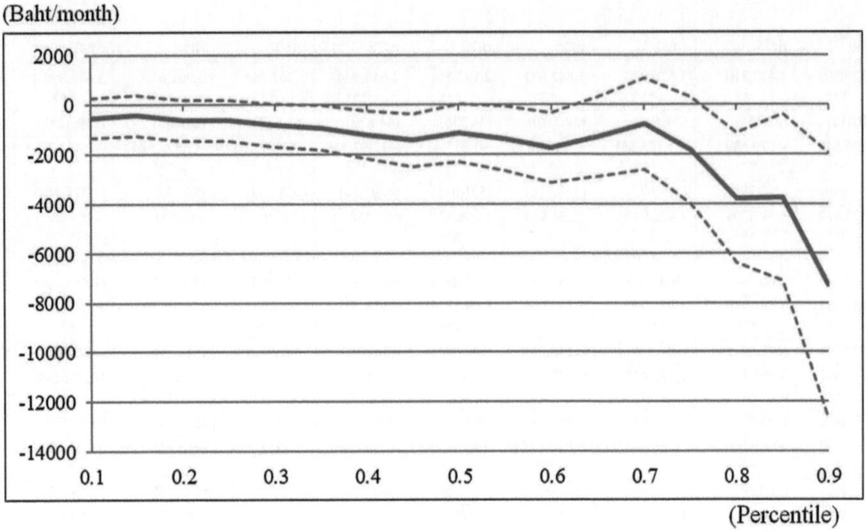

Fig. 5.3 Flood effect on household income. *Source*: Estimated from the quintile regressions of household income, wage and salary income business profit using the 2011 Socio-economic Survey

All coefficients in the farm profit regressions are not statistically significant (not shown here). One drawback to using the 2011 Socio-economic Survey to measure the impact of floods on agricultural income is that the 2011 flood destroyed most, if not all, of the paddy output in the main crop which would be harvested in November and December. The use of regression to control for the socio-economic variables may not be able to capture the pure flood effect because the treatment groups, i.e., the affected farmers in the flat land of the Chao Phraya River basin, have rather different physical farm characteristics from the farmers in the controlled (non-flood areas) group. This issue will be resolved in the following section by using the data on farm households in two different years.

4.8 *Effect of Flood on Household Income and Expenditure: Comparing 2009 and 2011*

Our tabulations shows that the real net farm income (or farm profit) in the 2011—flood year was substantially lower than that in 2009, by more than 60 %. Although the result does not yet control for the changes in prices of agricultural products and cultivated land, it implies that the 2011 flood had a severe impact on the farmers in the Lower Northern and Central provinces along the Chao Phraya river basin. The households' business income also declined by less than 7 % between 2009 and 2011.

We compared the real income of households in 2009 and 2011 in two periods, i.e., a 12 month period, and the 3 months of October to December. In general the fourth quarter income of households in the flooded areas declined more than their annual income. The fourth quarter real income of households in 19 flooded provinces declined by 11.4 % between 2009 and 2011. Surprisingly, household income in 26 provinces also declined, and by a larger percentage, i.e., 12.8 %, despite the fact that flood in the Northeast was not as severe as that in the Central Plains. On the other hand, the income of households in the non-flooded provinces increased between 2009 and 2011.

Except for the annual expenditure of households in the non-flooded areas, household expenditures of those in both the flooded and non-flooded areas declined between 2009 and 2011, implying that the 2011 flood had a widespread impact on household expenditure throughout the country. The monthly household expenditures of households in the 19 flooded provinces in the fourth quarter declined by a larger percentage than their average monthly expenditures over twelve months. The average 12-month expenditures of households in the non-flooded provinces in 2011 were slightly higher than that in 2009. But their fourth quarter monthly expenditures declined by almost 3 % between 2009 and 2011.

The above tabulation does not control for other factors affecting real farm income. The researchers therefore use quantile regressions based on the "difference-in-difference" approach to estimate the effect of the 2011 flood on farm profits in 2011, using the households' farm profit in 2009 and 2011. The rationale is that most agricultural outputs are harvested during October and December of every year. Therefore, the full impact of a flood can be measured only when one has complete information on annual farm income of the farm households in 2009 and can compare this with farm income in 2011. The results show that the coefficients of the interaction between the time (flood period) and area (flooded areas) dummies are statistically significant with expected negative sign in only six regressions, i.e., 55th to 80th percentiles. The negative impact on farm profit of the middle income farmers is consistent with the estimated effect of floods on household expenditures of the middle income households. Another interesting variable is the flooded area dummy. The coefficients in all the regressions have the expected negative sign, but only 9 out of 20 regressions are statistically significant. They are in the 5th to 45th percentiles. The coefficients of time dummy (2011 equals 1) also have the expected negative sign in all regressions, but are statistically significant in eight equations, i.e., from the 15th to the 75th percentile. The impact of floods on farm profit in 2011 relative to that in 2009 is calculated and shown in Fig. 5.4.

Although the results for all the flood variables have the expected negative sign, they are not significant, except the coefficient of interaction dummy (flooded area*flooded period) in two regressions. Estimated regressions of farm profit can be obtained upon request.

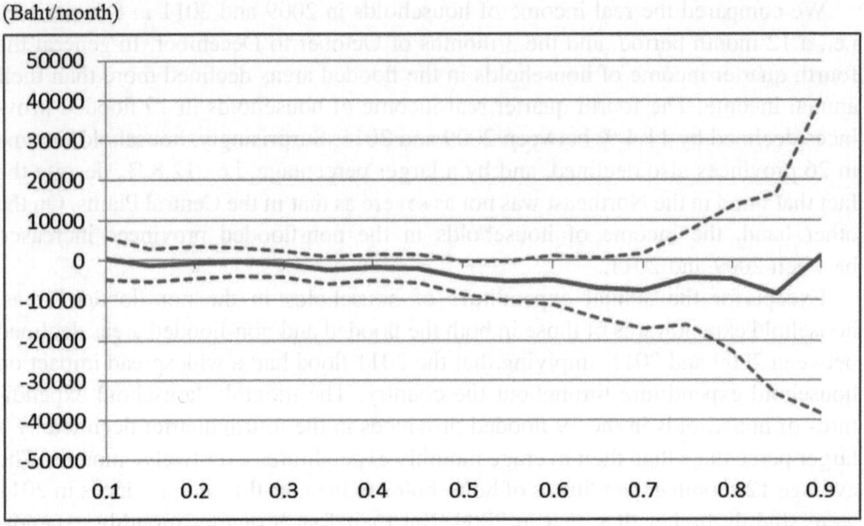

Fig. 5.4 Flood effect on farm profit in 2011 relative to that in 2009. *Source*: Calculated by the authors

5 Conclusion and Policy Implications

This chapter described the causes of Thailand's 2011 flood, and the government's response, revised the World Bank's estimated agricultural loss, and estimated the impact of the 2011 flood on household expenditure and income, using the "difference-in-difference" method.

The 2011 flood-the biggest and worst flood in Thailand's modern history-resulted in total damage and loss of USD46.5 billion. It was caused by the highest recorded rainfall, including five tropical storms which were concentrated in a short period of 106 days in the mid rainy season. But man-made mistakes worsened the situation, particularly the unregulated changes in land-use pattern and flood mismanagement. Political pressure has forced the government to allocate USD 11.29 billion for assistance of, and compensation to flood victims, restoration of damaged property, and flood management action plans, under a comprehensive flood management master plan, all of which were drafted in relatively few months following the flood.

This chapter revises the World Bank's estimates of agricultural loss, using satellite radar images which allow researchers to identify districts (and sub-district tambons) that were flooded for at least two consecutive weeks. The revised estimates of loss are lower than those of the World Bank. World Bank estimates were based solely on the size of farm lands that were flooded without taking into account the flood's duration. Using the 2-week duration of flood from the satellite images, the study also argues that the MOAC reported loss of agricultural output might be too high, thanks to the moral hazard of farmers' self-reports that were filed for compensation from the government. Compensation for farmers accounted for most (49 %) of the government compensation for households. But our estimates also suffer from the problem of outdated information on agricultural land use, which recently has rapidly been taken up by non-agricultural uses, particularly in some rapidly developed provinces.

Finally, the study used the "difference-in difference" method to estimate the impact of the flood on expenditure and income of households in 26 flooded provinces. Because the 2011 Socio-economic Survey did not contain questions regarding the impact of floods, the researchers have had to identify households that were affected by the flood in the fourth quarter of 2011. Thanks to the satellite radar images, the households in the flooded sub-districts (tambons) can be matched with the flooded areas in the satellite images. The estimated results confirm that the 2011 flood had a significant negative impact on expenditures of not only households in the flooded provinces but also those in non-flooded areas, indicating the interdependence between families in the flooded areas and those in non-flooded areas. One explanation is that the 2011 flood seriously affected Bangkok and its vicinity, which are the main economic activity zones of the country, where workers from every province come to work. When their income declined significantly, their families in the non-flooded areas received smaller repatriation income and thus had to reduce their expenditures. The study also finds that the 2011 flood had a negative impact on money income and wage income of households in the flooded areas. The results for business income are not statistically significant. Using the Socio-economic Survey in 2009 and 2011, the study also finds that the 2011 flood had a large negative impact on the farm profits of households in the flooded provinces.

One interesting finding is that the 2011 flood had relatively more impact on the expenditures and incomes of middle income households than other income classes, thus explaining why the government paid billions of baht for compensation, has been very active in formulating the flood management master plan, and plans to spend more almost $17 billion in the coming years.

Finally, the study finds several weaknesses in the current information for flood management. Despite the huge volume of information on the impact of flooding on output and damage to property, as reported by millions of flooded citizens, no government agency has paid attention to computerizing the flood data-base and information system and strengthening the capability of their information centers. As a result, valuable individual data have been discarded and were not brought into use for the policy making process.

Next, GISTDA still lacks some crucial information on flooding that will allow users to measure the true impact of a flood. Two important areas need to be urgently implemented. These are the construction of a digital elevation map, and investment in ground truthing activities to validate the information from satellite images. Some of the most important information urgently needed includes updated land-use patterns and the digitization of village boundaries. There is additionally a need to explore the possibility of using new techniques to identify and measure flooding in the cities.

We conclude with two policy recommendations. First, the capability of statistical agencies and agencies that are responsible for flood management should be urgently strengthened in the following areas: data collection, data base development, data processing and reporting using IT, and human resource development. Secondly, these agencies should be encouraged to communicate and exchange information and ideas with data users. Given that communities can work collectively to share information and overcome collective action problems, they serve as the basis for any disaster preparation plans.

Appendix 1

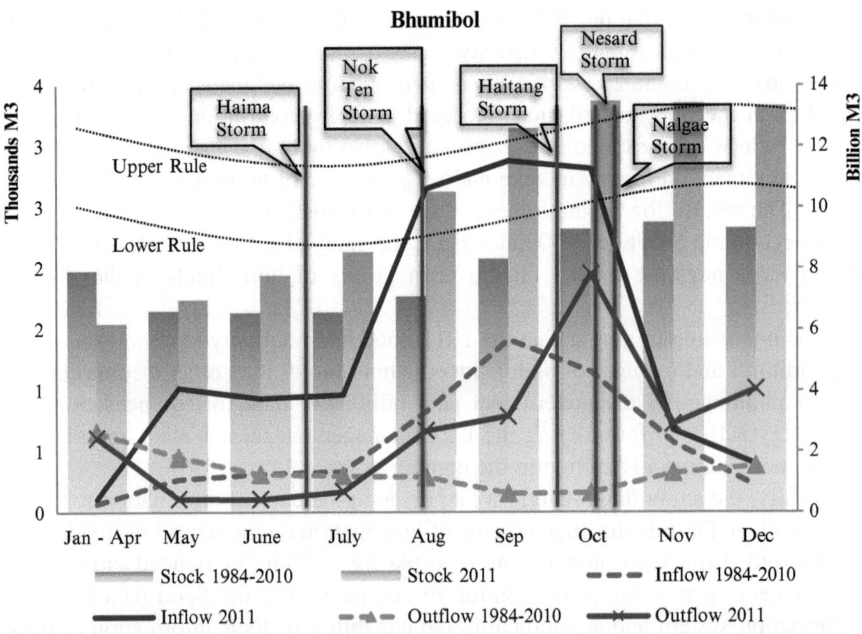

Fig. A.1 Water inflow, outflow and stock in the Bhumibol Dam, 1984–2010 and 2011. *Source*: EGAT 1984-2011 (calculated from monthly data)

Appendix 2

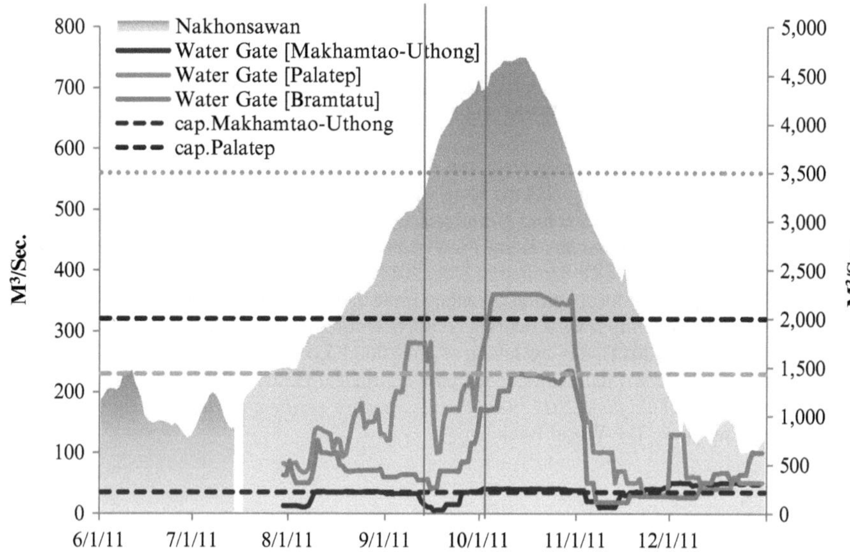

Fig. A.2 Water flowing through gates on the western side of Chao Phraya River and Chao Phraya River in Nakorn Sawan. *Source*: RID 2011

References

Bangkok biznews. (2011). Mismanagement-wrong decision, great flood resulted from politics (in Thai). *Bangkokbiznews*, 8th Nov. 2011, N.p. http://www.bangkokbiznews.com/home/detail/politics/analysis/20111108/418193/mismanagement-wrong decision...flood caused by politics (in Thai).html (accessed June 29, 2012).

Department of Agricultural Extension. (2012). Report on Impact of Flood on Farmers. Ministry of Agriculture and Cooperative. May-December 2011. Bangkok, n.p.

Department of Disaster Prevention and Mitigation, Ministry of Interior (DDPM). (2011). *Report on flood in 2011*. January 2012.

Department of Land Development. (2010). Land Use Survey 2006-2009. Ministry of Agriculture and Cooperative. Bangkok.

EGAT. (2012). *Fact: Water drainage management of Bhumibol and Sirikit dams, (in Thai)* Power Purchase Agreement Division. EGAT, n.d. http://www.ppa.egat.co.th/Pr-Egat/2554/1-11-54Water-drain-fact/waterdrain facts on water discharge from Bhumibol and Sirikit Dams (in Thai)-htm (accessed June 29, 2012)

Electricity Generating Authority of Thailand (EGAT). (1984–2011). *Data on irrigated water management at major dams.*

Firpo, S., Fortin, N., & Lemieux, T. (2009). Unconditional quantile regression. *Econometrica, 77*(3), 953–973.

GISTDA. (2011). *Radar satellite images and flood maps of the 2011 flood*, May-December 2011.

Komchadluek. (2011). Banhan criticizes scholars, Says Prime Minister pass the test (in Thai) *Komchadluek Online*. N.p., n.d. http://www.komchadluek.net/detail/20111105/114095/Banharn criticized academia - prime minister passes the test (in Thai).html. Accessed 29 June 2012.

National Statistical Office (NSO). (2011). The 2011 Socio-economic Survey.

Royal Irrigation Department (RID). (2011). *Information on the irrigated water management at major sluice gates and canals.*

Strategic Committee for Water Resource Management. (2012). Master Plan on Water Resource Management. Office of the SCWRM and National Economic and Social Development Board. Bangkok, n.p. January 2012.

Suppaisarn, C. (2008). Land management and flood plain development project for Chao Phraya Basin's flood relief following HM the King's monkey cheek concept at Bang Ban. *Manual of Development Project: Process and Maintenance of Monkey Cheek Reservoirs at Bang Ban* 5.

Suppaisarn, C. (2011). *Medium and heavy flood management in Chao Phraya river basin following the royal initiative*. TRF Seminar, 2 Dec. 2011.

Thairath. (2011). Chainart locals furious, Banhan protects Suphanburi (in Thai). *Thairath Online*. 24th Sept. 2011. N.p. http://www.thairath.co.th/content/region/204220. Accessed 29 June 2012.

Tobunmee, Weerapan (2012). Review lesson of 2011 flood: Look forward to the future, *Dailynews* [Bangkok] 25 Jan www.dailynews.co.th/content/Article/133222/index.html.

World Bank. (2012). *Thai flood 2011. Rapid assessment for resilient recovery and reconstruction planning*. Bangkok: The World Bank.

Part II
Market and Production Networks

Chapter 6
Impact of Recent Crises and Disasters on Regional Production Networks and Trade in Japan

Mitsuyo Ando

1 Introduction

Japan has recently encountered several crises and disasters. First, Japan faced a worldwide economic crisis, namely the 2008–2009 Global Financial Crisis (GFC) that primarily started as a demand shock due to drastic falls in demand in the US and EU markets. The 2008–2009 GFC seriously affected the world economy including Japan and other East Asian countries, as well as international production/distribution networks, mainly in machinery industries in the region. Second, Japan experienced a natural and technological disaster in March 2011, i.e., the 2011 Great East Japan Earthquake (EJE). The 2011 EJE brought about a supply shock due to the devastation of production plants located in the disaster areas caused by the tsunami, and had negative impacts on domestic/international production networks. Moreover, the 2011 EJE was not a simple natural disaster; the Fukushima nuclear accident resulting from the Tsunami caused a serious technological disaster and significantly affected Japan's agriculture and food exports. Third, the Japanese economy suffered from another natural disaster that occurred in Thailand in October 2011 (the 2011 Thailand floods) because many Japanese firms have operations in the disaster areas of Thailand, playing important roles in supply chains.

Given the fact that serious negative impacts of these crises/disasters were transmitted through domestic/international production/distribution networks, some people, including researchers and government officials, claimed that production networks had revealed their vulnerability toward shocks. As Ando and Kimura (2012) demonstrate, by analyzing the impacts of the 2008–2009 GFC and the 2011 EJE on Japan's exports, however, international production/distribution networks demonstrated their resiliency in the face of these two massive shocks despite their

M. Ando (✉)
Faculty of Business and Commerce, Keio University, Tokyo, Japan
e-mail: m-ando@fbc.keio.ac.jp

D.P. Aldrich et al. (eds.), *Resilience and Recovery in Asian Disasters*, Risk, Governance and Society 18, DOI 10.1007/978-4-431-55022-8_6

initial negative impacts. Where the initial section of the book focused more on the role of family and community ties during disaster, this chapter begins the section focused on the role of markets and networks. As discussed in Chap. 1, markets can quickly reach equilibrium under standard circumstances, but under severe pressure may fail.

This chapter sheds light on domestic/international production networks in machinery industries and examines how these economic crises and natural disasters affected the networks, mainly from the viewpoint of Japan's exports. More specifically, the chapter first decomposes changes in exports into "extensive and intensive margins," i.e., the quantity effect, the price effect, the effect due to exiting products, and the effect due to new products entering the market, in order to capture the features of trade declines and recoveries resulting from the crises for machinery parts and components and machinery final products. The chapter also examines the probability of trade declines and recoveries, using a logit estimation, to formalize the natures of international production/distribution networks under the crises. I also discuss domestic activities as well as the impacts of the 2011 Thailand floods. Furthermore, as mentioned above, the 2011 EJE was not only a natural disaster but also a technological disaster that seriously affected Japan's agriculture and food exports. The chapter therefore also investigates the impacts on their exports as well.

The rest of the chapter is organized as follows: Section 2 describes the patterns of Japan's exports. Sections 3 and 4 provide analyses of reduction and recovery of machinery exports resulting from the 2008–2009 GFC and the 2011 EJE, using the decomposition approach as well as a logit estimation. Section 5 in turn focuses on agriculture and food exports and examines the impacts of the two crises, using the same methodologies used in the previous sections. Section 6 briefly investigates the impacts of the GFC and the EJE on domestic activities, and the impacts of the 2011 Thailand floods, using indices of industrial production, regional input-output tables, and the Japan External Trade Organization (JETRO) survey. Section 7 concludes the chapter.

2 Patterns of Japan's Exports[1]

We analyzed the trends of Japan's real exports in US dollars for all products, machinery parts and components, and machinery final goods (in total and automobiles only) from January 2007 to October 2011.[2] While the data clearly show the existence of significant negative impacts from the 2008–2009 GFC on Japan's

[1] Sections 6.2–6.4 are based on Ando and Kimura (2012).

[2] Machinery goods are composed of general machinery, electrical machinery, transport equipment, and precision machinery (see Ando and Kimura (2012) for the definition of machinery parts and components). Machinery final products are defined as machinery goods other than machinery parts and components. Automobiles are final products only in HS87.

Table 6.1 By-region values and shares of Japan's real exports

	The value of exports, indexed to 2007=1				Share in total exports (%)			
Destinations	2007	2008	2009	2010	2007	2008	2009	2010
All products								
East Asia	1.00	1.18	1.09	1.53	47	48	53	54
US	1.00	1.01	0.78	1.01	20	18	16	15
EU	1.00	1.10	0.82	1.00	15	14	12	11
World	1.00	1.16	0.97	1.31	100	100	100	100
Machinery parts and components								
East Asia	1.00	1.13	1.06	1.54	56	56	59	62
US	1.00	1.04	0.85	1.13	18	17	16	15
EU	1.00	1.11	0.83	1.13	15	15	13	13
World	1.00	1.11	0.99	1.38	100	100	100	100
Machinery final products								
East Asia	1.00	1.19	1.02	1.55	22	23	28	30
US	1.00	0.97	0.66	0.86	29	24	23	22
EU	1.00	1.06	0.69	0.78	18	16	15	12
World	1.00	1.15	0.81	1.12	100	100	100	100
HS87 final goods only								
East Asia	1.00	1.38	1.20	2.00	7	8	12	14
US	1.00	0.96	0.64	0.86	37	31	34	31
EU	1.00	1.01	0.62	0.76	17	15	15	12
World	1.00	1.14	0.70	1.02	100	100	100	100

Note: export values are in USD
Data: Ando and Kimura (2012)

exports, they display a V-shaped recovery for all products, particularly for machinery parts and components. East Asia is the most important destination for Japan's exports in machinery parts and components, and a very quick recovery of exports to East Asia contributes to the rapid recovery of Japan's exports in machinery parts and components (see Table 6.1).[3] In addition, East Asia is growing in terms of the value of exports as well as the share in total exports of machinery final products; the value in 2010 was 1.6 times as high as that in 2007, and the share increases from 22 % in 2007 to 30 % in 2010.[4] The corresponding value and share in 2010 for automobiles only (final products) doubled from those in 2007. With the GFC as a trigger, East Asia is

[3] East Asia in this chapter includes the following 14 countries/economies: Association of South-East Asian Nations (ASEAN) 10, China, Korea, Hong Kong, and Taiwan.

[4] East Asia itself also became a major contributor to the recovery of East Asian trade, not only for machinery parts and components but also for machinery finished products (Ando 2010). Also see Haddad and Shepherd (2011) for an interesting series of analyses of trade and economies under the GFC.

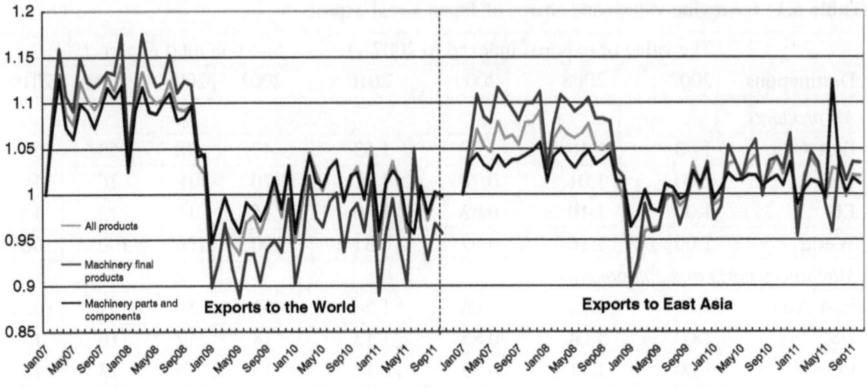

Fig. 6.1 The number of exported product-country pairs, indexed to January 2007=1. *Data*: Ando and Kimura (2012)

gaining importance as a market for machinery final products, though the United States (US) and European Union (EU) remain as important markets.[5]

While machinery export values per se recovered their pre- GFC levels, there exists a permanent change in the "extensive margins" of machinery exports. The number of exported product-country pairs for all products exported to the world significantly dropped in the 2008–2009 GFC, with a minimum in January 2009 (Fig. 6.1). Although the number of exported product-country pairs has had a tendency to increase since January 2009, it has not returned to the level of 2007 or 2008. The number of product-country pairs for exports to East Asian countries only dropped significantly as well, though the decline was not as pronounced as in the case of exports to all countries in the world. These reflect the fact that the geographical distribution of activities by Japanese firms, including those in East Asia, was reshuffled and the basis of Japan's exports has been narrowed down with the GFC as a trigger.

The negative effects of the EJE are reflected in exports particularly in April and May 2011. Exports rapidly increased in June, however, achieving a positive growth in terms of both changes from the previous month and from the previous year. Compared with the 2008–2009 GFC, the magnitude of the fall in overall exports, including exports in machinery parts and components, was much smaller, recovery was more rapid, and no distinctive change in the extensive margins of exports is observed.

Machinery final product statistics depict a somewhat different picture; their exports suffered from both the GFC and the 2011 EJE, and exports of automobiles, in particular, were even lower in April 2011 than they were at their lowest point resulting from the 2008–2009 GFC. As critical small and medium-sized enterprises

[5] EU refers to the EU27 in this chapter.

(SMEs) were located in the disaster areas of the 2011 EJE, negative supply shocks affected exports through production chains. Exports of machinery final products, including automobiles, however, rapidly recovered after May and even exceeded the level of the previous year in June. There also seems to be very little evidence of any long term affect on their exports

3 Machinery Exports: Decomposition of Trade Reduction and Recovery

This section investigates patterns of trade reduction and recovery, using the decomposition approach. For the analysis of the 2008–2009 GFC, the chapter sets the period of trade reduction from October 2008 to January 2009 and the period of trade recovery from January to October 2009. For the analysis of the 2011 EJE, this chapter focuses on monthly changes, or changes from previous months, to capture features of trade movements within a short period.

3.1 Methodology and Data

The decomposition approach used in this section is the one proposed by Haddad et al. (2010). As a first step, the category of a product exported to a given partner country is identified as "continuing", "entry", or "exit". If a product is exported to a given country in both period $t-1$ and period t, the category of the product for the corresponding country (the product-country pair) is defined as "continuing". Similarly, the category is defined as "entry" if the product is exported only in t, and the category is defined as "exit" if the product is exported to the corresponding country only in $t-1$. Changes in export values from period $t-1$ to period t are then decomposed into extensive and intensive margins, based on the categories defined above. Intensive margins are composed of effects due to changes in quantity and price; that is, changes in export values for country-product pairs in the category "continuing" due to changes in quantity (the quantity effect) and changes in price (the price effect). On the other hand, extensive margins consist of an effect due to exiting products (exit effect hereafter) and an effect due to new products (entry effect hereafter); that is reduction in export values due to no exports in t for product-country pairs in the category "exit", and an increase in export values due to new exports in t for product-country pairs in the category "entry." According to the decomposition approach, the percentage change in the total value of exports can be expressed as the sum of the quantity effect, the price effect, the entry effect, and the exit effect:

$$\frac{dv_t}{v_{t-1}} = \frac{\sum_{c=1}^{C} \frac{p_t^c + p_{t-1}^c}{2} \Delta q_t^c}{v_{t-1}} + \frac{\sum_{c=1}^{C} \Delta p_t^c \frac{q_t^c + q_{t-1}^c}{2}}{v_{t-1}} + \frac{\sum_{n=1}^{N} p_t^n q_t^n}{v_{t-1}} - \frac{\sum_{x=1}^{X} p_{t-1}^x q_{t-1}^x}{v_{t-1}}$$

$$(I = C + N + X)$$

where v_t stands for the total value in t, which is the sum of value of each product i, c for products that are traded in both $t-1$ and t (in the category "continuing"), n for products that are traded only in t (in the category "entry"), x for products that are traded only in $t-1$ (in the category "exit"), I for the total number of products, C for the total number of products in the category "continuing," N for the total number of products in the category "entry", and X for the total number of products in the category "exit."

To decompose changes in values of Japan's exports by applying this method, monthly data of Japanese bilateral exports at the most disaggregated level or the Harmonized System (HS) 9-digit level, which are available from the Trade Statistics of Japan, the Ministry of Finance, Japan, are employed.[6] The nominal export values in Japanese Yen are converted into real export values in US dollars, using an export price index, available from the Bank of Japan, and exchange rates that are the monthly average of public rates announced by Japan Customs, available from the Ministry of Finance, Japan.

3.2 Results

We investigated export changes during the periods of trade reduction and recovery, together with export changes in the same period of the previous year, to partially consider seasonal fluctuations. The data clearly demonstrate that exports declined from October 2008 to January 2009 by almost 40 %. Even in normal years, Japanese exports tend to fall from October to January; for instance, exports declined in the same period of the previous year by 5–10 %. A 40 % drop, however, is certainly far beyond a drop due to seasonality. In particular, exports of automobiles dropped by more than 50 %, which is much larger than the decline in the same period of the previous year (3 %). The 2008–2009 GFC therefore did have significant negative impacts on Japanese exports.

[6] The decomposition of changes in trade into extensive and intensive margins may change when data at a different level of disaggregation are used. For instance, the results based on data at the most disaggregated level (HS 9-digit level in the case of Japan) may be more likely to make the extensive margins appear larger than the results based on data at more aggregated levels such as the HS 6-digit level. Also, if we use some cutoff point to identify the extensive margins, the results may change. However, the major findings discussed here do not change even if we use different levels of aggregation.

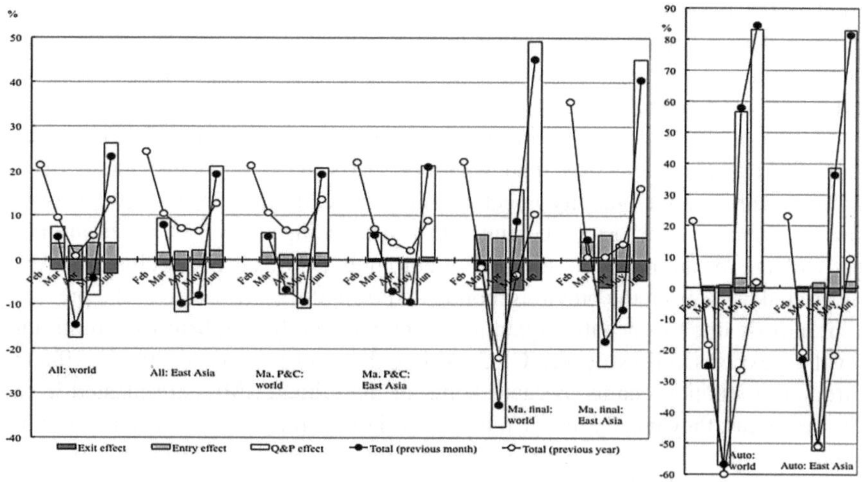

Fig. 6.2 Decomposition of changes in Japanese real exports under the 2011 EJE (USD). *Data*: Author's preparation, based on the results in Ando and Kimura (2012)

The figure also demonstrates that the exit effect is much smaller in absolute terms for machinery parts and components than for other products; the exit effect is only −1.6 % for the world. Moreover, the exit effect is even smaller for East Asia with −0.7 %, and is almost at the level of the same period of the previous year. Although large intensive margins induced a significant decline in their exports, particularly for East Asia, such a small exit effect suggests the robustness of trade relationships for machinery parts and components within dense production/distribution networks in the region. Furthermore, the pattern of export recovery shows a symmetric picture to the export fall; the extensive margin was quite small, and a large positive quantity effect was observed for machinery parts and components exported to East Asia.

Figure 6.2 in turn represents monthly changes in real exports to the world after the EJE from March to June 2011, and the change in real exports to East Asia only. Unlike the GFC, monthly changes, i.e., changes from the previous month are decomposed into extensive and intensive margins, since drastic fluctuations in a short period are observed. Similarly to the analysis for the GFC, however, changes from the corresponding month of the previous year (changes from previous year) are also considered, as monthly changes tend to be significantly influenced by seasonality.

As is the case of the GFC, the exit effect is much smaller for machinery parts and components than for other products: the exit effect is only around −1.5 % in a month. Moreover, the exit effect for machinery parts and components is more or less equal to the low level in the same month of the previous year 2010. Although their exports decreased in April and May 2011, they significantly expanded in June 2011, reflecting a large and positive quantity effect. As a result, exports in June 2011 exceeded those in June 2010 by 14 %. Furthermore, the exit effect was even smaller for East Asia, i.e., less than −0.5% in a month, compared with other regions. These findings suggest that trade relationships for machinery parts and components are robust, and that firms prioritize international production networks even following the EJE, just as is the case of the GFC.

On the other hand, exports in machinery final goods substantially declined in April 2011 by a greater extent than machinery parts and components, mainly due to a significant negative quantity effect as well as an exit effect. A dramatic recovery was seen, however, in May and June. The outstanding recovery can be observed particularly for automobiles. Exports of automobiles drastically declined in April by around 60 % from the previous month, and from the same month of the previous year, mostly due to a negative quantity effect, which fell even below the minimum level of exports following the GFC. Although exports were negatively affected through production chains, because some of the critical SMEs are located in the disaster areas, they mostly returned to the level of the previous year in June. Behind such a dramatic recovery for automobiles, there were great "private" efforts to restore supply chains by private companies.

One symbolic episode comes from the case of Japan Renesas. This company produced several key electronic parts and components called micro-processing units (MPU), memory control units (MCU), and application specific standard products (ASSP) for automobiles and various ICT products. The EJE severely damaged its factories, including the Naka Factory in Ibaraki Prefecture. In order to resume their supply chains, the Japan Automobile Manufacturers Association (JAMA) and others gathered workers from a number of companies and sent them to the Naka Factory to help restore the operation; the number of such helpers exceeded 2,500 a day at maximum. Thus a strong incentive to maintain the supply chains worked even beyond the boundaries of individual firms, even if negative impacts were transmitted through the supply chains at the beginning of the crisis.

4 Machinery Exports: Probability of Trade Fall and Recovery

To formalize the features of machinery exports in responding to the crises, this section first investigates probability of reduction and recovery of machinery exports resulting from the two crises, using a logit estimation.

4.1 Methodology and Data

For the analysis of trade reduction as a result of the 2008–2009 GFC [the 2011 EJE], those product-country pairs at the HS 9-digit level with exports in October 2008 (and/or 1 month before and after) [March 2011 (and/or 1 month before and after)] are employed to examine whether or not their exports existed in January 2009 [May 2011]. For the analysis of trade recovery under the GFC [the EJE], on the other hand, those product-country pairs at the HS 9-digit level with exports in October 2008 (and/or 1 month before and after) [March 2011 (and/or 1 month before and after)] and no exports in January 2009 [May 2011] are used to investigate whether their exports recover by October 2009 [July 2011].

The equation for our logit estimation analyses is as follows:

$$EXchange_{i,j} = \beta_0 + \beta_1 \ln Dist_i + \beta_2 Parts_j + \sum\nolimits_n^N \alpha_n Country_n + \varepsilon,$$

where $EXchange_{i,j}$ is a binary variable representing fall/recovery of exports; $EXchange_{i,j}$ is 1 if no export of product j to country i is observed in January 2009 [May 2011] and 0 otherwise for the analysis of trade fall at the 2008–2009 GFC [the 2011 EJE]. In contrast, $EXchange_{i,j}$ is 1 if exports of product j to country i are observed in October 2009 (July 2011) and 0 otherwise for the analysis of trade recovery under the 2008–2009 GFC (the 2011 EJE). $\ln Dist_i$ denotes the distance between Japan and country i in the form of a natural logarithm. $Parts_j$ is 1 if product j is machinery parts and components, and 0 otherwise. In addition, country/region dummies expressed as $Country_n$ are included for 14 East Asian countries, the US, and EU to capture the features of trade relationships with these countries/region at the crises.

4.2 Results

Given the control for distance, the results (see Ando and Kimura (2012)) imply that machinery parts and components trade is less likely to be discontinued and is likely to recover even if it stops once, regardless of whether due to demand shock or supply shock. The coefficient for parts is negative for the analysis of trade decline and positive for the analysis of trade recovery with statistical significance, suggesting robust trade relationships for machinery parts and components, compared with machinery final products. This is consistent with the results of the decomposition analysis.

The results also indicate that, among East Asian countries, those who are heavily involved in the regional production networks tend to maintain their trade relationships and tend to recover trade even if they stop briefly. The coefficients for East Asian countries are mostly negative for the analysis of trade fall and positive for the analysis of trade recovery with statistical significance. In particular, the absolute values of coefficients for countries such as China, Thailand, Korea, Taiwan, and Vietnam are large for the analysis of the GFC, indicating the strong trade relationships in the production networks. Similarly, the absolute values of coefficients for countries such as China, Korea, Thailand, Taiwan, and Vietnam are large for the analysis of the EJE. On the other hand, the coefficients for countries such as Brunei,

Cambodia, Laos, and Myanmar are either statistically insignificant, small in absolute terms, or even opposite. This implies that these countries are not deeply involved in regional production networks in machinery industries.

In addition to the logit analysis mentioned above, Ando and Kimura (2012) conducted a survival analysis to investigate the long term probability of trade recovery, focused on the timing of recovery. Their results also demonstrate that trade in machinery parts and components has a lower probability of being discontinued and has a higher probability of recovery even if briefly stopped. All findings in this section confirm that regional production networks are resilient against shocks to save transaction costs of firms' setting-up production networks even if negative impacts are transmitted through the production networks at the outset of a crisis.

5 Agriculture and Food Exports

Unlike other commodities, destinations of exports in agriculture and food products are limited to specific countries/regions; major destination countries/regions are Hong Kong (24 % of total exports in 2010), the US (14 %), ASEAN (13 %), Taiwan (13 %), China (11 %), Korea (10 %), and the EU (5 %), accounting for 90 % of the total. In addition, the seasonality is typical for exports in agriculture and food products, with a peak in December every year mainly due exports to Hong Kong.

While agriculture and food exports seem to have been less affected by the 2008–2009 GFC, they were significantly affected by the Fukushima nuclear accident caused by the Tsunami component of the 2011 EJE. The negative impacts of this technological disaster are clearly shown in a significant decline of exports in April and May; exports in April and May declined from the respective previous month by almost 20 %. The negative impacts are also reflected in the number of exported product-country pairs; the number for agriculture and food products drastically decreased in April and May, though the seasonality is stronger than other products (Fig. 6.3).

The decomposition of trade reductions resulting from the EJE demonstrates that the serious decline in agriculture and food exports in April and May 2011 was largely induced by the exit effect or the effect by products for which exports discontinued, in addition to the negative quantity effect (Fig. 6.4); the exit effect explains half of the export decline. Many countries introduced safety inspections and trade restrictions in various ways, including the obligation of submitting certificates of inspection for radioactive materials and/or certificates of origin at the prefecture level, sampling inspection on the import side, and import prohibition, for imports in agriculture and food products produced in Japan. Besides safety inspections and trade restrictions, there seem to have been exit blows from unfounded (but partially understandable) rumors induced by the nuclear disaster. Most of the major partner countries/regions also introduced import prohibition for specific agricultural and food products produced in specific prefectures (all products

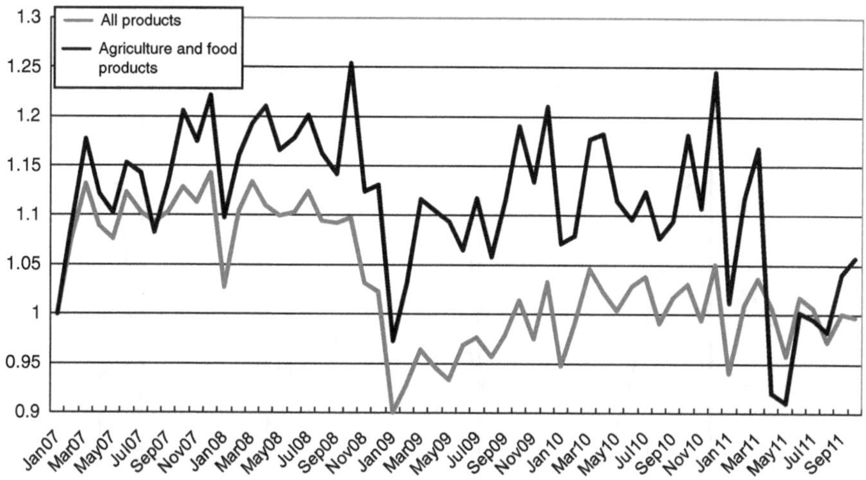

Fig. 6.3 The number of exported product-country pairs for agriculture and food products, indexed to January 2007=1. *Data*: author's calculation, using data available from the Ministry of Finance

produced in specific areas in the case of China and Taiwan), in addition to the obligation of submitting certificates of origin and safety inspection. The effects of these trade restrictions are directly reflected in the significant reduction of exports.

Table 6.2 confirms how the number of exported products declined in each country/region. Even if the trend in the previous year is considered, the number of exported products is indeed low particularly for May and June in China (0.60 and 0.54, respectively), May in Korea (0.65), April in the EU (0.63), and April and May in the Middle East (0.59 and 0.65).[7] On the other hand, an upward trend is observed by June for some countries such as Korea and the EU, and also the reduction is rather marginal in terms of the number of products exported to the US and the ASEAN 10. As a result, agriculture and food exports were rapidly recovering in June.

6 Domestic Activities and the 2011 Thailand Floods

While previous sections in this chapter focused on the patterns of exports, this section briefly investigates domestic activities from the perspective of industrial production and regional input-output tables.[8] As with the patterns of exports, the

[7] Some countries in the Middle East imposed import prohibition on any agriculture and food products produced in Japan, regardless of where they were produced in Japan. Such strict trade restrictions should directly influence the number of exported products.

[8] Indices of industrial production and regional input-output tables are available from the following websites, respectively;

http://www.meti.go.jp/english/statistics/tyo/iip/index.html, and
http://www.meti.go.jp/statistics/tyo/tiikiio/result/result_02.html.

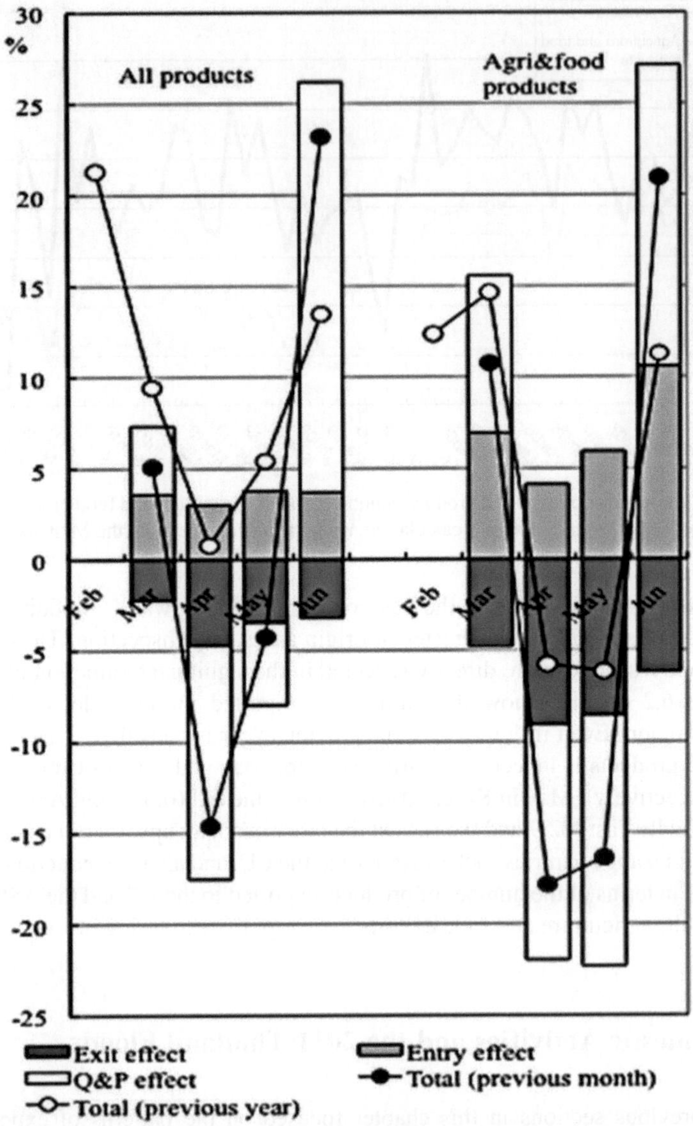

Fig. 6.4 Decomposition of changes in exports to the world in agriculture and food products under the 2011 EJE(USD). *Data*: author's calculation, using data available from the Ministry of Finance and the Bank of Japan

index of industrial production for the whole Japan suggests that the direct impacts of the 2008–2009 GFC were more serious than those of the 2011 EJE. As Fig. 6.5 clearly displays, the impacts of the EJE are indeed more serious if analysis is

Table 6.2 The number of exported agriculture and food products for selected countries/region in 2011

Destination	Share in total exports (%)	The number of exported products							
		March		April		May		June	
Hong Kong	24	1.03	(1.00)	0.95	(1.05)	0.92	(1.08)	0.97	(1.03)
US	14	1.05	(1.14)	1.02	(1.12)	1.01	(1.08)	1.03	(1.04)
ASEAN10	13	1.34	(1.31)	1.12	(1.30)	1.10	(1.19)	1.25	(1.24)
Taiwan	13	0.95	(0.90)	0.87	(0.96)	0.83	(0.95)	0.84	(0.90)
China	11	1.06	(1.04)	0.80	(1.04)	0.60	(1.03)	0.54	(1.06)
Korea	10	0.95	(0.95)	0.98	(1.00)	0.65	(0.86)	0.81	(0.91)
EU27	5	1.18	(1.24)	0.63	(1.33)	0.95	(1.15)	1.02	(1.00)
Middle East	2	1.76	(1.57)	0.59	(1.35)	0.65	(1.61)	0.78	(1.37)

Notes: The number of exported products is indexed to January 2007. The figures in *parenthesis* are those for 2010. The shares are based on export values in 2010
Data: author's calculation, using data available from the Ministry of Finance

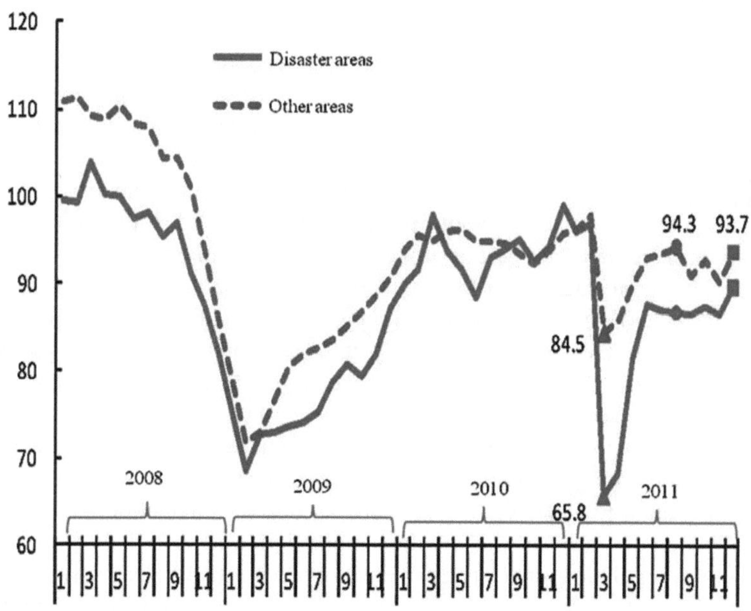

Fig. 6.5 Indices of industrial production by disaster and non-disaster areas: Mining and manufacturing (2005=100). *Data*: Ministry of Economy and Trade, Industry (METI) (2012)

focused only on the disaster areas.[9] The magnitude of the direct impacts of the GFC, however, was more serious, at least from the perspective of production as well as exports for the whole country.

[9] The disaster areas in this figure are the designated regions to which the Disaster Relief Act may apply.

Production activities in the disaster areas are of course connected with those in other areas. I analyzed regional connections of production activities in terms of output in 2005: regional shares of demand for the production in the Tohoku (Northeast) region that had significant direct damage from the Tsunami. In many of the machinery sectors, a large portion of the products produced in the Tohoku region go to the Kanto region (where Tokyo is located): 51 % for office electric appliance, 49 % for industrial electric machinery, 40 % for household electrical machinery, 42 % for communication electronics equipment, and 55 % for auto parts. In the case of other transport equipment, 20 % of the products go to the Chubu region (where Toyota is located).

I also analyzed the regional connections of production activities in terms of input in 2005: that is, the shares of manufacturing inputs from the Tohoku region in the production of machinery sectors for all regions as well as the Kanto region. In machinery sectors, the manufacturing input from the Tohoku region is large: in particular, in sectors of communication electronics equipment, electronic computing equipment, and electronic parts, the Tohoku region has a share of 10 % of the production in the whole Japan. Interestingly, electronic parts produced in the Tohoku region are used in various machinery sectors. Moreover, auto parts produced in the Tohoku region are used in various transport equipment sectors, though the portion of input is smaller than in the case of electric machinery sectors.

When we focus only on the production in the Kanto region, the share of input from the Tohoku region exceeds 4 % in total in sectors of the communication electronics equipment, electronic computing equipment, and electronic parts. In particular, electronic parts and auto parts that are produced in the Tohoku region seem to form an important part of production; the share of input of auto parts from the Tohoku region is larger for the production in the Kanto region than the average (the whole Japan). All of these analyses suggest that non-disaster areas, particularly the Kanto region, are tightly connected with disaster areas in domestic production networks, and thus they had negative impacts on production activities particularly in the machinery sector through supply chains.

Insufficient supply of intermediate goods from the disaster areas had direct negative effects on production in non-disaster areas, particularly just after the EJE from March to June. What was more serious for production activities from July to September in Japan was the implementation of an electricity saving policy (compulsory regulation on the usage of electric power to save electricity). Although firms made great efforts to cope with this regulation and took various actions, this regulation apparently resulted in the reduction of production.[10]

The 2011 Thailand floods, which occurred in October 2011, also had negative impacts on production networks and Japanese firms, because many Japanese

[10] See Ministry of Economy and Trade, Industry (METI) (2012) for the detailed analysis of industrial activities in F/Y2011.

Table 6.3 Damage of Japanese firms in Thailand from the 2011 Thailand floods

	Manufacturing		Non-manufacturing	
	Number of firms	Share	Number of firms	Share
Directly damaged	**40**	**49.4%**	**8**	**16.7%**
Inside of industrial estates	36	44.4%	6	12.5%
Outside of industrial estates	4	4.9%	4	8.3%
Indirectly damaged	**33**	**40.7%**	**11**	**22.9%**
Damage by firms to supply	13	16.0%	5	10.4%
Damage by firms to purchase	18	22.2%	2	4.2%
Damage by a part of supply chains	13	16.0%	4	8.3%
Not damaged	**8**	**9.9%**	**29**	**60.4%**
The number of effective answers (firms)	81		48	

Notes: multiple answers are allowed. The rate of effective answers in total is 69.3 %
Data: JETRO Bangkok (2012)

firms have operations in the disaster areas and play important roles in supply chains. The JETRO conducted an interesting survey on the firms suffering from the floods in Thailand. Table 6.3 presents the situation of the damage of Japanese firms in Thailand (multiple answers were allowed). Some firms were directly affected, while others were indirectly affected. 41 % of the manufacturing firms in the sample (81 firms) had indirect negative impacts; 16 % was due to the damage of the firm to which a firm in the survey sells its products, 22 % was due to the damage of the firm from which the corresponding firm purchases products, and 16 % are due to the damage of some firms in a line of supply chains. These figures confirm that many firms were indirectly affected even if they did not have direct damage from the floods. It implies that when production networks exist, negative impacts are likely to expand through supply chains.

On the other hand, the existence of the production networks seems to confer robustness. Among firms that directly suffered from the floods, more than half of the firms in the sample (40 %) were planning to maintain the size of operations before the crisis, which is higher than the share for non-manufacturing firms (38 %) (Table 6.4). Moreover, more than three-quarters of the firms in the sample were planning to maintain operations at the same locations, and 15 % of the firms at different locations in Thailand, rather than going other countries (multiple answers were allowed). Even those who were going to move some production blocks to other countries as a risk-diversification measure were also intending to keep some production sites in Thailand.

The major reason why firms were intending to stay in the same places or at least to stay in Thailand was that most of them were already involved in supply chains in Thailand, and thus the movement of production blocks abroad would require a change in transactions, i.e., the origins of purchases and the destinations of sales, which would lead to large transaction costs. In practice, other countries also have

Table 6.4 The expected size of operations and locations for firms directly damaged

	Manufacturing		Non-manufacturing	
The expected size of operations				
Steady	21	52.5 %	3	37.5 %
Shrinkage	16	40.0 %	3	37.5 %
Expansion	0	0.0 %	0	0.0 %
Not decided yet	3	7.5 %	2	25.0 %
The number of effective answers (firms)	40		8	
The expected location of operations				
Same place	31	77.5 %	7	87.5 %
Other place in Thailand	6	15.0 %	2	25.0 %
Relocation to other countries	3	7.5 %	0	0.0 %
Exit	0	0.0 %	0	0.0 %
Not decided yet	3	7.5 %	0	0.0 %
The number of effective answers (firms)	40		8	

Note: Multiple answers are allowed
Data: JETRO Bangkok (2012)

risks, such as political risks and natural disasters, while Thailand has advantages in infrastructure and industrial clustering. Thus, with a consideration of these elements, firms tended to choose to stay in the same places, or to move only to different places in Thailand.

Actually, those firms that suffered seriously from the 2011 Thailand floods are making great efforts to restore operations as quickly as possible. Japan's exports to and imports from Thailand declined in October and November 2011. In order to replace capital goods and other machinery damaged by the floods, however, Japan's exports to Thailand are drastically increasing in 2012. In other words, involvement in production networks and the existence of industrial clustering generate strong incentives to maintain the networks in order to avoid transactions costs, even if the networks tend to spread negative shocks, at least temporarily, when they encounter supply or demand shocks.

7 Conclusion

This chapter has focused on domestic/international production networks in machinery industries, and has examined how the economic crisis and natural/technological disaster that Japan encountered in recent years affected the networks and trade, mainly from the viewpoint of Japan's exports. Regardless of whether creating demand shock or supply shock, the economic/natural disasters revealed the stability and robustness of markets and production networks in machinery sectors. It is true that the shocks seriously damaged production networks, and their negative impacts were transmitted through production networks, at their outset. Strong forces, however, worked to keep production networks in being, and quick adjustments for recovery were implemented. As the extended fragmentation theory states, the fragmentation of production takes advantage of the reduction in production cost within production blocks, while it should pay for the network set-up/adjustment cost and the service link cost.[11]

The latter two costs are particularly high for transactions in parts and components compared with transactions in final products. In order to respond to massive shocks, firms try to save these costs by keeping existing transaction channels for parts and components. As a result, exports in machinery parts and components tend to be sustained, and are likely to recover rapidly even if they are temporarily discontinued. Even the behavior of firms involved in the production networks and suffering from the Thailand floods also confirms the existence of strong continuation or centripetal forces and the deployment of efforts to keep production networks in being, in consideration of the various transaction cost implications of discontinuing a network.

Conversely, once production networks are moved away from Japan, it is not easy to get them back. Therefore, it is quite important to deal with various concerns in the business environment. Indeed, in the case of the EJE, there still remains the risk of "hollowing-out" due to continuing the shortage of electricity supply and substantial JP Yen appreciation. The same discussion can be applied to countries involved in the production networks, such as Thailand. To rebuild infrastructure and implement policies that help restart operations, such as tax-exemptions for imports of capital goods or what needs to make factories restart operations as quickly as possible, is important. So far, Thailand has relatively great advantages, particularly due to a better business environment in terms of infrastructure and industrial clustering, compared with that in surrounding countries, but it is important to recover the better business environment as soon as possible and further improve it. Otherwise, private firms may utilize the crisis as a trigger for removing production blocks to other countries.

The 2011 EJE and its aftermath as a technological disaster also remind us of the importance of reliable safety guarantees and of nurturing international credibility on export products such as agriculture and food products.

References

Ando, M. (2010). Machinery trade in East Asia and the global financial crisis. *Korea and the World Economy, 11*(2), 361–394.

Ando, M. S., Arndt, W., & Kimura, F. (2009). Production networks in East Asia: Strategic behavior by Japanese and U.S. firms. In The shorter version in Japanese is available in Kyoji Fukao and Japan Center for Economic Research (JCER) (Eds.), *Keio Business Review No.*

[11] See Ando et al. (2009) for the two-dimensional fragmentation and their costs in terms of fixed costs, services link costs, and production cost per se.

45-2, *Japanese firms' strategy in East Asia: A comparison with US and European firms: Nihon Keizai Shinbun Sha*. 2008.

Ando, M., & Kimura, F. (2012). How did the Japanese exports respond to two crises in the international production network?: The global financial crisis and the East Japan Earthquake. The *Asian Economic Journal*, *26*(3), 259–285.

Haddad, M., Harrison, A., & Hausman, C. (2010). *Decomposing the great trade collapse: Products, prices, and quantities in the 2008–2009 crisis*, NBER Working Paper Series No. 16253.

Haddad, M., & Shepherd, B. (Eds.). (2011). *Managing openness: Trade and outward-oriented growth after the crisis*. Washington, DC: The World Bank.

JETRO Bangkok. (2012). *Survey on firms damaged by the Thailand floods*. JETRO Bangkok (In Japanese).

Ministry of Economy, Trade, and Industry (METI). (2012). *Report on the analysis of industrial activities in F/Y2011. In Japanese*. Available at: http://www.meti.go.jp/statistics/toppage/report/bunseki/oldrepo_23.html#menu04.

Chapter 7
Impact of Natural Disasters on Production Networks and Urbanization in New Zealand

Brent Layton

1 Introduction

1.1 Geography

New Zealand is a string of islands situated in the South West Pacific Ocean approximately 1,600 km east of mainland Australia[1] and approximately 1,000 km south of New Caledonia, Fiji and Tonga. The distance between the northernmost point of New Zealand (Nugent Island) and its southernmost point (Jacquemart Island) is 2,813 km. The islands making up the country lie in a northwest-southeast direction between latitudes 29° and 53° South on the boundary of the Pacific and Indo-Australian continental plates.

The edges of the Pacific plate define most of the 'Ring of Fire'. This is the active volcanic and seismic area that encircles the Pacific Ocean and includes Japan, the Aleutian Island chain, the southern coast of Alaska, and the west coast of North America (California). Virtually all of New Zealand's 4.4 million population lives on the two major islands—the North and South Islands. These are situated very close to one another near the center of the string of islands that make up the entire territory. The Pacific and Indo-Australian plates meet under the South Island and under and close to the southeast coast of the North Island.

[1] The shortest distance between Australian and New Zealand territory is the 617 km between the Auckland Islands (New Zealand) and Macquarie Island (Australia) in the Southern Ocean, well away from the major land masses and population centres of both countries.

B. Layton (✉)
The Electricity Authority, Wellington, New Zealand
e-mail: brent.layton@xtra.co.nz

D.P. Aldrich et al. (eds.), *Resilience and Recovery in Asian Disasters*, Risk, Governance and Society 18, DOI 10.1007/978-4-431-55022-8_7

1.2 Vulnerability to Natural Disasters

1.2.1 Geophysical Hazards

In the region of New Zealand, the Pacific plate is currently moving slowly westward and sliding under the Indo-Australian plate. The result is that New Zealand experiences frequent earthquakes, often of significant magnitude, and contains several active volcanic and geothermal areas. The outlying islands are all volcanic in origin; some of them, like Raoul Island and White Island, are very active but others are dormant or extinct.

The major city, Auckland, with a population of 1.5 million, is spread across a field of 49 dormant volcanoes. All have erupted during the last 250,000 years; the most recent and largest eruption was approximately 600 years ago, after inhabitation of the area by humans. The very violent last eruption produced the same amount of lava as the eruptions that created the rest of the volcanic field.[2]

The capital city, Wellington, with a population of 0.35 million, lies directly above the boundary of the Pacific and Indo-Australian plates. As a result, it has three major fault-lines in close proximity to it: the Ohariu, Wairarapa, and Wellington Faults.[3] There are frequent movements on these faults and since 1855 there have been three significant events generating earthquakes with magnitudes between 7.2 and 8.2 on the Richter scale.[4]

Christchurch, which until recently was thought to be most vulnerable to a tsunami and not significantly at risk from earthquakes, experienced four major and approximately 11,000 other earthquakes in the 21 months after 4 September 2010. The largest quake, with a magnitude of 7.1, struck on 4 September 2010. Its epicenter was approximately 40 km west of the city center near the small country town of Darfield. It caused significant property damage in the city but no loss of life. The most destructive, with a magnitude of 6.3, struck on 22 February 2011. Its epicenter was directly under the city. It caused very significant damage to most buildings in the Central Business District (CBD) and significant destruction to many housing areas in the suburbs, especially in the south and east of the city. The death toll was 185 with 134 of the deaths occurring in the collapses of just two relatively modern buildings in the CBD.[5]

New Zealand has experienced approximately ten tsunami with waves higher than 5 m since 1840. The four major cities are all located close to the sea and contain areas vulnerable to inundation by tsunami. Christchurch has the largest area

[2] Geonet (2012)a.

[3] Wellington City Library (2012).

[4] Geonet (2012)d.

[5] Coronial Services of New Zealand (2012). The initial toll was 181 dead but subsequently the coroner (the official investigator into the causes of death) has classified four additional deaths as directly attributable to the 22 February 2011 earthquake. See Lynch et al. (2011) and Stylianou (2011).

and most vulnerable population. Most tsunami that have impacted on New Zealand recently have been generated by distant events on the Ring of Fire, for which there have been ample and effective warnings. There is potential, however, for tsunami to be generated by many numerous local sources. There could be very little or no effective warning of these events.[6]

1.2.2 Biological Hazards

The major islands of New Zealand have been submerged below sea-level at various points in their geological history as a result of the movements relative to one another of the tectonic plates beneath the country. The consequence of this, and the relative isolation of the country, is that much of New Zealand's flora and fauna are unique and many plant and animal diseases found elsewhere in the world are not present in New Zealand.

The economy is heavily dependent on agricultural production, forestry and fishing and the processing of the products of these industries. As a result, the economy is almost uniquely vulnerable to introduced insect, animal and plant species and diseases. New Zealand has a modern and effective health system and the last occasion on which an epidemic caused significant mortality was the "Spanish" influenza epidemic in 1918. An estimated 8.600 people died in that event.[7] The "SARS", avian-flu and swine-flu scares in the early years of this century impacted on travel and tourism but had little effect on the economy as a whole. SARS and avian-flu were not introduced into the New Zealand population[8] but a total of 19 deaths were recorded as due to the 2009 outbreak of swine-flu.[9]

1.2.3 Hydrological and Meteorological Hazards

The climate and maritime location of New Zealand can occasionally produce "weather bombs." These involve ultra-high rainfall in localized areas in a short period of time, high winds and, when near the coast, high surf and coastal erosion.[10] The combination of weather bombs and steep terrain can produce flash floods in small streams and rivers, and disasters involving multiple deaths can occur. Weather bombs can also cause extensive erosion or silting of pastureland and have a significant economic effect on farm production at a local level. The impacts can last several years. The East Coast was badly affected this way by Cyclone Bola

[6] GNS Science (2012)b.

[7] New Zealand History online (2012)b.

[8] According to World Health Organization (2012) there was one death from SARS recorded in the country.

[9] Wikipedia (2014).

[10] The Weather Network (2012).

in March 1988.[11] New Zealand is not, however, vulnerable to any significant extent to tornadoes and hurricanes. Nor is it as vulnerable to widespread and multi-year droughts as are parts of Australia. Drought can materially impact agricultural production in some areas, but its bigger potential threat to the economy is through its impact on electricity supply.

2 Natural Disaster Risk Management

2.1 *Monitoring*

New Zealand has a comprehensive natural hazards monitoring regime.

2.1.1 Geophysical Hazards

All the active volcanoes in the country are monitored by GeoNet, a service of the Institute of Geological and Nuclear Sciences (GNS), a Crown Research Institute. A variety of techniques are used: high resolution GPS instruments to detect deformation of the volcano's shape; seismographs to detect movements in magma; and gas and water sampling to detect changes in chemical composition.[12] The Crater Lake on Mt Ruapehu is monitored, also by GeoNet, in order to provide warnings of lahar (volcanic mud) floods in the streams and rivers below the mountain.[13] The Auckland volcanic field is monitored by the regional government using in-ground and surface seismographs to detect signs of magma build up below the earth's surface.[14]

GeoNet provides a country-wide network of seismic stations that transmit their data to the GeoNet Data Management Centre where it is analyzed by automated processes. If the automated processes detect an earthquake of material strength, the Duty Response Team is notified and if the Duty Officer confirms that the earthquake is real and significant, the earthquake information is released.[15]

New Zealand is linked to the Pacific Ocean tsunami warning system which is based in Hawaii. It also has a network of 17 gauge stations around the coastline and on the outlying Kermedec and Chatham Islands. The network is operated by GNS as part of GeoNet[16] in conjunction with Land Information New Zealand and the National Institute of Water and Atmospheric Research (NIWA).[17]

[11] Wikipedia (2012)c.

[12] GNS Science (2012)a.

[13] GNS Science (2012c).

[14] Auckland Regional Council (2012).

[15] Geonet (2012)b.

[16] Geonet (2012)e.

[17] Morse (2008)

2.1.2 Hydrological and Meteorological Hazards

The Meteorological Service of New Zealand Ltd (MetService),[18] a State-owned Enterprise, undertakes short- and medium-term weather forecasting, including forecasting extreme weather events such as weather bombs, tornado strikes, lightning, and sea surges. There are also a number of private sector providers of short- and medium-term weather forecasts that compete with MetService.

NIWA, a state-owned research and consultancy company, undertakes long-term weather forecasts. It bases these largely on the state of the Southern Oscillation and whether the weather pattern is likely to follow a *La Nina* or *El Nino* pattern in the next few months, or whether it will be in a transition phase between these states.[19] GeoNet monitors areas with significant potential for damaging and life-threatening landslips.[20]

2.2 *Warnings*

The principal vehicles for warning and informing the public about natural hazards are the public media: radio, television, the internet and print. GeoNet operates a website that is updated in real time with information about the risks it monitors.[21]

There are also some specialized communications channels. GeoNet, for example, provides eruption warnings directly to the aviation industry, and lahar warnings directly to those responsible for bridges and roads that are vulnerable. The hydrological information of relevance for electricity production is communicated to market participants over the system used to trade electricity and by websites and e-mail. Warnings about tsunami generated distant from New Zealand are distributed over the radio and television media. There is currently no system to warn the public about tsunami originating close to New Zealand as it is considered the warning times would be too short to be useful.

2.3 *Ex-Post Rescue and Recovery*

The Ministry of Civil Defence and Emergency Management (CDEM) is responsible for the management of major disasters due to earthquakes, volcanic eruptions, tsunami, floods and landslides. It does this by coordinating the capabilities of other emergency management organizations, such as the fire service, ambulance service,

---

[18] http://www.metservice.com/national/index (accessed 28 March 2012).

[19] http://www.niwa.co.nz/our-science/climate (accessed 28 March 2012).

[20] Geonet (2012)c.

[21] http://www.geonet.org.nz/ (accessed 28 March 2012).

urban search and rescue (USAR), search and rescue (SAR), police, local authorities, gas, water, electricity and telecommunications utility operators, the military and local civil defense officials and volunteers.[22] CDEM has very wide powers to require co-operation in the provision of support and compliance with its instructions during a declared civil defense emergency.

In a very major natural disaster, CDEM will call on international support when the size of the task is beyond New Zealand's internal capacity to respond. For example, in the rescue phase following the 22 February 2011 Christchurch earthquake, USAR teams from Australia, Japan, China, Singapore, Taiwan, the United Kingdom and the United States, in addition to New Zealand's USAR team, searched for injured persons and bodies in the rubble. At the peak there were 600 USAR personnel, most of whom came from outside New Zealand.[23]

In a more limited and local disaster of the kind dealt with by CDEM, the local civil defense organization, which is part of the local government authority of an area, is responsible for management of the emergency and coordinating the capabilities of the other emergency management organizations. It fulfills a role similar to the role of CDEM in more major events.

2.4 *Ex-Post Recovery and Reconstruction*

There have been two very major natural disasters in New Zealand in the last 100 years, along with numerous more minor ones. The first was a 7.8 scale earthquake on 3 February 1931. This killed 256 persons and destroyed Napier and much of Hastings in the Hawkes Bay, an area which at the time was home to 5 % of the country's population.[24] The capital loss amounted to approximately 2.3 % of New Zealand's annual GDP or 45 % of the region's annual GDP at the time.[25]

The second was the series of sizeable earthquakes between September 2010 and December 2011 that killed 185 people and destroyed much of Christchurch's CBD and severely damaged some of the surrounding region, an area which at the time was home to approximately 12 % of New Zealand's population. The loss at replacement cost in this case is currently estimated to be approximately 15.8 % of New Zealand's GDP in 2010/2011 and 114 % of the region's annual GDP.

On both occasions, the central Government appointed a special body with wide powers to organize and oversee the recovery and reconstruction. In Napier in 1931, the power was placed in the hands of two commissioners—a judge and an engineer.[26] Recovery was relatively swift and successful, especially compared

---

[22] http://www.civildefence.govt.nz/ (accessed 28 March 2012).

[23] Guy (2011).

[24] Wikipedia (2012)a.

[25] Chapple (1997: 27).

[26] Sharpe (2011)

with Hastings, which had suffered less damage, and where the local authority was left to organize recovery. Following the Christchurch earthquakes, the power has been placed by legislation in the hands of a special government body—the Canterbury Earthquake Reconstruction Authority (CERA)—headed by a Cabinet Minister but subject to oversight of its exercise of its special powers by a review panel of highly respected citizens.[27] It is too early to judge whether CERA has been a success or not.

3 Impact of Natural Disasters on Urbanization

3.1 Economic Impacts of Disasters: Case Study

3.1.1 Impact on Christchurch

The sequence of major earthquakes in Christchurch that started in September 2010 provide an instructive case study of the short-term and medium-term economic impacts of a major natural disaster in New Zealand and of the effectiveness of the country's regime for the management of natural disasters. The area directly affected by these earthquakes is home to around 12 % of New Zealand's population and includes Christchurch, New Zealand's second largest city after Auckland.

Each of the four major earthquakes over the course of this disaster, and many of the smaller quakes, caused some property damage. The event on 22 February 2010 caused by far the most damage. By 24 June 2012 orders requiring the total demolition of 798 commercial and industrial buildings and partial demolition of 208 more had been issued by the authorities.[28] A large proportion of the buildings in the CBD, which took the main force of the 22 February 2011 earthquake, have been demolished or are in the process of being demolished. This includes most of the high-rise buildings and a good proportion of the CBD's hotel accommodation capacity, along with several large public buildings, such as the Anglican and Catholic Cathedrals, the Town Hall and the Convention Centre.

Many roads were extensively damaged, and there was major damage to the underground sewage and water pipes. Christchurch does not have a piped gas supply except in small areas in isolated suburbs. The local electricity distribution system suffered some damage to underground and overhead cables, but greater damage to substations. The national electricity grid suffered only very minor damage.

Very little damage was sustained by plant, machinery and equipment in manufacturing plants and offices. Partly this was because virtually all office buildings and factories remained upright so their contents remained largely intact, despite the structures being damaged in many cases beyond repair. This is what

[27] http://cera.govt.nz/ (accessed 28 March 2012).

[28] http://cera.govt.nz/demolitions/list (accessed 25 June 2012).

the building codes had been designed to achieve—the preservation of structural form sufficient not to endanger human life and not necessarily the ability to repair the building. It is also partly because manufacturing in Christchurch is concentrated in the west of the city, which was less severely affected.

The public was not allowed into the CBD area for several months after 22 February 2011, not even to recover equipment and personal belongings. As a result, many businesses and local and central government agencies were required to replace their office equipment in order to remain functioning. They have since been able to recover their equipment, stocks and files.

The four most significant earthquakes all resulted in liquefaction of the ground in many of the lower lying areas close to rivers in the greater Christchurch area. As a result, by the end of June 2012, 6,791 residential properties,[29] or 3.7 % of the approximately 185,000 in the area, had been declared as unfit sites on which to rebuild because geo-technical problems with the soils upon which they are built mean it would be uneconomic to do so. These sites are mainly clustered adjacent to the lower reaches of two major rivers. The result will be that several areas of the greater metropolitan area will be abandoned and allowed to return to farmland or be converted to parks and reserves.

The Government has offered to purchase these residential sites at their 2008 market valuation, which it considers to be a good approximation of their market value at the time of the February 2011 earthquake. Approximately 3,000 other residential sites await final geotechnical assessment, so the total number of residential sites to be abandoned is likely to be between 7,000 and 9,000.

There are also several thousand houses in the city which require very substantial renovation or complete re-building on their existing sites, if they are to be occupied again. Approximately 165,000 residential properties suffered some degree of damage.

3.1.2 Classification of Economic Costs

Hallegatte and Przyluski (2010) distinguish direct and indirect losses. The former they define as "the immediate consequences of the disaster physical phenomenon."[30] They further distinguish between direct market losses—losses to goods and services that are traded on markets, and for which a price can be observed—and direct non-market losses—all damage that cannot be repaired or replaced through purchases on a market.[31]

Hallegatte and Przyluski propose two criteria to help identify indirect losses. First, indirect losses are caused by secondary effects, not by the hazard itself. Secondly, costs are indirect if they span a longer period of time, a larger spatial

[29] Recovery Canterbury (2011) and Mann and Mathewson (2012).

[30] Hallegatte and Przyluski (2010), p.2.

[31] Hallegatte and Przyluski (2010), pp.2-3.

area or a different economic sector than the disaster itself. They note that for capital destroying disasters, the term "indirect losses" is often used as a proxy for "output losses" or the reduction in economic production provoked by the disaster, including the costs of business interruption and the longer term consequences of infrastructure and capital damages. Like direct losses, indirect losses may be market or non-market losses. Indirect losses can have "negative-costs" components, i.e. gains from additional activity created by the reconstruction. These gains can occur in the affected region or in another region.[32]

Hallegatte and Przyluski note that to implement these definitions of costs it is necessary to define a baseline or counterfactual scenario; the scenario of what would have occurred in the absence of a disaster. They also note that identifying the relevant costs of a disaster cannot be done independently of the purpose of the assessment. The costs relevant to insurance companies, households, firms and the Government can all differ depending on their purpose.[33]

3.1.3 Cost Estimates

I estimated in mid-2012 the measurable direct and indirect costs of the earthquakes in the greater Christchurch area in New Zealand dollars. New Zealand has a floating exchange rate and its value against other currencies, including the United States dollar, moves widely. The daily average exchange rate between the United States dollar and the New Zealand dollar in the calendar year 2011 was $NZ1 = $US0.7916.[34]

For most depreciable assets like buildings, network assets and commercial and industrial plant and equipment two cost estimates are provided: a replacement cost (RC) and a depreciated replacement cost (DRC) estimate. The RC estimates for these assets reflect the cost of replacing those destroyed in the earthquake with equivalent new assets at current market prices. The DRC estimates are the RC estimates adjusted for the estimated extent to which these replaced assets were already depreciated at the time they were destroyed or damaged.

The DRC estimates for the assets for which they are given can be considered to be approximate current market value estimates. This is because the value of an asset to a firm is generally the present value of the expected future cash flows. If, however, as is usually the case, this is above the DRC of the asset, the firm will not pay more than DRC, assuming it can buy (or lease) second hand assets. The estimates of the other cost components are at current market values. The result is that the estimates labeled Replacement Cost are reasonable indicators of the costs that would be incurred restoring the damage that resulted from the earthquakes.

[32] Hallegatte and Przyluski (2010), p.4.

[33] Hallegatte and Przyluski (2010), pp. 4–5.

[34] Calculated from Reserve Bank data published in http://www.rbnz.govt.nz/statistics/exandint/b1/index.html (accessed on 10 July 2012).

The estimate labeled "Depreciated Replacement Cost," however, is an indicator of the economic costs of the earthquakes, taking into account that some of the assets that were destroyed were part way through their useful economic lives but will be replaced by new assets, which will generally have a longer remaining economic life.

Only the costs (and benefits) that have been able to be expressed in monetary terms are included in the estimates. Other costs include loss of life and serious injury, the disruption to lifestyle, loss of heritage architecture and the stress from the experience and the on-going uncertainties around the future.

I estimated the contributions by different groups—insurers, households, Government, local authorities, donors, and commercial and industrial firms—to the estimated total replacement cost of the impact of the earthquakes in New Zealand dollars.

By far the major contribution to the total replacement cost of $NZ30.9 billion will come from insurers; in total $NZ24.1 billion, or 78 %. The central Government (i.e. the New Zealand taxpayer) is the second most significant contributor when the fact it tops up EQC's funds for all claims against it exceeding $NZ4.0 billion dollars for any one event. The third most significant contributor group is households, which bear an estimated 7.7 % of the total replacement cost or about $NZ2.4 billion. A significant component of the cost to households is the reduction in incomes.

Households will also indirectly bear the costs of the other groups through future taxes (central government), future rates (local government property taxes), higher charges or rates (monopoly infrastructural providers) and higher future insurance premiums (insurance). The table does not reflect the indirect incidence of the costs.

A significant point to emerge is that an estimated 78 % of the $NZ30.9 billion of direct and indirect costs of the earthquakes at replacement cost will be covered by insurance of one form or another.

My estimate of the cost as $NZ30.9 billion at replacement cost is not out of line with other aggregate estimates. To date there are no other estimates for which a detailed breakdown is available. In October 2011, the Reserve Bank of New Zealand's estimated, before the final major quake, the costs to rebuild as between $NZ15 billion and $NZ25 billion.[35] Subsequently, however, in late January 2012, the Reserve Bank revised its figure upwards to $NZ30 billion. It is clear this estimate is on a replacement cost basis.[36] Swiss Re, a reinsurance provider, estimated in late 2011 that the economic losses from the Christchurch earthquakes, excluding the December 2011 earthquake, was approximately $US18 billion[37] ($NZ22.9 billion). In late October 2011, Treasury warned that the costs of the quakes could be as high as $NZ30 billion.[38] It is clear from the context that

[35] Bollard and Ranchhod (2011).

[36] Hickey (2012).

[37] Wood (2012).

[38] One News (2011a).

Treasury's estimate was on a replacement cost basis as it refers to changes in building standards increasing costs.[39]

3.1.4 Loss of Population

According to official estimates by Statistics New Zealand,[40] a government agency, the population of the Canterbury Region, which includes Christchurch City, fell by an estimated 5,000 in the year to June 2011. The components of this change were natural increase of 2,600, as births exceeded deaths by this number, and net emigration of 7,600 from the region. In the 4 years ended 30 June 2010, the population of the Canterbury Region is estimated to have increased on average by 6,400 with 3,200 of the increase being from net immigration and 3,200 from natural increase. These figures suggest that the earthquakes resulted in a reduction in the natural increase in the region by approximately 600, a turn-around in migration of 10,800 and a gross reduction in regional population of around 11,400 from what it otherwise would have been if normal growth as experienced in the previous 4 years had continued. On the 30 June 2010 the population of the Canterbury Region was 565,700, so a reduction of 11,400 amounts to a change of 2.0 %.

According to the same source,[41] the population of Christchurch City was 376,700 on 30 June 2010, but fell by 8,900 in the subsequent year to 30 June 2011. The reduction was composed of a natural increase of 1,700 and net emigration of 10,600. In the 4 years ended 30 June 2010, the population of Christchurch City is estimated to have increased on average by 3,700 with natural increase accounting for 2,200 per year and net immigration for 1,600. These figures suggest that the earthquakes resulted in a reduction in the natural increase in Christchurch City by approximately 500, a turnaround in migration of 12,200 and a gross reduction in the city's population of around 12,700 (3.4 %) from what it would have been if 'normal' growth had continued. There are currently no official estimates of the populations of the Canterbury Region and Christchurch City after June 30 2011. The indications from media reports are that there has been further net emigration from the region and the city since 30 June 2011, and that the population losses in both have increased in absolute and percentage terms.

3.1.5 Changes in Labor Inputs

Employment in the Canterbury Region fell by 26,800 persons, or 8.0 %, in the year to September 2011 and reached its lowest level since June 2004. A very slight

---

[39] One News (2011a).

[40] Statistics New Zealand (2011b).

[41] Statistics New Zealand (2011b).

increase in employment occurred in the December 2011 quarter followed by a substantial increase of 15,900 persons, or 5.1 % in the March 2012 quarter. In the rest of the country, employment grew by 51,200 persons, or 2.8 % over the year to September 2011 and was relatively static in the following 6 months to March 2012.

During 2010 employment had been relatively static in the Canterbury Region, having fallen prior to this by about 4 % from its peak in mid-2008. This suggests that over the year to September 2011, employment in Canterbury fell below what it would have been without the earthquakes by between 30,000 and 35,000 persons, or around 10 %. A 10 % reduction in labor inputs is a significant change, as is the increase of 17,200 persons, or 5.6 %, in the 6 months after September 2011.

I also looked at the sector breakdown of the Canterbury labor force of 335,200 in September 2010. The sector with the largest share of employment was retail trade and accommodation (16.9 %). This reflected the importance of tourism to the Canterbury economy. In the rest of New Zealand, 15.1 % of employees were engaged in this activity. The next largest proportion of employees in Canterbury were engaged in manufacturing and operating utilities (12.8 %), followed by professional, etc. services (10.4 %) and education and training (9.4 %). Both manufacturing and education and training had larger shares of total employment in Canterbury than in the rest of the country.

The impact of the earthquakes on employment in the region had diverse effects. This can be seen from Fig. 7.1. The job losses in the Canterbury Region in the 12 months ended September 2011 were widespread among sectors, but particularly prevalent in the retail trade and accommodation sector that is more heavily concentrated in the extensively damaged CBD. In percentage terms, the losses in information media etc. approached 50.0 %, but the sector was a relatively small percentage of total employment (1.7 %). The only sectors to show job gains in the 12 months ended September 2011 were construction, public administration and professional services. Employment in manufacturing was relatively static.[42] In the rest of New Zealand over the same period there was employment growth in almost all sectors.

In the period from September 2011 until March 2012, employment grew in the Canterbury region in most sectors. The exceptions in addition to the small information media sector were public administration and safety, education and training and health care and social assistance. Employment in the rental, hiring and real estate sector, which has fallen over 40 % in the year to September 2011 rose by roughly the same amount in the 6 months to March 2012. This reflected the return of activity to the property market as people abandoned red-zoned and other residential properties and moved elsewhere, often within Christchurch.

[42] Statistics New Zealand (2011a).

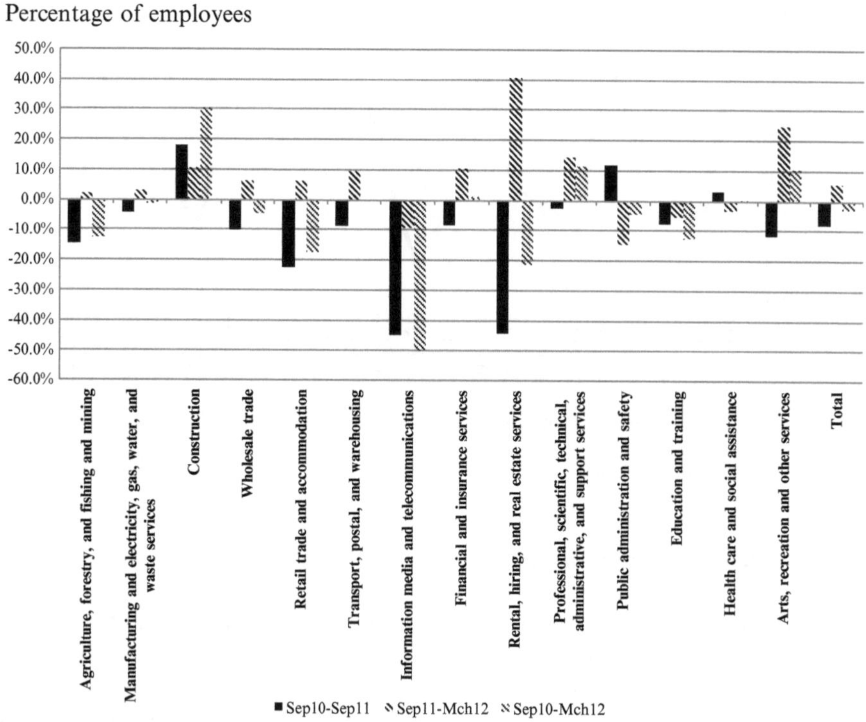

Fig. 7.1 Changes in Canterbury employment by sector, Sept 2010–March 2012. *Source*: Statistics New Zealand

3.1.6 Loss of Output

Regional GDP data are not officially compiled in New Zealand. However, the New Zealand Institute of Economic Research (NZIER) has long produced and published its own estimates. According to these estimates the GDP of the Canterbury region fell by around 5–7 % in the year to September 2011. The decline in Canterbury was, however, partly offset by resilience elsewhere in New Zealand.[43]

NZIER's *Quarterly Survey of Business Opinion* for the September 2011 quarter showed that Canterbury businesses were expecting a bounce back from the initial disruption in the 6 months to March 2012 and that investment activity in the region would pick up sharply, especially for building investment and construction labor hiring intentions.[44]

[43] NZIER (2011).

[44] NZIER (2011).

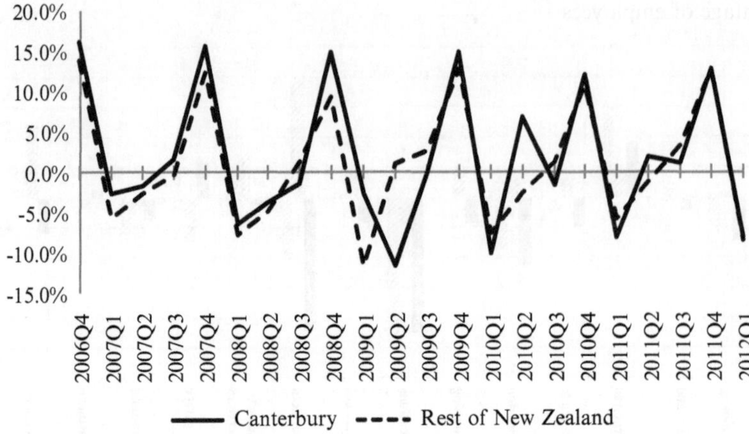

Fig. 7.2 Changes in retail sales, 2007–2012 (Quarterly percentage changes). *Source*: Statistics New Zealand

3.1.7 Other Economic Indicators

Electronic transaction data appears to indicate that retail spending in Canterbury dropped below what it would have been if it had of followed the national trend by between $NZ25 million and $NZ40 million per month, or by approximately 7–11 %.[45] However, no similar drop in expenditure is evident in the quarterly retail sales statistics shown in Fig. 7.2. The drop off in electronic transactions reflected a reduction in payments by this means as access to electronic payment facilities was disrupted.

House sales nearly stopped in Canterbury immediately after the major quakes but in recent months have bounced back to be more in line with national trends. House prices appear to be rising in Canterbury, compared to flat prices elsewhere but the increase is still very modest at less than 5 % per year. The inventory of houses for sale relative to numbers of house sales has declined in Canterbury much more than in the rest of the country.[46]

The number of bed nights in accommodation places in the Canterbury region fell sharply after the earthquakes and had not completely recovered by the December quarter 2011 (Fig. 7.3). This is despite the people who have been brought in to Christchurch temporarily to undertake assessments and help with the recovery phase.

The number of bed nights in New Zealand reaching an all-time monthly high of approximately 2.5 million in October 2011, whereas those in Canterbury were 27 % below their previous peak.[47]

[45] NZIER (2011).

[46] NZIER (2011).

[47] NZIER (2011).

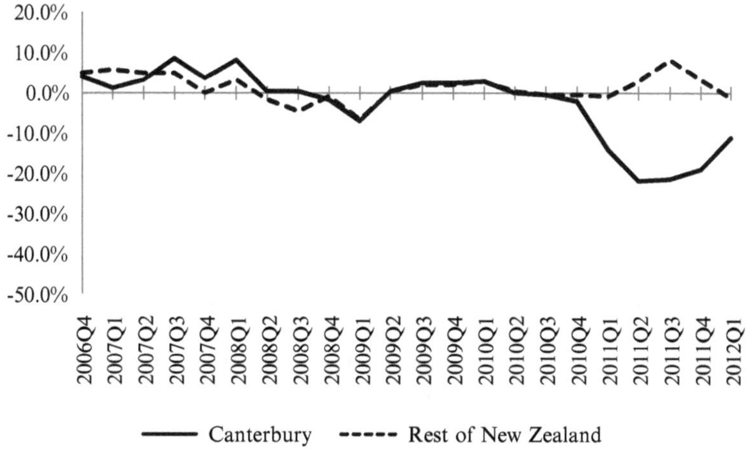

Fig. 7.3 Changes in total guest nights, 2006–2012 (Annual percentage changes). *Source*: Statistics New Zealand

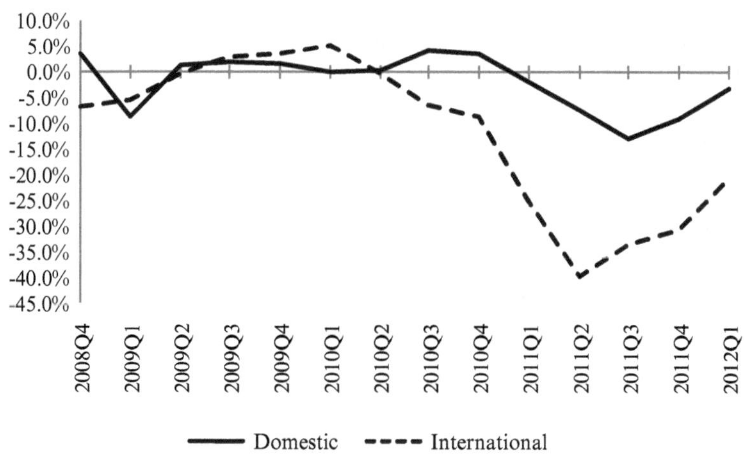

Fig. 7.4 Changes in Canterbury Guest Nights, 2008–2012 (Annual percentage changes). *Source*: Statistics New Zealand

From Fig. 7.4 it is clear that the fall in the number of international guest nights in Canterbury was far more significant than the fall in the number of domestic guest nights. Of the major population centers in New Zealand, Christchurch is the one most dependent upon international tourism and the earthquakes severely disrupted this industry.

Despite very significant damage to the physical assets of the region's major port at Lyttelton, exports through the port were reasonably resilient after the earthquakes and reached an all-time high by value late in 2011.[48] In terms of volumes of cargo, the throughput of Lyttelton has always been quite volatile. This is partly due to the importance of coal exports to the port; these vary significantly depending on the arrival times of ships. It is also partly due to the importance of primary produce in the exports through the port. Small variations in the timing of the seasonal meat kill and grain harvest can have a large impact on volumes exported in a quarter.

My analysis illustrates the volatility of trade through Lyttelton and that there has been no obvious impact on this trade as a result of the earthquakes until the March quarter 2012. In that quarter total trade through the port was 67.2 % greater than in the corresponding quarter the previous year. Import volumes rose 105 % and export volumes by 55 %. It is likely that imports for reconstruction activities contributed to the sharp increase in imports and total trade.

The impact of the earthquake on the Government's fiscal position has been significant. Both central and local government faced large costs. The central government has purchased residential properties in the zones that will be abandoned for geotechnical reasons. This is estimated to have cost approximately $NZ840 million. It has also offered financial support to AMI, a major insurer of households based in the region affected by the earthquakes. AMI held inadequate re-insurance to cover the string of earthquakes. The cost to the Government will be approximately $NZ100 million.

In addition to these costs, the Government faced significant expenses for welfare and emergency services and has to fund the on-going operation of the Canterbury Earthquake Recovery Authority (CERA), the special statutory body the Government established to manage the recovery of the region. In addition, the Government is the owner of EQC, a New Zealand Government agency providing natural disaster insurance to residential property owners, and underwrites the claims on it in excess of $NZ4.0 billion for any single event. The earthquakes in Christchurch have been considered to be several different events for the purposes of EQC liability.

The Reserve Bank estimated the Government's earthquake-related expenditure at $NZ13.6 billion in the June 2011 fiscal year.[49] This figure includes the expenses of EQC. Earthquake-related expenditure were a major contributor to the marked deterioration in the Government's operating deficit in the 2010/2011 year and this contributed to a downgrading of New Zealand's long term sovereign rating by Standard and Poor's to AA.[50] The Government has tightened its expenditure in general in response to the deterioration in its fiscal position.

---

[48] NZIER (2011).

[49] Bollard and Ranchhod (2011).

[50] Bollard and Ranchhod (2011).

3.2 *Impacts of Disasters on Urbanization in New Zealand*

3.2.1 Short-Term Relocations

It is too early to identify the longer-term impact of the September 2010–December 2011 earthquakes on the pattern of urbanization and production networks in Christchurch and New Zealand. However, the short-term impacts that have emerged are interesting, and suggest a number of points.

The earthquake on 22 February 2011 was by far the most destructive. It very nearly demolished the Christchurch CBD and led to it being subject to a 24 h a day curfew that was still in place in March 2012 in the worst affected areas. Apart from members of the emergency services required to be in the area for their work, the public were excluded from most of the CBD for several months. This included all those that owned or worked in buildings in the city center.

Within hours of the very damaging February 2011 earthquake, service industry businesses located in the CBD—lawyers, accountants, financial advisers, banks, architects, dentists, doctors etc.—began relocating, mainly to the western side of the city, where damage to infrastructure such as roads, sewage, water and electricity was less severe and most buildings were either lightly or not damaged. They moved into former warehouses and distribution centers; in fact, into almost any space they could find. Other businesses relocated to garages and parts of dwellings in the suburbs, again mainly in the west of the city. Within days of the earthquake, a large proportion of former CBD located businesses, apart from retail shops, were operating from temporary premises elsewhere in the city.

A local commercial radio station set space aside on its webpage for firms to record where they had relocated from and to.[51] The service was provided free. The number of firms which used this service was small—approximately 90—but the majority were originally located in the CBD. An analysis of the data reveals that of the 72 CBD firms, no less than 50.0 % shifted to addresses in Sydenham, Addington or Riccarton. These three areas are adjacent to the CBD and form an arc to its south and west. No less than 77.8 % of the CBD firms shifted to a suburb adjacent to the CBD.

The Christchurch telephone directory covers the greater Christchurch area and is usually produced annually. The yellow pages volume of the directory list businesses by the industry or service they provide. The 2010/2011 volume was collated in August 2010, just before the first earthquake. The 2011/2012 volume was collated in September 2011.

Table 7.1 contains a comparison of the listing in these directories of the accountants and auditors, lawyers and solicitors, barristers and dentists recorded as located in the CBD in the 2010/2011 volume. The popularity of relocating to the CBD fringe suburbs of Sydenham, Addington and Riccarton, especially by lawyers and solicitors can be seen from the data. Interestingly, while no accountants and

[51] The Breeze (2012).

Table 7.1 Relocation of selected professional firms from Christchurch CBD, 2010–2011. Numbers and percentages of firms

Professional occupation	Same location	New location				No location	Total
		Elsewhere in CBD	Sydenham, Addington and Riccarton	Merivale and Papanui	Other		
Accountants and auditors	28	6	13	0	30	3	80
Lawyers and solicitors	21	7	26	8	16	11	89
Barristers	20	2	7	6	4	10	49
Dentists	11	2	3	8	5	2	31
Total	80	17	49	22	55	26	249
Accountants and auditors	35.0 %	7.5 %	16.3 %	0.0 %	37.5 %	3.8 %	100.0 %
Lawyers and solicitors	23.6 %	7.9 %	29.2 %	9.0 %	18.0 %	12.4 %	100.0 %
Barristers	40.8 %	4.1 %	14.3 %	12.2 %	8.2 %	20.4 %	100.0 %
Dentists	35.5 %	6.5 %	9.7 %	25.8 %	16.1 %	6.5 %	100.0 %
Total	32.1 %	6.8 %	19.7 %	8.8 %	22.1 %	10.4 %	100.0 %

Source: Calculated from Christchurch yellow page phone books for 2010/2011 and 2011/2012

auditors were recorded as having moved to the Merivale-Papanui area,[52] and only 9.0 % of firms of lawyers and solicitors, 25.8 % of dentists are recorded as having done so.

Prior to the earthquakes, Riccarton already had clusters of legal and accounting firms, and this, along with the larger size of offices available in the area was undoubtedly an attraction to those firms that had to relocate. Dental practices tend to be small and not dissimilar in terms of the office space they require to medical specialists. Merivale-Papanui is a popular location for medical specialists because of its proximity to the two major private hospitals in Christchurch. That a significant proportion of dental practices needing to relocate should have been drawn here by the kinds of space available is not surprising.

Those recorded in the yellow pages as "barristers" rather than as "barristers and solicitors" or as "lawyers" are sole practitioners. It is common for several barristers to operate from the one building or chamber, and when they do they usually share secretarial and other support. However, they are sole practitioners. Many of those with no location recorded in the 2011/2012 yellow pages have undoubtedly set up practice from their home address. There are also several instances of barristers recorded as shifting to the same building as others with whom they were formerly co-located.

Despite the disruption created by the series of major earthquakes and the speed with which decisions often had to be made, what is very clear is that the forces that lead to agglomeration of businesses were still at work when sites for relocation by professional firms and sole practitioners were being chosen.

In October 2011 the Department of Labour conducted a telephone survey of 1,689 employers trading before 4 September 2010 in the greater Christchurch area.[53] The survey did not cover owner operated businesses without any staff. One of the questions related to whether the workplace had partly or fully relocated as a result of the earthquake. Tables 7.2 and 7.3 summarize the results according to staff size and industry in which the workplace operates.

On average, 27.6 % of the surveyed workplaces relocated, and 72.4 % did not. In general, the larger workplaces—those with staff of 50 or more—were more likely to have relocated than smaller workplaces. Approximately 35 % of the larger workplaces relocated compared with approximately 25 % of the smaller ones. Of the workplaces that relocated, 36.4 % thought in October 2011 that the change was permanent, 51.6 % that it was temporary and 12.0 % were unsure.

No less than 59.8 % of the workplaces engaged in professional, scientific and technical services relocated as a result of the earthquake. Of the public, health and education workplaces, which are predominantly in the government sector, 33.7 % relocated. At the other end of the scale, only 11.6 % of the hospitality workplaces shifted and only 16 % of those engaged in manufacturing.

---

[52] Also includes addresses described as in Strowan.

[53] Department of Labour (2011).

Table 7.2 Proportion of workplaces that relocated following the earthquakes by staff size, October 2011. Percentage of workplaces

Staff size	Did not relocate (%)	Relocated Permanent (%)	Temporary (%)	Unsure (%)	Total (%)
1–5	72.0	9.8	15.1	3.0	100.0
6–9	77.9	10.0	8.8	3.3	100.0
10–24	70.3	12.0	15.5	2.2	100.0
25–49	74.9	5.5	13.7	5.9	100.0
50–99	68.2	12.6	14.3	4.8	100.0
100+	62.9	7.7	18.8	10.6	100.0
Total	72.4	10.0	14.2	3.3	100.0

Source: Department of Labour (2011, p. 13), Table A5

Table 7.3 Proportion of workplaces that relocated following the earthquakes by industry, October 2011. Percentage of workplaces

Industry	Did not relocate (%)	Relocated Permanent (%)	Temporary (%)	Unsure (%)	Total (%)
Primary, transport, utilities	87.6	7.1	4.8	0.4	100.0
Public, health, education	66.3	6.1	23.8	3.7	100.0
Professional, scientific and technical services	40.2	13.3	39.3	7.2	100.0
Manufacturing	84.0	10.9	2.7	2.4	100.0
Construction	78.0	5.2	13.2	3.6	100.0
Retail, wholesale	79.4	12.2	5.9	2.5	100.0
Hospitality	88.4	7.5	3.6	0.5	100.0
Other	64.8	13.3	17.5	4.4	100.0
Total	72.4	10.0	14.2	3.3	100.0

Source: Department of Labour (2011, p. 13), Table A6

The new locations did not initially have the car parking facilities, bus services, coffee shops, and restaurants, lunch bars etc. that were a feature of the CBD and supported its service industry. However, the coffee bars, lunch bars and restaurants very quickly followed their customers. In some instances they did this by subleasing space from new tenants, the employees of whom they had served in the CBD. In other cases, they relocated to trucks and vans on the street side.

The CBD retailers found it much harder to relocate. Some were able to move to vacant shops in the suburbs and in suburban malls, but there was a limited supply of these, and some of the malls had also sustained damage and were temporarily shut. After several months a temporary shopping area was opened in the former heart of the retail area of the CBD. Shops from all over the former CBD agglomerated into a new center made up of 40 very colorfully painted and decorated shipping containers. They decided to relocate to one relatively small area rather than re-open close to their former locations because they considered this would attract customers. This has turned out to be the case. The opening of the temporary shopping center—Re:Build—was timed to coincide with a festival and public holiday in the city and with the re-opening of a major department store whose relatively modern building was able to be repaired.[54]

3.2.2 Longer-Term Issues: Theory

One interesting issue raised by the literature on natural disasters is whether the Christchurch CBD will ever be completely reconstructed and how long it will take for the city more generally to recover.

Kennedy School of Government students and faculty have worked on the recovery of New Orleans following its devastation in 2005 by Hurricane Katrina and the flooding it produced. The director of Harvard's New Orleans Recovery Initiative, Douglas Ahlers, and colleagues have developed several concepts relating to the dynamics of recovery, repopulation and reinvestment following natural disasters.[55] Ahlers argues that much of disaster recovery where there has been a major loss in physical capital, as there has been in Christchurch, is an investment problem, and, more specifically, an investor confidence problem. Following a major natural disaster of this type, thousands of individuals have to make the decision of whether to re-build or not. Because of the existence of agglomeration benefits, the pay-off to an investor from a decision to re-build is influenced by the decisions of all the others in a similar locality as to whether they will rebuild or not.

Agglomeration benefits are the economic advantages in terms of higher productivity and lower costs firms (and individuals) obtain from locating near each other; i.e. from agglomerating. The advantages arise because of positive externalities through:

- the increased size of the pool of skilled labor available to the firms;
- the improved access to specialized goods and services and their lower cost due to increased competition among suppliers;
- the improved ability to specialize; and
- technological spill-overs in the form of quicker diffusion or adoption of new ideas.

The more people deciding to re-build in a locality, the higher the pay-off, and vice versa. So the probability an individual will decide to re-build is a function of his or her assessment of whether others will decide to rebuild or not. The situation is analogous to the prisoner's dilemma problem often analyzed using game theory.

---

[54] One News (2011b).

[55] See Douglas Ahlers' slide presentation to a public meeting in Christchurch entitled 'Disaster recovery: what the research shows', August 2011. Available at: http://futurechristchurch.wordpress.com/2011/10/11/douglas-ahlers/ (accessed 28 March 2012).

The upshot is that there can be two equilibrium positions. One in which "everyone" tips in, and decides that they will re-build because they believe everyone else will re-build. The other one in which "everyone" tips out, and decides that, since it is unlikely that others will re-build, they will not re-build but instead invest elsewhere, where agglomeration benefits are known to be available, or in another activity.

In the short-term, investors can decide to "wait-and-see". In fact, from the point of view of an individual investor, this is the dominant strategy. However, the longer an investor "waits-and-sees" the more others faced with the same decision will take their inaction as evidence that they will not be re-building and this will lower the probability that re-building will actually occur.

The implication of this analysis is that uncertainty over time will slow and may even kill a recovery and reconstruction. For this reason, policy makers should avoid or rectify factors that will increase investor uncertainty, such as:

- lack of a clear leader of the recovery in whom or which people have confidence;
- where and what can be re-built not being settled quickly;
- who will provide affordable insurance for re-built structures and infrastructure, and on what terms; and
- how quickly infrastructure needed to support any rebuilding will be restored or provided in new locations.

A second implication is that recovery will tend to occur in pockets, interspersed among pockets not yet recovering. The resulting patch-work quilt of areas where re-building is occurring interspersed with other areas not currently being re-built was a noticeable feature of the recovery of the lower income areas of New Orleans.

A policy implication is that focusing recovery efforts on particular areas is likely to be more successful. Moreover, the most effective place to concentrate policy interventions is in the areas which are closest to the tipping point; closest to the point where the balance of investor decisions will be easiest to switch from "wait-and-see" to a decision to re-build.

Recovery and reconstruction are less likely the easier it is for people to:

- abandon an area or decide not to re-build because, for example, the area was already in decline and/or still had surplus fixed assets relative to needs after the disaster;
- migrate elsewhere because they have the opportunity to do so as jobs are readily available; and
- shift because they have limited financial capital locked up in land or other assets in the area affected by the natural disaster that they will have to abandon or sell for a low return if they do not re-build.

In regard to the last factor, holding insurance cover for disaster damage to buildings, chattels, etc. means that, in the event the insured property is destroyed in a disaster, what was previously a fixed asset becomes a liquid and highly mobile one immediately the insurance pay-out is received.

For this reason, an implication of the Harvard Kennedy School model of recovery and reconstruction is that high levels of assets covered by insurance may not translate into rapid re-building following a disaster. The insurance pay-outs may facilitate re-building by giving parties the financial resources to do so, but they may also make it easier for people to relocate. This will be particularly the case if "insurance" compensation covers not only losses of buildings and chattels but also covers land and, for businesses, lost income and profits, as has been the case to some degree in Christchurch.

Ahlers et al. are not the only ones to note the relevance of the new economic geography concept of agglomeration to the study of the impact of natural disasters, and specifically that one of its implications is that the shock associated with a natural disaster may in some circumstances lead to the relocation of an industry. Okazaki, Ito and Imazuimi have investigated the long-run impact of the Great Kanto Earthquake of 1923 on the geographic distribution of industries in the Tokyo Prefecture.[56] They found that while the effects of the temporary shock on most economic aspects had basically dissipated by 1936, the re-location of the machinery and metal industry following the earthquake was persistent and remained even in 1936.[57]

3.2.3 Longer-Term Issues: Application to Christchurch

Will the Christchurch CBD ever be completely reconstructed and how long will it take for the city more generally to recover? Will the professional service organizations that shifted from the CBD to new locations in the days after the 22 February 2011 earthquake ever return to the CBD? Some have had to take long leases to secure new office accommodation and once the transport and other services are more fully developed in and around their new locations it is likely many will want to stay, especially since they have agglomerated at the new locations with other compatible organizations.

Will the mainly private owners of the city's numerous two and three storey masonry-fronted buildings invest to replace them or use the proceeds from their insurance policies to invest elsewhere, or in other assets? These buildings were generally old and had poor lighting, heating and space utilisation. Many were not heavily occupied and the economics of rebuilding them in a modestly growing city like Christchurch appears to be challenging.

Will the retail activity in the CBD fully recover? Retailing in the Christchurch CBD has been an activity in decline since the 1960s as a result of the local government encouraging the development of suburban shopping malls. Christchurch currently has eight major suburban malls ringing the CBD. One of the lessons from previous natural disasters is that an activity in decline at the time

[56] Okazaki et al. (2011).

[57] Okazaki et al. (2011), p.10.

may never recover, and at best will take a very long time to do so. A scenario the Harvard School literature suggests is more than possible is that the CBD, even when fully redeveloped, will have a smaller and more focused retail shopping area than it had prior to the earthquakes.

Will the people with houses in the residential red zone, where the Government has offered to buy the land at 2008 market value, relocate within Christchurch or shift elsewhere? Property owners in this situation, who have replacement insurance on their buildings, will be compensated for the land at 2008 market value by the Government and for the buildings at current replacement cost by their insurance company. In short, they will receive close to their entire equity in their residential property in cash. This applies to virtually all the estimated 8,200 residential red zone owners, as insurance coverage in New Zealand is extremely high, and is usually on a replacement basis for houses.

However, the replacement cost of the land in Christchurch is likely to be higher than most will receive from the Government. This is partly because land prices in Christchurch are likely to increase in response to demand relative to the reduced supply and partly because the areas condemned were among the areas with the lowest values in the city. This suggests there is a real possibility that some will decide to relocate elsewhere in New Zealand or Australia, rather than relocate within Christchurch. There are, however, only about 8,200 houses in the residential red zone, out of nearly 200,000 impacted directly. There could therefore be too few people in this situation to have more than a minor impact on the population growth and recovery of Christchurch overall.

The manufacturing sector, historically important in Christchurch, was not affected in a significant manner because it is largely located on the western side of the city outside the CBD. These areas suffered much less damage and, as a result, manufacturing is unlikely to be materially affected in future. Comparison of the Business New Zealand Performance of Manufacturing Index (PMI) for Canterbury with the index for New Zealand as a whole is consistent with the impact on Canterbury manufacturing being limited. The PMI is an early indicator of levels of activity in New Zealand manufacturing.

However, tourism is in the opposite situation. Most major hotels have had to be demolished. In addition, virtually all the city's stone heritage buildings, a major attraction to tourists from within New Zealand and beyond, have been destroyed or, at best, will be very many years in the process of being restored. Unless the city re-invents its attractions to tourists this important industry for the local economy will take a long time to recover to its former level. It is not impossible. Napier, which was devastated by an earthquake in 1931, rebuilt in Art Deco style and this is now a major tourist attraction in itself.

3.2.4 Disaster Insurance

One unusual feature of New Zealand is the widespread level of insurance against damage from geophysical, hydrological and meteorological disasters. In 1945, the

New Zealand Government established the Earthquake Commission (EQC) to provide insurance for residential dwellings (including apartments and holiday houses), most personal property, and the land immediately around a dwelling against damage caused by earthquake, volcanic eruption, hydrothermal activity, tsunami, natural landslips, storm or flood damage and fire caused by any of these natural disasters. All parties with fire insurance over a dwelling and insurance over household goods and personal property are required to pay for insurance from EQC. The levy used to be $NZ0.05 per $NZ100 insured but following the Christchurch earthquakes the rate has been tripled in order to restore the fund.

There are limits on the level of cover provided. For dwellings (i.e. house alone), the maximum is $NZ100,000. In November 2011, the median residential property (i.e. house and land) price was $NZ367,500. For personal property, the maximum is $NZ20,000. Most insured parties top-up the EQC cover with private insurance so they are fully covered on a replacement basis. This extra insurance was in the past relatively cheap because insurance with EQC meant that only large claims above the maximums of EQC's coverage would fall on the private insurer. Since the Christchurch earthquake the rates for this kind of insurance have risen to reflect the greater perception of risk, but they are still affordable and obtainable by most parties outside Christchurch.

Insurance coverage levels are very high, however, partly because of the availability of EQC cover—in order to access EQC the party must hold house and/or contents insurance—and partly because New Zealand lending institutions will not advance funds against uninsured properties, and most dwelling owners borrow money to finance the purchase of a property, whether it is for their own occupation or to rent to tenants. Although the EQC only covers residential and personal property, most businesses also carry property insurance and business interruption insurance for losses due to geophysical, hydrological and meteorological risks. This reflects the requirement of lenders that businesses hold adequate insurance cover before they will advance funds.

Over the years, EQC built up its own pool of funds as a result of its levies exceeding its pay-outs. In more recent years it bought additional cover on the international market through reinsurance organizations. Losses in excess of $NZ1.5 billion up to $NZ4.0 billion for any one event have been covered by international reinsurance. The Government covers losses in excess of $4.0 billion for any one event. Private insurance providers of the top ups to EQC cover and commercial disaster insurers also largely pass on the risks they cover to international reinsurers. Much of the financial burden of the earthquakes in Christchurch will fall in the first instance on international reinsurance businesses. I estimate that insurers and reinsurers, including EQC and the Government-owned Accident Compensation Corporation (ACC) will contribute $NZ24.1 billion of the total $NZ30.9 billion, or 78.0 % of the total cost at replacement cost.

I have already noted one of the potential consequences of the high level of insurance coverage. Parties receiving insurance payments may be tempted to use their liquidity in the asset they now hold to relocate elsewhere in New Zealand or overseas in places such as Australia.

Another related issue is that because of the size of the losses sustained, and the on-going seismic activity in the Canterbury regions, many insurers and reinsurers are reluctant to extend cover to new or replacement buildings in the region. This is now starting to hold back redevelopment and, as a result, creating uncertainty among investors; uncertainty which could lead to an unwillingness to invest and retard the time of the recovery, possibly, significantly. It remains to be seen how long it will take for the insurers and reinsurers to re-enter the Christchurch market.

4 Policy Recommendations

4.1 National Level

New Zealand has a comprehensive disaster monitoring and management regime, and while it is always possible to improve any regime of this kind, the only obvious policy points to emerge from the Christchurch experience are the need to more adequately assess the geotechnical characteristics of land when determining the use to which it should be put and the danger of unreinforced masonry fronts on "historic" buildings.

Of pressing concern at present is the need to create and maintain momentum in the reconstruction of Christchurch, to avoid the risk of the city never returning to its full economic strength and potential. There are several factors working against momentum in reconstruction that need to be overcome.

First, the extended period over which aftershocks have occurred, and the sizable magnitude of several of them, has delayed the return to the market of insurers and reinsurers. According to the telephone survey of workplaces in the greater Christchurch area conducted by the Department of Labour in October 2011, of the respondents that had had to renew insurance policies since 4 September 2010, 14.6 % had experienced difficulty renewing existing policies.[58] Obtaining insurance on new and reconstructed buildings has been widely reported to be significantly more difficult than renewing an existing policy. Banks will not fund redevelopment of buildings in the absence of adequate insurance, including insurance against earthquakes.

Secondly, the high level of insurance and the fact that much of it is on a replacement basis, mean that many potential investors in the redevelopment of Christchurch have the funds to progress their aspect of the investment. The longer the delay the more likely they will decide to invest elsewhere.

Thirdly, New Zealanders are generally quite mobile and willing to shift residence and migrate overseas to places like Australia. Most New Zealanders are entitled to live and work in Australia without obtaining a visa. The slower the

[58] Department of Labour (2011, p. 16), Table A11.

momentum of reconstruction in Christchurch the greater the number of residents who are likely to migrate to other parts of New Zealand or overseas.

Finally, the CBD of Christchurch has been in relative decline for a long period of time. This is an added barrier to stimulating investment in this part of Christchurch.

4.2 *Regional*

4.2.1 Regional Co-operation in Disaster Management

New Zealand's experience is that regional co-operation on search and rescue, maintaining security for people and property and victim identification in the period immediately after a major natural disaster is very worthwhile. Trained experts in these fields can provide much needed assistance. It is unlikely that even a medium sized country would have natural disasters frequent enough to warrant maintaining the number of people required for these tasks with the appropriate expertise.

Drawing on people with these skills on a regional basis, and sending local teams with these skills to assist in other countries in the region is a good means of maintaining high quality capacity and access to sufficient numbers on the relatively rare occasions they are required. Regional co-operation in setting standards and ensuring that personnel providing these specialist services have the required level of expertise and access to the necessary resourcing would also be desirable.

4.2.2 Disaster Insurance

New Zealand's experience with EQC and disaster insurance contains some lessons for others:

- high levels of disaster insurance properly backed by international reinsurance can go a long way to ameliorating the financial costs of a disaster;
- the provision of a national scheme, like New Zealand's EQC, encourages high levels of coverage by private parties;
- high penetration of insurance brings its own issues for the recovery task:
  - considerable resources are required to assess the numerous claims in a large event;
  - it increases the liquidity of the assets of persons affected by the disaster and this can stimulate migration to other regions rather than rebuilding the affected region; and
  - delays in re-establishing access to insurance can retard the recovery process.

This chapter has shown how market-provided insurance can serve as an accelerant of recovery provided that authorities listen to signals from broader society and move policy forward as efficiently as possible.

References

Auckland Regional Council (2012) Volcanoes of Auckland. Auckland Regional Council. http://www.arc.govt.nz/environment/volcanoes-of-auckland/monitoring.cfm. Accessed 28 March 2012

Bollard, A., & Ranchhod, S. (2011). *Economic impacts of seismic risk: Lessons for Wellington. Speech by Dr. Bollard to the Rotary Club of Wellington and Victoria University of Wellington. Organisational Effectiveness in Times of Seismic Risk*, 18 October 2011. http://www.rbnz.govt.nz/speeches/4559383.html. Accessed 28 March 2012.

Chapple, S. (1997). *The economic effects of the 1931 Hawkes Bay Earthquake, NZIER Working Paper*, No. 97/7. Wellington: NZIER.

Coronial Services of New Zealand. (2012). *Media updates from the Chief Coroner*. New Zealand: Ministry of Justice Home. http://www.justice.govt.nz/courts/coroners-court/christchurch-earthquake/media-updates-from-the-chief-coroner. Accessed 28 March 2012.

Department of Labour. (2011). *A changing landscape: The impact of the earthquakes on Christchurch Workplaces, December 2012*. Wellington: Department of Labour.

Geonet. (2012)a. *Auckland volcanic field*. Wellington New Zealand: GeoNet. http://www.geonet.org.nz/volcano/our-volcanoes/auckland-volcanic-field.html. Accessed 28 March 2012.

Geonet. (2012)b. *Earthquake*. New Zealand: GeoNet. http://www.geonet.org.nz/earthquake/. Accessed 28 March 2012.

Geonet. (2012)c. *GeoNet's current landslide monitoring projects and the reports from earlier responses*. New Zealand: GeoNet. http://www.geonet.org.nz/landslide/. Accessed 28 March 2012.

Geonet. (2012)d. *Historic earthquakes*. New Zealand: GeoNet. http://www.geonet.org.nz/earthquake/historic-earthquakes/. Accessed 28 March 2012.

Geonet. (2012)e. *Tsunami*. New Zealand: GeoNet. http://www.geonet.org.nz/tsunami/. Accessed 28 March 2012.

GNS Science. (2012)a. *Natural hazards*. Wellington, New Zealand: GNS Science. http://www.gns.cri.nz/Home/Our-Science/Natural-Hazards. Accessed 28 March 2012.

GNS Science. (2012)b. *Tsunami in New Zealand*. New Zealand: GNS Science. http://www.gns.cri.nz/Home/Our-Science/Natural-Hazards/Earth-s-Forces/Tsunami/Tsunami-in-New-Zealand. Accessed 28 March 2012.

GNS Science (2012)c Volcano monitoring. GNS Science. http://www.gns.cri.nz/Home/Our-Science/Natural-Hazards/Alert-Nation/Volcano-Monitoring. Accessed 28 March 2012

Guy, H. N. (2011). *Last international USAR team leaves Christchurch*. Scoop Parliament [online], 17 March. http://www.scoop.co.nz/stories/PA1103/S00297/last-international-usar-team-leaves-christchurch.htm. Accessed 28 March 2012.

Hallegatte, S., & Przyluski, V. (2010). *The Economics of Natural Disasters: Concepts and Methods. World Bank Policy Research Paper*, No. 5507, Washington D.C.: World Bank.

Hickey, B. (2012). *RBNZ Governor Alan Bollard Says Bank now estimates ChCh quake claims at NZ$30 bln and delays rebuild forecasts by "few months" to 2013*. Interez.co.nz [online], 27 January. http://www.interest.co.nz/news/57652/rbnz-governor-alan-bollard-says-bank-now-estimates-chch-quake-claims-nz30-bln-and-delays. Accessed 28 June 2012.

Lynch, K., Mathewson, N., & Williams, D. (2011). Quake toll lifted to 184. New Zealand: Fairfax NZ News. http://www.stuff.co.nz/the-press/news/christchurch-earthquake-2011/6365058/Quake-toll-lifted-to-184. Accessed 28 March 2012.

Mann, C., & Mathewson, N. (2012). *New riverside Red Zone*. Fairfax NZ News [online], 23 March. Availabe at: http://www.stuff.co.nz/the-press/news/christchurch-earthquake-2011/6624862/New-riverside-red-zone. Accessed 28 March 2012.

Morse, K. (2008). *NZ's tsunami monitoring network*. Wild Land blog [blog], 18 February. http://wildland.owdjim.gen.nz/?p=568. Accessed 28 March 2012.

New Zealand History online. (2012)b. *The 1918 Flu Pandemic*. New Zealand: Ministry for Culture and Heritage. http://www.nzhistory.net.nz/culture/influenza-pandemic-1918. Accessed 28 March 2012.

NZ army. (2011). *Singapore armed forces assistance appreciated*. New Zealand army [online], 15 March. http://www.army.mil.nz/at-a-glance/news/media-releases/media-release.htm@guid=%7Bfab412fa-01a3-40f0-b8ea-dcfa9fbe9060%7D.htm. Accessed 28 March 2012.

NZIER. (2011). *Canterbury after the earthquakes, November 2011*. Wellington: NZIER.

Okazaki, T., Ito, K., & Imaizumi, A. (2011). *Impact of Natural Disasters on Industrial Agglomeration: The Case of the 1923 Great Kanto Earthquake, CIRJE Discussion Paper*. Tokyo: CIRJE. http://www.cirje.e.u-tokyo.ac.jp/research/03research02dp.html. Accessed 28 March 2012.

One News. (2011a). *Chch Quake Cost could hit $30 billion*, One News [Online], 25 October. http://tvnz.co.nz/national-news/christchurch-quake-cost-could-hit-30-billion-4482971. Accessed 28 March 2012.

Recovery Canterbury. (2011). *Further 758 Christchurch Properties Rezoned*. Recovery Canterbury [online], 17 November. http://www.recovercanterbury.co.nz/news/126/further-758-christ church-properties-rezoned.aspx. Accessed 28 March 2012.

Sharpe, M. (2011). *What Napier can teach Christchurch about earthquake recovery*. Fairfax NZ News [online], 26 March. http://www.stuff.co.nz/dominion-post/news/4811992/What-Napier-can-teach-Christchurch-about-earthquake-recovery. Accessed 28 March 2012.

Statistics New Zealand. (2011a). *Household labour force survey, December 2011*. Wellington: Statistics New Zealand.

Statistics New Zealand. (2011b). *Sub-national population estimates: 30 June 2011*. Wellington: Statistics New Zealand. See http://www.stats.govt.nz/browse_for_stats/population/estimates_and_projections/SubnationalPopulationEstimates_HOTPJun11.aspx. Accessed 28 March 2011.

Stylianou, G. (2011). *Woman's death lifts earthquake Toll to 185*. New Zealand: Fairfax NZ News. http://www.stuff.co.nz/the-press/news/christchurch-earthquake-2011/6395047/Womans-death-lifts-earthquake-toll-to-185. Accessed 28 March 2012.

The Breeze (2012). *Christchurch business relocation directory*. The Breeze [online]. http://www.thebreeze.co.nz/Regions/Christchurch/RelocationDirectory/tabid/578/Default.aspx. Accessed 10 July 2012.

The Weather Network. (2012). *Glossary: weather bomb*. The Weather Network. http://www.theweathernetwork.com/glossary/weatherbomb. Accessed 28 March 2012.

Wellington City Library. (2012). *Heritage > earthquakes*. Wellington: Wellington City Library. http://www.wcl.govt.nz/heritage/earthquakes.html. Accessed 28 March 2012.

Wikipedia. (2012)a. *1931 Hawke's bay earthquake*. Wikipedia [online]. http://en.wikipedia.org/wiki/1931_Hawke%27s_Bay_earthquake. Accessed 28 March 2012.

Wikipedia. (2012)c. *Cyclone bola*. Wikipedia [online]. http://en.wikipedia.org/wiki/Cyclone_Bola. Accessed 28 March 2012.

Wikipedia. (2014). 2009 flu pandemic in New Zealand. Wikipedia [online]. http://en.wikipedia.org/wiki/2009_flu_pandemic_in_New_Zealand. Accessed 8 July 2014.

Wood, A. (2012). *February quake 'Third most expensive'*. Fairfax NZ News [online]. http://www.stuff.co.nz/business/rebuilding-christchurch/6663626/February-quake-third-most-expensive. Accessed 28 March 2012.

World Health Organization. (2012). *SARS cases worldwide*. USA Today [flash data. http://www.usatoday.com/news/health/sarscases/flash.htm. Accessed 28 March 2012.

Chapter 8
Long-Run Economic Impacts of Thai Flooding on Markets and Production Networks: Geographical Simulation Analysis

Ikumo Isono and Satoru Kumagai

1 Introduction

After the Great East Japan Earthquake and the flooding in Thailand in 2011, many media outlets reported interruptions in production networks and manufacturing industries in Japan and Thailand. Disruption of a single factory in a value chain may lead to the halt of the total production and sales chains, and the media claimed that the vulnerability in production networks must be a serious risk to Japan and Thailand. However, as Ando (2014) pointed out, production networks have recovered very quickly and have demonstrated the inherent resiliency of the value chain as the value chain itself has a strong self-recovering function from disconnection.

This chapter discusses another aspect of the economic impacts of disasters, namely, the long-term economic impact of natural disasters on markets and producers in affected countries. If the damage caused by disasters is severe, industries will move out from the countries in question, and the outflow of economic activities may cause a negative impact on the national economies in the long run. By using quantitative modeling based on spatial simulations we can estimate the seriousness of the disasters in terms of the long-term economic performance.

IDE/ERIA-GSM, a simulation model based on spatial economics, is also known as new economic geography. The model is used as a tool for policy makers to judge what sorts of trade and transport measures (TTFMs) must be

I. Isono (✉)
Institute of Developing Economies, Chiba, Japan
e-mail: Ikumo_Isono@ide.go.jp

S. Kumagai
Research Fellow Sent Abroad (Kuala Lumpur), Economic Integration Studies Group, Inter-disciplinary Studies Center, IDE-JETRO

D.P. Aldrich et al. (eds.), *Resilience and Recovery in Asian Disasters*, Risk, Governance and Society 18, DOI 10.1007/978-4-431-55022-8_8

undertaken, how to prioritize them and how to combine them. It can also simulate possible negative impacts of disasters in the long run. The model consists of an original microeconomic model with a general equilibrium setting, original simulation programs, a huge dataset including 1,654 regions, 3,156 nodes and 5,029 routes, and several parameters obtained by econometric estimations. It covers 16 countries/economies in Asia and two non-Asian economies, namely; Bangladesh, Brunei Darussalam, Cambodia, China, Hong Kong, India, Indonesia, Japan, Lao PDR, Macao, Myanmar, Malaysia, the Philippines, Singapore, Thailand, Vietnam, the United States and the European Union (EU). The model provided the theoretical foundation for the prioritization of infrastructure projects in the Comprehensive Asia Development Plan (CADP) and was also referred to in the Master Plan on ASEAN Connectivity (MPAC) report (ERIA 2010; ASEAN 2010).

We adopt the same methodology as Isono and Kimura (2011) to estimate the economic impacts of the 2011 flooding in Thailand. Isono and Kimura (2011) assessed the economic effects of the Great East Japan Earthquake and concluded that the earthquake might cause a shift of industrial structure from the east to the west of Japan, and to China and other East Asian counties. They claimed that further enhancement of the linkages between Japan and East Asia could mitigate this shift and for Fukushima, Miyagi and Iwate prefectures, tighter connections between Sendai Airport and Okinawa's logistics hub would positively stimulate electronics industries in the Tohoku area.

In addition to adopting the methodology in Isono and Kimura (2011), we reinforced our base settings with using the Current Quarter Model (CQM) by Kumasaka (forthcoming, 2014). By applying this short-run forecast as of December 2011 for the GSM, we can obtain a rough image of the magnitude of the damage to Thailand at a very early stage following the disaster. Here we estimate the long-run impacts and show that these long-run impacts would be moderate because many companies' first reaction to the flood is to seek possible relocation of their production sites within Thailand. In fact, simulation results reveal that, at the national level, because some provinces in Thailand experienced positive economic impacts following the flood, it mitigated the negative impacts on the affected provinces. At the time of writing, observations and surveys on the ground in Thailand report that some companies, including multinational enterprises, are relocating from the affected areas to safer provinces in Thailand, which clearly supports our estimations.

This chapter is structured as follows: Sect. 2 gives a brief explanation of the model. Section 3 provides the baseline scenario, the flooding scenario and alternative scenarios concerning recovery from the flood by enhancing connectivity. Section 4 concludes with some policy implications.

2 Simulation Model

2.1 Basic Structure of Our Simulation Model[1]

In our economic model, there are 1,654 locations, indexed by r in 18 countries/economies. There are two productive factors: labor and arable land. Labor is mobile within a country but stays immobile across countries.

Consumer preferences, which are identical across the world, are described by a Cobb-Douglas consumption function for an agricultural product, a manufacturing aggregate and a services aggregate. The manufacturing aggregate and services aggregate are expressed by a constant elasticity of substitution (CES) consumption function for individual manufactured goods or services. There are three sectors: agriculture, manufacturing, and services, and the manufacturing sector is divided into five sub-sectors; automobile, electronics and electrical appliances, garment and textile, food processing and other manufacturing. The agricultural sector produces a single and homogeneous agricultural product from arable land and labor, using a constant-returns technology under perfect competition. Manufacturing firms produce differentiated products using an increasing-returns technology under monopolistic competition where they use their labor forces and intermediate goods as inputs. Manufacturing intermediaries are procured from all manufacturing firms. Services are produced with using an increasing-returns technology under conditions of monopolistic competition where they use labor only. Economies of scale arise at factory levels. Labor can move to the sectors that offer higher nominal wage rates within the region.

All products in the three sectors are tradable. Transport for an agricultural good is assumed to be costless. Note that the price of an agricultural good selected in such a way that the price of the good is unitary across regions. Transport costs for manufactured goods and services are supposed to be of the iceberg type. An increase in purchaser's price compared to the manufacturer's price is regarded as the transport cost. Transport costs within a region are considered to be negligible.

2.2 Parameters

We have a number of critical parameters in the model. The consumption share of consumers by industry is uniformly determined for the entire region in the model. Of the seven industries in the model, the service industry takes up the largest share (0.55) while the automotive industry takes up the smallest (0.009); agriculture comes in second (0.16) with other manufacturing after (0.15).

[1] This section is excerpted and modified from Kumagai et al. (forthcoming, 2014)

The labor input share for each industry is uniformly determined for the entire region in the model, according to that of Thailand in the year 2000, taken from the International Input Output Table by IDE-JETRO. Because the simulation is run for more than 20 years, however, it may not be realistic to fix the labor input share for such a long period of time, especially for a developing country. However, we do not have a method to change the share with confidence. We therefore decided to use an "average" value, in this case that of Thailand as a country at the middle-stage of economic development. Labor input is largest for the service industry (1.0) followed by the food processing industry (0.796); the smallest share comes from the automotive industry (0.621).

We adopt the elasticity of substitution for manufacturing sectors from Hummels (1999) and estimate that for services as follows: 5.1 for food, 8.4 for textiles, 8.8 for electronics, 7.1 for transport, 5.3 for other manufacturing, and 5.0 for services. The estimates for the elasticity for services are obtained from the estimation of the usual gravity equation for services trade, including importer's GDP, exporter's GDP, importer's corporate tax, geographical distance between countries, a dummy for free trade agreement, a linguistic commonality dummy, and the colonial dummy as independent variables.

For the transport costs, we first estimate the multinomial logit model of firms' behavior in shipping their products by using firm-level data, based on the Establishment Survey on Innovation and Production Network (Intarakumnerd 2010). Next, we estimate some parameters such as holding time across borders. By employing these estimates in addition to the multinomial logit results, we specify a transport cost as a function for calculating the transport costs between regions. After that, we estimate Policy and Cultural Barriers (PCBs). Finally, we derive the transport costs between regions to be used in the simulation. Specifically, the transport cost in industry s by mode M between regions i and j is assumed as

$$C_{ij}^{s,M} = \underbrace{\left[\left(\frac{dist_{ij}}{Speed_M}\right) + (1 - Abroad_{ij}) \times ttrans_M^{Dom} + Abroad_{ij} \times ttrans_M^{Intl}\right]}_{\text{Total Transport Time}} \times ctime_s$$
$$+ \underbrace{dist_{ij} \times cdist_M}_{\text{Physical Transport Cost}} + \underbrace{(1 - Abroad_{ij}) \times ctrans_M^{Dom} + Abroad_{ij} \times ctrans_M^{Intl}}_{\text{Physical Transshipment Cost}}$$

where $dist_{ij}$ is the travel distance between regions i and j, $Speed_M$ is travel speed per one hour by mode M, $cdist_M$ is physical travel cost per one kilometer by mode M, and $ctime_s$ is time cost per one hour perceived by firms in industry s. The parameters ${ttrans_M}^{Dom}$ and ${ctrans_M}^{Dom}$ are the holding time and cost, respectively, for domestic transshipment at ports or airports. Similarly, ${ttrans_M}^{Intl}$ and ${ctrans_M}^{Intl}$ are the holding time and cost, respectively, for international transshipment at borders, ports, or airports. The parameters in the transport function are determined by estimation and adaptation from the ASEAN Logistics Network Map 2008 by

JETRO (2008, 2009). $Abroad_{ij}$ is a dummy taking a value of one if the transaction is international while zero if domestic.

In addition, $ttrans^{Dom}$ and speed of railway are estimated by the same dataset and the same estimating equation. Due to the minimal usage of railways in international transactions in the dataset, we adopted the same value for the time and cost of international transactions. Finally, we set the cost per km as half the value of road transport.[2] We use the estimated values as a general rule and additionally set the speed of land, sea, air and rail transport of each section differently from the data from UNESCAP and other various institutions, reflecting the gaps of the quality of infrastructure and the frequency of transport modes. For example, we assume most land trunk routes in Thailand can be run at 60 km/h, while some mountainous routes or poor roads can be run at only 19 km/h.

So far, we have estimated several components of transport costs including cost for transportation time, cost for transshipment time (holding time), physical transport cost, and physical transshipment cost. These costs are collectively called "GSM transport cost" in this subsection. However, some important components of the broadly defined "transport costs" remain excluded in the model. Examples include tariffs, non-tariff trade barriers (e.g. quota restrictions), procedures before shipping, costs arising from political situations or from certain risks, cost arising from preference differences and cost arising from commercial customs differences. We call these collectively "Policy and Cultural Barriers" (PCBs). We employ the "log odds ratio approach", as initiated by Head and Mayer (2000), in order to avoid the problem of data availability in the estimation of the model, similar to our GSM model. We first estimate the values for Thailand, the Philippines, Malaysia, and Indonesia by using per capita GDP data from the World Development Indicator (World Bank) and input–output data from the Asian International Input–output Table published by the Institute of Developing Economies, JETRO (IDE-JETRO). We regress days for customs clearance in importing (Days), for which data are drawn from the "Doing Business Indicator" from the World Bank, to get the other sample countries' PCBs.

We are then able to obtain the transport costs between regions, by industry, to be used in the simulation, using the transport cost function, several parameters, and PCBs. Firstly, we choose the economically shortest routes between regions by industry, adopting the transport cost function to all possible routes between regions. The shortest routes and utilized modes may differ among industries, even in the same regional pairs. Next, we calculate the transport costs between regions by industry. This cost is defined as the monetary cost when shipping products using a 20-ft container. Due to the fact that transport costs in this simulation are the ratio associated with the value of products being shipped, we need to transform the costs

[2] The ASEAN Logistics Network Map 2008 offers an example where the cost per km for railway is 0.85 times that of trucks. However, this is only the case when we ship a quantity that can be loaded onto a truck. Railways have much greater economies of scale than trucks in terms of shipping volume, so some industries such as coal haulage incur much lower cost per ton-kilometer. Therefore, we need to deduct this from the value in the ASEAN Logistics Network Map 2008.

Table 8.1 Average value in 20-ft container (USD)

	# of Sample	Average value
Automobile	6	89,691
E & E	11	92,746
Garment and textile	10	34,560
Agro and food processing	9	37,233
Others	8	59,450
Total	44	

Source: Preliminary survey results of FY2010 ERIA-GSM Project

to fit into the simulation. Except for the electronics and electrical appliance industry, we adopt the average values in a 20-ft container from the preliminary survey results of the FY2010 ERIA-GSM Project, as in Table 8.1. In the case of the electronics and electric appliance industry, we assumed that firms ship 2 t per 20-ft container. The value in 20-ft container for the electronics and electric appliance industries is calculated independently as USD 376,611 based on the trade value and volume data in Thailand. The reason why we adopt another value for those industries is the fact that some electronics firms answered in the survey that they selected mainly air transport, and that they did not utilize containers. This implies the existence of a sample selection bias in this survey for those industries. Finally, we transform the transport costs associated with the value of the products. PCBs are multiplied by the factors when the products are imported to corresponding countries.

Wage equations in the model include the variable A, which represents technology, or the productivity of each region, and is set by industry. A is calibrated at the beginning of the simulation to match the expected wage rate from the wage equation and the actual wage rate. It is a kind of "residual," including everything that affects the wage level, other than the variables explicitly included in the wage equation.

The parameters for labor mobility are set out at three levels, namely, international labor mobility (γ_N), intra-national (or intercity) labor mobility (γ_C), and inter industry labor mobility (γ_I) within a region. If $\gamma = 0.1$, it means that a country/region/industry with twice as high real wages as the average attracts 10 % labor inflow per year.

We set γ_N at 0. This means that the international migration of labor is prohibited. Although this looks like a rather extreme assumption, it is reasonable enough, taking into account the fact that most ASEAN countries strictly control incoming foreign labor. We set γ_C as 0.02. This means that a region with twice as high real wages as the national average induces 2 % labor inflow a year. Finally, we set γ_I to 0.05 too. This means that an industrial sector with twice as high real wages as the average in the region induces 5 % labor inflow from other industrial sectors per year.

We assume exogenous population growth, given the predicted rate of population growth provided by the United Nation Population Division

3 Baseline Scenario, Flood Scenario and Recovery Scenarios

In this section, we provide simulation results based on the settings and assumptions in the last section. The relationships between scenarios in terms of economic impacts are shown in Fig. 8.1. Every simulation starts from 2005. We assume that there were some infrastructure projects completed by 2010. In the baseline scenario, we do not assume additional damage or infrastructure development and run a simulation toward 2020. In the alternative scenario of flooding in Thailand, we assume damage to production in 2011 and recovery in 2012, and run a simulation up to 2020. We compare the economic situations between the baseline scenario and the alternative scenario in 2020 and derive the economic impact of the flooding as a difference between the two scenarios. We also conduct various simulations to identify effective recovery measures, assuming various physical and institutional connectivity enhancements in addition to the damage caused by the flood.

3.1 *Flood Scenario*

First we set the flood scenario (Scenario 0). We assume that local infrastructure including the production infrastructure of the factories in affected provinces were damaged in 2011 and recovered in 2012. We describe the situation by lowering the technological parameter A in 2011 and restoring it in 2012. Parameter A includes elements as follows:

- Education level/skill level
- Logistics infrastructure within the region
- Communications infrastructure within the region
- Electricity and water supply

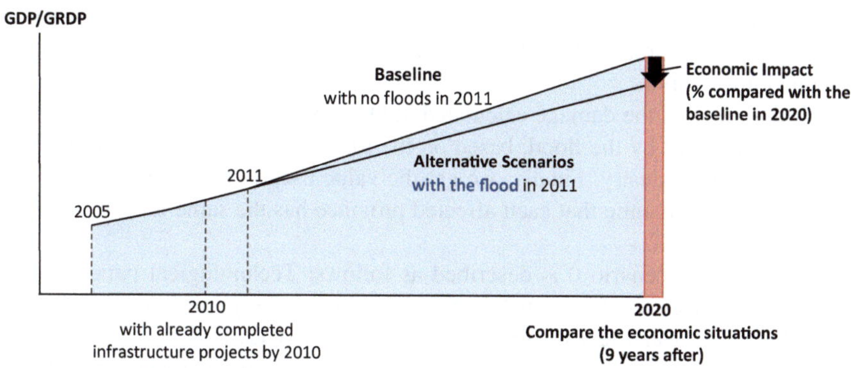

Fig. 8.1 Baseline scenario and alternative scenarios. *Source*: Authors

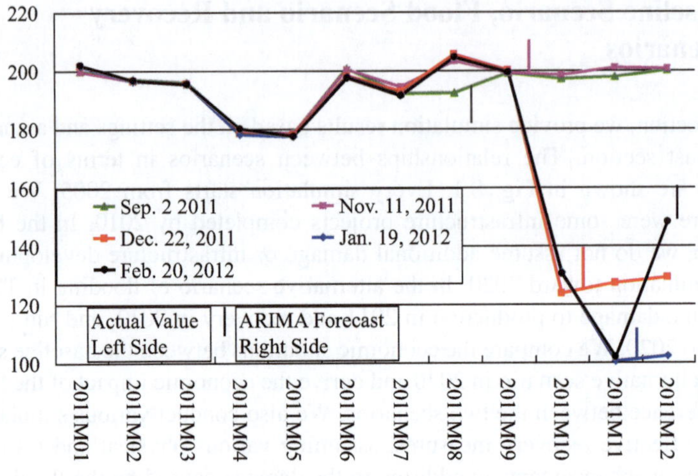

Fig. 8.2 Production value index by CQM. *Source*: Kumasaka (forthcoming, 2014)

- Equipment in firms
- Utilization ratio/efficiency of this infrastructure and equipments

To set the magnitude of the damage, we use CQM of Thailand by Kumasaka (forthcoming, 2014). CQM, updating estimations by an ARIMA type analysis from various partially available information, can estimate very short run impacts of economic shocks to production or GDP. It can provide estimated values before actual official reports are released. As of December 22, 2011, CQM estimated the impacts on real and nominal GDP values in Q4 in 2011, where we had no official reports on GDP yet.

Figure 8.2, the estimated production value index of Thailand, explains how CQM adjusts the estimated values using available sources. After getting additional available data, CQM updates its estimations to more reliable values. On September 2 and November 11, CQM did not have data of the damage caused by the flood and it could not assess the possibility of decreasing production. On December 22, CQM got partial information on the damage and revised the estimation values. Also, on January 19 and February 20, CQM revised its values accordingly from additionally obtained information.

We assume that the damage calculated in Q4 is proportionally distributed in the provinces affected by the flood, based on the total share of these provinces of the country in each industry. Finally, we get the value used in the assumptions of the simulations. We assume that each affected province has the same level of damage, as seen in Table 8.2.

In summary, Scenario 0 is described as follows: Technological parameters of affected provinces as shown in Fig. 8.3 decrease by the percentage provided in Table 8.2 in 2011 and recover to the former value in 2012.

Figure 8.3 illustrates the economic impacts of the flood evaluated in the year 2020, compared with the baseline scenario. Filled regions have positive impacts

Table 8.2 Assumptions of damage in the technological parameters in 2011

Agriculture	−17.6%
Automotive	−19.8%
Electronics and electrical appliances	−15.0%
Textiles and garments	−11.1%
Food processing	−13.6%
Other manufacturing	−13.6%
Services	−2.8%

Source: Author derived based on CQM short-run forecasts

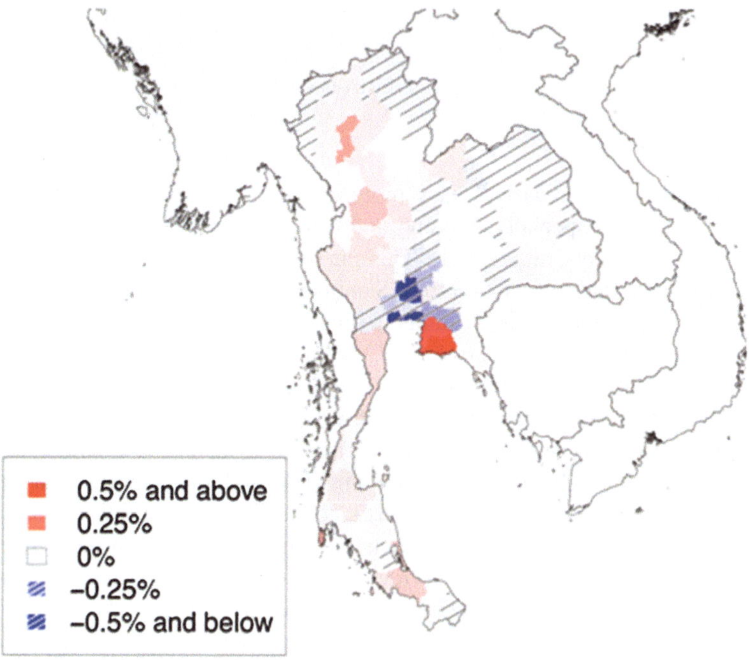

Fig. 8.3 Economic impacts of the flood (2020). *Source*: IDE/ERIA-GSM 4

and slashed regions have negative impacts. As explained in Fig. 8.1, a negative impact does not necessarily mean a GDP below the present level. Samut Sakhon, Samut Prakarn and Ayutthaya provinces have larger negative impacts, because they have large scale electronics industries. Bangkok has a slight negative impact, reflecting the idea that service industries had less damage caused by the flood, and that services has a dominant share in the Bangkok economy.

Table 8.3 shows the top seven negatively affected provinces and the top four positively affected provinces. Interestingly, there are many provinces positively affected, compared with the baseline scenario. This is because some households and firms move away from severely affected provinces to other areas, and thus

Table 8.3 Top seven negatively affected provinces and top four positively affected provinces

Region	Impact in GRDP (%)
Samut Sakhon	−0.5
Samut Prakarn	−0.5
Ayutthaya	−0.5
Pathum Thani	−0.3
Chachoengsao	−0.1
Saraburi	−0.1
Nakhon Pathom	−0.1
Phuket	0.1
Lamphun	0.1
Chonburi	0.3
Rayong	0.7

Source: IDE/ERIA-GSM 4

some of these other areas will have more industrial activities than shown in the baseline scenario. Especially, Rayong and Chonburi are predicted to see 0.7 and 0.3 % positive impacts, respectively. This can be interpreted as indicating that many companies move their production from Samut Sakhon, Samut Sakhon or Ayutthaya provinces to safer and better locations in other provinces. Lamphun, which has an electronics cluster, follows Rayong and Chonburi. Phuket also gets positive impacts from tourism shifting from Bangkok.

As in Fig. 8.3, other countries, such as Cambodia, Laos, Myanmar and Vietnam, have negligible impacts.[3] This means that replacement of the production lost in Thailand will be largely accomplished within Thailand, mainly led by Rayong and Chonburi provinces. In sum, Thailand as a country has almost 0 % impact. China and Indonesia will have positive impacts though they are almost negligible. This can be supported by JETRO's interview survey of affected companies in January 2012; it reported that among 50 affected companies, 39 answered they would restart operations at their existing locations, while and the other 8 replied that they planned to relocate their production site to other areas of Thailand. The Japan Chamber of Commerce, Bangkok released another survey result showing that among 48 affected manufacturing companies, 41 answered that they would restart operations at their existing production sites and 12 reported they would restart in other areas in Thailand.[4]

[3] We could not obtain flood damage data for Cambodia in terms of economic values, so we do not assume any damage for Cambodia.

[4] Multiple answers were allowed.

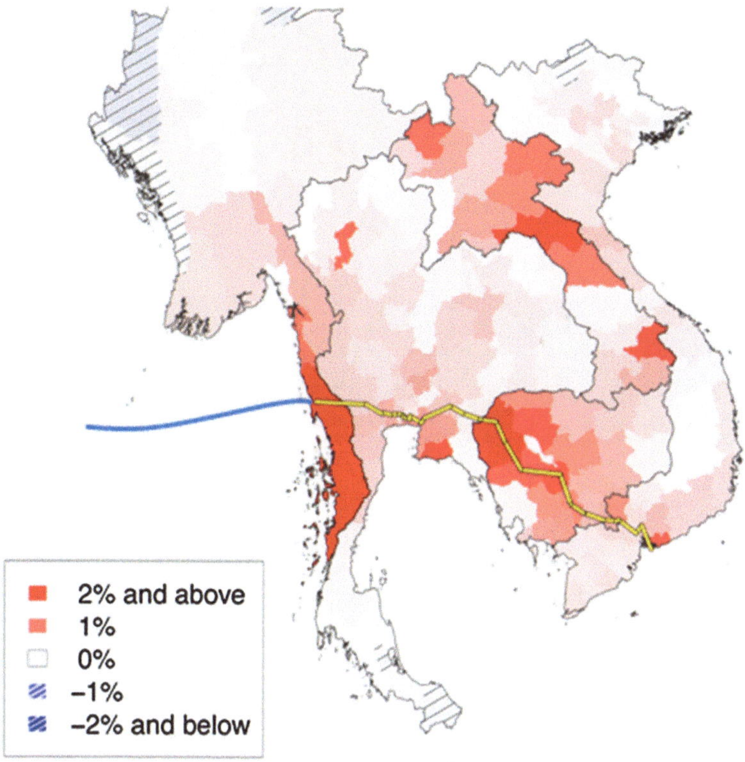

Fig. 8.4 Economic impacts of MIEC (2020). *Source*: IDE/ERIA-GSM 4

3.2 Recovery Scenario (1): MIEC and NSEC

At present Thailand, the Greater Mekong Sub-region and ASEAN have many connectivity enhancement projects in hand. To assess the net effect of the negative impacts of the flood and the expected positive impacts from the connectivity enhancement, we run simulations including improving the Mekong-India Economic Corridor (MIEC, Scenario 1A) and the North–south Economic Corridor (NSEC, Scenario 1B). These scenarios are set as follows:

We set up scenario 1A for the Mekong-India Economic Corridor (MIEC). Here a new bridge over the Mekong River at Neak Loueng in Cambodia is constructed. The speed of trucks along MIEC is raised in Cambodia and Vietnam to 60 km/h. Dawei and Kanchanburi are connected by a road, and border crossing facilitation along the MIEC is introduced. Dawei and Chennai (India) are connected via a sea route that is equivalent to other international routes between equally important ports.

Scenario 1B involves the North–south Economic Corridor (NSEC). In this scenario, the speed of trucks along the NSEC is raised in Lao PDR, Myanmar and Vietnam to 60 km/h. Border crossing facilitation along the NSEC is introduced.

Figures 8.4 and 8.5 present economic impacts of the MIEC and the NSEC, given the impact of the flood in the last subsection, respectively. In these scenarios, we do

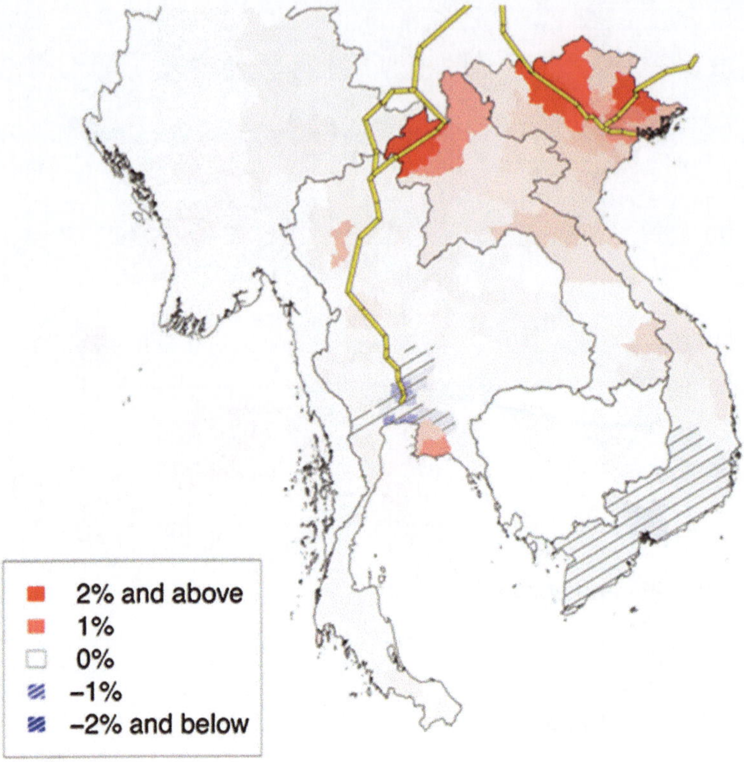

Fig. 8.5 Economic impacts of NSEC (2020). *Source*: IDE/ERIA-GSM 4

not assume increasing speeds of trucks within Thailand, because Thailand already has good national road networks. Even though we recognize some negative impacts of the flooding in these simulations and have no speed enhancement in Thailand, Fig. 8.4 shows that Thailand will overcome the negative shock of the flood through the MIEC development. By comparing Fig. 8.4 with Fig. 8.5, we find that the NSEC has a relatively smaller positive impact on Thailand, because connecting Ho Chi Minh City, Phnom Penh and Bangkok and providing a new gateway toward India, the Middle East and Europe yield much larger benefits to Thailand.[5]

[5] The CADP report (ERIA 2010) also compared the MIEC and the NSEC using IDE/ERIA-GSM version 3 and concluded that the MIEC has much larger economic impacts than the NSEC.

3.3 Recovery Scenario (2): MIEC, NSEC and Soft Infrastructure Development

We conduct another simulation of soft infrastructure development, together with the MIEC and the NSEC, given the impact of the flood. We assume Thailand, Cambodia, Lao PDR, Myanmar, Vietnam and India will reduce PCBs by 2 % per year, presuming the situation that they are cooperatively improving institutional connectivity. Our second scenario involves Soft infrastructure improvement in addition to the other development and enhancement. Countries participating in the MIEC and NSEC reduce Policy and Cultural Barriers (PCBs) by 2 % per year, in addition to the other development and link enhancement mentioned above.

We also calculated the economic impacts of the MIEC, the NSEC and soft infrastructure development. These measures will help Thailand overcome the negative impact of the flood. Ayutthaya will have a 4.9 % net positive impact, even allowing for the implicit negative impact of the flood. Samut Prakarn and Samut Sakhon have 4.8 and 4.6 % positive impacts, respectively. Rayong, Chonburi and Lamphun which have relatively larger positive impacts caused by the flood will also see further economic benefit.

4 Policy Recommendations and Concluding Remarks

Simulation results show that the long-run impact of the flood in Thailand on markets and production networks may not be as great as previously thought. Positive impacts in Rayong or Chonburi, for example, can only be simulated by a model with CGE setting, including many provinces. At an early stage of the disaster, many partial observations or interviews are collected in severely damaged areas, which may lead to exaggerating the long-run damage. Utilizing IDE/ERIA-GSM with an assumption from the Current Quarter Model (CQM) provides a solution to cope with this bias. In fact a preliminary report of this study, with the message that the long-run impact of the flood might not be as great as previously thought, was conveyed to the National Economic and Social Development Board (NESDB) and the Committee of Permanent Representatives (CPR) member of Thailand in January and February 2012.

We conclude with our findings, policy recommendations and some limitations or challenges. First, minimizing the damage arising from the flood and minimizing future risk are essential. We assume smooth recovery from the flood. If the Thai government had not offered good recovery measures, the flood's negative impacts would be larger. In fact many companies in JETRO's interview survey responded that they wanted to ask the Thai government to provide a good disaster insurance scheme and to develop tangible flood countermeasures.

Secondly, some facilitation measures to help firms move some production blocks from affected provinces to Rayong or Chonburi may contribute to

Thailand's recovery. This does not mean, of course, that we recommend the forced relocation of firms. As reported in the media, many companies are already seeking production sites in industrial estates in Chonburi, Rayong and Lamphun, and developers are planning to establish new industrial estates. Our recommendation is that these movements should not be impeded, even though the government must be aiming for an equitable development of the country.

Thirdly, stimulating R&D activities and innovation is indispensable. In the simulations we assume full recovery of production infrastructure in 2012. However, if Thailand saw a delay in conducting R&D activities and other countries went ahead in 2011, possible negative impacts compared to the baseline scenario would be much larger.

Fourthly, even though we forecast a favorable result from the MIEC, several conditions are required to make it possible. There needs to be a smooth transaction flow between Dawei and the Kanchanburi border. Dawei port should be large and efficient enough to host international carriers, as in Laem Chabang port or Tanjung Priok port because Dawei itself is located far from the major international sea lines.

Fifthly, and finally, the assumptions used in this chapter need to be reviewed repeatedly in order to produce more reliable results. For example, we assumed that Samut Prakan was affected by the flood, based on information from JETRO as in November 2011. Actually Samut Prakan was affected by the flood, but no industrial estates in Samut Prakan were damaged. In this regard, the result for Samut Prakan in Fig. 8.3 should be overestimated, even though some companies in Samut Prakan are in fact now seeking alternative sites considering their vulnerability to flooding. Similarly, the result as of January 2012 did not detect booming demand for construction in 2012. Nevertheless, IDE/ERIA-GSM can be a good tool for assessing the long-run effects of severe disasters and identifying possible remedies.

References

Ando, M. (2014). *Impacts of recent crises and disasters on regional production/distribution networks and trade in Japan*. Chapter 9 in this report.

ASEAN. (2010). *Master plan on ASEAN connectivity: One vision, one identity, one community*. Jakarta: ASEAN Secretariat.

ERIA. (2010). *The comprehensive Asia development plan*, ERIA Research Project Report 2009 No. 7–1. Jakarta: ERIA.

Head, K., & Mayer, T. (2000). Non-Europe: The magnitude and causes of market fragmentation in Europe. *Weltwirschaftliches Archiv, 136*, 285–314.

Hummels, D. (1999). *Toward a geography of trade costs*, GTAP Working Paper No. 17.

Intarakumnerd, P. (Ed.) (2010). *Fostering production and science & technology linkages to stimulate innovation in ASEAN*, ERIA Research Project Report 2009 No. 7–4. Jakarta: ERIA.

Isono, I., & Kimura, F. (2011). *Links with East Asia for a recovery from the Great East Japan earthquake: Geographical simulation analysis*, ERIA Policy Brief 2011–03. Jakarta: ERIA.

JETRO. (2008). *ASEAN logistics network map*. Tokyo: JETRO.

JETRO. (2009). *ASEAN logistics network map* (2nd ed.). Tokyo: JETRO.

Kumagai, S., Gokan, T., Isono, I., Hayakawa, K., Tsubota, K., & Keola, S. (forthcoming, 2014), *"IDE/ERIA-GSM v4.0" in geographical simulation analysis for logistics enhancement in ASEAN, China and India.* In R. Banomyong , I. Isono, & S. Kumagai (Eds.), ERIA Research Project Report 2011.

Kumasaka, Y. (Ed.) (forthcoming, 2014). *CQM construction and forecasts for the economies of Malaysia, Philippines, and Thailand*, ERIA Research Project Report 2011.

Chapter 9
Index-Based Risk Financing and Development of Natural Disaster Insurance Programs in Developing Asian Countries

Sommarat Chantarat, Krirk Pannangpetch, Nattapong Puttanapong, Preesan Rakwatin, and Thanasin Tanompongphandh

1 Introduction

There is growing evidence that the frequency and intensity of natural disasters continue to rise over the past decades (Swiss Re 2011a). This trend is likely to continue as the impact of climate change drives greater volatility in weather-related hazards (IPCC 2007). The low-income and developing countries suffered an increase of disaster incidence at almost twice the global rates large proportion of population still rely on agriculture and live in vulnerable environments (IFRCRCS 2011). Overall, costs per disaster as a share of GDP are considerably higher in developing countries (Gaiha and Thapa 2006). Over the past decade, Asia has been the most frequently and significantly hit region occupying 80 % of the major natural disasters worldwide.

Less than 10 % of natural disaster losses in developing countries are insured as several markets imperfections have served to impede development of markets for transferring natural disaster risks. Adverse selection and moral hazard are inherent to any form of conventional insurance products when insured have total control of

S. Chantarat (✉)
Crawford School of Public Policy, The Australian National University, Canberra, Australia
e-mail: sommarat.chantarat@anu.edu.au

K. Pannangpetch
Faculty of Agriculture, Khon Kaen University, Khon Kaen, Thailand

N. Puttanapong
Faculty of Economics, Thammasat University, Bangkok, Thailand

P. Rakwatin
Geo-Informatics and Space Technology Development Agency, Ministry of Science and Technology, Bangkok, Thailand

T. Tanompongphandh
Faculty of Economics, Kasetsart University, Bangkok, Thailand

D.P. Aldrich et al. (eds.), *Resilience and Recovery in Asian Disasters*, Risk, Governance and Society 18, DOI 10.1007/978-4-431-55022-8_9

and private information on the indemnified probability. Transaction costs of financial contracts necessary for controlling these information asymmetries and for verifying claimed losses are extremely high relative to the insured value especially for smallholders. Limited spatial risk-pooling potential resulted from covariate nature of natural disaster losses further impedes the development of domestic insurance market, unless local insurers can transfer the risks to international markets.

Without effective insurance market, public disaster assistance and highly subsidised public insurance programs have been the key supports for affected population in developing countries. The increasing frequency and intensity of these covariate shocks, however, could jeopardise the adequacy, timeliness and sustainability of these programs (Cummins and Mahul 2009). These public programs are largely prone to moral hazard, which could easily alleviate the program costs through induced risk taking incentives or underinvestment in risk mitigating activities among vulnerable populations. Without proper targeting, these programs could further crowd out private insurance demand impeding the development of healthy domestic insurance market.

Households in developing countries, thus, are disproportionally affected by disasters due to larger exposures but limited access to effective risk management strategies. While literatures analyse the wide array of informal social arrangements and financial strategies that households employ to manage risk, in nearly all cases these mechanisms are highly imperfect especially with respect to covariate shocks and in many cases carry very high implicit insurance premiums. The resulting long-term impacts of catastrophic shocks on their economic development thus have been widely evidenced in the literatures (cf. Barrett et al. 2007 for a review).

This chapter explores the potentials of the increasingly used index-based risk transfer products (IBRTPs) in resolving the key market imperfections that impede the development and financing of sustainable natural disaster insurance programs in developing countries. Unlike conventional insurance that compensates individual losses, IBRTPs are financial instruments, e.g., insurance, insurance linked security, that make payments based on an underlying index that is transparently and objectively measured, available at low cost and not manipulable by contract parties, and more importantly highly correlated with exposures to be transferred. By design, IBRTPs thus can obviate asymmetric information and incentive problems that plague individual-loss based products, as the index and so the contractual payouts are exogenous to policyholders. Transaction costs are also much lower, since financial service providers will only need to acquire index data for pricing and calculating contractual payments. There will be no need for costly individual loss estimations. Properly securitising natural disaster risk into a well-defined, transparently and objectively measured index could further open up possibilities to transfer covariate risks to international reinsurance and financial markets at competitive rates.

As natural disaster losses are covariate, it would be possible to design IBRTPs based on a suitable aggregated index. These opportunities, however, come at the cost of basis risk resulting from imperfect correlation between an insured's actual loss and the behaviour of the underlying index on which the contractual payment is based. IBRTPs will be effective only when basis risk is minimised. The contracts need to also be simple enough to hold informed demand among clients with limited literacy in developing countries, and to be scalable to larger geographical settings to ensure efficient market scale. Trade-offs among basis risk, simplicity and scalability thus constitute the key challenges in designing appropriate IBRTPs for developing countries.

Over the past decade, IBRTPs have emerged as potentially market viable approaches for managing natural disaster risk in developing countries. The growing interests among academics, and development communities have resulted in at least 36 projects in 21 countries worldwide covering risks of droughts, floods, hurricanes, typhoons and earthquakes based on objectively measured area-aggregated losses, weather and satellite imagery products.[1] Contracts have been designed to enhance risk management at various levels ranging from farmers and homeowners as target users to macro level, allowing governments and humanitarian organisations to transfer their budget exposures in provision of disaster relief programs to the international markets.

The consensus, however, has not been reached if and how IBRTPs could work in developing country settings for several reasons. First, current literature[2] tends to either lack rigorous analysis of basis risk and welfare impacts or use aggregated data to perform such analysis. Hence, less could be learnt ex ante about the value of the contracts to the targeted population. Second, contract designs to date are context specific, making it very difficult to be scaled up in other heterogeneous settings. Finally, as most of the current studies are small in scale, less has been explored on the potentials for portfolio risk diversifications, transfers and financing.

This chapter complements existing literatures, especially on the rigorous analysis and applications of IBRTPs in Asia. We provide an analytical framework and show empirically how to use a combination of disaggregated and spatiotemporal rich sets of household and disaster data, commonly available in developing countries, to design nationwide and scalable IBRTP contracts, to analyse hedging effectiveness and welfare impacts at a disaggregated level and to explore cost effective disaster risk-financing options. We explore the potentials for development of nationwide index insurance program for rice farmers in Thailand. We analyse contract design based on three forms of indices: (1) government collected provincial-averaged rice yield, (2) estimated area yield constructed from scientific

[1] Much literature has depicted opportunities and challenges of implementing IBRTPs. See IFAD and WFP (2010), Barnett et al. (2008), for example, for review. See Chantarat et al. (2007, 2008, 2011, 2013), Clarke et al. (2012) and Mahul and Skees (2007) for examples related to IBRTP designs in the developing world, and Mahul (2000) for examples related to agriculture in high-income countries.

[2] With the exception of some on-going new projects, see for example, Chantarat et al. (2013) and various piloted projects funded by USAID-I4 Index Insurance Innovation Initiative at http://i4.ucdavis.edu/projects/. These ongoing pilot projects undertake rigorous contract design and ex-ante evaluation using high-quality household welfare data in addition to their proposed ex-post evaluation through multi-year household-level impact assessment.

crop-climate modelling and (3) various constructed parametric weather variables. These indices differ in risk coverage, exposure to basis risk, level of simplicity and scalability. Disaggregated welfare dynamic data obtained from the multi-year repeated cross sectional household survey are then used to estimate basis risk and to evaluate the relative hedging effectiveness of these indices given the above trade-offs.

The nationwide design coupled with spatiotemporal rich indices data further allows us to explore portfolio risk diversification and transfers through reinsurance and securitisation of insurance-linked security in the form of catastrophe bond. And through simulations based on disaggregated nationwide household dynamic data, we finally explore potential impacts of the optimally designed index insurance program under various public–private integrated risk financing arrangements. Except for the existing literature on Mongolia (Mahul and Skees 2007) and India (Clarke et al. 2012), this chapter is among the very first to study IBRTPs using a countrywide analysis. Using commonly available data sets further enhance scalability of our analysis to other settings in the region.

The rest of the chapter is structured as following. Section 2 presents the main empirical results illustrating the potentials of IBRTPs for rice farmers in Thailand. Section 3 concludes with discussions on challenges and opportunities in implementing IBRTPs and implications of our studies for the rest of Asia.

2 Index-Based Disaster Insurance Program for Rice Farmers in Thailand

Rice is the country and region's most important food and cash crop. In Thailand, rice production occupies the majority of arable land with the largest proportion of farmers (18 % of the population) relying their livelihoods on. Improving and stabilising rice productivity is thus one of the core prerequisites for the country's economic development. Thai rice production, however, has been increasingly threatened by natural disasters, especially droughts and floods.

Thai farmers typically take out input loans and expect to pay back with income raised through the harvested crop. Production shocks thus usually bring about increasing level of accumulated debt, as farmers could face difficulties in repaying their loans and in smoothing their consumption. These translate directly to high default risk facing rural lenders, especially the Bank of Agriculture and Agricultural Cooperatives (BAAC) holding the majority of agricultural loan portfolios in the country. While instruments that allow rice farmers to hedge other key risks are largely available—e.g., public rice mortgage program for hedging price risk—sustainable insurance that could insure farmers' production risks without distorting their incentives to improve productivity are still largely absent.

2.1 Rice Production, Exposures to Natural Disasters and the Current Programs

There are about 9.1 million hectares of rice growing areas in Thailand in 2010.[3] Figure 9.1 presents variations in rice paddy areas and production systems across the country's 76 provinces.[4] The key growing provinces, where rice paddy occupies at least 50 % of the total arable areas, are clustered mainly in the central plain especially around Chao Phraya River basin and the lowland Northeast. Small numbers of rice growing provinces are also scattered around the upland North and the South.

Production regions vary in cropping patterns due to heterogeneous irrigation systems, ecology, soil and weather patterns. Irrigation is available in less than 25 % of the total growing areas. These occupy most of the central provinces and some areas in the North and the South, allowing farmers to cultivate two crops a year. Yields thus tend to be higher in these regions. The majority of rain-fed production occupies almost the entire key growing areas in the lowland Northeast, relies extensively on rainfall and so harvests lower yields. The main crop cycles typically start with the onset of annual rain, which usually comes during mid-May to November and varies slightly across regions. The second crop can then be grown throughout the rest of the year depending on water availability. As the key growing areas around Chao Phraya River basin are flood prone, crop cycles deviate slightly in order to avoid extended flood periods.

Rice cropping cycle spans about 120 days from seeding to harvesting (Siamwalla and Na Ranong 1980). Long dry spells and extended flood periods appear as the two key shocks affecting productions with increasing frequency. Sensitivity to these key disasters varies across different stages of crop growth. According to World Bank (2006)'s collective scientific findings,[5] the first 105-day period from seeding to grain filing critically requires enough water, and thus is vulnerable to long dry spells that could result from late or discontinued rain. Farmers are also already well adapted to small dry spells by adjusting their planting periods or re-planting when loss occurs early in the cycle. As cycle progresses to maturity and harvesting (during the 105–120 day period that typically fall into the peak of seasonal rain), plants become vulnerable to extended flood that could come about at least when 4-day cumulative rainfall exceeds 250 mm.

[3] Data are obtained from the Office of Agricultural Extension, Ministry of Agriculture and Cooperatives, Thailand. There is no significant trend from the annual areas since 1980.

[4] The number of provinces has just recently increased to 77 with one additional province added in the Northeast 2011. Our spatiotemporal data are extracted using the un-updated 76-province GIS information.

[5] These results are obtained from PASCO, Co.'s study using a combination of scientific literature reviews, agro-meteorological model (DSSAT) with detailed geographical information and ground checking with the local experts in the key-growing province, Phetchabun, and flood plain modelling.

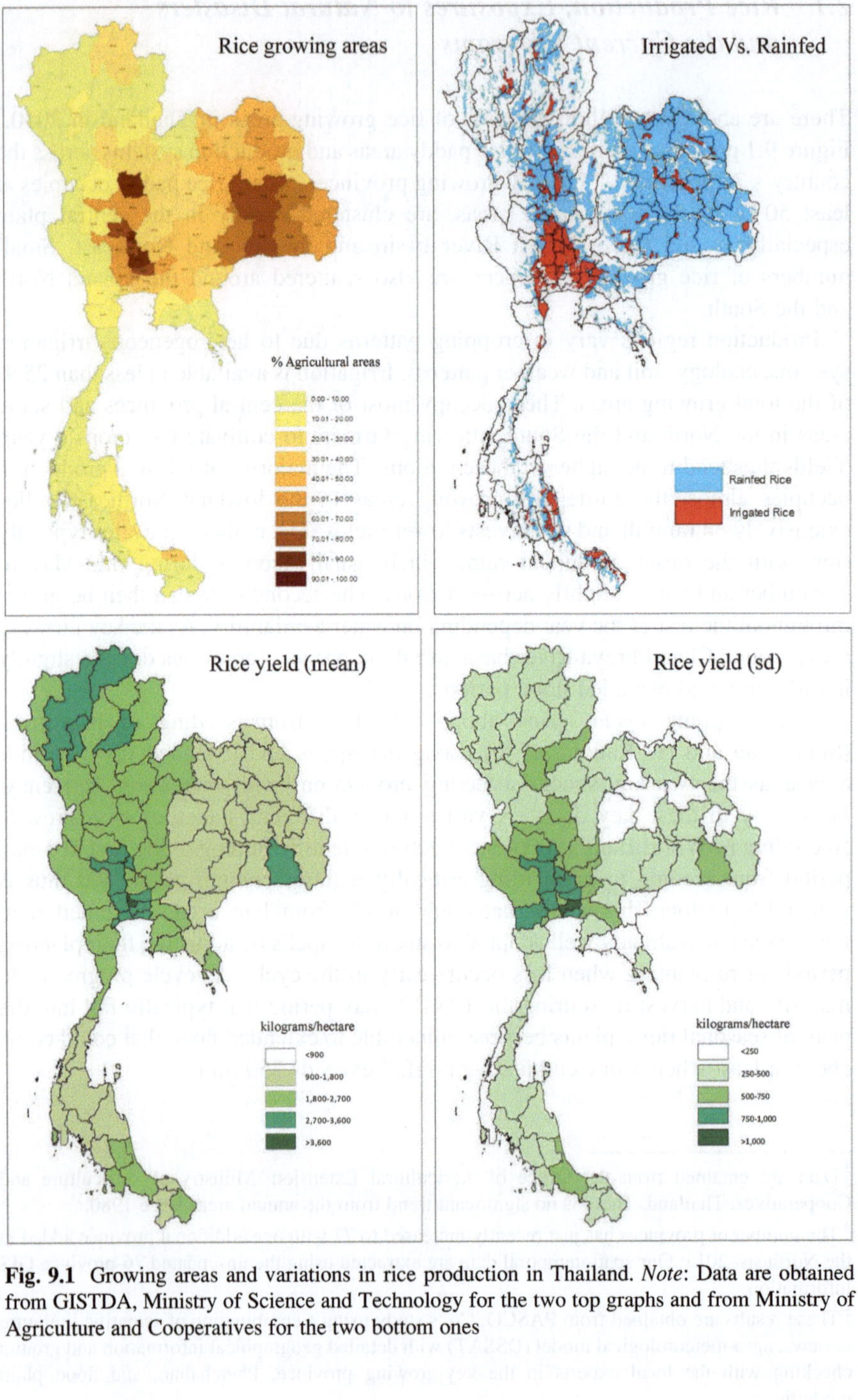

Fig. 9.1 Growing areas and variations in rice production in Thailand. *Note*: Data are obtained from GISTDA, Ministry of Science and Technology for the two top graphs and from Ministry of Agriculture and Cooperatives for the two bottom ones

Catastrophic crop losses from dry spells typically occur in the rain-fed areas during the onset of rain in July–August, whereas, losses from extended floods occur in the peak of rain during September–October. Exposures differ across regions. The north-eastern rain-fed production are especially vulnerable to long dry spell, while most of the irrigated production in the central plain are subject to long periods of deep flooding annually. Productions in the South are vulnerable to floods caused by thunderstorms (Siamwalla and Na Ranong 1980). Pest also serves as one of the key covariate risks for rice production. Figure 9.2 presents government records of incidences and spatial variations of actual rice crop losses from these three main shocks in 2005–2011. Flood losses occur with the highest frequency and significance relative to others.

Over the past decade, the Thai government has provided disaster relief program for farmers when disaster strikes. The program compensates about 30 % of total input costs for farmers, who live in the government declared disaster provinces and are verified by local authorities to experience total farm losses. Government spends about 3,350 million baht[6] on average per year for rice farmers affected by droughts, floods and pests. And the program cost could increase up to 40 % in some extreme years. Despite these tremendous spending, results from randomised farmer survey imply that the compensation is largely inadequate and subjected to serious delay especially from loss verification process (Thailand Fiscal Policy Office 2010). There are also increasing evidence of moral hazard associated with the program, especially as farmers start growing the third crop off suitable season.

The nationwide rice insurance program—a top-up program for disaster relief—was piloted in 2011. The program was underwritten by a consortium of local insurers and reinsured by Swiss Re (2011b). At 50 % subsidised premium rate of 375 baht/ha nationwide, the program covered main rice season, and compensated farmers up to 6,944 baht/ha (about 30 % of farmers' input costs) should they experience total farm losses from droughts, floods, strong winds, frosts and fires during the cropping cycle. About 1.5 % of growing areas were insured in 2011. The flood resulted in a loss ratio of as high as 500 % for the first year. Reinsurance prices thus inevitably increased more than double making it not market viable for the following years. This program continued in 2012 at the same (highly subsidised) rate but with government now taking the role as an insurer.

The current program thus resumes various inefficiencies and market problems, commonly evidenced in the traditional crop insurance to jeopardise the program's sustainability (Hazell et al. 1986). First, like other conventional insurance, the program would be subjected to moral hazard, e.g., when it induces additional risky off-season rice cropping, etc. Second, high direct subsidisations distorted market prices and thus could reduce sustainability of the market in the longer run. This could further exacerbate incentive problems. Third, this voluntary program is offered at one single premium rate for farmers with different risk profiles. It could

[6] USD 1 = 31.81 baht (Bank of Thailand as of May 29, 2012).

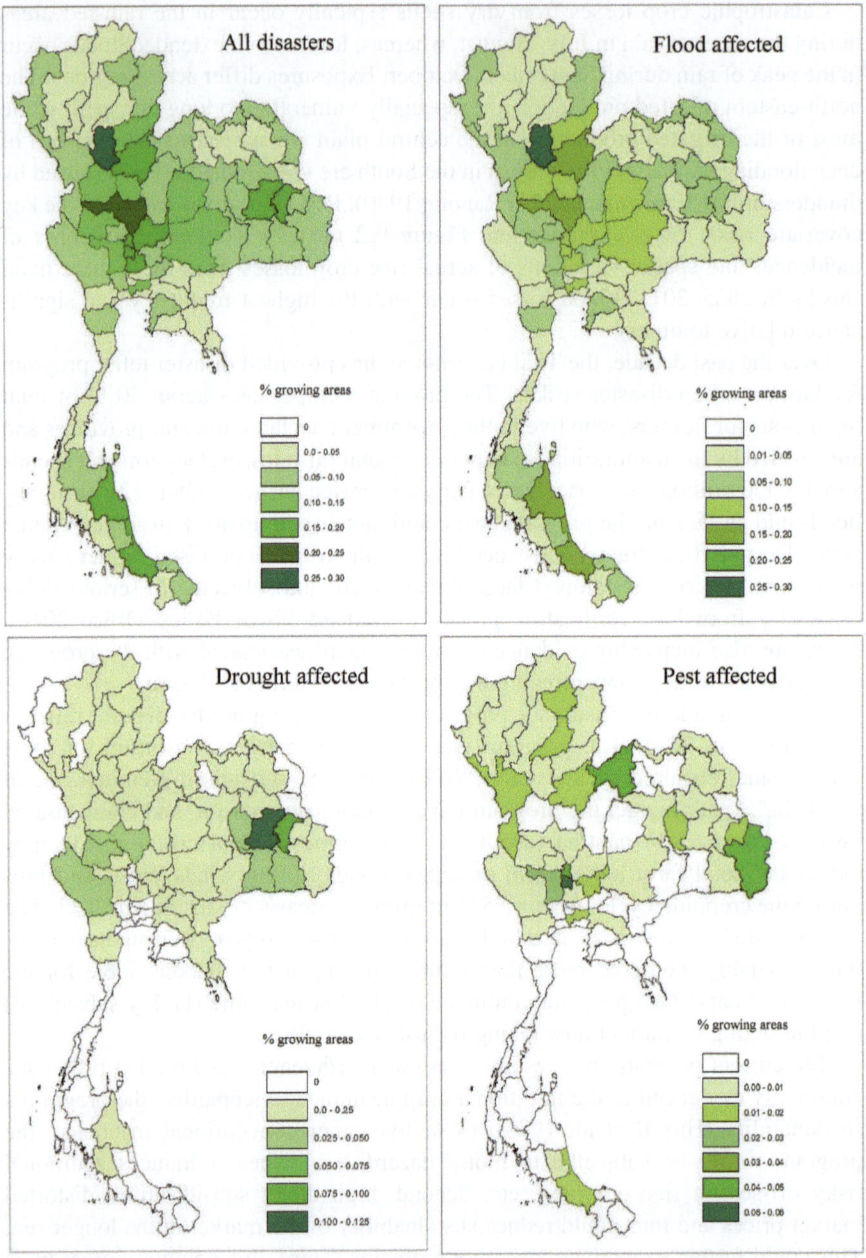

Fig. 9.2 Rice growing areas affected by key disasters (2005–2011). *Note*: Data are obtained from Thailand Ministry of Agriculture and Cooperative

potentially signify adverse selection and moral hazard.[7] Fourth, because the government's declaration of disaster areas can be subjective in nature, asymmetric information at the government level could further arise. The highly subjective local verification of losses could potentially induce rent seeking at various levels, further affecting the commercial sustainability of this program. The highly subjective and non-transparent nature of loss measures would no doubt lead to increasing risk pricing in the international market. Finally, the program resumed inefficiencies in time and cost of loss verification in the relief program.

2.2 Data

We use five disaggregated nationwide datasets in this study. The first four sets are used to construct objectively measured indices for index insurance design, and the last set represents variations in households' incomes from rice production, and thus is used to establish optimal contract design, basis risk and hedging effectiveness associated with various designed contracts.

First, measures of area-yield indices are drawn from the provincial rice yield data collected annually by the Office of Agricultural Extension at Thailand Ministry of Agriculture and Cooperatives (MoAC). The data are available for all the provinces nationwide from 1981 to 2010 and were collated from a combination of an annual survey of randomised villages in each province and official records by local agricultural extension offices. They are thus representative at the provincial level. Yield data reflect total yield from all crops harvested each year. To remove time trends potentially resulting from technical change, improvements in varieties, irrigations and other management practices, we de-trend the data using a robust Iterative Reweighted Least Squares Huber M-Estimator[8] to first estimate the time trend.

Second, objective measures of weather indices are drawn from 20×20 km gridded daily rainfall data obtained from the simulated regional climate model ECHAM4-PRECISE constructed by Southeast Asia System for Analysis, Research and Training (START) as part of their regional climate change projections. These simulated climate data were verified and rescaled to match well with the comparable data from observed weather stations (Chinvanno 2011). These simulated weather data are available from 1980 to 2011.[9]

[7] Farmers in the risky areas would, in expectation, tend to be the majority of the purchasers of the cheaper contract relative to their risk profiles. And the heavily subsidised insurance contracts for those in the risky zones could further induce excessive risk taking behaviours.

[8] This trend estimation has been commonly used in agricultural time series especially when the underlying data are not normally distributed (Ramirez et al. 2003).

[9] These also include projected future climate data and are available at http://www.start.or.th/. The resolutions of these data could be improved. Attempts are current made in gridding weather data at lower resolutions.

Third, estimated rice yield data were then constructed using an integrated crop-climate model developed by Pannangpetch (2009). High resolution GIS maps of soil types (1999), rice growing areas constructed by LANDSAT 5TM (2001) and ECHAM4-PRECISE weather were first overlaid in order to cluster geographical areas into distinct simulation mapping unit (SMU)[10] representing the smallest homogenous areas, where crop response to weather conditions could be uniform. DSSAT crop model was then used to estimate longitudinal estimated rice yields driven by ECHAM4-PRECISE weather controlling for exogenous time-invariant SMU-specific GIS characteristics and crop management. These estimated yields reflect total yields from one (two) crops harvested in the rain-fed (irrigated) SMUs. As the simulated yield variations are driven solely by variations in weather, these data can serve as objectively measured index for IBRTPs.

Fourth, the remote sensing Normalised Difference Vegetation Index (NDVI)[11] data are extracted from Tera MODIS satellite platform every 16 days from 2000 to 2011 throughout the country at a 500-meter resolution. NDVI data provide indicators of the amount and vigour of vegetation, based on the observed level of photosynthetic activity (Tucker et al. 2005). This knowledge is critical in the construction of appropriate weather indices that ally well with different stages of crop growth. Some GIS information characterising production systems that could condition the sensitivity of rice production to shocks and records of annual crop cycles are also obtained from MoAC for cross checking with NDVI data.

Fifth, household-level incomes from rice production data are obtained from multi-year repeated cross-sectional Thai Socio-Economic Survey (SES) surveyed nationwide every 2–3 years from 1998, 2000, 2002, 2004, and 2006 to 2009 Thailand's National Statistical Office. Each round, a total of 34,000–36,000 households were randomly sampled from the sampled villages in all provinces (10–25 sampled households per village; 30–50 sampled villages per province). Because no household is sampled more than once during these surveys, our analysis thus can be based on repeated household cross sectional data. Subset of households from the six rounds, who reported their socioeconomic status as farm operator and rice farming as the main household enterprise, are used in this study. The subsample size in each round ranges from 2,500 to 3,100 households with households per province varying from 5 in the non-rice provinces to 150 in the key rice growing provinces. Because there is no direct measure of rice production, we use household's annual[12] income from crop production per hectare as a representation of y_{it}. This annual income measure thus includes income from more than one cropping seasons in irrigated areas. Other household and area characteristics are also extracted from SES data.

All of the GIS variables are first constructed at pixel level before downscaling to provincial level, so that these can all be merged with household-level data. Table 9.1

[10] This results in 9,254 SMUs covering all the 9.1 million hectares of rice growing areas nationwide. The size of constructed SMUs ranges from 0.16 to 35,900 ha.

[11] Data are available worldwide and cost free. See https://lpdaac.usgs.gov/content/view/full/6644.

[12] Farm incomes from the last month are also available, but the large variations in cropping patterns as well as survey timing constitute great difficulties in controlling for seasonality effects.

Table 9.1 Summary statistics of key variables

Variables		N	Mean	S.D.	Minimum	Maximum
Rice production and rainfall						
Rice growing areas, 1981–2010	– Country (million hectare)	30	9.2	0.2	8.7	9.5
	– Province (% total area)	2,240	53 %	24 %	2 %	92 %
Annual cumulative rainfall (cm), 1980–2011		2,432	425	124	179	889
Provincial yield (kg/ha/year), detrended 1981–2010		2,240	2,622	868	710	5,398
Rice farming households						
Household crop production income (baht/ha/year)		18,216	40,246	31,541	0	98,137
Rice cropping land size (hectare)		18,216	1.92	3.56	0.16	47.00
Number of times cultivated rice per year		18,216	1.64	1.13	1.00	3.00
Number of members working on farm		18,216	2.75	1.24	1.00	6.00
Input and operating cost per cropping season (proportion of income)		18,216	0.49	0.31	0.37	0.89
Household takes out loans for input cost each season = 1		18,216	0.89	0.23	0.00	1.00
Total outstanding agriculture loans (proportion of annual income)		18,216	1.41	6.94	0.00	256.25
Annual Interest rate on 12-month agricultural loan		18,216	0.06	0.03	0.02	0.15
Household size		18,216	3	1	1	6
Head age		18,216	50	14	17	94
Head female = 1		18,216	0.17	0.38	0.00	1.00
Head highest education—primary = 1		18,216	0.85	0.38	0.00	1.00
Head highest education—secondary = 1		18,216	0.05	0.20	0.00	1.00
Head highest education—university = 1		18,216	0.00	0.00	0.00	0.00
Head highest education—vocational = 1		18,216	0.00	0.06	0.00	1.00
Own house = 1		18,216	0.96	0.18	0.00	1.00
Own agricultural land = 1		18,216	0.81	0.42	0.00	1.00
Provincial production characteristics						
Households' farm located in the irrigated areas = 1		77	0.22	0.43	0.00	1.00
Upland areas (% total rice paddy)		77	6 %	27 %	0 %	100 %
Flood plain areas (% total rice paddy)		77	12 %	47 %	0 %	100 %
River basin areas (% total rice paddy)		77	19 %	41 %	0 %	100 %
Indices (% of provincial long-term mean)						
Provincial yield index, 1981–2010		2,240	100 %	14 %	41 %	146 %
Estimated yield index, 1980–2011		2,432	100 %	24 %	57 %	146 %
Cumulative rainfall index, 1980–2011		2,432	100 %	27 %	29 %	154 %
Moving dry spell index, 1980–2011		2,432	100 %	35 %	38 %	165 %
Moving excessive rain spell index, 1980–2011		2,432	100 %	31 %	41 %	179 %

provides summary statistics of the key variables extracted from these five data sets. Overall, mean de-trended provincial averaged rice yield stands at 2,622 kg/ha with high standard deviation capturing the variations across households and years. Household's averaged income from rice production is at 40,246 baht per hectare per year. This results from cultivating 1–3 crops (with 1.64 crops on average) a year. Total input costs are averaged as high as 49 % of income[13] implying that households earn about 20,525 baht as farm profit per hectare per year. Mean rice-growing areas per household is about 1.92 ha. About 89 % of households take out input loan each season. And critically, their accumulated agricultural debt stands at an average of 141 % of annual income in any given year. Apart from the lowland majority, 6 % of total rice growing areas are upland, 12 % is flood prone and 19 % locates near river basin.

2.3 Index Insurance Designs for Thai Rice Farmers

Various spatiotemporal data sets allow us to explore various standard index insurance contracts for Thai rice farmers based on the following constructed indices.

First, direct measures of area yields $\bar{y}_t$ can be constructed from annual provincial yield data. As it offers protection against any covariate risks affecting provincial yield, not just from weather, it could perform well in the case of Thai rice, where pest constitutes one of the key covariate threats. Second, estimated provincial yields $y(w_t)$ can be constructed from the SMU-specific modelled yields. To the extent that the complex crop-climate predictive model performs well in predicting weather-driven yield shocks, this index could provide good hedging effectiveness for farmers. Third, we explore various parametric weather indices w_t. But because the sensitivity of plants to weather shocks varies across stages of crop growth, knowledge of cropping cycles and how they vary spatially and temporally are thus critical.

2.4 Cropping Cycles and Weather Indices

Smoothing [14] the provincial NDVI data in a 1-year window results in uni- or bi-modal patterns. Each of these NDVI modes corresponds well with one full 120-day crop cycle. These smoothed provincial NDVI patterns can then be clustered into six distinct zones with homogenous crop cycles. Normal starts of the main and second crops in the irrigated areas vary across flood prone lower Central

[13] These statistics align well with findings in Isvilanonda (2009).

[14] Simple local polynomial smoothing is used over all the pixels that fall into provincial boundary over 2000–2011.

(mid May, December), upper Central and North (July, January) and South (August, March). Normal starts of the main crop in the rain-fed areas follow those of the irrigated zones with those of Northern Province sallying well with those of the North. The variations of crop cycles observed objectively from the patterns of NDVI also align well with the MoAC-collected records of cropping patterns in some key provinces.

These six distinct zone-specific crop cycles then form a basis for constructing provincial weather indices. For each crop cycle, we extend World Bank (2006)'s crop scientific findings and so explore two provincial dry spell indices covering weather conditions in the first 105 days and a flood index covering those in the 106–120 days of the cycle. These indices are constructed for both main and second crops in the two-crop zones opening a possibility that farmers can obtain insurance protection for both crops. All weather indices are constructed first at pixel level and then averaged toward provincial indices.

First, a simple cumulative rainfall index (CR) can be constructed from daily rainfall. The level of CR below some critical strikes thus could reflect the extent of dry spell that could in turn damage rice production. The key advantage of this is its simplicity. Hence this index has been used in various piloted projects including one in the north-eastern province in Thailand.[15] This simple index, however, might not reflect the extent of dry spell well, as it fails to take into account how rainfall is distributed within 105-day period. In particular, high CR could result from couple large daily rains and a long dry spell (that would otherwise damage crop).

Alternatively, a moving dry spell index (MD), which measures the extent that 10-day cumulative rainfall falls below the crop water requirement (30 mm for 10-day period) in each and every 10-day dry spell in the 105 cropping days, can be constructed. MD above some critical strikes thus could better reflect the extent of dry spell that really matters to rice production. This index has widely been identified to better quantify the extent of dry spells. But because of its relatively more complexity, this index has not been used widely.[16]

Continuous excessive rainfall is the key cause of extended flooding periods in the paddy fields. World Bank (2006) found that the 4-day cumulative rainfall above 250 mm can trigger high probability of extended flood causing losses to harvesting rice crops. We thus quantify flood index using a moving excessive rain spell index (ME) to measure the extent that 4-day cumulative rainfall excess 250 mm. But the extent that ME could determine extended flooding period and crop losses should also vary across production systems, which in turn determine soil type, drainage system, crop variety, etc.

The three weather indices so far are constructed based on the assumption that insured cropping cycles in each year and province follow the six smoothed zone-specific patterns. Because famers tend to adjust their production annually in order to

---

[15] Current contract piloted by JBIC and Sompo Japan insurance in Khon Kaen relies on simple cumulative rainfall are taken from July to September.

[16] For example, drought index insurance for maize piloted in Thailand since 2007.

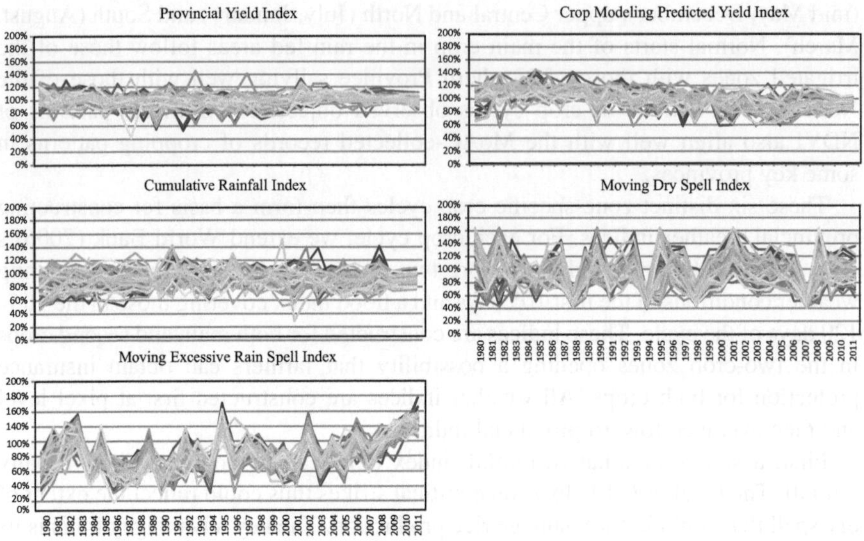

Fig. 9.3 Temporal and spatial distributions of the key indices

adapt to small inter-year variations in rainfall patterns, using fixed crop cycles as a basis for index construction might result in misrepresentations of crop losses from drought and flood events. Alternatively, indices can be constructed based on a dynamic crop cycle. Because successful seeding critically requires at least 25 mm of rainfall (World Bank 2006), the first day from the fixed zone-specific starting date when a 1-day, 2-day or 3-day cumulative rainfall exceeding 25 mm can be used to trigger the start of an insured cropping cycle, during when the underlying weather indices will be constructed. We experiment among the three choices above and choose the optimal threshold that yields the highest explanation power of the constructed indices in predicting actual losses.

In order to effectively compare contracts designed with various indices, we standardise these indices into relative percentage forms with respect to their provincial-specific expected value.[17] Table 9.1 provides statistics of these standardised indices. Figure 9.3 plots the five indices and their spatial distributions across all rice growing provinces.[18] Overall, provincial averaged, estimated yield indices and CR exhibit lower temporal variations relative to weather indices. Their spatial variations, however, are larger than the last two weather indices. MD seems

[17] Note that for $y(w_t), CR_t, MD_t, ME_t$, we standardise at the SMU and pixel first (using SMU and pixel specific moments) before aggregate them into provincial indices. This is different from taking average of index first then dividing by overall long-term average later. The latter case will result in index with lower variations since most the SMU-level variations are already smoothed out in the aggregation process.

[18] There are two values for each of the weather indices in the two-crop zones, one for each crop cycle.

to well capture the key covariate drought events in the country especially in 2008, 2001, 1995 and 1990. ME captures the key flood years well especially the catastrophic floods in 1995 and 2010–2011.

2.5 Basis Risks and Hedging Effectiveness

How well might these indices explain variations in household's annual crop income per hectare? Household data are merged with these indices at the provincial level in order to estimate (9.1). Without household panel, we instead use 6-year repeated cross sectional data to estimate, for each index, the following equation[19]

$$lny_{ilt} = X_{ilt}\gamma + D_l\mu + \eta_t + \lambda z_{lt} + \kappa D_l z_{lt} + \varepsilon_{ilt}. \quad (9.1)$$

The first three terms capture household's long-term expected income with X_{ilt} absorbing characteristics of households entered in each survey round, D_l absorbing provincial time invariant characteristics especially with respect to rice production systems (e.g., upland, flooded plain, closure to river basin) and η_t absorbing time effect that captures trend in income common across all households. The last three terms reflect stochastic shocks to household income. We also interact D_l with the index in order to capture variations in sensitivity of income to weather shocks across different production systems. This equation is estimated separately for irrigated and rain-fed regions using simple linear least squared with standard deviations clustered at provincial level.[20]

Different regressions explore how different indices can explain variations in farm income of the rice growing households controlling for household and provincial characteristics and time effects that determine household's long-term mean income. The first column shows that these controls explain about 40 % and 48 % of the income variations for households in the irrigated and rain-fed areas respectively, implying a maximum of 60 % and 52 % of income variations that households are still unable to manage using existing mechanisms. Except CR, all the indices significantly explain income variations though with different significant level. At 1 % significant level, the provincial yield index explains an extra 13 % and 11 % of income variations in the irrigated and rain-fed areas. The estimated yield perform relatively worse, explaining an extra 7 and 9 %.

Among weather indices constructed based on the fixed 6-zone crop cycles, CR performs the worst among all albeit its relative advantage in simplicity. While

[19] We reintroduce provincial subscript l here for clarification. The alternative approach of using pseudo provincial panel in estimating (1) controlling for provincial fixed effect would not take full advantage of these rich household data, as it would not yield household-level variations of basis risks.

[20] Ideally, we want to estimate provincial-specific β_l. The temporal observations per province are simply not enough with 6 years in Thai SES data.

explaining only 8 % of income in the irrigated areas, MD significantly explain up to 13 % of the income variations in the rain-fed areas, where cropping rely extensively on rainfall. ME explains only about 10 % of income variations in both areas. This raises question if it could serve as appropriate index for insuring flood losses in these areas. Combining MD and ME, we found that the two-peril index combination outperform others and explain 14 % and up to 19 % of income variations in irrigated and rain-fed areas respectively. Despite the added complexity, using dynamic crop cycles in determining index coverage does not add substantial improvement (if at all) to the explanation powers of the constructed weather indices.[21] Overall, the two-peril index combination MD + ME based on fixed zone-specific crop cycle thus strikes us as the potential basis risk-minimising underlying index for Thai rice contract.

How might hedging effectiveness of the optimal contracts based on these indices vary given the observed variations in household-level basis risks? The 6-year household data are limited in temporal variations, and so might under-represent the incidence of extreme events. Using the established relationship and distributions of household-level basis risk estimated in (16), we thus expand our data temporally and spatially by simulating 32-year income dynamics of representative households based on 32-year index data. In specific, for each year t from 1980 to 2011, 1,000 idiosyncratic shocks are randomly drawn for each province l from the province-specific empirical distributions $f(\varepsilon_{ilt})$ estimated using bootstrapping. Using the 32-year index data, provincial averaged household characteristics and provincial characteristics along with the estimated coefficients in (16), we then simulate 32-year income dynamics of 1,000 households in each province l from 1980 to 2011. Households' optimal coverage scales for various contracts and strike levels can then be estimated according to (7).[22] These then allow us to compute household-specific certainty equivalent values of consumption with and without various insurance contracts.

Figure 9.4 presents our results from 32-year income dynamics of 76,000 simulated households with assumed risk aversion $\theta = 3$ and actuarially fair contract prices. The two top panels compare averaged utility-based hedging effectiveness in term of increasing certainty equivalent values gained from obtaining insurance contract relative to no contract. The bottom two compare effectiveness based on simple variance reduction. Contracts are compared at the same level of payout frequency thus controlling for the same level of risk coverage and cost despite varying underlying risk distributions across indices and provinces.[23] Overall, both measures of hedging effectiveness of these actuarial fair priced contracts increase at

[21] Two-day cumulative rainfall exceeding 25 mm is chosen to trigger the start of each crop cycle, as it provides the best results comparing to others. This chosen trigger might not serve as an appropriate trigger for crop cycle just yet.

[22] As the estimated coefficients are specific at provincial level (not household), the simulated households' optimal coverage scales are specific at provincial level.

[23] And so we would expect that specific strike level for each payout frequency to be different across indices and provinces depending on their specific underlying distributions.

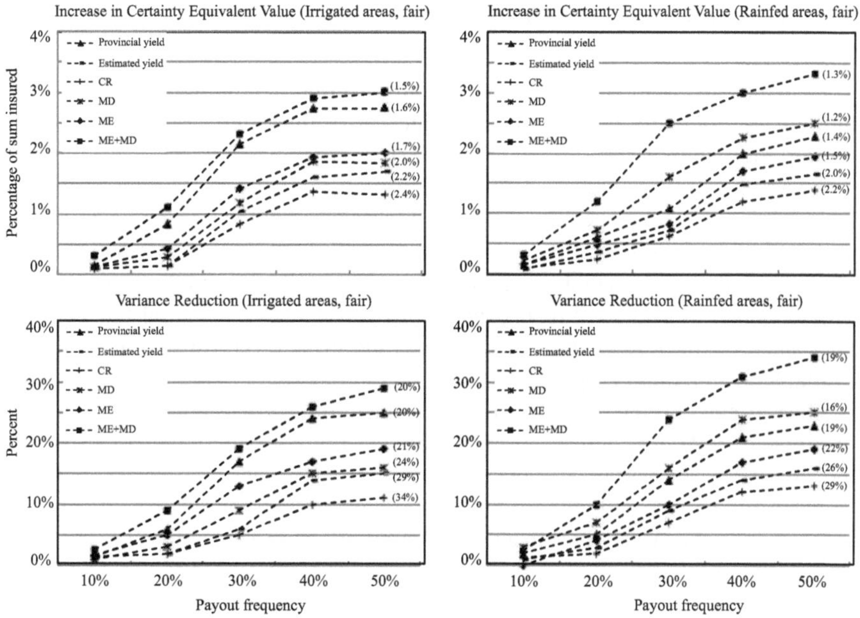

Fig. 9.4 Comparison of hedging effectiveness across optimal contracts. *Note*: Plots are averaged across 76,000 simulated households with CARA = 3. Average standard deviations around the estimated series in *parentheses*

a decreasing rate as payout frequency increases. Hedging effectiveness is very minimal for contracts with low payout frequency, e.g., of less than once every 5 years. This is due to the nature of systemic shocks on rice production, which tend to be less extreme but occur quite often. Variations of hedging effectiveness across households are high and vary across indices.

The optimal contracts with MD + ME index exhibit the highest hedging effectiveness in both measures. The provincial yield index, which was originally perceived to provide larger coverage for non-weather location systemic shock, performs almost as good as MD + ME in the irrigated zones but worse in the rain-fed zones. The simplest contracts based on CR perform the worst in all cases. On average, the optimal MD + ME contracts covering 1-in-3 year losses could result in 2.3 % and 2.5 % increase in households' average certainty equivalent values in irrigated and rain-fed areas respectively. This could imply that the rates that households are willing to pay for the contracts on top of the fair rates. Up to 20 % and 25 % reduction in consumption variance in irrigated and rain-fed areas are possible, respectively. The MD + ME contract also appears with the lowest variations in contract performance across households. These results are also robust with respect to other underlying risk aversion and premium loading assumptions.

2.6 Optimal Contract Designs

The two-peril MD + ME contract is thus chosen as appropriate basis risk minimising contracts for Thai rice production in this study. For each cropping season, MD index is constructed for the first 105 days and ME index for the 105–120 days of the cycle. The fixed period of insurable crop cycle for each province is drawn from the zone-specific patterns. A seasonal contract payout per insured hectare is thus a combination of payouts from the two indices optimally scaled with α^*_{MD} and α^*_{ME} estimated using the risk profiles of 76,000 simulated households. The top panel of Table 9.2 reports mean provincial scales, actuarial fair premium rates and probable maximum losses by zones and strike levels for seasonal contracts available for the main crop.

Overall, the optimal coverage scales for the rain-fed zones are larger than those of irrigated zones due to their larger income sensitivities to these indices, especially the MD index. Actuarial fair rates are, however, larger at all strike levels for the irrigated zones, especially the irrigated flood prone lower central zone due to larger index variations. Mean provincial fair premium rates vary from 12–16 % for 1-in-2 year coverage to 6–9 % for 1-in-3 year coverage to 2–5 % for 1-in-5 year coverage. The variations of mean provincial premium rates across zones also imply spatial variations of the exposures to floods and droughts. The extent of catastrophic risks of the provincial contracts can be shown by estimated MPLs at $VaR_{99\%}$. The PMLs range from as high as 68 % of total sum insured for 1-in-2 year coverage to 56 % for 1-in-3 year coverage.

2.7 Portfolio Pricing and Potentials for Risk Diversifications

Making the seasonal contracts available for both main and second crops in the irrigated areas could further allow for temporal risk pooling across seasons within a year. The bottom panel of Table 9.2 reflects these results. While the optimal coverage choices remain the same (as they are established from an annual model (16)), the fair rates and PMLs reduce slightly for the seasonal contracts available for both crops in the three 2-crop zones. A nationwide portfolio of provincial contracts is then constructed with provincial weights established from combining provincial optimal scales and provincial share of rice growing area. The bottom row in each panel of Table 9.2 reflects the spatial risk pooling benefits. Catastrophic layers of the insurable risk of the nationwide portfolio reduce for all strikes relative to those of the individual provincial contracts.

How might the annual portfolio payouts co-move with annual returns of various tradeable goods in capital, commodity, future and weather markets? We found no significant pair-wise relationship between the portfolio of Thai rice insurance and the key market indices, e.g., Thai Stock Index (SET), NASDAQ, and securities in commodity or future markets. Our key results are the significant and negative

Table 9.2 Optimal seasonal contracts and actuarial fair rates

Zone	Strike = 110 % (Avg. payout freq. = 50 %)				Strike = 120 % (Avg. payout freq. = 30 %)				Strike = 130 % (Avg. payout freq. = 20 %)			
	α*(MD)	α*(ME)	Fair rate	PML	α*(MD)	α*(ME)	Fair rate	PML	α*(MD)	α*(ME)	Fair rate	PML
Contracts available for main crop only												
Irrigated Lower Central	0.7	0.8	16 %	68 %	0.8	0.9	9 %	56 %	0.8	0.9	5 %	38 %
Irrigated Upper Central-North	0.6	0.8	16 %	65 %	0.7	0.8	8 %	52 %	0.7	0.8	4 %	35 %
Irrigated South	0.8	0.9	14 %	59 %	0.8	1.0	7 %	49 %	0.8	1.0	3 %	32 %
Rainfed Lower Central	1.1	0.9	15 %	57 %	1.1	0.9	7 %	46 %	1.1	0.9	3 %	27 %
Rainfed Northeast-North	1.1	0.9	12 %	48 %	1.1	0.9	6 %	37 %	1.1	0.9	2 %	23 %
Rainfed South	1.0	1.0	12 %	46 %	1.0	1.0	6 %	32 %	1.0	1.0	2 %	19 %
Nationwide	0.9	0.9	14 %	59 %	1.0	1.0	7 %	47 %	1.0	1.0	3 %	29 %
Contracts available for both main and second crops												
Irrigated Lower Central	0.7	0.8	15 %	64 %	0.8	0.9	8 %	53 %	0.8	0.9	4 %	33 %
Irrigated Upper Central-North	0.6	0.8	14 %	59 %	0.7	0.8	7 %	48 %	0.7	0.8	3 %	31 %
Irrigated South	0.8	0.9	12 %	57 %	0.8	1.0	5 %	48 %	0.8	1.0	2 %	28 %
Rainfed Lower Central	1.1	0.9	14 %	57 %	1.1	0.9	7 %	46 %	1.1	0.9	3 %	27 %
Rainfed Northeast-North	1.1	0.9	12 %	48 %	1.1	0.9	6 %	37 %	1.1	0.9	2 %	23 %
Rainfed South	1.0	1.0	12 %	46 %	1.0	1.0	6 %	32 %	1.0	1.0	2 %	19 %
Nationwide	0.9	0.9	12 %	55 %	1.0	1.0	6 %	43 %	1.0	1.0	2 %	27 %

Note: Payout frequencies are for both perils from MD + ME. Optimal scales are estimated at fair rates using annual data. Hence, they are similar for both contracts. Optimal scales, fair rates are averaged across provincial rates. PMLs are maximum provincial values. Prices are based on 1980–2011 historical burn rates. Price estimates from Monte Carlo simulations are comparable so omitted. The nationwide scales is averaged provincial scales weighted by shares of growing areas

Table 9.3 CAT bond linked with stop-loss reinsurance

	Capped (%)	100 % Stop-loss reinsurance on nationwide portfolio		
Required return	Principle losses	110 %	120 %	130 %
4 %	100 %	0.8412	0.8729	0.8898
	50 %	0.8823	0.8942	0.9064
6 %	100 %	0.8276	0.8511	0.8688
	50 %	0.8667	0.8818	0.8997
10 %	100 %	0.8096	0.8212	0.8389
	50 %	0.8532	0.8734	0.8935

Note: Bond prices are calculated assuming market rates of stop-loss reinsurance = fair rates + 3 % PML

relationships between the portfolio and various actively traded weather indices from around the world. While these results are based on low frequency (aggregated annually) data, they could signal potential diversifying values of Thai rice insurance portfolio in the portfolio of global weather risks.

2.8 *Risk Financing and Transfer*

The net payout position of risk aggregators, e.g., local insurers, appears with great exposures especially during the key catastrophic years. For example, the occurrence of both catastrophic drought and flood in 1995 result in net payouts of as high as 43 % of total sum insured for contracts with 1-in-3 year coverage (120 % strike). This signals the importance of international market risk transfers in ensuring the sustainability of the program.

Because the underlying risks are not as catastrophic as that of earthquakes, etc., with reasonable PMLs of about 49 % sum insured, we assume an optimistic case, where the potential market rates for these reinsurance contracts are established with an additional catastrophic load at 3 % of the estimated PMLs. This could reflect the potential costs of capital for reinsurer in holding necessary reserve or obtaining other risk financing instruments. At these potential market rates, we can illustrate some designs of a zero-coupon cat bond with principle payments linked with 100 % stop-loss reinsurance contracts for the nationwide portfolios.

Table 9.3 reports cat bond prices for various specifications of required rate of returns for investor, a cap (% of principle) that limit investor's principle loss if reinsurance contract triggers payouts and strike levels of nation wide insurance portfolio for the linked 100 % stop-loss reinsurance contracts. Cat bond with 100 % cap is thus riskier comparing to that with 50 % cap since an investor would be exposed to losing all of his/her principle should the catastrophic events triggered reinsurance payout. The required rates of return are set at 4, 6 and 10 % translating into risk premiums between 2.93 and 8.93 % at the current LIBOR rate of about 1.07 %.[24] Comparing with other existing cat bonds (with relatively more catastrophic underlying risks) and the Mexican cat bond with as low as 2.35 % premium above LIBOR, it seems this chosen range of risk premiums is sufficiently representative of spreads required by investors in the market (Froot 1999). We note that the total return realised by investors when the bond is not triggered is always higher than the required return used in computing bond prices. The difference between the two presents the added premium associated with the catastrophic risk.[25] The bond prices thus decrease (hence the bond yields increase) with riskiness of the underlying reinsurance contract, the cap value and the required rates of return.

These results are, however, only for illustration of how Thailand's nationwide rice insurance portfolio might be securitised and transferred to international capital market. The actual potential of cat bond will also rely on the costs associated with securitising the contract relative to other means. The key feature that deviates this cat bond from others is its coverage of less extreme shocks relative to other earthquake- or hurricane-linked products in the market.

2.9 How Might This Nationwide Rice Index Insurance Program Work?

Our results so far imply that (1) the basis risk minimising contract with two-peril MD + ME index could provide up to 35 % reduction in the insured's consumption variance, (2) households are willing to pay between 2 and 4 % of total sum insured on top of the fair rates for contracts with 1-in-2 year to 1-in-3 year payout frequency, (3) it could be cost effective to price provincial seasonal contracts as part of a pooled nationwide portfolio and (4) opportunities could exist in transferring portfolio risks to international markets through some forms of illustrated reinsurance and securitisation. We now illustrate the potential market rates, how the designed program and public support can be integrated in the risk financing in order to enhance market viability, and more importantly, how the program could benefit farmers, agricultural lenders and government.

Table 9.4 reports potential market rates for the provincial contracts priced as part of the nationwide portfolio under various market arrangements. With a working assumption that the additive catastrophic load for a contract equals to the market

[24] LIBOR rate as of May 30, 2012 from www.global-rate.com.

[25] For example, an investor who purchased a cat bond with required return of 4 %, 50 % cap with 110 % strike at the price = USD0.8823 and received USD1 principle back 1 year later when reinsurance is not triggered, would realise a total compounded return of 12.4 %. The rate can be interpreted as including a risk free LIBOR rate of 1.07 %, 2.93 % premium associated with bond default and other risks not associated with the insured reinsurance risk, and an additional 8.4 % premium associated with this catastrophic risk associated with the reinsurance.

Table 9.4 Potential market pricings and arrangements for nationwide index insurance

		Market Arrangements							
		Potential market rates		With Public Financing of Tailed Risk beyond Capped Payout at					
				20 %		30 %		40 %	
Strike	Payout freq.	Mean	SD	Mean	SD	Mean	SD	Mean	SD
110 %	50 %	17.8 %	(4.6 %)	11.9 %	(3.1 %)	14.3 %	(3.3 %)	16.9 %	(3.7 %)
120 %	30 %	8.8 %	(3.7 %)	**4.2** %	(**2.3** %)	**6.4** %	(**3.1** %)	8.8 %	(3.7 %)
130 %	20 %	**3.1** %	(**2.1** %)	3.1 %	(2.1 %)	3.1 %	(2.1 %)	**3.1** %	(**2.1** %)
		Increase in certainty equivalent value, $CE^{insured}$-$CE^{uninsured}$ (% sum insured per season)							
Low risk aversion (θ = 1)		0.1 %		3.6 %		1.4 %		0.1 %	
Med. risk aversion (θ = 3)		0.2 %		4.2 %		2.0 %		0.2 %	
High risk aversion (θ = 5)		0.4 %		4.9 %		2.7 %		0.4 %	
		Simulated impacts of insurance on households, agricultural loans and government (θ=3)							
Net income for consumption (*No I = 25,314 baht/year*)		24,275 (28,978)		33,052 (24,464)		31,278 (26,464)		24,275 (28,978)	
5-years loan outstanding (*No I = 90 % 1-year income*)		39 % (57 %)		0 % (0 %)		9 % (17 %)		39 % (57 %)	
Input loan default rate (*No I = 47 % per year*)		21 % (12 %)		0 % (0 %)		8 % (4 %)		21 % (12 %)	
Government spending (*No I = 0 million baht*)		0 (0)		843 (3,249)		297 (1,580)		0 (0)	

Note: The potential market rates = fair rates + market rates for 100 % stop-loss reinsurance. Reinsurance market rates = fair rates + 3 % PML. Payouts are capped as % of total sum insured. Those in *bold* are welfare maximising contract strike for each market arrangement. CE and impacts of insurance are for the welfare maximising coverage. Results vary across provinces. Mean reported with standard deviations in parentheses rate for 100 % stop-loss reinsurance coverage for that contract, our pricing results in an additional 50 % mark up from the fair rates.[26] As catastrophic loads drive high mark-up rates, insurable risk can then be layered so that complementary public financing of tailed risk beyond some capped indemnity payouts from insurers could result in reduction of market rates. As shown in Table 9.4, when insurer's payouts are capped at 30 % of total sum insured, market rates for the 1-in-2 year and 1-in-3 year contracts reduce dramatically to their fair rates (and even below their fair rates for a cap of 20 %).[27]

We now base an analysis on 32-year income dynamics of 76,000 simulated households with welfare maximising contract strike level under each market arrangement. The associated increases in certainty equivalent consumption are also reported for farmers with low, medium and high levels of risk aversion. The 1-in-5 year contract appears optimal under fully market-based index insurance program. But with low risk coverage, its utility-based hedging effectiveness is low but still positive, implying that on average households are willing to buy this contract at the market rate and contribute up to 0.4 % of total sum insured on top of the current rate. With government financing indemnity payouts beyond 20–30 % caps, the welfare maximising strike shifts to 1-in-3 year contract. These market arrangements also result in larger hedging effectiveness through lower insurance prices and larger resulting optimal risk coverage.

Which market arrangement is appropriate for this nationwide index insurance program? We explore this further by simulating the potential impacts on farmers, agricultural loan portfolios and government of these market arrangements for the nationwide index insurance program, as well as the existing program. To do so, several assumptions are made. First, we assume that all 76,000 simulated farmers are clienteles of BAAC. Each year, they take out a loan to finance total input cost and to obtain insurance coverage for income from all cultivated rice crops (one or two). Total production income is then used to pay back the loan. From SES data, total input cost is assumed to be 49 % of averaged provincial crop production income, which also vary across provinces. Household is assumed to pay back their loan as much as is feasible—the maximum repayment is reached when net income available for consumption drop to zero.

With these assumptions, household's production income available for consumption per hectare per year thus reflects total income after receiving insurance payout

[26] This mark up is comparable to other existing index insurance programs in other part of the world. These market rates are comparable to other pilot projects for rice insurance in Thailand. For example, 4.64 % rate changed for recently piloted deficit rainfall index insurance covering only drought peril for only the main rice production in Khon Kaen province during July–September.

[27] Because the extreme layers of risk are not so catastrophic, capping at higher level beyond 40 % of sum insured will result in more or less the same effects to market premium rates. The market premium rates for 130 % strike contract do not change with payout caps, as the contracts' maximum payout rates are already well below the caps.

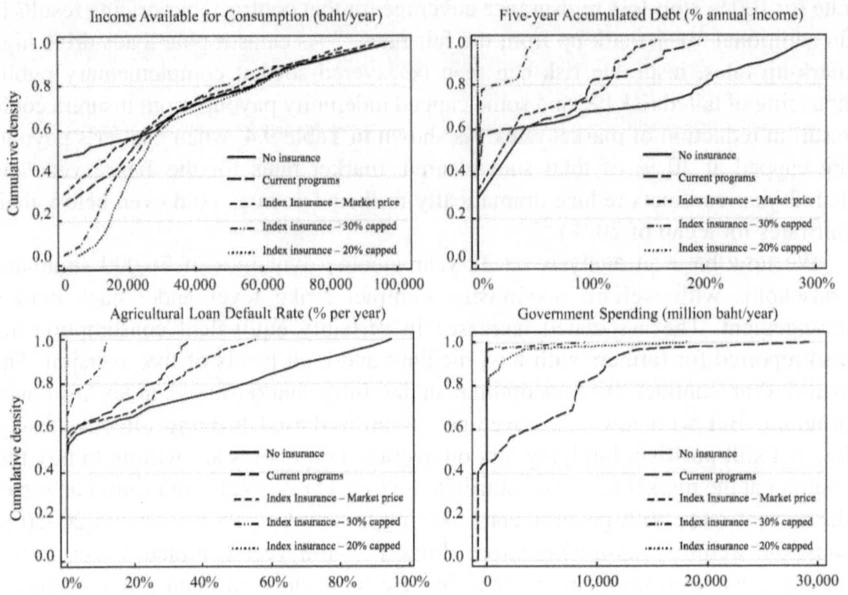

Fig. 9.5 Simulated impacts of various nationwide index insurance arrangements. *Note*: Cumulative densities based on 32-year dynamic data of 76,000 simulated households in 76 provinces nationwide

and netting out all the accumulated loans outstanding up to that year: The nominal interest rate r is at 6.75 % per year. From SES data, we assume that household cultivates 1.92 ha of rice paddy each year.

Based on 32-year dynamic data of 76,000 simulated households, Fig. 9.5 plots cumulative densities of income available for household consumption, 5-year accumulated debt position realised at any given year, BAAC's annual loan default rates and annual government spending[28] under various schemes. The bottom panel of Table 9.4 also reports means and SDs of these impacts. With no disaster insurance market and government support, there is about 50 % probabilities that income available for consumption of Thai rice farming households could collapse to zero. Household's 5-year accumulated debt realised in any given year is almost always positive with an average of 90 % of annual production income. This outstanding debt could be as high as 300 % of average annual income in any given year. And BAAC's loan default rate is estimated at 47 % per year on average. The existing program with a combination of government's disaster relief and subsidised

[28] We rescale the simulated representative sample to represent the current 9.2 ha of growing areas nationwide. The current sample represents 63 similar households (9,200,000/(76,000 × 1.92)).

insurance[29] results in favourable distributional impacts that almost always first order stochastically dominate those of the baseline. The key drawback, however, is the tremendous government budget exposure, which stands at an average of 8,890 million baht per year, and could reach 29,930 million baht in some key years.

The market driven index insurance program without government support could also result in dramatically improvement in distributional impacts relative to the baseline case of no market and government support. The probabilities of zero income available for consumption, the averaged long-term debt accumulation and BAAC's loan default rates reduce by half and also with great reduction in variations. These distributional impacts are, however, relatively smaller on average but not necessarily first order stochastically dominated by those of the existing program. This is because, on the one hand, farmers pay higher market prices for market-based index insurance product that covers smaller sets of disasters relative to the existing product. On the other hand, compensations from index insurance (based on provincial averaged income) tend to be larger than those of the existing program (based on 30 % of input cost) when the contract is triggered. With comparable impacts but no cost to the government, this purely market driven index insurance product could be appealing as one of the risk management tools for Thai rice farmers.

These distributional impacts further improve substantially for the index insurance program with integrated public financing of tailed risk beyond insurer's payout caps. At 30 % (20 %) payout cap, the resulting lower insurance prices and larger optimal risk coverage lead to more than 80 % (almost 100 %) reduction in probabilities of zero income available for consumption, long-term accumulated debt and BAAC's loan default rates relative to the baseline. The required public financing of these tailed risks are also substantially smaller in means and variations comparing to those required in the existing program. A case for public financing of tailed risk for Thailand's nationwide index insurance program thus could be strong. First, these public–private market arrangements are no doubt superior in both potential impacts on households and BAAC loan and on government's budget exposure relative to the existing program. And second, their distributional impacts are substantially larger than those under purely market-driven program.

[29] Without actual payout statistics, we assume that under the existing program, if household's actual crop income falls below its 1-in-3 year trigger level, they will be paid 3,787 baht per hectare (606 bath/rai) under disaster relief program and an extra 6,944 baht per hectare (1,111 baht/rai) if they pay for disaster insurance coverage at a subsidised price of 375 baht per hectare (60 baht/rai). We believe this assumption is reasonable, as (1) the program covers larger sets of disasters and (2) it makes payout conditional on government's declaration of disasters at very local levels with required actual loss verification. Because government disaster insurance is offered at highly subsidised price, our welfare optimisation implies that all representative risk-averse households will purchase full coverage. Hence 100 % insurance penetration rate is used. Note that we abstract from all the incentive problems associated with existing program that could result in larger exposure on government spending.

3 Conclusions and Implications for the Rest of Asia

This chapter laid out why index based risk transfer products could be attractive as a means to address important insurance market imperfections that have precluded the emergence and sustainability of formal insurance markets in developing countries. It then illustrated how disaggregated and spatiotemporal rich sets of household and disaster data, commonly available in developing countries, could be used to design and analyse nationwide, scalable disaster index insurance program for rice farmers in Thailand.

Relative to the direct measures of provincial yield and the estimated yield based on climate-crop modelling, we found that objectively measured weather data could be carefully constructed as basis risk minimising indices for index insurance contract. Objectively measured remote sensing data also proved to be useful in controlling for heterogeneous cropping patterns across larger geographical areas nationwide. The transparency of these weather indices and control measures along with their spatiotemporal availability could hold further advantages in scaling up contract designs to wider settings.

Using household level data in estimating basis risk and so in simulating contracts' hedging effectiveness, we found the resulting contract performance, optimal contract scales and pricings to vary largely across provinces and households. Contract designed at the provincial level—the most micro level given our representative data—was thus considered. Overall, the optimal provincial contract based on basis risk minimising combination of moving dry spell and moving excessive rain spell indices could result in up to 25 % reduction in the variations of household's income available for consumption. Simple cumulative rainfall, widely used in marketable contracts worldwide, however, appeared with the lowest performance. This raised concerns on the extent of basis risk associated with currently available contracts.

We found evidence of temporal and spatial diversification benefits, as we scaled insurance portfolio to cover all provinces nationwide and to cover the second crop grown among farmers in the irrigated areas each year. Thus return to scale in term of cost effective portfolio pricing can thus be achieved as part of nationwide, multi-seasonal coverage insurance program. Our finds could imply, on the one hand, that local risk aggregators could diversify their portfolio risk with appropriate hedging portfolio of global weather indices. On the other hand, tradable security linked with Thai nationwide insurance portfolio, e.g., cat bond, could be appealing in the international market as diversifiable security in various diversifying global portfolios.

The transparency of these weather indices and control measures in fact could further promote the possibility of cost effective risk transfers in the international market. We thus designed the corresponding reinsurance contracts and cat bonds, and illustrated their potentials and how these might be useful as risk transfer instruments. The key distinction of our cat bonds from others is the coverage of relatively higher frequency but lower impact losses from floods and droughts, comparing to other earthquake- or hurricane-linked products (cf. Skees et al. 2008).

Bringing all the results together, we asked what might appropriate market arrangement be to ensure sustainable implementation of this nationwide insurance program? Using disaggregated spatiotemporal rich data, we simulated the potential impacts on household welfare, agricultural loan portfolio and government of this nationwide program under various market arrangements relative to the current program. The purely market driven program was found to result in more than 50 % reductions in probabilities that household consumption collapsing to zero, in means and variations of 5-year accumulated debt and BAAC's annual loan default rates. As these impacts are comparable to those of the current program, albeit no budget exposure to the government, the market-driven program thus already proved as one of the effective disaster risk management tools for the setting. Properly layering insurable nationwide risk, we further found public financing of tailed risk beyond the 20–30 % capped to insurer's payout rates to result in substantial reduction in market premium rates. These in turn resulted in up to twice the impacts of the purely market-driven program, though with substantial smaller budget exposures to the government relative to the current government program. There could thus be a strong case for public financing of tailed risk in enhancing development values and market viability of Thailand's nationwide index insurance program.

How might this nationwide insurance program be implemented? An insurance indemnity pool of the nationwide index insurance contract could be created to allow local insurers to diversify their risks and contribute capital to the reserve pool, from where indemnity payments can be drawn. Reinsurance could potentially be acquired when indemnity payments exceed the pool but for the risk up to some appropriate capped level. Government could then finance the low frequency but catastrophic tailed risk through various options, e.g., offering complementary disaster insurance coverage for this tailed risk, providing the insurers direct coverage or financing of the transfers of this tailed risk.

The design and market arrangement of this nationwide index insurance for Thai rice farmers thus deviate largely from the current program. First, unlike direct premium subsidisation, public financing of the tailed risk does not distort market prices. The capped commercialized contracts are still sold at their market rates and the rates differ across provinces with different risk profiles. This prevents the potential adverse selection problem, likely to occur under the current scheme with one price for all. Second, the public financing of the tailed risk provides complementary, rather than substituting, coverage. This would not crowd out private demand for insurance, especially for the risk layer that should appropriately be absorbed by the households and market. Third, the government's budget exposure to financing of the tailed risk could be insured through some forms of IBRTPs. This, in turn, could enhance sustainability of the program. And more importantly, the key advantages of these index insurance design relative to the current loss-based insurance program are (1) relatively lower transaction cost, especially in loss verifications, (2) relatively lower adverse selection and moral hazard, (3) the contract still preserves insured household's incentive to take good care of their farms and so to adjust their cropping patterns to avoid risk since the indemnity is regardless of their actions and (4) contract could potentially make timely payout as verification of these indices are in near real time.

Various limitations of the current study are worth noting with the goal to stimulate future required research ideas. First, our analyses are based on simulated rainfall data, not the actual data observed at various stations. Despite its relative advantage in the relatively richer spatial distribution, simulated data need to be verified with actual weather experienced at the micro level. Efforts are also underway in many developing countries, including Thailand, in constructing appropriate gridded data from observed station data in order to improve spatial distribution of the station data. Second, the current analysis mapped the relatively higher spatial resolution weather data with household data at provincial level, due to the lack of sub-district locators in the SES data. Efforts should be made in matching weather or disaster variables at the most micro level possible. Third, various spatiotemporal available remote sensing products, could have high potential in improving the measures and performance of the underlying indices. Efforts are underway in using these products to detect inter and intra year variations of rice growing areas, stage of crop growth, paddy losses and the extent of natural disasters (see Rakwatin et al. 2012, for example). And fourth, the observed increases in frequency and intensity of natural disasters imply the need for incorporating simulated impacts of climate change in the modelling and pricing of insurable risks.

The analytical framework as well as the empirical methodology proposed in this chapter should be replicable in other settings and in other developing Asian countries, where exposures to covariate natural disaster risks remain uninsured. The data sets used in this chapter should well be available in other Asian countries. The extended time series of spatiotemporal rich weather data as well as remotely sensed data are available worldwide at high quality and low cost.[30] And the high quality, national representative household dynamic welfare data similar to Thai SES data should well be available in the key Asian countries. Some examples include repeated cross-sectional household data from Indonesia National Socioeconomic Survey (SUSENAS), available every year from 1990 to 2010, from Vietnam Household Living Standards Survey (VHLSS), available every 2 years from 2002 to 2010.

This chapter offers an optimistic view of the potentially optimal designs, market viability and impacts of IBRTPs designed at a large nationwide scale. These results could deviate largely from actual implementation in the real world. At least, four key implementation challenges are worth noting. First, it could be difficult to establish informed effective demand among clientele with relatively low financial literacy in developing countries. Second, the presence of large basis risk could still

[30] Gridded weather data from WMO stations across Asia are available online at NOAA Global Daily Climatology Network (daily, 1900–present). Various satellite imagery Normalised Difference Vegetation Index (NDVI) available from NASA MODIS at 250 m resolution (15-day; 2000–present) and from NOAA AVHRR at 8 km resolution (10-day; 1982–2000). RADARSAT-1 and RADARDAT-2 with cloud-penetrating SAR sensor at 25 m resolution (every 15 day, 1995–present) have been increasingly used for flood monitoring.

be possible in some coverage areas. Third, cost of marketing and delivery mechanisms of the contract could still be high in developing countries. And fourth, the targeted clientele could have financial constraints in paying insurance premium.

These key challenges thus place significant implications on how index insurance program should be implemented in developing country settings. Should the insurance contracts be offered as a stand-alone or linked with other financial products? Linking with other existing financial products might resolve high implementation costs and relax some financial constraints among targeted clientele. Should the program be established at the micro, meso or macro levels? Extended investment in education, training and extension tools are thus critical if contracts are sold directly to households. At the meso level, rural banks like BAAC could obtain insurance contract to insure their loan portfolio, so that they can then lend insured loans to households. Groups and cooperatives can obtain coverage for their group saving or credit schemes. One testable assumption is that group-sharing network could potentially smooth out individual basis risk associated with index insurance contracts. Necessary randomised impact evaluation research has been launched around the world in attempt to address these questions. Extended discussion of key implementation challenges of IBRTPs in developing countries to data are summarised in Miranda et al. (2012) and IFAD and WFP (2010). Overall, the challenges are significant, but the considerable prospective gains associated with IBRTPs for enhancing development of sustainable disaster insurance programs in developing countries would seem to justify considerable new effort in this area.

References

Barnett, B. J., Barrett, C. B., & Skees, J. R. (2008). Poverty traps and index-based risk transfer products. *World Development, 36*(10), 1766–1785.

Barrett, C. B., Barnett, B. J., Carter, M. R., Chantarat, S., Hansen, J. W., Mude, A. G., et al. (2007). *Poverty traps and climate risk: Limitations and opportunities of index-based risk financing* (IRI Technical report 07-02). IRI, New York: Columbia University.

Chantarat, S., Barrett, C. B., Janvilisri, T., Mudsri, S., Niratisayakul, C., & Poonswad, P. (2011). Index insurance for pro-poor conservation of Hornbills in Thailand. *Proceedings of the National Academy of Sciences United States of America, 108*(34), 13951–13956.

Chantarat, S., Barrett, C. B., Mude, A. G., & Turvey, C. G. (2007). Using weather index insurance to improve drought response for famine prevention. *American Journal of Agricultural Economics, 89*(5), 1262–1268.

Chantarat, S., Mude, A. G., Barrett, C. B., & Carter. M. R. (2013). Designing index-based livestock insurance for managing asset risk in Northern Kenya. *Journal of Risk and Insurance 80*(1): 205–237.

Chantarat, S., Turvey, C. G., Mude, A. G., & Barrett, C. B. (2008). Improving humanitarian response to slow-onset disasters using famine-indexed weather derivatives. *Agricultural Finance Review, 68*(1), 169–195.

Chinvanno, S. (2011). *Developing regional climate change scenario and dilemma in climate change adaptation planning*. Bangkok, Thailand: Mimeo, Southeast Asia System for Analysis, Research and Training (START) Regional Center.

Clarke, D. J., Mahul, O., & Verma, N. (2012). *Index based crop insurance product design and ratemaking* (World Bank Policy Working Paper 5986). Washington DC: World Bank.

Cummins, J. D., & Mahul, O. (2009). *Catastrophe risk financing in developing countries: Principles for public intervention*. Washington DC: The World Bank.

Froot, K. A. (Ed.). (1999). *The financing of catastrophic risk*. Chicago/London: The University of Chicago Press.

Gaiha, R., & Thapa, G. (2006). *Natural disasters, vulnerability and mortalities – A cross-country analysis* (International Fund for Agricultural Development Working Paper). Rome: IFAD.

Hazell, P. B., Pomareda, C., & Valdes, A. (1986). *Crop insurance for agricultural development: Issues and experience*. Baltimore: The Johns Hopkins University Press.

IFRCRCS (International Federation of Red Cross and Red Crescent Societies). (2011). *World disaster report 2011*. Bloomfield, CT: Kumarian Press, Inc.

Intergovernmental Panel on Climate Change. (2007). *Climate change: Impacts, adaptation and vulnerability. Contribution of Working Group II to the 4th Assessment Report of the IPCC*.

Isvilanonda, S. (2009). *Dynamic change of rice production in Thailand*. Bangkok: Lerd Sin Inc.

Mahul, O., & Skees, J. R. (2007). *Managing agricultural risk at the country level: The case of index- based livestock insurance in Mongolia* (Policy Research Working Paper 4325). Washington DC: The World Bank.

Miranda, M. J., Farrin, K., & Romero-Aguilar, R. (2012). *Weather index insurance for developing countries* (Working Paper). Ohio: Ohio State University.

Pannangpetch, K. (2009). *Impacts of global warming on rice, sugarcane, cassava and maize production in Thailand* (Project report. 31 October 2009). Bangkok: The Thailand Research Fund.

Rakwatin, P., Sansena, T., Marjang, N., & Rungsipanich, A. (2012). *Using multi-temporal remote sensing data to estimate 2011 flood area and volume over Chao Phraya river basin, Thailand* (Working Paper). Bangkok: GISTDA.

Ramirez, O. A., Misra, S. K., & Nelson, J. (2003). Efficient estimation of agricultural time series models with nonnormal dependent variables. *American Journal of Agricultural Economics, 85* (4), 1029–1040.

Siamwalla, A., & Na Ranong W. (1980). *Rice handbook* (published manuscript in Thai).

Skees, J. R., Barnett, B. J., & Murphy, A. G. (2008). Creating insurance markets for natural disaster risk in lower income countries: The potential role for securitisation. *Agricultural Finance Review, 68*(1), 151–167.

Swiss Re. (2011a). *Natural catastrophes and man-made disasters in 2011*, Sigma [online]. http://www.swissre.com/sigma/.

Swiss Re. (2011b). *Filling stomachs worldwide with agriculture risk transfer solutions* (Economist Intelligence Unit - Executive Briefing, Singapore Management University. 16 July 2011). Singapore: SMU.

Thailand Fiscal Policy Office. (2010). *Developing a financial instrument for farmers: A case of weather index-based insurance for agriculture in Thailand*. Thailand: Ministry of Finance.

Tucker, C. J., Pinzon, J. E., Brown, M. E., Slayback, D. A., Pak, E. W., Mahoney, R., et al. (2005). An extended AVHRR 8-km NDVI data set compatible with MODIS and SPOT vegetation NDVI data. *International Journal of Remote Sensing, 26*(14), 4485–4498.

WFP, & IFAD. (2010). *Potential for scale and sustainability in weather index insurance*. Rome: IFAD & WFP.

World Bank. (2006). *Earth observation based multi peril crop index development for agricultural insurance– Project development study*. Japan: PASCO Corporation.

Chapter 10
On the Design of Regional Insurance Markets for East Asia

Hiroyuki Nakata

1 Introduction

East Asia has been hit numerous times by catastrophic natural disasters over its long history. In 2011 alone, the region suffered from the 3/11 great earthquake, tsunami and nuclear meltdowns in Japan and massive flooding in Thailand. Whilst it would be impossible to prevent the occurrence of a natural disaster itself, every effort should be made to prevent and limit the level of damages natural disasters could inflict. Nevertheless, some damage or loss from natural disasters is inevitable—especially for catastrophes, which implies the need for an insurance mechanism.

Catastrophe insurance or insurance for natural disasters, however, is not very common in practice. The fact that a catastrophe typically incurs a macro risk invalidates the application of the strong law of large numbers, on which a typical insurance mechanism is based. This is the reason why catastrophe insurance is often backed or indirectly supplied by the government. Nevertheless, there is evidence that the demand for catastrophe insurance is often weak, even though the insurance premium is apparently set favourably to the (potential) buyers.

This chapter examines the key issues in designing a regional insurance scheme for catastrophes or natural disasters. The presumed target of the possible insurance schemes examined in the chapter is the household sector, rather than the corporate sector. Nevertheless, many issues raised in this chapter would remain valid for insurance schemes that target the corporate sector. In the analysis, I apply the theoretical explanation for the weak demand for catastrophe insurance given by Nakata et al. (2010). The key observation of Nakata et al. (2010) is that rare events by definition take place very infrequently, which implies that no robust probability estimate of a rare event would be readily warranted by empirical or scientific evidence. Thus, diverse probability beliefs would be inevitable, which in turn

H. Nakata (✉)
The University of Tokyo, Tokyo, Japan
e-mail: hnakata@stanfordalumni.org

D.P. Aldrich et al. (eds.), *Resilience and Recovery in Asian Disasters*, Risk, Governance and Society 18, DOI 10.1007/978-4-431-55022-8_10

results in a weak demand for catastrophe insurance. Based on this observation, I compare several insurance schemes that differ in terms of the payment structure and also regarding the subscription structure. To be more specific, I compare conventional indemnity insurance and index insurance with respect to the payment structure, whilst I also compare direct subscription by households, subscription by local governments, and subscription by national governments with respect to the subscription structure.

Allowing for diverse beliefs, the welfare evaluation of a regional insurance scheme is not straightforward. Because the standard Pareto optimality is based on the ex ante preferences of the agents that govern their decisions, the standard Pareto optimality is inherently an ex ante criterion. With diverse beliefs, agents would be making 'incorrect' decisions or 'mistakes', although such 'mistakes' are not understood as mistakes a priori by the agents themselves. If we know the true probability, then we may still be able to evaluate how agents are making mistakes, and consequently we may evaluate the insurance schemes with respect to the true probability. However, it is rather unreasonable to assume such knowledge, especially for rare events.

Thus, the use of the standard Pareto criterion calls for a significant value judgement, since ex ante preferences do not capture regrets or pleasure arising from the outcomes of decisions made in accord with incorrect subjective beliefs. Such arguments can be found in Diamond (1967) and Drèze (1970), while Starr (1973) introduces the notion of ex post optimality, which is based on realised allocations rather than prospects of future allocations, with which the standard ex ante optimality is defined. Starr (1973) shows that the two concepts do not coincide generically, when beliefs are heterogeneous. Hammond (1981) introduces the notion of the ex post social welfare optimum, which is based on an expected social welfare function, where the expectation is with respect to the social planner's probability (or the social probability) rather than with respect to the subjective beliefs of the agents. Hammond (1981) shows that the ex post social welfare optimum does not coincide with the usual ex ante social welfare optimum when the subjective beliefs are heterogeneous. However, the choice of the social probability for the ex post social welfare function is not trivial. Thus, it is important to identify the conditions under which a reasonably high level of ex post social welfare can be assured, even when we do not know the social probabilities.

In this regard, the absence of personal catastrophe states for everyone would assure a reasonably high level of ex post social welfare, as Nakata (2013) shows in a dynamic general equilibrium model with diverse beliefs.[1] Note that the existence of a personal catastrophe state is not very damaging from the ex ante point of view if the agent believes that the probability of such a state is extremely low, which implies that an agent may choose to allow for the emergence of personal catastrophe states.

[1] The term a 'personal catastrophe state' describes a state in which an agent is left with an extremely low level of wealth.

Based on the above observations, this paper therefore compares the various insurance schemes from the viewpoint of the ex post social welfare. In particular, I examine conventional indemnity insurance and index insurance. In doing so, this chapter pays attention to the subscription structure, i.e. direct subscriptions by households, subscriptions by local governments, and subscriptions by national governments.

2 Insurance Demand Under Diverse Beliefs

This section first reviews the three stylised facts regarding demand for catastrophe insurance based on aggregate data. Then, I show that the willingness-to-pay for insurance is almost linear in the subjective loss probability when the loss probability is very small, by numerical examples. By following Nakata et al. (2010), I then show that subjective loss probabilities may well be very diverse and unstable for rare loss events, which in conjunction with the almost linear property of the willingness-to-pay, provides a consistent explanation for the three stylised facts.

2.1 *Stylised Facts About Catastrophe Insurance*

It is well reported that there are some anomalies regarding the demand for insurance that appear to be incompatible with the standard expected utility framework. First, there is evidence that insurance for catastrophes, such as earthquakes or flooding, is not very widely purchased, even though many policies against catastrophes are subsidised by governments to keep the premiums favourable to the buyers, e.g. earthquake insurance in Japan and the National Flood Insurance Program (NFIP) in the United States.[2] In contrast, it is widely known that commonly sold insurance policies such as travel insurance, home insurance and medical insurance, have a substantial mark-up. Yet, many people voluntarily elect to purchase such policies. Hence, insurance for catastrophes is purchased with less frequency compared to insurance for moderate risk (e.g. travel insurance), even if the premium is often set more favourably for catastrophe insurance (stylised fact 1). Furthermore, (a) market penetration is much lower in areas that have historically been less frequently hit by catastrophes, even if the premiums are adjusted to reflect the lower frequencies (stylised fact 2), and (b) market penetration jumps up immediately after a catastrophe (stylised fact 3).[3]

---

[2] Kunreuther et al. (1978) provide one of the pioneering works that reported this "anomaly." Also, see Michel-Kerjan (2010) for the history of NFIP.

[3] See for instance, Dixon et al. (2006), and Browne and Hoyt (2000).

The above three stylised facts present difficulties in designing a catastrophe insurance scheme that would enjoy a wide subscription. Although it appears that these facts are in contradiction with the model of insurance demand based on the standard expected utility framework, the apparent incompatibility becomes less straightforward allowing for diverse subjective beliefs. In what follows, I introduce a simplified version of the framework by Nakata et al. (2010), which attempts to explain the three stylised facts above simultaneously within the subjective expected utility framework.[4]

2.2 *The Willingness-to-Pay for Catastrophe Insurance*

Consider an agent who is facing some uncertainty. I assume for simplicity that there are only two states, state 1 (the no-loss state) and state 2 (the loss state), with $x > 0$ being the loss in state 2. Let W denote the initial wealth of the agent. Then, the final wealth is W in state 1 and $W - x$ in state 2 when there is no insurance.

Assume that the agent is a risk-averse expected utility maximizer, who makes some probability estimate of the two states; π is the agent's subjective probability of the no loss state. Now, assume that any loss up to $b\,(\leq x)$ can be covered by insurance with a premium of ρ_b. With this insurance, the final wealth becomes $W - \rho_b$ in state 1 and $W - x + b - \rho_b$. Agent h purchases the insurance if

$$\pi \cdot u(W) + (1 - \pi) \cdot u(W - x) \leq \pi \cdot u(W - \rho_b) + (1 - \pi) \cdot u(W - x + b - \rho_b),$$

while the agent is indifferent between purchasing and not purchasing when an equality holds. This observation leads us to define the agent's willingness-to-pay for this insurance as $\hat{\rho}_b$, satisfying the following equation:

$$\pi \cdot u(W) + (1 - \pi) \cdot u(W - x) = \pi \cdot u(W - \hat{\rho}_b) + (1 - \pi) \cdot u(W - x + b - \hat{\rho}_b)\hat{\rho}_b.$$

The willingness-to-pay is almost linear in the loss probability $(1 - \pi)$ when $(1 - \pi)$ is very small as the following numerical example illustrates.

Example: Effects of Loss Probability and Degree of Risk Aversion Suppose an agent possesses a property of 100, but it is subject to a damage of 30 with subjective probability π. I assume that the loss can be fully insured (i.e. $x = b = 30$), and the willingness-to-pay for such an insurance policy $\hat{\rho}^{\pi}$ is computed by

$$\hat{\rho}^{\pi} := 100 - u^{-1}[\pi \cdot u(100) + (1 - \pi) \cdot u(70)].$$

[4] Some existing studies based on the standard expected utility framework explained the anomalies, e.g. Brookshire et al. (1985) and Kunreuther and Pauly (2004).

Table 10.1 Effects of loss probability and degree of risk aversion

$1-\pi$	10^{-1}	10^{-2}	10^{-3}	10^{-4}	10^{-5}	10^{-6}
$\gamma=1$	3.50	3.56×10^{-1}	3.57×10^{-2}	3.57×10^{-3}	3.57×10^{-4}	3.57×10^{-5}
$\gamma=2$	4.11	4.27×10^{-1}	4.28×10^{-2}	4.29×10^{-3}	4.29×10^{-4}	4.29×10^{-5}
$\gamma=3$	4.83	5.16×10^{-1}	5.20×10^{-2}	5.20×10^{-3}	5.20×10^{-4}	5.20×10^{-5}

Table 10.1 reports the values of $\hat{\rho}^{\pi}$ for different values of loss probability π and those of the degrees of relative risk aversion γ for a power utility $u(w)=w^{1-\gamma}/(1-\gamma)$.

Note that a catastrophe is typically rare, but causes a huge damage. In the example, this is characterised by a very small true loss probability $(1-\pi^*)$. The trouble is that no one really knows the true probability π^* even if we may all agree that $(1-\pi^*)$ is 'very small'. However, both 1 in 1 million (or 10^{-6}) and 1 in 10,000 (or 10^{-4}) are small probabilities, yet the willingness-to-pay for the latter is approximately 100 times of the former, regardless of the degree of relative risk aversion in the above example. Nakata et al. (2010) focuses on this feature to explain the above three stylised facts within the subjective expected utility framework. In what follows, I briefly explain the argument of Nakata et al. (2010).

2.3 Diverse Beliefs and Rationality

The main idea of Nakata et al. (2010) is simple. It is based on the fact that rare events are by definition observed very infrequently.[5] More specifically, rare events tend to be unprecedented even if the probability is not zero; thus, the empirical relative frequency tends to be zero. This implies that both a loss probability of 1 in 1 million and that of 1 in 1 billion would be consistent with data of no loss out of 100 observations. However, an insurance premium based on a probability of 1 in 1 million and that based on a probability of 1 in one billion will be very different in scale. In contrast, just one occurrence of a rare event will typically result in an inflated empirical relative frequency. This is compatible with stylised fact 3, i.e. an immediate jump in the market penetration upon occurrence of a catastrophe. The key observation is that the empirical data for rare events would not be sufficiently large to warrant a robust probability estimate, which would restrict diversity in terms of insurance premium or willingness-to-pay for insurance.

I illustrate the point more specifically by the following simplified version of the model in Nakata et al. (2010). Suppose there are two states for each period, where state 1 is the no-loss state and state 2 is the loss state. The sequence is known to be i.i.d. Let π denote the probability of state 1 in each period. Table 10.2 reports

[5] In the macroeconomics literature, Rietz (1988) introduced a rare disaster state to resolve the equity premium puzzle. His framework has attracted renewed attention recently—e.g., Weitzman (2007) and Barro (2009).

Table 10.2 Probability of observing no loss in 100 period

π	$P_{\pi}\{\text{no loss}\}$
0.999999999	0.999999900
0.999999	0.999900050
0.9999	0.990049339
0.999	0.904792147
0.99	0.366032341

$P_{\pi}\{\text{no loss}\}$, the probability of observing no losses for different levels of π, when I fix the length of the sequence as 100. Observer that when π is as low as 0.9999 (i.e. the probability of the loss states is 1/10,000), the probability of observing no loss for 100 observations is approximately 0.99. This means that for any $\pi \geq 0.9999$, up to about 99 % there will be no loss for 100 periods. Hence, the scale of loss probabilities that are compatible with the empirical frequency may vary substantially for rare events, particularly unprecedented events (any probability less than 1/10,000 is very plausible when there are 100 periods). In other words, the diversity of beliefs may well be very large in terms of the scale of the loss probability even if all agents are rational in the sense that their beliefs are compatible with the empirical data.

The large diversity in the subjective loss probability has a significant implication for the insurance demand. Recall that the willingness-to-pay for the insurance is almost linear in the loss probability when the loss probability is very small. Thus, a large diversity in the scale of subjective loss probability will imply a large diversity in the willingness-to-pay for the insurance. It follows that there may well be many agents whose willingness-to-pay is lower than the insurance premium offered by the insurance provider, even if the premium is set at an actuarially fair level with respect to the subject probability of the insurance provider.

Next, I observe the large impact of just one loss event on the class of subjective loss probabilities that are compatible with the empirical data. Table 10.3 reports the upper bound Eq. (10.2) of the proposition in the appendix for the probability of observing exactly one loss event in 100 periods for different values of π. It is obvious that one realisation of the loss state out of 100 periods/samples is not compatible with any π greater than 0.999. This means that one occurrence of a rare event is typically incompatible with beliefs that assign a very low probability to such an event. As a result, one occurrence of a rare event may well result in a substantial revision of beliefs of the agents so that their willingness-to-pay for the insurance rises rapidly since the willingness-to-pay is almost linear in $(1 - \pi)$ for small $(1 - \pi)$ as the above numerical example illustrates. Note that this is consistent with stylised fact 2, and particularly, stylised fact 3.

As noted above, the key observation is that the empirical data for rare events would not be sufficiently large to warrant a robust probability estimate that restricts diversity in terms of insurance premium or willingness-to-pay for insurance. Mathematically, the rate of convergence matters even if (we know that) the strong law of large numbers holds.

Table 10.3 Probability of observing exactly one loss in 100 periods

π	Upper bound
0.999999999	2.70468×10^{-7}
0.999999	0.000270441
0.9999	0.026780335
0.999	0.244962197

3 Welfare Measure Under Diverse Beliefs

Let U^h denote the utility of agent h, which may or may not have an expected utility form. It is then standard that a Pareto optimal allocation is characterised as a solution to the social planner's problem, which is based on a social welfare function such that $Z = \sum_{h=1}^{H} \lambda^h U^h$, where λ^h is some positive weight attached to agent h. When U^h has an expected utility form and the beliefs are homogeneous, the above social welfare function can be described as follows:

$$Z = E\sum_{h=1}^{H} \lambda^h u^h = \sum_{h=1}^{H} \lambda^h E u^h$$

since $U^h = Eu^h$ for all h. In contrast, when beliefs are heterogeneous, each utility function U^h is based on a subjective probability.

However, as explained briefly in the introduction, heterogeneity of beliefs invalidates the standard ex ante Pareto optimality and/or social welfare criterion. This is because by allowing for heterogeneous beliefs some agents inevitably hold incorrect beliefs, and such incorrect beliefs cause 'mistakes', which may results in regrets or pleasure ex post, even if they act optimally ex ante in accord with their beliefs. I use the term 'mistakes', since it is impossible to identify exactly if and how they made 'mistakes' by data when the beliefs are compatible with the data. Ignoring such regrets or pleasure calls for a significant value judgment, since it requires that the inability to hold the correct belief be penalised. In the context of natural disasters, the ex ante Pareto optimality requires that any ex post relief efforts would typically distort the allocation provided that the insurance policy was available prior to any very rare catastrophes.

Instead of taking such a strong value judgment, and to take ex post regrets or pleasure into account, it is probably reasonable to measure the welfare of the agents and the society as a whole with respect to an ex post measure. An ex post social welfare function is defined by

$$\hat{E}\, V\left(u^1, u^2, \ldots, u^H\right)$$

where $\hat{E}$ is the expectation operator with respect to a social probability measure, u^h is the ex post utility of agent h (a random variable), and V is a von Neumann-Morgenstern social welfare function, which is a function of the ex post utilities of the individuals.

Hammond (1981) shows that a socially optimal allocation based on an ex post social welfare function is not Pareto optimal in terms of the ex ante expected utilities of the agents unless all agents agree on the probability and the ex post social welfare function takes a special form such that

$$\hat{E}\,V(u^1, u^2, \ldots, u^H) = \hat{E}\sum\nolimits_{h=1}^{H} \lambda^h u^h = \sum\nolimits_{h=1}^{H} \lambda^h \hat{E}\,u^h \qquad (10.1)$$

Note that when all agents hold rational expectations, the probability measure that defines $\hat{E}$ is identical to the one in the ex ante expected utility function of each agent, and consequently, the ex post optimal allocation is identical to the ex ante optimal allocation.

Even if we assume that the ex post social welfare function takes the form as Eq. (10.1) above, the choice of the social probability measure is not trivial, since there is no way to learn the true probability, and one can only *believe* that his probability belief is the true probability, although one may happen to hold the true probability as his belief. One easy resolution would be to *assume* that the modeller knows the true probability, while the agents in the model don't, and then specify the true probability as the social probability measure. However, such an assumption is not plausible, since apparently no objective justification can be given for the assumption. In other words, *I propose to take a view that the modeller and the agents in the model have equal knowledge and/or ability, rather than taking a paternalistic view that the modeller takes care of the agents in the model by assuming the modeller's possession of superior knowledge and/or ability.*

To follow the principle that the modeller and the agents in the model have equal knowledge and/or ability, the choice of the social probability must be objective, and at least the procedure must be one that can be agreed upon by anyone rational. The rationality requirement here should be a weak one, that the view must not be contradictory to evidence or empirical data. In other words, by taking a frequentist view of probability, and then I can define the acceptable range of subjective probabilities that are compatible with the empirical data. As Nakata et al. (2010) argued and as was explained above, the range of acceptable subjective loss probabilities for rare events would be very large in terms of scale; for instance, 1 in 1,000 and 1 in 1 million are both compatible with the empirical data if the loss event concerned is unprecedented. One way is to define the social loss probability as the average of these acceptable subjective loss probabilities. In doing so, by assuming that the subjective loss probabilities are uniformly distributed, I will be effectively taking the least biased view, since a uniform distribution has the maximum entropy.

Moreover, the lack of knowledge of the subjective probability beliefs of the agents will cause a mechanism design issue, especially when designing a decentralised insurance mechanism. This is because I need to be able to predict the behaviour of the agents, which will be influenced by the subjective probability belief. In contrast, the lack of knowledge regarding tastes or degrees of risk aversion would not be too problematic as the above numerical example illustrates.

Suppose there are S states (i.e. the set of all states is defined by $\mathcal{S} := \{1, 2, \cdots, S\}$), and let $u^h(w_s^h)$ denote agent h's ex post utility in state $s \in \mathcal{S}$ when its wealth level is w_s^h.

The ex post social welfare is characterised by the utility frontier $(\langle u_1^h\rangle_h, \langle u_2^h\rangle_h, \ldots, \langle u_S^h\rangle_h)$, where $\langle u_s^h\rangle_h := (u_s^1, u_s^2, \ldots, u_s^H)$ for all s. The ex post social welfare would be not too far away from the ex post social optimum if there is no state s in which w_s^h is extremely low for some agent h, regardless of the functional form of u^h. This is a sufficient condition, not a necessary condition, to maintain a reasonably high level of ex post social welfare.

Note that this remains the same even if the ex post social welfare function does not have an expected utility form Eq. (10.1). Thus, a reasonably high level of ex post social welfare is maintained even if preferences of some or all agents do not have a standard expected utility representation and exhibit ambiguity aversion.[6] However, in the case of unawareness or unforeseen contingencies, the set S itself is unknown.[7] Thus, it is impossible to describe a full state contingent plan, and also the utility frontier $(\langle u_1^h\rangle_h, \langle u_2^h\rangle_h, \ldots, \langle u_S^h\rangle_h)$ is not well defined. The distinction between unawareness/unforeseen contingencies and the known state space may be important as the empirical study on insurance demand by Nakata, et al. (2010) suggests; the willingness-to-pay for flooding insurance is by and large consistent with the subjective expected utility framework, whilst it is not really the case for avian flu insurance, which appears to involve unforeseen contingencies, since mutation is not a foreseen contingency.

4 Comparisons of Regional Insurance Schemes

This section compares several insurance schemes for catastrophes or natural disasters from the viewpoint of the ex post social welfare.

4.1 The Macro Risk and the Strong Law of Large Numbers

As stated in the introduction, a typical insurance scheme is based on the strong law of large numbers. Namely, by letting X^h denote the loss of household h, and assuming that X^h is independent for all h,

$$\frac{1}{H}\sum_{h=1}^{H} X^h \to \overline{X} \text{ almost surely as } H \to \infty,$$

where $\overline{X}$ is some constant. In other words, by expanding the membership of the insurance mechanism $\{1, 2, \ldots, H\}$, the average loss per household will converge to

[6] The Ellsberg paradox by Ellsberg (1962) illustrates the distinction between risk and ambiguity. The latter is formally described by Choquet integral; see Gilboa (1987) and Schmeidler (1989).

[7] See Kreps (1979) and Dekel et al. (2001).

a constant with probability one (with respect to a probability measure). In the language of economics, the assumption of independence of X^h across h is stating that each household's loss entirely consists of idiosyncratic risk. However, a catastrophe or a natural disaster typically violates the assumption of independence, which in turn implies the failure of the almost sure convergence of the average loss per household. In other words, a catastrophe incurs some macro risk.

Moreover, the treatment of the idiosyncratic part of the household loss requires great care. This is because it is not obvious at all under what probability measure the strong law of large numbers holds for the idiosyncratic part of the household losses. In other words, the precise properties of the idiosyncratic and the systematic risks of each household's loss are not very straightforward. The diversity of beliefs is inevitable and we need to take into account the impacts of the diversity of beliefs, as the numerical examples in Sect. 2 illustrate.

4.2 Indemnity and Index Insurance

Consider two insurance contracts with different payoff structures: (a) indemnity insurance, and (b) index insurance. A conventional insurance contract is based on the actual loss or the indemnity, and I call the conventional insurance contract as indemnity insurance. Hence, a typical payoff structure of indemnity insurance that covers disaster type(s) k for policyholder i in state s is

$$r^i_{k,s} = \min\{\max\{x^i_{k,s} - d,\ 0\}, b\} = \begin{cases} 0 & \textit{if } x^i_{k,s} \leq d; \\ x^i_{k,s} - d & \textit{if } x^i_{k,s} \in [d, b]; \\ b & \text{otherwise,} \end{cases}$$

where $x^i_{k,s}$ is the loss from type k disaster policyholder i incurs, d is the deductible and b is the maximum coverage. Thus, the payoff will exactly match the loss when $d = 0$ and $b \geq \max\{x^i_{k,s},\ s \in S\}$. Moreover, the price of the insurance (the insurance premium) is described as $\rho^i_k(d, b)$, i.e. it is a function of (i, k, d, b). For standardised indemnity insurance, the premium is not exactly personal to the policyholder i, but is a function of the attributes of i. In such a case, $\rho_k(\theta, d, b)$, where θ is the attributes of the policyholder.

Meanwhile, index insurance is a contract whose payment is contingent on a set of pre-determined conditions, and is not based on the actual loss the policyholder incurs. Usually the pre-determined conditions (i.e. the trigger event) are easily observable and/or verifiable. For instance, a pre-determined amount (e.g. USD one million) of an earthquake index insurance contract will be paid to the policyholder if an earthquake that is at least as powerful as the specified level (e.g. magnitude 7.0) occurs in a specific location (e.g. the epicentre is within 100 miles from Tokyo's city centre). Thus, the payoff structure of a typical index insurance contract for the trigger event k (i.e. the set of states $S^k \subset S$) is

$$r_{k,s} = \begin{cases} c & \text{if } s \in \mathcal{S}^k; \\ 0 & \text{otherwise.} \end{cases}$$

Note that the payoff $r_{k,s}$ is not a function of i, i.e. it is the same across the policyholders. There will be a discrepancy between the payment of the index insurance and the actual loss from the perspective of the insurance policyholder, and such discrepancy is often referred to as a basis risk in this context.

Each index insurance k can be described as a zero-net supply security:

$$\sum\nolimits_{i \in \mathcal{J}} z_k^i = 0,$$

where $\mathcal{J}$ is the set of all economic agents (households, firms, local governments, etc.) and is economic agent i's position of index insurance k. Indeed, the market structure of the index insurance can be either (a) a competitive market along the line of a standard general equilibrium model, where all economic agents are price takers, or (b) a typical market for insurance products, where insurance companies control prices and hold short positions. Practically, the former case would require that the index insurance to be traded on the capital market, just like the catastrophe (CAT) bonds. In the latter case, we may fix the identity of the supplier of each index insurance k, i.e. we can simply add conditions such that $z_k^i < 0$ for the particular supplier i.

In the former case, the price q^k satisfies the following equation in equilibrium:

$$q^k = \sum\nolimits_{s \in \mathcal{S}} \pi_s^i \frac{\partial u^i\left(w_s^i\right)}{\partial w_s^i} r_{k,s},$$

where π_s^i is economic agent i's subjective probability of state s, w_s^i is agent i's wealth in state s, and u^i is agent i's (indirect) utility function. This equation states that the agent may choose to allow for the occurrence of a state with a very low w_s^i when π_s^i is very small. In other words, agents that underestimate the catastrophe states would limit the purchase of index insurances that could compensate for the losses in those states.

It is clear that both types of insurance contracts are state contingent claims. Thus, the verification of the state is crucial. However, verification is much costlier and is more prone to moral hazard for the indemnity insurance than for the index insurance, since the latter only requires the verification of $s \in \mathcal{S}$, whilst the former requires the verification of $x_{k,s}^i$.

4.3 Evaluations of Different Insurance Schemes

Next, I attempt to compare and evaluate the indemnity and index insurance. In so doing, this chapter considers three different cases concerning the identity of the policyholders: (a) households, (b) local governments, and (c) national governments. The first case is the most obvious one, in which each household directly purchases insurance policies. The second and the third are the cases in which the insurance policies are purchased by the governments (local or national), and the purchases may be financed by tax.

Let N denote the set of countries (that participate in the regional insurance scheme), and n its typical element, i.e. country n. Let $\mathcal{L}$ denote the set of all local governments in the region, and l its typical element, i.e. local government l. If necessary, let $\mathcal{L}^n$ denote the set of all local governments in country n. We may let $\mathcal{H}^l$ denote the set of all households in the area of the local government l.

4.3.1 Direct Subscriptions by Households

First consider the case in which each household is the potential policyholder of the insurance, either indemnity or index insurance. This is desirable with respect to the ex ante Pareto optimality criterion, since the choice made by each household will reflect its ex ante preference.

However, as seen above, the subjective loss probability would be rather diverse especially for households who have experienced no major losses in the past. When the insurance premium is set by the supplier, this would result in a rather low level of subscription rate, since a large number of households would deem the premium too high. Also, for index insurance, when the market structure is competitive (i.e. all economic agents are price takers), households whose probability estimates for the catastrophe states are very low would not hold a position that would sufficiently cover the losses in the catastrophe states. In these cases, the ex post welfare of the economy would become very low, since some households would be left in a disastrous condition, if no relief efforts are made ex post.

4.3.2 Subscriptions by Local Governments

Next, examine the case in which local governments are the potential policyholders of the insurance, instead of the households. For every local government l, the aggregate loss of the households in the governing area is $X^l := \sum_{h\in\mathcal{H}^l} X^h$. When there is no macro risk at each local government level, this quantity is a constant. However, there typically remains a macro risk at this level especially for natural disasters. Thus, there are incentives for the local governments to share risk with other local governments within the country or within the whole East Asian region.

Moreover, to finance the insurance premium, the local government would either use its general tax income or impose a separate tax specific to the insurance. For index insurances, it is possible conceptually that the cost of the portfolio of index insurances may be zero, $\sum_{k\in\mathcal{K}} q^k z^i_k = 0$, where $\mathcal{K}$ is the set of all index insurances.

Either way, this scheme is effectively a two-tier risk sharing scheme. That is, (a) the risk sharing scheme amongst local governments, and (b) the risk sharing scheme within the governing area of each local government. The latter scheme should be designed so that it eliminates idiosyncratic risk at the household level.

One major advantage of this scheme over the one with direct subscriptions by households is that the subjective probability of X^l would be less diverse than that of X^h for household h with no or very limited prior loss experience, since the empirical loss probability of X^l is larger than that of X^h for households with no or very little prior loss experience. Thus, the conflict between the ex ante and ex post welfare measure would be less severe, at least in terms of decision making. However, many households with no prior loss experience may well view the scheme ex ante as a wealth transfer mechanism that would be disadvantageous to them.

The implementation of the risk sharing scheme within the governing area of each local government may be very costly and prone to moral hazard if it follows the design of indemnity insurance, i.e. the payments to the households are made against the claims made by the households. However, if the payments are made so that no household would be left in a devastating state even if they are not exactly matching the actual losses, the ex post welfare would be reasonably high.

4.3.3 Subscriptions by National Governments

Finally, I examine the case in which national governments are the potential policyholders of the insurance. For every national government n, the aggregate loss of the households in the governing area is $X^n := \sum_{h \in \mathcal{H}^n} X^h$. Clearly, the subjective probability of X^n would be less diverse than that of X^l for all $l \in \mathcal{L}^n$. In this case, the regional insurance scheme aims at sharing the macro risks at the country level, whilst the risk sharing within the country will be done through the tax system that would finance the regional insurance premium.

One major problem is that the determination of the insurance premium would be very political, as we observe in many international frameworks. This applies also to index insurance, since no national government would act as a price taker.

5 Conclusion

This chapter has examined the possible issues that are key to design regional insurance schemes for catastrophes or natural disasters that mainly target the household sector. It first introduced a simplified version of the insurance demand model by Nakata et al. (2010), which is consistent with the three stylised facts about catastrophe insurance demand. The key observation is that the robustness of a probability estimate of a rare event is very limited, which would result in a large diversity and variability in the scale of subjective loss probabilities for rare events.

When the probability beliefs are diverse, the standard Pareto criterion becomes dubious, because it is based on the ex ante preferences, which govern the decisions of the agents, but ignore the regrets for the mistakes made due to the 'incorrect' beliefs. Thus, it would be sensible to use the ex post welfare measure proposed by Starr (1973) and Hammond (1981). However, the choice of social probability for the ex post social welfare function with an expected utility form is not straightforward. Nevertheless, by making everyone avoid any catastrophe state would ensure that the ex post social welfare would be close to the ex post social optimum, regardless of the true social probability or the functional form of the ex post utility.

With this in mind, the chapter evaluated various insurance schemes. For both the indemnity and index insurance schemes, voluntary direct subscriptions by the households are not desirable, since voluntary subscriptions by the households would most likely to lead to insufficient level of insurance coverage and the occurrence of personal catastrophe states for some agents due to the large diversity in subjective loss probabilities. Since the diversity in the loss probabilities would be less for aggregate losses at the local government level, an insurance scheme with subscriptions by local governments in conjunction with ex post payments/compensations to the affected households would be more desirable. Considering the possible moral hazard issues inherent to indemnity insurance, schemes based on index insurance appear to be more desirable. However, the underwriting costs for index insurance may well not be low, whether the index insurance will be supplied and priced by insurance suppliers or traded on the capital market.

The current paper leaves several important issues unexamined. First, supply side issues, including but not limited to the issues related to underlying costs, are not examined, and they require both empirical and theoretical examinations. Moreover, analyses based on a dynamical model would be needed. As noted above, catastrophes or natural disasters tend to incur risk at the aggregate level (i.e. macro risk). Thus, it is impossible to exactly match the insurance payment of indemnity insurance with fixed insurance premiums in every period. Hence, a dynamical model is needed to analyse the level of reserves needed to ensure smoothing of aggregate wealth or consumption over time, without falling to insolvency. Also, for index insurances traded on the capital market, the impacts of possible fluctuations in (relative) prices should be analysed by a dynamical model, since the fluctuations may well have significant impacts.

Appendix: The Large Deviation Property

In what follows, we reproduce the exposition of Lemma 1.1.9 of Dembo and Zeitouni (1998) in Nakata, et al. (2010). Let random variable X_t denote the loss in period t, and let $X_1, X_2, \ldots, X_T$ be an i.i.d. sequence. Also, let $\mathcal{P}(\mathcal{A})$ denote the space of all probability laws on $\mathcal{A} := \{a_1, a_2, \ldots, a_S\}$. Furthermore, for a finite sequence (of realisations) $\mathbf{x}^T = (x_1, x_2, \ldots, x_T)$, we define the empirical measure of a_s as follows:

$$m_T^{\mathbf{x}}(a_s) := \frac{1}{T}\sum_{t=1}^{T} 1_{a_s}(x_t), \ \forall s,$$

where $1_{a_s}(\cdot)$ is an indicator function such that

$$1_{a_s}(x_t) = \begin{cases} 1 \text{ if } & x_t = a_s; \\ 0 \text{ otherwise.} \end{cases}$$

Then, we define type $m_T^{\mathbf{x}}$ of $\mathbf{x}^T$ as

$$m_T^{\mathbf{x}} := \left(m_T^{\mathbf{x}}(a_1), m_T^{\mathbf{x}}(a_2), \ \ldots, m_T^{\mathbf{x}}(a_S)\right).$$

Let $\mathcal{M}_T$ denote the set of all possible types of sequences of length T, i.e.

$$\mathcal{M}_T := \left\{\nu : \nu = m_T^{\mathbf{x}} \text{ for some } \mathbf{x}^T\right\}.$$

Also, the empirical measure $m_T^{\mathbf{x}}$ associated with a sequence of random variables $\mathbf{X}^T := (X_1, X_2, \ldots, X_T)$ is a random element of $\mathcal{M}_T$.

Let P_π denote the probability law associated with an infinite sequence of i.i.d. random variables $\mathbf{X} = (X_1, X_2, \ldots)$ distributed following $\pi \in \mathcal{P}(\mathcal{A})$. Also, the relative entropy of probability vector ν with respect to another probability vector π is $H(\nu|\pi) := \sum_{s=1}^{S} \nu_s \ln\frac{\nu_s}{\pi_s}$.

Proposition (Lemma 1.1.9; Dembo and Zeitouni 1998) *For any* $\nu \in \mathcal{M}_T$,

$$(T+1)^{-S} e^{-TH(\nu|\pi)} \le P_\pi\left(m_T^{\mathbf{x}} = \nu\right) \le e^{-TH(\nu|\pi)} \tag{10.2}$$

The proposition states that the probability of observing type ν for a sequence of length T with respect to probability law π^π has the lower and upper bounds as specified in Eq. (10.2).[8] Clearly, both the lower and upper bounds are decreasing in $H(\nu|\pi)$. Note that this result (and the results in the literature of large deviations) is very useful, since it may well be rather difficult to compute the exact probability $P_\pi(m_T^{\mathbf{x}} = \nu)$ in many cases. This difficulty arises from the fact that we need to consider all possible paths/sequences that belong to the specified type, which involves combinatorics. Moreover, from this result, we know that the relative entropy $H(\nu|\pi)$ characterises the probability $P_\pi(m_T^{\mathbf{x}} = \nu)$, although the bounds may not be very tight in some cases.

[8] $P_\pi(m_T^{\mathbf{x}} = \nu)$ is a likelihood function in the language of Bayesian statistics, in which case an explicit updating of beliefs is modelled. However, we do not assume such an explicit belief updating mechanism in the current paper.

References

Barro, R. J. (2009). Rare disasters, asset prices, and welfare costs. *American Economic Review, 99*, 243–64.

Brookshire, D. S., Thayer, M. A., Tschirhart, J., & Schulze, W. D. (1985). A test of the expected utility model: Evidence from earthquake risks. *Journal of Political Economy, 93*, 369–89.

Browne, M. J., & Hoyt, R. E. (2000). The demand for flood insurance: Empirical evidence. *Journal of Risk and Uncertainty, 20*, 291–306.

Dekel, E., Lipman, B. L., & Rustichini, A. (2001). Representing preferences with a unique subjective state space. *Econometrica, 69*, 891–934.

Dembo, A., & Zeitouni, O. (1998). *Large deviations techniques and applications* (2nd ed.). New York: Springer.

Diamond, P. A. (1967). Cardinal welfare, individualistic ethics and interpersonal comparisons of utility: A comment. *Journal of Political Economy, 75*, 765–66.

Dixon, L., Clancy, N., Seabury, S. A., & Overton, A. (2006). *The national flood insurance program's market penetration rate–estimates and policy implications*, Technical Report, Rand Corporation.

Drèze, J. (1970). Market allocation under uncertainty. *European Economic Review, 2*, 133–65.

Ellsberg, D. (1962). Risk, ambiguity, and the savage axioms. *Quarterly Journal of Economics, 75*, 643–69.

Gilboa, I. (1987). Expected utility with purely subjective non-additive probabilities. *Journal of Mathematical Economics, 16*, 65–88.

Hammond, P. J. (1981). Ex-ante and ex-post welfare optimality under uncertainty. *Economica, 48*, 235–50.

Kreps, D. M. (1979). A representation theorem for "preference for flexibility". *Econometrica, 47*, 565–76.

Kunreuther, H., Ginsberg, R., Miller, L., Sagi, P., Slovic, P., Borkan, B., et al. (1978). *Disaster insurance protection: Public policy lessons*. New York: Wiley.

Kunreuther, H., & Pauly, M. (2004). Neglecting disaster: Why don't people insure against large losses? *Journal of Risk and Uncertainty, 28*, 5–21.

Michel-Kerjan, E. O. (2010). Catastrophe economics: The national flood insurance program. *Journal of Economic Perspectives, 24*, 165–86.

Nakata, H. (2013). Welfare effects of short-sale constraints under heterogeneous beliefs. *Economic Theory, 53*, 283–314.

Nakata, H., Sawada, Y., & Tanaka M. (2010). *Entropy characterisation of insurance demand: theory and evidence*, RIETI Discussion Paper 10-E-009.

Rietz, T. A. (1988). The equity premium: A solution. *Journal of Monetary Economics, 22*, 117–131.

Schmeidler, D. (1989). Subjective probability and expected utility without additivity. *Econometrica, 57*, 571–87.

Starr, R. M. (1973). Optimal production and allocation under uncertainty. *Quarterly Journal of Economics, 87*, 81–95.

Weitzman, M. L. (2007). Subjective expectations and asset-return puzzles. *American Economic Review, 97*, 1102–1130.

Part III
Government Policy and Risk Management

Chapter 11
Natural Disaster and Economic Policy for ASEAN and the Pacific Rim: A Proposal for a Disaster Risk Reduction 'Seal of Approval' Fund

Ilan Noy

1 Disasters in South–East Asia

Many of the most destructive natural disasters of the past few decades occurred in Pacific Rim countries. During the past century for example, the most lethal earthquake (Tangshan, China, 1976), the most lethal tsunami (Aceh, Indonesia, 2004), and some of the most lethal storms and floods have all occurred in Asia bordering the Pacific.[1] Other catastrophic natural disasters like the exceptionally strong earthquake in Chile in 1960 that generated a Pacific-wide tsunami, the most destructive natural disaster in modern history in terms of destroyed property (Tohoku, Japan, 2011), or the Mexico City earthquake of 1985, are all examples of how natural disasters play a significant part in the economies of almost all the Pacific Rim countries.

Even without these catastrophic infrequent events, some Pacific Rim countries are buffeted by repeated and very frequent natural disasters (e.g., the Philippines experiences, on average, 5.8 destructive tropical storms annually). The countries of the Pacific Rim, as well as the volcanic islands and coral atolls of the Pacific Ocean itself, are also some of the most vulnerable to future disasters that may be associated with the changing climate and most are within the Ring of Fire—the globally most geologically active region.[2]

[1] The five most lethal events in Pacific Rim nations (1970-2008) were all initiated by earthquakes: China 1976, Indonesia 2004, China 2008, Peru 1970 and Guatemala 1976. In these five events, 585,000 people died.

[2] The Ring of Fire is an inverted U-shape region, whose Western tip is New Zealand. The region then encompasses the archipelagos of Indonesia, the Philippines, and Japan, the Russian Far East, the Aleutian Islands, Alaska, and then down the Western Coast of the Americas all the way to

I. Noy (✉)
Victoria University of Wellington, Wellington, New Zealand
e-mail: ilan.noy@vuw.ac.nz

D.P. Aldrich et al. (eds.), *Resilience and Recovery in Asian Disasters*, Risk, Governance and Society 18, DOI 10.1007/978-4-431-55022-8_11

Robert Barro has argued that the infrequent occurrence of economic disasters leads to much larger welfare costs than continuous economic fluctuations of lesser amplitude (Barro 2006, 2009). He estimated that for the typical advanced economy, the welfare cost associated with large economic disasters such as those experienced in the twentieth century amounted to about 20 % of annual GDP, while normal business cycle volatility only amounted to a still substantial 15 % of GDP. For developing countries, which usually suffer from more frequent natural disasters of all types, and of even greater magnitude than in advanced economies, these events have an even greater effect on the welfare of the average citizen.

Understanding the history of disasters in the Pacific Rim, their impact on development, on the spatial evolution of income, and the risks that the region faces in terms of future events and their likely consequences all seem to be important components of an understanding of the region's economy. After all, the disruptions in many multinationals' supply chains that occurred after the 2011 Tohoku earthquake/tsunami and the 2011 Bangkok floods demonstrated persuasively the potentially global impact of these types of disasters—especially for a region whose countries' level of trade integration within the global economy is very high.

I employ a typology of disaster impacts that distinguishes between direct and indirect damages. Direct damages are the damage to fixed assets and capital (including inventories), damages to raw materials and extractable natural resources, and of course mortality and morbidity that are a direct consequence of the natural phenomenon. Indirect damages refer to the economic activity, in particular the production of goods and services, that will not take place following the disaster and because of it. These indirect damages may be caused by the direct damages to physical infrastructure or harm to labor, or because reconstruction pulls resources away from the usual production practices. These indirect damages also include the additional costs that are incurred because of the need to use alternative and potentially inferior means of production and/or distribution for the provision of normal goods and services (Pelling et al. 2002).

These costs can be accounted for in the aggregate by examining the overall performance of the economy, as measured through the most relevant macroeconomic variables. These are GDP, the fiscal accounts, consumption, investment, and, especially important for the comparatively globalized countries of the Pacific Rim, the balance of trade and the balance of payments. These costs can also be further divided, following the standard distinction in macroeconomics, between the short run (up to several years) and the long run (typically considered to be at least 5 years, but sometimes also measured in decades). I use these distinctions in the discussion that follows.

Tierra Del Fuego at the very southern tip of the continent. This region experiences by far the majority of the volcanic activity and earth movements recorded worldwide.

2 Data on Regional Disasters

2.1 *The Past*

The Emergency Events Database (EM-DAT), maintained by the Centre for Research on the Epidemiology of Disasters (CRED) at the Catholic University of Louvain, is the most frequently used resource for disaster data.[3] EM-DAT defines a disaster as an event which overwhelms local capacity and/or necessitates a request for external assistance. For a disaster to be entered into the EM-DAT database, at least one of the following criteria must be met: (1) 10 or more people are reported killed; (2) 100 people are reported affected; (3) a state of emergency is declared; or (4) a call for international assistance is issued. Natural disasters can be hydro-meteorological, including floods, wave surges, storms, droughts, landslides and avalanches; geophysical, including earthquakes, tsunamis and volcanic eruptions; and biological, covering epidemics and insect infestations (these are much less frequent). The data report the number of people killed, the number of people affected, and the amount of direct damages in each disaster. Since biological events are much more anthropogenic, and the data collected on them are much less reliable; we will not discuss these in what follows.

We present disaster data for all the countries of the Pacific Rim, but exclude the small island-nations of the Pacific itself.[4] The disaster-types we include are earthquakes, temperature extremes, floods, storms, volcanic events, and wildfires. Natural disasters, as defined in the EM-DAT database, are common events. The five worst disasters (in terms of the three measures of disaster magnitude) are given in Table 11.1. In the Pacific Rim region, the five disasters with the highest mortality are all earthquakes, with a total of almost 600,000 people killed. In terms of people affected, floods in China dominate the list, although aggregate mortality for these is fairly low (about 10,000 people in total). Hurricane Katrina in the U.S., and the Kobe earthquake in Japan were by far the costliest disasters (in terms of damage to infrastructure) until the March 2011 earthquake/tsunami in Tohoku, which dwarfs both disasters with damages estimated at more than US$200 billion, about twice as much as the amount estimated for Katrina.

A list of the three worst disasters for each Pacific Rim country and their aggregate toll (in terms of mortality), is provided in Table 11.2. It provides some limited insight into the vulnerabilities of each country both in terms of the kinds of disasters that are likely to wreak the most damages and how big these damages are likely to be. Not surprisingly, there are very few Pacific Rim countries for which earthquakes are not part of the most dangerous disaster list: these are Australia,

[3] The data is publicly available at: http://www.emdat.be/

[4] The following are included: Australia, Canada, Chile, China PR, Colombia, Costa Rica, Ecuador, El Salvador, Guatemala, Honduras, Indonesia, Japan, Korea (South), Malaysia, Mexico, New Zealand, Nicaragua, Panama, Papua New Guinea, Peru, Philippines, Russia, Taiwan, United States, and Vietnam.

Table 11.1 Worst disasters in the Pacific Rim 1970–2008

Country (year)	Type	# Killed	# Affected	Damages
Worst disasters (# of people killed)				
China PR (1976)	Earthquake	242,000	164,000	5,600
Indonesia (2004)	Earthquake	165,708	532,898	4,451.6
China PR (2008)	Earthquake	87,476	45,976,596	30,000
Peru (1970)	Earthquake	66,794	3,216,240	530
Guatemala (1976)	Earthquake	23,000	4,993,000	1,000
Worst disasters (# of people affected)				
China PR (1998)	Flood	3,656	238,973,000	30,000
China PR (1991)	Flood	1,729	210,232,227	7,500
China PR (1996)	Flood	2,775	154,634,000	12,600
China PR (2003)	Flood	430	150,146,000	7,890
China PR (1995)	Flood	1,437	114,470,249	6,720
Worst disasters (damages in US$ million)				
United States (2005)	Storm	1,833	500,000	125,000
Japan (1995)	Earthquake	5,297	541,636	100,000
China PR (1998)	Flood	3,656	238,973,000	30,000
China PR (2008	Earthquake	87,476	45,976,596	30,000
United States (1994)	Earthquake	60	27,000	30,000

Source: Author's calculations from EMDAT

Canada, Honduras, Korea, New Zealand, the U.S. and Vietnam. But, after the 2011 earthquake in Christchurch, New Zealand can no longer be considered relatively earthquake safe, and most predictions are that a large West Coast quake in the U.S. will also dwarf any impact from other American disasters. Thus, past recent experiences is only of limited use in assessing future vulnerabilities in the face of catastrophic but rare events.

The last column in Table 11.2 measures vulnerability differently, by counting the number of large events in the past 40 years. In this case, we adopt a threshold that is ten times higher than the one used by EM-DAT, since the dataset includes many relatively minor events (from a macroeconomic perspective). Using this measure, Indonesia, China and the Philippines stand out as highly vulnerable.

Figure 11.1, taken from Cavallo and Noy (2011), plots the average number of natural disaster events (hydro-meteorological and geophysical) per country in the period 1970–2008. The figure shows that the incidence of disasters has been growing over time everywhere in the world. In the Asia-Pacific region for example, which is the region with the most events, the incidence has grown from an average of 11 events per country in the 1970s to over 28 events in the 2000s. In other regions, while the increase is less dramatic, the trend is similar. However, these patterns appear to be driven to some extent by improved recording of milder events, rather than by an increase in the frequency of disasters. Furthermore, truly large

Table 11.2 Vulnerability A—worst disasters per country

Country	Worst three disasters (1970–2008)[a]			# Killed[b]	# of large disasters[c]
Australia	Wildfire 1983	Storm 1974	Flood 1984	176	0
Canada	Storm 1998	Storm 1987	Storm 1975	68	0
Chile	Earthquake 1971	Earthquake 1985	Flood 1993	374	1
China	Earthquake 1976	Earthquake 1974	Earthquake 2008	349,476	84
Colombia	Volcano 1985	Earthquake 1970	Earthquake 1999	23,416	10
Costa Rica	Storm 1988	Storm 1996	Earthquake 1991	126	0
Ecuador	Earthquake 1987	Flood 1983	Flood 1998	5,525	3
El Salvador	Earthquake 1986	Earthquake 2001	Flood 1982	2,444	5
Guatemala	Earthquake 1976	Storm 2005	Flood 1982	25,133	4
Honduras	Storm 1998	Storm 1974	Flood 1993	22,974	4
Indonesia	Earthquake 2004	Earthquake 2006	Earthquake 1992	173,986	20
Japan	Earthquake 1995	Flood 1972	Flood 1982	6,100	10
Korea	Flood 1972	Flood 1998	Storm 1987	1,558	9
Malaysia	Storm 1996	Earthquake 2004	Flood 1970	411	0
Mexico	Earthquake 1985	Flood 1999	Storm 1976	1,736	22
N Zealand	Storm 1988	Flood 1985	Storm 1997	13	0
Nicaragua	Earthquake 1972	Storm 1998	Storm 2007	13,520	4
Panama	Flood 1970	Earthquake 1991	Storm 1988	108	0
Papua NG	Earthquake 1998	Storm 2007	Earthquake 1993	2,407	2
Peru	Earthquake 1970	Earthquake 2007	Storm 1998	67,831	6
Philippines	Earthquake 1976	Storm 1991	Earthquake 1990	14,368	17
Russia	Earthquake 1995	Ex temp 2001	Ex temp 2001	2,597	3
Taiwan	Earthquake 1999	Storm 2001	Storm 2000	2,453	2
U. S.	Storm 2005	Ex temp 1980	Ex temp 1995	3,763	19
Vietnam	Storm 1997	Storm 1985	Storm 1989	5,231	20

Note:
[a]The worst three disasters in terms of the number of fatalities
[b]Measures the sum of fatalities in the three worst disasters experienced in each country
[c]Measures the number of disaster events for which there were more than 100 fatalities, more than a thousand people affected, and damages of more than a million US$ (this is a significantly higher threshold than the one used by EMDAT—we further did not count disasters for which the number of fatalities was unavailable)
Source: Author's calculations from EMDAT

events—i.e., conceivably more catastrophic—are rarer. At this point, there is no credible evidence that the frequency of catastrophic events is increasing, though that is most clearly a possible prediction given the projected evolution of climatic conditions in the next century.

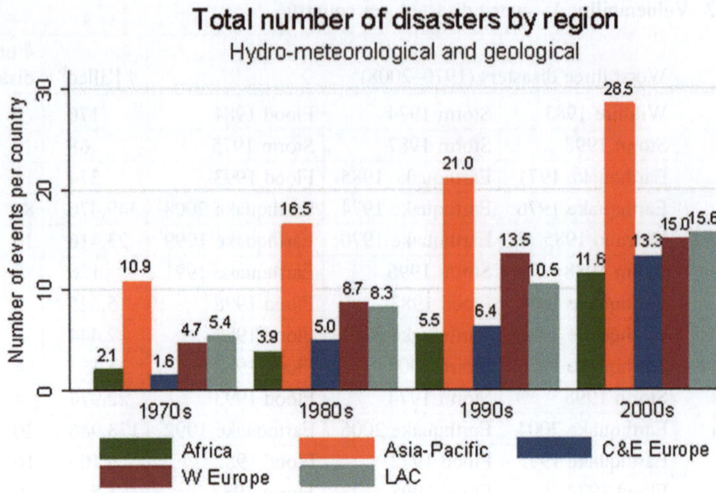

Fig. 11.1 Frequency of disasters by geographic region. *Source*: Cavallo and Noy (2011)

2.2 *The Future*

A recent report by the Intergovernmental Panel on Climate Change (IPCC 2012), the *Special Report on Managing the Risks of Extreme Events and Disasters to Advance Climate Change Adaptation* concludes that there will be a "likely increase heat wave frequency and very likely increase in warm days and nights across Europe….likely increase in average maximum wind speed and associated heavy rainfall (although not in all regions)…. very likely contribution of sea level rise to extreme coastal high water levels (such as storm surges)…." (IPCC 2012).[5] While the report is fairly skeptical about the robustness of many of the predictions available in the scientific literature about catastrophic high-risk low-probability natural disasters, it does argue that "For exposed and vulnerable communities, even non-extreme weather and climate events can have extreme impacts".

In its latest comprehensive report from 2007, the IPCC states that: "Warming of the climate system is unequivocal, as is now evident from observations of increases in global average air and ocean temperatures, widespread melting of snow and ice, and rising global average sea level" (IPCC 2007). The IPCC report projects that by the year 2100, average global surface temperature will increase by between 1.8° Celsius and 4° Celsius depending on the success of emissions mitigation strategies.[6]

[5] By 'very likely' the IPCC refers to 90–100 % probability, while 'likely' means 66–100 % probability (IPCC 2011).

[6] Different climate models, yield somewhat different results, but the consensus is well represented by this range.

The projected increase in sea surface temperatures will potentially impact both the frequency and intensity of tropical storms. Several studies posit that, as global sea surface temperatures rise, hurricanes may become more numerous or intense, the range of hurricanes will increase to the north and south of the current "hurricane belt", or their location and typical paths will change (e.g., Webster et al. 2005; Li et al. 2010; Mendelsohn et al. 2012; Elsner et al. 2008; Emanuel et al. 2008).

More recent predictions than the 2007 IPCC report regarding global sea level rise are considerably more alarming as more information on glacial melting has become available. Rahmstorf (2007), for example, predicts a sea level rise of 0.5–1.4 m by 2100 while Vermeer and Rahmstorf (2009) predict rises of up to 1.9 m. These sea level rises, besides posing ongoing difficulties to low-lying areas, will certainly also increase the damages caused by storm wave surges and earthquake induced tsunamis. Whatever climate models are used, however, there is wider agreement that the combination of sea level rise and deterioration in coral reef ecosystems will make coastal areas considerably more vulnerable to storms, regardless of whether storms will indeed be more frequent or more intense (or both).

The impact of global climate change on the incidence of other types of natural disasters is even less well understood., but there is some preliminary evidence, mostly from model exercises, that droughts and floods will become more common and more severe (e.g., IPCC 2007). For now, we have no evidence that the incidence of geophysical disasters is likely to change over time or be affected by any of the climatic changes that are predicted to occur. The frequency of large earthquakes appears to be fairly constant with, on average, 17 large earthquakes (magnitude 7.0–7.9) and about one mega earthquake (magnitude 8.0 and above) per year.[7] However, as we already observed about the future damages from earthquake-generated tsunami waves, one can easily conclude that even if the probability of geophysical events will not be impacted, the ways in which these natural events will interact with the local economy may clearly change over time.

3 Determinants of Initial Disaster Costs

When evaluating the determinants of disasters' direct costs, most research papers estimated a model of the form: $DIS_{it} = \alpha + \beta \mathbf{X}_{it} + \varepsilon_{it}$; where DIS_{it} is a measure of direct damages of all disasters in country i and time t; using measures of primary initial damage such as mortality, morbidity, or capital losses. $\mathbf{X}_{it}$ is a vector of control variables of interest with each research effort distinguishing different

[7] A one point increase in earthquake magnitude entails a 10 times increase in earth movement and a 32 times increase in the amount of energy released, so a 9.0 earthquake is dramatically different from an 8.0 one. For historical information about earthquake frequencies, see: http://earthquake.usgs.gov/earthquakes/eqarchives/.

independent variables. Typically $\mathbf{X}_{it}$ will include a measure of the disaster magnitude (e.g., Richter scale for earthquakes or wind speed for hurricanes) and variables that capture the "vulnerability" of the country to disasters (i.e., the conditions which increase the susceptibility of a country to the impact of natural hazards). ε_{it} is generally assumed to be an independently and identically distributed (iid) error term.

Kahn (2005) estimates a version of this model and concludes that while richer countries do not experience fewer or less severe natural disasters, their death toll is substantially lower. In 1990, a poor country (per capita GDP < US$2,000) typically experienced 9.4 deaths per million people per year, while a richer country (per capita GDP > US$14,000) would have had only 1.8 deaths. This difference is most likely due to the greater amount of resources spent on prevention efforts and legal enforcement of mitigation rules (e.g., building codes). In particular, some of the policy interventions likely to ameliorate disaster impact, including land-use zoning, building codes and engineering interventions are rarer in less developed countries.

This finding, however, does not imply that higher damages in developing countries are inevitable. The contrast between storm preparedness in Cuba vs. Haiti, or in Burma vs. Bangladesh, clearly demonstrates that even poor countries can adopt successful mitigation policies and that successful mitigation does not only depend on financial resources and the ability to mobilize them. Even in wealthier countries, there are dramatic differences in the degree of preparedness; Japan, for example, has constructed a nation-wide earthquake warning system that successfully managed to stop all high-speed rail a few seconds before the damaging earthquake shock waves arrived in the Sendai region on March 11th, 2011—no other country has installed such a system.

A consistent finding of several studies (i.e., Kahn 2005; Raschky 2008; Strömberg 2007) is that better institutions—understood, for instance, as more stable democratic regimes or greater security of property rights—reduce disaster impact. Typhoon Nargis that hit Burma in May 2008 provides a tragic contrast to this insight. Apparently, the Burmese government was warned about the nearing storm 2 days before it arrived, but did little to warn coastal residents. In addition, the government interrupted post-disaster relief efforts and restricted access by international NGOs to the affected area; more than 138,000 people were killed. Nargis is an extreme case, but other countries that experience periodic storms and flooding, such as the Philippines, also appear comparatively unprepared.

Anbarci et al. (2005) elaborate on the political economy of disaster prevention. They conclude that inequality is important as a determinant of prevention efforts: more unequal societies tend to have fewer resources spent on prevention, as they are unable to resolve the collective action problem of implementing costly preventive and mitigation measures. Collective action difficulties may be overcome in communities whose inter-communal ties are stronger. As Aldrich (2012 and Chap. 2) discusses, when people feel an affinity with their neighbors, organizing them to act communally both in preparing for disasters, mitigating their consequences and reconstructing are all done more easily.

Besley and Burgess (2002), using data from floods in India, observe that disaster impacts are lower when newspaper circulation is higher, which leads to more accountable politicians and a government that is more active in preventing and mitigating impacts.[8] Compounding this question of accountability is the apparent unwillingness of the electorate to punish politicians who had under-invested in preparedness while failure to provide generous post-disaster reconstruction funds does appear to be an important determinant of post-disaster electoral success (Healy and Malhotra 2009, 2010). The benefits of generous post-disaster government intervention also appear to be long-lasting (Bechtel and Hainmueller 2011). Not surprisingly, politicians respond to these incentives, and thus increase their generosity in allocating post-disaster assistance in election years (Cole et al. 2012). Thus, even in democracies, politicians rarely face the optimal incentives in terms of disaster prevention and/or mitigation.

To summarize, while the damage caused by disasters is naturally related to the physical intensity of the event, a series of economic, social, and political characteristics also affect vulnerability. A by-product of this analysis, of course, is that these characteristics are therefore potentially amenable to policy action. In particular, the collective action problems that the literature identifies can potentially be overcome with the design of decision-making mechanisms that take these problems into account. Political incentives are probably more difficult to alter, but robust public scrutiny with the assistance of an activist and investigative media can assist in that process. There is growing awareness among the Pacific Rim countries' policymakers of the importance of not only mitigation but of reducing vulnerability to the economic pain that is likely in a disaster's aftermath. In the November 2011 ministerial meeting of Asia-Pacific Economic Cooperation (APEC), the leaders issued a statement that details these concerns and describes the steps that APEC countries are encouraged to take in order to become more resilient (APEC 2011).

In addition to all these incentive problems that inhibit the desire to act, the resources needed are also typically only provided ex post rather than ex ante. Both private donations channeled through NGOs and public sector resources (from foreign or domestic sources, or both) generally become available only in the aftermath of catastrophic events, and are not available beforehand to prevent or mitigate any likely event.

4 Economic Impacts: Are Disasters a Poverty Trap?

A disaster's initial impact causes mortality, morbidity, and loss of physical infrastructure (residential housing, roads, telecommunication, and electricity networks, and other infrastructure). These initial impacts are followed by consequent impacts

[8] An equally plausible explanation for this finding is that newspaper circulation is a representation of more cohesive communities with higher 'social capital' (see Aldrich 2012).

on the economy (in terms of income, employment, sectoral composition of production, inflation, etc.). These indirect impacts, of course, are not pre-ordained, and the policy choices made in a catastrophic disaster's aftermath can have significant economic consequences. For example, by using a non-equilibrium dynamic growth model, Hallegatte et al. (2007) show that a country experiencing disastrous events may find itself unable to adequately reconstruct and may remain stuck in a post-disaster poverty trap. Thus, while post-disaster policy choices clearly have a direct economic impact in the short run, they potentially also have long-run consequences.

4.1 Short-run

The short-run impacts of disasters are usually evaluated in a regression framework of the form: $Y_{it} = \alpha + \beta \mathbf{X}_{it} + \gamma DIS_{it} + \varepsilon_{it}$; where Y_{it} is the measured variable of interest (e.g., per capita GDP), DIS_{it} is a measure of the disaster's immediate impact on country i at time t, $\mathbf{X}_{it}$ is a vector of control variables that potentially affect Y_{it}, and ε_{it} is an error term. Noy (2009) estimates a version of this equation and, in addition to the adverse short-run effect already described in Raddatz (2007), he describes some of the structural and institutional details that make this negative effect worse. Noy (2009) concludes that countries with a higher literacy rate, better institutions, higher per capita income, higher degree of openness to trade, higher levels of government spending, more foreign exchange reserves, and higher levels of domestic credit but with less open capital accounts are better able to withstand the initial disaster shock and prevent further spillovers into the macro-economy. These findings suggest that access to reconstruction resources and the capacity to utilize them effectively are of paramount importance is determining the speed and success of recovery.

Raddatz (2009) uses vector autoregressions (VARs) to conclude that smaller and poorer states are more vulnerable to these spillovers, and that most of the output cost of climatic events occurs during the year of the disaster. His evidence, together with Becerra et al. (2010), also suggests that, historically, aid flows have done little to attenuate the output consequences of climatic disasters.[9]

Even if aid inflows are typically not substantial enough to assist in complete reconstruction, bigger countries may be capable of engineering the inter-sectoral and inter-regional transfers required to fully mitigate the economic impact of natural disasters (Coffman and Noy 2010; Auffret 2003). The importance of inter-regional transfers was highlighted by the massive mobilization of reconstruction resources following the catastrophic Sichuan earthquake of 2008. The Chinese government

[9] Loayza et al. (2009) notes that while small disasters may, on average, have a positive impact (as a result of the reconstruction stimulus), large disasters always pose severe negative consequences for the economy in their immediate aftermath.

spent lavishly on reconstruction, with about 90 % coming from the central government and only 10 % financed locally in Sichuan.[10] The rebuilt infrastructure in the destroyed counties (which were remote and under-developed pre-quake) appears to be significantly superior to its previous state. Therefore, while direct losses may be high in large countries because of the increased wealth exposure, the greater capacity to absorb shocks means that indirect losses may be lower, and/or that the size of the damage may be lower relative to the size of the country.

Noy and Vu (2010) further focus on the importance of inter-regional transfers in Vietnam, and find that the post-disaster impact on economic activity across Vietnamese provinces appears to be determined by the provincial ability to attract reconstruction resources from the central government.

Very little research has attempted to examine household data and determine the effects of natural disasters on household expenditures. An important exception is Sawada and Shimizutani (2008) who examine household data after the 1995 Kobe earthquake in Japan. They find that, even in a rich country, credit-constrained households experienced significant reductions in consumption, while households with access to credit did not. Further evidence on the importance of credit is suggested by the Rodriguez-Oreggia et al. (2009) findings of a significant increase in poverty in disaster-affected municipalities in Mexico.

4.2 *Long-run*

Theoretically, the likely impact of natural disasters on growth dynamics is not clear. Standard neo-classical frameworks that view technical progress as exogenous—e.g. the Solow-Swan model with exogenous saving rate sand the Ramsey-Cass-Koopman model with consumer optimization—all predict that the destruction of physical capital will enhance growth since it will drive countries away from their balanced-growth steady states. In contrast, endogenous growth frameworks do not suggest such clear-cut predictions with respect to output dynamics depending on the approach used to explain the endogeneity of technological change. For example, models based on Schumpeter's creative destruction process may also ascribe higher growth as a result of negative shocks (Hallegatte and Dumas 2009), as these shocks can be catalysts for re-investment and upgrading of capital goods. Yet the AK-type endogenous growth models, in which the technology exhibits constant returns to capital, predict no change in the growth rate following a negative capital shock; though the economy that experiences a destruction of the capital stock will never go back to its previous growth trajectory. Endogenous growth models that have increasing returns to scale production generally predict that a destruction of part of the physical or human capital

[10] Data obtained from http://www.china.org.cn/china/earthquake_reconstruction/2010-01/25/content_19302110.htm (accessed on 11/11/11).

stock results in a lower growth path and consequently a permanent deviation from the previous growth trajectory.

To date, the empirical work on this question has also failed to reach a consensus. Skidmore and Toya (2002) uses the frequency of natural disasters in a cross-sectional dataset to examine long-run growth impacts of disasters, while Noy and Nualsri (2007) uses a panel of five-year country observations, as in the extensive literature that followed the work by Barro (1997). Intriguingly, they reach diametrically opposing conclusions, with the former identifying expansionary and the latter contractionary disaster effects. More recently, Jaramillo (2009) finds qualified support for the Noy and Nualsri (2007) conclusion.

Skidmore and Toya (2002) explain their somewhat counterintuitive finding by suggesting that disasters may be speeding up the Schumpeterian "creative destruction" process that is at the heart of the development of market economies. Cuaresma et al. (2008), however, find that for developing countries, disaster occurrence is associated with less knowledge spillover and a reduction in the amount of new technology being introduced rather than with an acceleration of these processes.

Cavallo et al. (2010) provide the most recent attempt to resolve this debate. They implement a new methodology based on constructing synthetic controls—i.e., a counterfactual that measures what would have happened to the path of the variable-of-interest in the affected country in the absence of the natural disaster. Using this methodology, they don't find any significant long-run effect of even very large disasters, except for very large events that were then followed by political upheavals. For these events, they find economically very substantial and statistically significant negative long run effects on per capita GDP.

Another possibility is suggested in Coffman and Noy (2012), where the question is the impact of a specific event (a hurricane) on an isolated Hawaiian island. In this instance, the authors conclude that while there was no long-term impact on per-capita variables, this is largely because the disaster led to an out-migration from which the island has never completely recovered (the net population loss was a very significant 15 %). Whether this pattern can be observed for other catastrophic events is not well established, though casual observation suggests that these irreversible out-migrations also happened in the case of New Orleans after hurricane Katrina, while in the city of Kobe after the earthquake of 1995 the population did not move away in spite of persistent decreases in incomes (see Vigdor 2008; Dupont and Noy 2012, respectively). There is much speculation that the same will be true for the Tohoku region of Japan that was hit by the March 2011 tsunami.

4.3 *Fiscal Impacts*

As we observed previously, disasters are likely to generate significant inter-regional transfers and/or international aid. Accurate estimates of the likely fiscal costs of disasters are useful in enabling better cost-benefit evaluation of various mitigation programs and in determining the appropriate level of insurance against disaster losses.[11]

On the expenditure side, publicly financed reconstruction costs may be very different from the original magnitude of destruction of capital, while on the revenue side of the fiscal ledger, the impact of disasters on tax and other public revenue sources has also seldom been quantitatively examined. Using panel VAR methodology, Noy and Nualsri (2011) and Melecky and Raddatz (2011) estimate the fiscal dynamics likely in an "average" disaster; they acknowledge, however, that the impacts of disasters on revenue and spending depend on the country-specific macroeconomic dynamics occurring following the disaster shock, the unique structure of revenue sources (income taxes, consumption taxes, custom duties, etc.), insurance coverage and the size of the financial sector, and government indebtedness.

The implications of these findings for the Pacific Rim region are quite obvious given the high degree of vulnerability of almost all countries in the region. Mexico's FONDEN (a disaster fund) provides an example of an ex-ante fiscal provisioning for disaster reconstruction, but this, while prudent, amount to a form of self-insurance, which may be very costly in the case of a developing economy with substantial borrowing costs.[12] Chile, in contrast, has used some of the funds available in its Sovereign Wealth Fund (the Copper Fund) to pay for reconstruction following the destructive earthquake of February, 2010. Japan, which can easily pursue counter-cyclical fiscal policy, resorted to additional borrowing to pay for the 2011 Tohoku earthquake reconstruction costs.

One way to overcome this lack of sufficient explicit insurance is for countries to mutually insure each other. While this is difficult to envision politically within any Pacific-Rim-wide grouping such as APEC, it may be more politically palatable and therefore practical in smaller and more geographically well-defined groupings like ASEAN (or ASEAN+3).

4.4 Disaster as an Opportunity?

Some argue that disasters provide an impetus for change, which can bring on positive economic changes that have long-term beneficial dynamic impact on the economy. Change can lead to "creative destruction" dynamics that entail replacing the old with new technologies and with upgrades of superior equipment, infrastructure, and production processes. The rapid growth of Germany and Japan after the

[11] Insurance could be purchased directly (maybe through re-insurance companies), indirectly through the issuance of catastrophic bonds (CAT bonds), or through precautionary savings

[12] In addition to FONDEN, Mexico is also one of the biggest issuers of CAT bonds. Even so, the provisioning of FONDEN has recently been insufficient to cover the costs of disasters in 2010 (see http://www.artemis.bm/blog/2010/09/16/fonden-mexicos-disaster-fund-exceeds-its-annual-bud get/ accessed 11/12/11).

destruction they experienced in World War II is widely used as an example of such beneficial dynamics. Even in these cases, however, empirical research failed to identify a long-term beneficial effect, at best finding a return to the pre-shock equilibrium (Davis and Weinstein 2002; Brakman et al. 2004).

Besides the potential 'creative' introduction of new technologies to replace the ones that had previously been destroyed, a large natural disaster changes political power dynamics in ways that may facilitate radical change. Rahm Emanuel, Barak Obama's former chief of staff, was often quoted as saying, "you never want a serious disaster to go to waste … it's an opportunity to do things you could not do before".[13] The evidence to date, however, does not suggest that after accounting for the loss of life and property, one can identify beneficial aspects to the destruction wrought by natural disasters.

5 A Disaster Risk Reduction Fund

Perrow (2007) argues that public policy should focus on the need to "shrink" the targets: lower population concentration in vulnerable (especially coastal) areas, and lower concentration of utilities and other infrastructure in disaster-prone locations. This advice also stems from the awareness that more ex-post assistance to damaged communities generates a "Samaritan's dilemma," i.e., an increase in risk-taking and a reluctance to purchase insurance when taking into account the help that is likely to be provided should a disaster strike.[14]

Constructing efficient and timely warning systems is clearly a desirable policy that is less controversial and more easily implementable. The 2004 South–East Asian tsunami, for example, led to an extension of the Pacific Tsunami Warning System to regions of Indonesia and the Indian Ocean that were previously unprotected. Operating warning systems, however, remains a long-term goal, and progress towards it can still be improved in cost-effective ways in most countries. A recent review of progress under the Hyogo Framework for Action adopted by the UN in 2005 concluded that in preparing early warning systems in the Asia Pacific: "achievement[s] are neither comprehensive nor substantial." (UNISDR 2011, p. 8).

The difficulty of developing an effective early-warning-system should not be underestimated. On April 11, 2012, a powerful earthquake (8.6 on the Richter scale) occurred not far offshore Banda Aceh, the city that was inundated by the 2004 South-East Asian tsunami with about 25,000 people killed (Doocy et al. 2007). By 2012, there was an early warning system in place for tsunami hazard in Aceh, but since everyone attempted to evacuate at the same time, roads became gridlocked very quickly as people were frantically trying to flee (Rondonuwu 2012). There were also wide-spread reports of various operational failures of the warning system

[13] Emanuel, at a Wall Street Journal event (see WSJ Nov. 21, 2008).

[14] See, for example, the discussion in Raschky and Weck-Hannemann (2007).

in this instance. Luckily, no significant tsunami was generated by the earthquake, but the inadequacy of a system developed specifically to prevent mortality if a repeat of the 2004 catastrophe were to occur was demonstrated quite starkly. Investment in effective mitigation and risk reduction is neither cheap nor easy as it also requires securing an effective response to the warnings that are supplied. Yet, the magnitude of benefits, in terms of life saved per dollar spent, are very large if these systems manage to prevent the very catastrophic disasters that occur all too frequently.[15]

If early-warning systems are indeed cost effective, why are they not being implemented wholeheartedly? As we discussed previously in analyzing the general underinvestment in preparedness, the answer is most likely political. In many cases, initiating the development of a disaster risk reduction (DRR) policy is clearly needed, and this can probably be best carried out with external support/incentives from the multilateral organizations. The World Bank, in particular, has been working on this front, but a dedicated fund, a Global Fund for DRR (GF-DRR), that will incentivize and support this work can and should result in the optimal allocation of resources for this task. Many developing countries lack coherent planning for disaster preparedness and risk reduction, and the knowledge collected by the international organizations (especially the World Bank), together with the funds to support this planning, can lead to a very cost effective implementation of a much more global DRR policy.

An appropriate DRR policy may primarily involve the funding of early warning systems in most cases, but may also involve other preparatory steps; DRR may mean retrofitting essential infrastructure for earthquakes (especially hospitals and other building where many people reside or work), moving people permanently away from wave-surge prone coastal regions or river flood-plains, or establishing more robust communication networks that will not collapse in the aftermath of a catastrophic event. Beyond costs, the appropriate steps needed depend on the broadly-defined institutional details, the current state of the economy, and predictions regarding likely future disaster risks.

Since all three factors (institutions, economy and disaster risk) are inherently local and widely varying, it would be difficult to attempt to devise a universally appropriate policy menu, or to argue for a universal implementation of any specific policy. Preparation of DRR is taking place, but much more needs to be done; especially since economic conditions are changing, and risk patterns are appearing to change as well. Future economic exposure to tropical storms, for example, is predicted to quadruple by 2100, with roughly half of this increase associated with higher population and property in vulnerable areas and half resulting from changing

[15] Kydland, Finn E., Robert Mundell, Thomas Schelling, Vernon Smith, and Nancy Stokey, 2012. Copenhagen Consensus: Expert Panel Findings. http://www.copenhagenconsensus.com/Admin/Public/DWSDownload.aspx?File = %2fFiles%2fFiler%2fCC12 + papers%2fOutcome_Document_Updated_1105.pdf

patterns in terms of new predicted storm tracks and storm intensities (Mendelsohn et al. 2012).

The International Monetary Fund (IMF) has been involved in post-crisis intervention for several decades. The lessons the IMF has learned, in terms of avoiding perverse incentives—e.g., moral hazard and adverse selection—and leading countries to adopt ex-ante sound policies, are as relevant to natural disasters. Essentially, the idea is that countries will be constantly evaluated for their DRR plans, and given 'Seals of Approval.' A country whose plans are favorably evaluated will have access to support for DRR projects and in addition will have access to an Emergency Disaster Fund should it be required (one can establish triggers that automatically provide affected countries access to pre-specified sums as grants or concessional loans). The evaluation process already undergoing through the Hyogo Framework umbrella may serve as a good starting point for developing the evaluation and scoring mechanisms that would allow a 'grading' of DRR policy and the allocation of the contingent 'seal of approval' for these policies.

An additional positive externality from such fund with its associated monitoring and evaluation functions, would be enabling countries who receive this DRR 'seal of approval' to more easily insure themselves explicitly (with re-insurers) or implicitly by issuing Catastrophic Bonds (CAT bonds) and further enable multi-year insurance. All three developments (re-insurance, CAT bonds and multi-year) will be made easier by having a 'seal of approval' since that seal will alleviate investors/insurers concerns regarding the moral hazard generated by the disaster-contingent financial support.

While macro-level explicit or implicit insurance has been growing in popularity in the last decade (see the discussion of a rice index insurance in a companion paper in this volume), the vast majority of CAT bonds, for example, are still issued by local organizations in developed countries or specialized insurance companies. Governments, at the local or national level, do not yet appear to avail themselves of these insurance opportunities, and the establishment of a 'seal of approval' may be the catalyst that will increase utilization of these new financial tools for handling catastrophic risk.

References

Aldrich, D. P. (2012). *Building resilience: Social capital in post-disaster recovery*. Chicago: University of Chicago Press.

Anbarci, N., Escaleras, M., & Register, C. A. (2005). Earthquake fatalities: The interaction of nature and political economy. *Journal of Public Economics, 89*, 1907–1933.

APEC. (2011). *APEC high level policy dialogue on disaster resiliency*. Singapore: APEC. http://www.apec.org/Meeting-Papers/Ministerial-Statements/High-Level-Policy-Dialogue/2011_disaster.aspx.

Auffret, P. (2003). *High consumption volatility: The impact of natural disasters?*, World Bank Policy Research Working Paper 2962. Washington D.C.: World Bank.

Barro, R. (1997). *Determinants of economic growth: A cross-country empirical study*. Cambridge: MIT.

Barro, R. (2006). Rare disasters and asset markets in the twentieth century. *Quarterly Journal of Economics, 121*, 823–866.

Barro, R. (2009). Rare disasters, asset prices, and welfare costs. *American Economic Review, 99* (1), 243–264.

Becerra, O., Cavallo, E., & Noy, I. (2010). *In the aftermath of large natural disasters, what happens to foreign aid?*, University of Hawaii Working Paper No. 10-18, Manoa: University of Hawaii.

Bechtel, M. M., & Hainmueller, J. (2011). How lasting is voter gratitude? An analysis of the short- and long-term electoral returns to beneficial policy. *American Journal of Political Science, 55* (4), 851–867.

Besley, T., & Burgess, R. (2002). The political economy of government responsiveness: Theory and evidence from India. *Quarterly Journal of Economics, 117*(4), 1415–1451.

Brakman, S., Garretsen, H., & Schramm, M. (2004). The strategic bombing of cities in Germany in World War II and its impact on city growth. *Journal of Economic Geography, 4*(1), 1–18.

Cavallo, E., Galiani, S., Noy, I., & Pantano, J. (2010). *Catastrophic natural disasters and economic growth*, Inter-American Development Bank Working Paper No. 183. Washington, D. C.: Inter-American Development Bank.

Cavallo, E., & Noy, I. (2011). The economics of natural disasters – A survey. *International Review of Environmental and Resource Economics, 5*(1), 63–102.

Coffman, M., & Noy, I. (2010). A hurricane hits Hawaii: A tale of vulnerability to natural disasters. *CESifo Forum, 11*(2), 67–72.

Coffman, M., & Noy, I. (2012). Hurricane Iniki: measuring the long-term economic impact of a natural disaster using synthetic control. *Environment and Development Economics, 17*, 187–205.

Cole, S., Andrew, H., & Werker, E. (2012). Do voters demand responsive governments? evidence from Indian disaster relief. *Journal of Development Economics, 97*(2), 167–181.

Cuaresma, J. C., Hlouskova, J., & Obersteiner, M. (2008). Natural disasters as creative destruction? evidence from developing countries. *Economic Inquiry, 46*(2), 214–226.

Davis, D., & Weinstein, D. (2002). Bones, bombs, and break points: The geography of economic activity. *American Economic Review, 92*(5), 1269–1289.

Doocy, S., Gorokhovich, Y., Burnham, G., Balk, D., & Robinson, C. (2007). Tsunami mortality estimates and vulnerability mapping in Aceh, Indonesia. *American Journal of Public Health, 97*, S146–S151.

Dupont, W., & Noy, I. (2012). *What happened to Kobe?*, University of Hawaii Working Paper No.201204. Manoa: University of Hawaii.

Elsner, J., Kossin, J., & Jagger, T. (2008). The increasing intensity of the strongest tropical cyclones. *Nature, 455*, 92–95.

Emanuel, K., Sundararajan, R., & Williams, J. (2008). Hurricanes and global warming: Results from downscaling IPCC AR4 simulations. *Bulletin of the American Meteorological Society, 89* (3), 347–367.

Hallegatte, S., & Dumas, P. (2009). Can natural disasters have positive consequences? Investigating the role of embodied technical change. *Ecological Economics, 68*(3), 777–786.

Hallegatte, S., Hourcade, J.-C., & Dumas, P. (2007). Why economic dynamics matter in assessing climate change damages: Illustration on extreme events. *Ecological Economics, 62*(2), 330–340.

Healy, A., & Malhotra, N. (2009). Myopic voters and natural disaster policy. *American Political Science Review, 103*, 387–406.

Healy, A., & Malhotra, N. (2010). Random events, economic losses, and retrospective voting: Implications for democratic competence. *Quarterly Journal of Political Science, 5*(2), 193–208.

IPCC. (2007). Summary for policymakers. In M. L. Parry, O. F. Canziani, J. P. Palutikof, P. J. van der Linden, & C. E. Hanson (Eds.), *Climate change 2007: Impacts, adaptation and vulnerability. Contribution of Working Group II to the fourth assessment report of the intergovernmental panel on climate change* (pp. 7–22). Cambridge: Cambridge University Press.

IPCC. (2011). Summary for policymakers. In C. B. Field, V. Barros, T. F. Stocker, D. Qin, D. J. Dokken, K. L. Ebi, M. D. Mastrandrea, K. J. Mach, G.-K. Plattner, S. K. Allen, M. Tignor, & P. M. Midgley (Eds.), *Managing the risks of extreme events and disasters to advance climate change adaptation. A special report of Working Groups I and II of the intergovernmental panel on climate change* (pp. 1–19). Cambridge and New York: Cambridge University Press.

IPCC. (2012). Managing the Risks of Extreme Events and Disasters to Advance Climate Change Adaptation. A Special Report of Working Groups I and II of the Intergovernmental Panel on Climate Change [Field, C.B., V. Barros, T.F. Stocker, D. Qin, D.J. Dokken, K.L. Ebi, M.D. Mastrandrea, K.J. Mach, G.-K. Plattner, S.K. Allen, M. Tignor, and P.M. Midgley (eds.)]. Cambridge University Press, Cambridge, UK

Jaramillo, C. R. H. (2009). *Do natural disasters have long-term effects on growth? Manuscript.* Bogotá: Universidad de los Andes.

Kahn, M. E. (2005). The death toll from natural disasters: The role of income, geography, and institutions. *Review of Economics and Statistics, 87*(2), 271–284.

Li, T., Kwon, M. H., Zhao, M., Kug, J.-S., Luo, J.-J., & Yu, W. (2010). Global warming shifts Pacific Tropical cyclone location. *Geophysical Research Letters, 37*, L21804.

Loayza, N., Olaberría, E., Rigolini, J., & Christiansen, L. (2009). *Natural disasters and growth-going beyond the averages*, World Bank Policy Research Working Paper 4980.Washington, D. C.: The World Bank.

Melecky, M., & Raddatz, C. (2011). *How do governments respond after catastrophes? natural-disaster shocks and the fiscal stance*, World Bank Policy Research Working Paper 5564. Washington D.C.: World Bank.

Mendelsohn, R., Emanuel, K., Chonabayashi, S., & Bakkensen, L. (2012). The impact of climate change on global tropical cyclone damage. *Nature Climate Change, 2*, 205–209.

Noy, I. (2009). The macroeconomic consequences of disasters. *Journal of Development Economics, 88*(2), 221–231.

Noy, I., & Nualsri, A. (2007). *What do exogenous shocks tell us about growth theories?*, University of Hawaii Working Paper No. 07-28. Manoa: University of Hawaii.

Noy, I., & Nualsri, A. (2011). Fiscal storms: Public spending and revenues in the aftermath of natural disasters. *Environment and Development Economics, 16*(1), 113–128.

Noy, I., & Vu, T. (2010). The economics of natural disasters in Vietnam. *Journal of Asian Economics, 21*, 345–354.

Pelling, M., Özerdem, A., & Barakat, S. (2002). The macroeconomic impact of disasters. *Progress in Development Studies, 2*(4), 283–305.

Perrow, C. (2007). *The next catastrophe: Reducing our vulnerabilities to natural, industrial, and terrorist disasters*. Princeton: Princeton University Press.

Raddatz, C. (2007). Are external shocks responsible for the instability of output in low-income countries? *Journal of Development Economics, 84*(1), 155–187.

Raddatz, C. (2009). *The wrath of god: Macroeconomic costs of natural disasters*, World Bank Policy Research Working Paper #5039. Washington D. C.: World Bank.

Rahmstorf, S. (2007). A semi-empirical approach to projecting future sea-level rise. *Science, 315* (5810), 368–370.

Raschky, P. A. (2008). Institutions and the losses from natural disasters. *Natural Hazards Earth System Sciences, 8*, 627–634.

Raschky, P. A., & Weck-Hannemann, H. (2007). Charity hazard—A real hazard to natural disaster insurance? *Environmental Hazards, 7*, 321–329.

Rodriguez-Oreggia, E., de la Fuente, A., de la Torre, R., Moreno, H., & Rodriguez, C. (2009). *The impact of natural disasters on human development and poverty at the municipal level in Mexico*, Manuscript. *Journal of Development Studies*, 49(3), pp. 442–455.

Rondonuwu, O. (2012). *Tsunami alerts pass Indonesia quake test, with luck.* Reuters [online]. http://www.reuters.com/article/2012/04/12/uk-asia-quake-idUSLNE83B00T20120412. Accessed on April 12, 2012.

Sawada, Y., & Shimizutani, S. (2008). How do people cope with natural disasters? Evidence from the Great Hanshin-Awaji (Kobe) earthquake in 1995. *Journal of Money, Credit and Banking, 40*(2–3), 463–488.

Skidmore, M., & Toya, H. (2002). Do natural disasters promote long-run growth? *Economic Inquiry, 40*(4), 664–687.

Strömberg, D. (2007). Natural disasters, economic development, and humanitarian aid. *Journal of Economic Perspectives, 21*(3), 199–222.

UNISDR. (2011). *HFA progress in Asia Pacific: Regional synthesis report 2009–2011.* Geneva: United Nations International Strategy for Disaster Reduction (UNISDR).

Vermeer, M., & Rahmstorf, S. (2009) Global sea level linked to global temperature. In W. C. Clark (Ed.), *Proceedings of the National Academy of Sciences* (PNAS) *Physical Sciences – Sustainability Science* (pp. 1–6). Washington D.C.: PNAS.

Vigdor, J. (2008). The economic aftermath of Hurricane Katrina. *Journal of Economic Perspectives, 22*(4), 135–154.

Webster, P. J., Holland, G. J., Curry, J. A., & Chang, H. R. (2005). Changes in tropical cyclone number, duration, and intensity. *Science, 309*(5742), 1844–1846.

Chapter 12
Impacts of Disasters and Disaster Risk Management in Malaysia: The Case of Floods

Ngai Weng Chan

1 Introduction

As floods are the single most severe of all disasters in Malaysia, the chapter specifically focuses on flood disaster management. This is followed by an emphasis on ex post and ex ante analysis of the past and potential socioeconomic impacts of flood disasters in Malaysia. This chapter then reviews and assesses the effectiveness of the Malaysian government's flood disaster management system with respect to risk identification, emergency preparedness, institutional capacity building, risk mitigation, and catastrophe risk financing. A detailed discussion on the current constraints that prevent people from engaging in post-disaster supports follows. Finally, the chapter ends with policy recommendations for reforms at the national level and explores the prospects for regional cooperation framework in disaster management.

1.1 Overview of Disasters in Malaysia

Malaysia lies in a geologically stable region which is free from earthquakes, volcanic activities, and strong winds such as tropical cyclones which periodically affect some of its neighbors. It lies geographically just outside the "Pacific Ring of Fire." It also lies too far south of the major typhoon paths, although tail-ends of tropical storms have occasionally hit it. However, that does not mean Malaysia is totally "free" from natural disasters and calamities, as it is often hit by floods, droughts, landslides, haze, tsunamis, and human-made disasters (Parker et al. 1997). Annually, disasters such as floods account for a significant number

N.W. Chan (✉)
Universiti Sains Malaysia, Pulau Pinang, Malaysia
e-mail: nwchan@usm.my

D.P. Aldrich et al. (eds.), *Resilience and Recovery in Asian Disasters*, Risk, Governance and Society 18, DOI 10.1007/978-4-431-55022-8_12

of casualties, disease epidemics, property and crop damage and other intangible losses (Chan et al. 2002a).

In the past few decades, the country has experienced various extreme weather and climatic events, including El Nino in 1997 (which led to severe droughts), La Nina in 2011 and 2012 (which brought floods), freak thunderstorms almost every year (which brought wind damage, flash floods and landslides), monsoonal floods (which brought about heavy losses, including loss of life in many parts of the country exposed to monsoon winds), and haze (which brought about poor air quality, extreme heat and drought). Monsoonal floods are an annual occurrence which varies in terms of severity, place and time of occurrences with a recent 2010 flood in Kedah and Perlis being among the worst flood ever experienced by the country. The total economic loss and the financial burden on the government were enormous. When two or more of these events coincide such as the "Terrible twins" (La Nina and the monsoon season) that hit the federal capital of Kuala Lumpur and Selangor in December 2011, the damage is compounded (The Star 2011). The haze phenomenon in 1997/1998 also caused significant problems due to losses in tourist income, health effects and hospitalization costs, and mitigation losses (Kunii et al. 2002). More recently, the 2005 haze episode in Malaysia was a week-long choking haze (at its worst on August 11) that affected mostly the central part of Peninsular Malaysia. The air quality in Kuala Lumpur was so poor that health officials advised citizens to stay at home. The event also led to crisis talks with Indonesia and caused widespread health effects and inconvenience (Ahmad and Hashim 2006). The Asian Tsunami which hit in December 2004 was also very severely felt on the coasts of Peninsular Malaysia, most notably in Penang, Kedah, Perlis and Langkawi (Chan 2009). Due to Malaysia's wet equatorial climate regime with frequent heavy rain storms of high rainfall intensities, landslide disasters are common. In recent decades, landslide disasters in the Klang Valley Region and elsewhere have caused significant loss of life, property and infrastructure damage, environmental destruction and anxiety (Chan 1998a; Periasamy 2011).

Arguably, of all the disasters in Malaysia, floods are most frequent and bring the greatest damage annually. In 1996, floods brought by Tropical Storm Greg in Keningau (Sabah State), claimed 241 lives, caused more than USD 97.8 million damage to infrastructure and property and destroyed thousands of houses. In 2000, floods caused by heavy rains killed 15 people in Kelantan and Terengganu, and caused more than 10,000 people to flee their homes in northern Peninsular Malaysia. The December 2006/January 2007 floods in Johor caused 18 deaths and USD 489 million in damage. In 2008, floods occurred in Johor again, killing 28 people and causing damage estimated at USD 21.19 million. In 2010, the floods affected transportation in and around Kedah and Perlis, shutting down rail, closing roads including the North-South Expressway (The Star 2010c) and the airport in Kedah's capital city of Alor Setar leaving helicopters as the only mode of aerial transport into Kedah and Perlis (The Star 2010d). Water supply in Kedah and Perlis was contaminated, forcing these two states to seek supplies from their neighbor Perak (Bernama 2010a). Kedah and Perlis are the "Rice Bowl" of Malaysia, and the floods destroyed an estimated 45,000 ha of rice fields with the government pledging USD8.476 million in aid to farmers (in both states (Bernama 2010c).

1.2 Literature Review

1.2.1 The Top-Down Government-Centric Model

Historically, disaster management in Malaysia has commonly been considered as a government function and is largely based on top-down government-centered machinery (Chan 1995). At the very top, the government agency responsible for disaster management (all sorts) is the National Security Division (NSD) under the Prime Minister's Department. The NSD is therefore responsible for coordinating activities related to the preparation for, prevention of, response to and handling of disasters, basically referring to natural and technological disasters. Currently, the handling and resolving of disasters in Malaysia are managed via the Committee System which emphasizes the concept of coordination and mobilization of agencies involved, in an integrated and coordinated manner. At the highest Federal level, the National Disaster Management and Relief Committee (NDMRC) is in charge of managing and handling national-level disasters. State-level disasters are managed by the State Disaster Management and Relief Committee (SDMRC). At the third level, district-level disasters are managed by at the District Disaster Management and Relief Committee (DDMRC). At the lowest village level, village-level disasters are managed by the DDMRC with inputs from the village committee.

All these committees at various levels are integrated via "Vertical Coordination" (e.g. between FDMRC and SDMRC) as well as via "Horizontal Coordination" (e.g. between the State Police Department and the State Drainage & irrigation Department). The above disaster management mechanism has been widely applied in flood disasters which is the major type of disaster affecting the country (Chan 2011). Before the country went through modernization and industrialization, there were also meteorological disasters, strong winds, rain-induced monsoon floods, and other natural disasters. However, since independence in 1957, other kinds of disaster have been experienced, such as fires, explosions, structural collapse, landslides, biological/disease-related disasters, flash floods and landslides caused by slope disturbance resulting from human activities. According to Yusof (n.d.), Malaysia has transformed radically from an agrarian economy to a modern industrialized nation. This rapid process of development and transformation has given rise to the occurrence of a range of man-made disasters that are considered as "landmark" disasters whereby various safety and emergency acts and regulations were proposed, amended or formulated, resulting also in the formation of specialized teams in disaster management. This government-centric approach is employed to address both the physical/natural (Sham 1973) as well as the human aspects of flood management (Leigh and Low 1983).

1.2.2 The Technocentric Model

In terms of flood disasters much of the relevant research literature reflects a technocentric approach which strongly emphasizes the use of structural/engineering methods in addressing floods (Chan 1995). Consequently, it is not surprising to find that the bulk of the literature on flood studies in Malaysia is largely focused on the field of engineering and hydrology. Some notable examples are Volker (1971), Drainage and Irrigation Department (1973, 1974, 1976), Japan International Cooperation Agency (1989, 1991), Syed Mohammad et al. (1988), Julien et al. (2010) and Ab. Ghani et al. (2012). Such an approach is central within the "Society over Nature" school of thought, or technocentricism, which asserts that science can solve all flood problems. This cannot be further from the truth in an ever-changing world, especially in the context of rapidly developing Malaysia. Despite the fact that technology plays an important role in flood hazard management, it is a fallacy that it can provide the means of total protection against all floods. In fact, Jones (1991) has observed that technology can increase vulnerability to floods.

1.2.3 The Natural Science Perspective

Against the background of the technocentric approach is the "natural science perspective," which is essentially the natural scientist's explanation to the occurrence of flood hazards. Alexander (1993) states that this approach focuses on how natural processes in the "Earth-Atmosphere System" create hazards. This approach also takes into account the importance of society in altering the physical processes, but the flood hazard is principally attributed to the natural causes (e.g. monsoon winds and rains). Some good examples of the natural scientist's approach to flood hazards in Malaysia are Chan (1998b) and Lim (1988). The natural science perspective is essentially a "tech-fix" approach, although in recent years it has incorporated ecological, biological, environmental and sustainability considerations. Because of its emphasis on technology as a means of alleviating hazards, it has often been criticized as being too narrow an approach. No field of science can predict the occurrence of hazard events with any level of certainty. Studies by others have also shown that disasters occur because of other factors such as the misapplication of technology, institutional ineffectiveness, warning ineffectiveness, and hazard generating socio-political systems (Winchester 1992).

1.2.4 The Organizational Perspective

Another flood disaster management approach is that of the organizational perspective, originally an approach used by organizational analysts in explaining hazards. This approach focuses upon the ways in which organizations such as government agencies, private companies, NGOs and other civil society voluntary bodies tackle hazards. Disaster managers in the field of economics, geography, systems analysis, planning and sociology who are concerned with "collective behavior" and "collective decision-making" are probably responsible for this perspective (Parker 1992). The role played by organizations cannot be underestimated because they are powerful and influential. The argument is that organizations may contribute in one way or another to the creation or worsening of hazards. Turner (1978) examined hazards arising out of organizational inefficiencies. Reasons for failures include organization inefficiencies (within and outside), existence of organizational "sub-cultures" which lead to "collective blindness" to the hazard, "organizational exclusivity", poor information dissemination and others. Handmer and Parker (1991) have documented the tendency for organizations to "groupthink," resulting in the narrowing of options, and noted the existence of a high level of secrecy amongst the bureaucracy of government organizations, all of which hinder emergency planning. In Malaysia, the organizational approach has been studied by Chan (1997a), who found that organizations tend to protect and safeguard self-interest rather than expose their weaknesses.

1.2.5 The Vulnerability Model and the Structural Paradigm

Vulnerability to flood disasters in Malaysia is another approach (Chan 2000). The study of disaster vulnerability originated from the "Structural Paradigm" in which disasters were believed to be subject to cultural, social, economic and political forces (Torry 1979). In developing countries and poor countries, it was discovered that broader structural forces (local and national) were more powerful and pervasive than local factors in affecting the outcome of hazards and disasters (Wadell 1983; Hewitt 1983). This radical view gave a new insight that went beyond the conventional geophysical cause of hazards and disasters. More recently, the recognition that structural forces at the international level can strongly affect local vulnerability has resulted in an expanded version of the structural paradigm, known as the "political economy paradigm" or the "political ecology perspective of hazards" (Blaikie et al. 1994; Varley 1994). All these approaches to disasters are essentially "structuralist" views that link social relations to disasters and are rooted in Marxist political economy. In Malaysia, Chan (2000) has used this paradigm to study flood hazards, and has proposed measures to reduce the exposure of people to flood hazards and also to reduce people's vulnerability to floods. Chan (1996) has found that vulnerability to flood disasters in Malaysia is not solely influenced by poverty, but more importantly by awareness, perception, attitude, experience, length of residence and social relations (Jamaluddin 1985).

2 Flood Disaster Risk in Malaysia

Malaysia is a country very prone to flood risks, mostly by nature of its physical (e.g. topography and drainage) as well as its human geography (e.g. settlement and land use patterns). The combination of natural and human factors has produced different types of floods, viz. monsoon, flash and tidal (Chan 1998b). Malaysians are historically a riverine people, as early settlements grew on the banks of the major rivers in the peninsula. Coupled with natural factors such as heavy monsoon rainfall, intense convection rain storms, poor drainage and other local factors, floods have become a common feature in the lives of a significant number of Malaysians. Monsoon and flash floods are the most severe climate-related natural disasters in Malaysia, with a flood-prone area of about 29,000 km^2 affecting more than 4.82 million people (22 % of the population) and inflicting annual damage of USD 298.29 million. With annual heavy monsoon rains averaging more than 3,000 mm and such a large flood-prone area, flood risk is indeed high, most notably in riverine areas and coastal flat lands. With such a large population living in flood-prone areas, flood exposure is high as well. Because of such high flood risks and exposure, the Malaysian Government is forced to spend a huge amount of its annual budget to mitigate against floods.

According to Hj Ahmad Hussaini, the Director General of the Drainage and Irrigation Department of the government of Malaysia, there are two major water-related problems affecting this country. These are excess water (floods) and water shortage (droughts). Both these problems have disrupted the quality of life and economic growth in the country and can result in severe damage and loss of property, and occasionally loss of human lives, as can be seen in the December 2006 and January 2007 floods in Johor (Hussaini 2007). Floods occur annually in Malaysia, causing damage to property and loss of life. It is useful to distinguish "normal" from "major" flood events. "Normal floods" are seasonal monsoon floods (November to March) whereby the waters do not normally exceed the stilt height of traditional Malay houses. Thus, people living in stilt houses in the rural areas are well adapted to normal floods. It is the major floods, which are "unusual" or "extreme" events that render people helpless. These floods are extensive, severe and unpredictable and result in significant loss of life, damage to crops, livestock, property, and public infrastructure (Winstedt 1927). In a major flood, people's coping mechanisms are totally ineffective and they are forced to rely on government relief for recovery. During major floods, a flood depth of 3 m is not uncommon, and hundreds of thousands of people are often evacuated. Historically, Malaysia experienced major floods in the years 1926, 1963, 1965, 1967, 1969, 1971, 1973, 1979, 1983, 1988, 1993, 1998, 2005 and most recently in December 2006 and January 2007. Recent urbanization amplifies the cost of damage in infrastructures, bridges, roads, agriculture and private commercial and residential properties. At the peak of the most recent Johor flood, around 110,000 people were evacuated to relief centers, and 18 people died. (Hussaini 2007).

In the past, natural causes such as heavy intense rainfall (monsoon or convective) and low-lying flat terrain were the main causes of flooding. However, deforestation reduces the role of forests as natural flood attenuation systems (Chan 2003; Chan et al. 2002b). As a result of deforestation, a very high proportion of rainfall becomes surface runoff, and this causes breaching of river capacity resulting in floods. Yet development has continued unabated. In more recent years, rapid development within river basins has further increased runoff and reduced river capacity, resulting in an increase in both flood frequency and magnitude. Urban areas are the most susceptible to flooding, and with more than 60 % of the Malaysian population now urban, flash flooding in urban areas has become a very serious problem (surpassing the monsoon floods) since the mid 1990s. This is reflected in flood frequency and magnitude, social-economic disruption, public outcry, media coverage and the government's escalating allocation of funds for flood mitigation.

3 Socioeconomic Impacts of Flood Disasters

Among all disasters, floods cause the most damage in Malaysia. The annual costs incurred by the Malaysian Government in rescue and flood relief operations, as well as rehabilitation of public works and utilities, are substantial. It is estimated that the costs of damage for an annual flood, a 10-year flood and a 40-year flood are USD 0.98 million, USD 5.87 million and USD 14.34 million respectively. The 1926 flood was perhaps the biggest flood in living memory in Malaysia. During this flood most parts of the country were affected. The 1971 flood was so serious that it was declared a national disaster by the Prime Minister. Total flood loss was estimated at USD 65.2 million then and there were 61 deaths. The 1967 flood damage estimated for the Kelantan River Basin alone was USD 25.43 million.

The socio-economic impacts of floods in terms of flood damage vary. However, there is now a considerable volume of literature on flood damage assessment (Chan and Parker 1996). Flood damage in terms of losses can be direct or indirect, and both categories include tangible and intangible losses. While the assessment of tangible losses is fairly straightforward, the evaluation of intangible losses can be problematic. Despite this, there have been attempts to quantify intangible flood damages so that they can be included in cost-benefit analysis (Green et al. 1988). In Northern Peninsular Malaysia, the 2004 flood resulted in tidal flooding that caused considerable damage to residential and commercial properties located on or near the eastern and northern coasts of the area. While the damage in rural areas was largely confined to residential properties (largely farms and fishermen's properties) resulting in the loss of livestock and crops, farm machinery, fishing vessels and equipment, and damage to building structure and contents, tsunami flooding in coastal urban areas involved damage to residential and commercial properties, vehicles, materials, machinery, goods and loss of business. And because of the high density of residential and commercial properties, infrastructure and public utilities in urban areas, the urban damage toll is expected to be much higher than in the rural areas. Though commercial properties suffered much greater damage in monetary terms, the households suffered the most in terms of damage in kind (intangible losses) and affected members of households are usually the victims that carry with them the trauma and mental damage for life. Jamaluddin (1985) suggests that victims need to respond positively and appropriately to flood disasters if they hope to have any chance of quick recovery.

In the flood damage assessment literature, damage or losses have been categorized as direct or indirect. Such damage is further categorized as tangible or intangible (Parker et al. 1987). According to Chan (1995), tangible flood damage refers to those effects of flooding which can be assigned monetary values. They can be direct as in the case of damage to building structures or indirect as in the case of the loss suffered as a result of drop in business volume. Direct flood damage results from the contact of flood water and its contents (sediment, oil etc.) with buildings and their contents, vehicles, livestock and crops, humans, memorabilia, etc. For residential properties, the pressure and contact of flood water may give rise to adverse effects on building structure (walls, floors, stilts etc.), damage to garden and house contents such as furniture, electrical appliances, household utensils, carpets, wiring systems and sockets, etc. In the case of commercial properties, additional effects may include damage to shop fittings, goods, raw material, machinery, etc.

In the case of residential properties, indirect damage includes the cost of alternative accommodation, costs of transportation (of family members and household contents), loss of income through disruption to work, costs of treatment for illness resulting from floods (especially children and the elderly being exposed to the cold waters), loss of schooling and subsequent costs of extra lessons to catch up with the syllabus, etc. Intangible flood damage refers to those effects of flooding to which it is not currently possible to assign acceptable monetary values (Pearce 1976). The only common property shared by "intangibles" is that they cannot be evaluated for one reason or another (Parker et al. 1987). As with tangible damages, it is possible to have both direct and indirect intangible damages. The damage of historical buildings by flooding is a direct effect but it would be difficult to evaluate the loss in monetary terms. This is then an intangible direct loss. On the other hand, the inconvenience caused by a flood is difficult to measure in monetary terms. This is then termed an intangible indirect loss.

According to findings by Green et al. (1988), the non-monetary (intangible) impacts of flooding are far more important to the households affected than the cost of the damage done. Physical damage to buildings and their contents are the most visible but not always the most serious effects of flooding (Green et al. 1983). Among the notable intangible damage is disruption to the household's life caused by a flood and the stress of the flood event itself; subsequent health damage; loss of memorabilia or of other irreplaceable and non-monetary goods; and possible evacuation. Furthermore, stress and worry about the risk and consequences of future flooding may also damage a person's health. Chan and Parker (1997) have evaluated the socio-economic aspects of flood disasters in Peninsular Malaysia and found that non-monetary and intangible effects are just as significant as monetary impacts.

4 Flood Disaster Risk Management

4.1 Background

In Malaysia, the Drainage and Irrigation Department's Flood Mitigation Policy and Strategy consists of both structural measures (for example dams and embankments to control flood flows) and non-structural measures (for example land use planning and flood forecasting and warning systems to mitigate the impact of flooding). Hence policy guidelines for implementing flood mitigation measures include the following: (i) implementation of structural flood mitigation in terms of engineering and socio- economic environment; (ii) implementation of complementary non-structural measures; (iii) implementation of non-engineering measures where there is no engineering solution; and (iv) continuation of strengthening flood forecasting and warning systems (Hussaini 2007).

In terms of flood mitigation and management, Malaysia conducted a National Water Resources Study in 1982 on structural and non-structural measures for flood mitigation and management (Japan International Cooperation Agency 1982). The government also conducted a number of flood mitigation projects but these were mostly structural mitigation measures such as canalization of rivers, raising river embankments and the building of multi-purpose dams. Interestingly, despite their high costs compared to non-structural measures, structural measures continue to this day to be favored. The financial allocations for such projects have consequently increased significantly in every one of Malaysia's subsequent five yearly development plans. Such escalating expenditures put a heavy strain on the government, and there have been suggestions that strategies be re-examined with the objective of developing a more proactive approach in finding ways and means to address the flood disasters in a holistic manner. The current government machinery allows the Economic Planning Unit of the Prime Minister's Department to coordinate all aspects of planning, design and implementation of water resources (including flood management) in the country.

4.2 Malaysian Flood Disaster Relief and Preparedness Machinery

The Malaysian Flood Disaster Relief and Preparedness Machinery (MFDRPM) was set up after the disastrous flood of 1971 when the National Disasters Management and Relief Committee (NDMRC) was formed. This committee was entrusted with responsibility for planning, coordinating and supervising relief operations during floods. Unfortunately, this was an entirely top-down approach as most of the organizations in the committee were governmental departments/agencies and social organizations that are able to provide shelter, rescue, food and medical supplies. Through the various government levels, the NDMRC, SDMRC and DDMRC committees coordinate between government departments and various voluntary organizations. In terms of early warning, the Flood Forecasting and Warning Systems have been upgraded (Chan 1997b).

The Department of Irrigation and Drainage Malaysia is responsible for providing flood forecasting and warning service to the public. It has established an Internet-based National Flood Monitoring System known as Infobanjir (http://infobanjir.moa.my), enabling rainfall and water level data can be collected for the whole country. The government has been working closely with the Canadian government to establish the GEOREX Monsoon Flood System for the Kelantan River Basin, a flood monitoring system integrating remote sensing, hydrological modeling and geographical information systems (GIS). This system allows the merging of hydrological data, such as river water levels and potential flooded areas, with geographical data on demography and transportation infrastructure.

Flood management activities undertaken include the following: (i) the National Water Resources Study; (ii) development of infrastructure for flood forecasting and warning systems; (iii) "Infobanjir" (the National Flood Monitoring System); (iv) "Flood Watch" (a flood forecasting and warning system); and (v) the Urban Storm-water Management Manual for Malaysia (MSMA) (Hussaini 2007). All these flood management activities are basically a combination of structural methods aimed at "controlling" floods and non-structural methods aimed at reducing flood impacts. One famous example of a structural method is the Storm-water Management and Road Tunnel (also known as the SMART Project), developed by the Drainage and Irrigation Department to alleviate flash flood problems in the Federal capital of Kuala Lumpur (Umar 2007). The 9.7 km long, 11.83 m diameter tunnel integrates both storm water management and a motorway in the same tunnel. In contrast, an example of a non-structural method is the flood forecasting and warning system (Drainage and Irrigation Department 1988).

In Malaysia, disaster management is almost entirely based on a top-down approach. At the very top is the NDMRC running a National Crisis and Disaster Management Mechanism (NCDMM). According to Chia (2004), this machinery was established with the objective of co-coordinating relief operations at the Federal, state and district levels so that assistance can be provided to flood victims in an orderly and effective manner. In the case of floods, the NCDMM would be called the National Flood Disaster Relief Machinery (NFDRM). The NFDRM is basically a reactive system, as it reacts to major floods when they occur. The coordination of flood relief operations is the responsibility of the National Flood Disaster Management & Relief Committee (NFDMRC), headed by the Minister of Information with its secretariat at the National Security Council (NSC). The committee is empowered, among other things, to declare any district, state or even the whole nation to be in a state of disaster so as to be eligible for financial assistance from the Federal Government. Members of this committee include government departments/agencies and social organizations which provide shelter, rescue and food supplies in case of disaster.

The NFDRM is theoretically responsible for all operations at the national, state, district, *mukim* and village levels. In reality, however, it coordinates operations at the national level and overseas operations at the state level. Much of the activity in each state is left to be run by the respective state authorities. Its main task is to ensure that assistance and aid are provided to flood victims in an orderly and effective manner from the national level downwards. As a result, its approach to disaster mitigation is largely reactive (Chan 1995). For example, this body meets annually just before the onset of the northeast monsoon season to organize flood disaster preparedness, evacuation and rehabilitation work. It is also more of a welfare body than it is a flood management organization. The Disaster Relief and Preparedness Committee (DRPC) coordinates all relief operations from the Malaysian Control Centre in Kuala Lumpur. At the state level, there are 13 State Disaster Relief and Preparedness Committees (SDRPC) for Malaysia. Each state is given funds by the Federal Government every year to enable it to run its own disaster relief operations. At the district level, there are several district committees under each state, depending on the number of districts in a particular state.

Each district will have its own District Disaster Relief and Preparedness Committees (DDRPC) which receives funds and directives from the SDRPC. Below the district level, there are several *mukim* Disaster Relief and Preparedness Committees (MDRPC), again depending on the number of *mukim* in each district. Each MDRPC is headed by a penghulu (County Head). Finally, there are many Village Disaster Relief and Preparedness Committees (VDRPC) under each *mukim*. Each VDRPC is headed by a ketua kampong (village Head). The National Disaster Response Mechanism (NDRM) is basically a system responding to disasters, as its name suggests. As such, its approach towards disaster management/reduction is largely reactive. Because Malaysia's main type of disaster is flooding, the NDRM is largely targeted at handling monsoon flooding. Consequently, this mechanism is less than effective and should be re-modeled into something more pro-active. There is also a serious lack in terms of stakeholder participation, although the authorities have recognized the important role of NGOs, particularly that of MERCY, the Red Cross, the Red Crescent and other NGOs. This is likely due to heavy the dependence of communities on government, and the reluctance of government to relinquish responsibilities to the public. Public apathy may also be a reason for low public participation in disaster management. Capacity building is therefore necessary. NGOs and other stakeholders should be involved right from the beginning, from pre-disaster preparedness to rescue and reconstruction. NGOs would be particularly effective in creating awareness and education on disasters. The disaster management mechanism should also adopt more non-structural measures, use state-of-the-art technology and cooperate internationally with other countries for addressing transboundary disasters.

4.2.1 Limitations of the Malaysian Flood Disaster Management Model

As a country which is almost annually affected by flooding, Malaysia employees countless measures and strategies to reduce floods. While many of these strategies have been responsible for reducing some of the impacts of flooding, they have not been entirely successful in the overall management of floods. This is largely due to an outdated reactive approach based on evacuation, relief and rehabilitation, the low salience of floods on government agendas, the lack of interaction and cooperation amongst government agencies dealing with floods, the bureaucratic nature of government agencies, and the victims' reluctance to relocate. In fact, floodplain encroachment has even exacerbated flood hazards, as more and more people are forced to occupy floodplains due to the shortage of land, high rents and rural–urban migration. Urban floodplains have also extensively developed as a result of rapid urbanization leading to greater flood damage potentials (Chan 1996; Chia 2004).

In Malaysia, flood forecasting and warning systems have also not developed as quickly as expected (Drainage and Irrigation Department 1988). Currently, two flood forecasting models have been developed and used by the Drainage and Irrigation Department Malaysia, viz. the Linear Transfer Function Model (LTFM) at Pahang River and the Tank Model at Kelantan River (Umar 2007). The agencies involved in flood relief have used information from the models to decide when they should mobilize their staff and equipment to the areas that are potentially to be hit. The flood warning system consists of dissemination systems such as automatic warning sirens, the Short Messaging System (SMS), telephone, fax and the website (http://infobanjir.water.gov.my, Accessed 16 May 2012). The current system being used is not state-of-the-art technology, as it does not have radar or satellite rainfall forecasts as inputs into computer models. Rather, it uses river levels as inputs. The number of automated telemetric rain gauges and river level recorders is also short of the required number. As a result, the advantages of flood forecasting and warnings have not been maximized and the current system appears cumbersome and ineffective. This has led to a lack of confidence amongst floodplain users and flood victims in flood forecasts and warnings (Chan 1997c). While every effort is made by relevant authorities to improve formal (official) FWESs, there has been little attempt to incorporate traditional (informal) FWESs into them. Traditional FWESs are an integral part of the Malaysian cultural heritage and are closely knitted into the fabric of rural societies. Due to years of responding to flood hazards, traditional FWESs are based on practical knowledge of adaptation and have served people well. As such, the authorities should incorporate them into formal FWESs in order to maximize the effectiveness of overall flood warning and evacuation response from the people.

As a developing country, Malaysia's flood mitigation policy can be described as commendable. Since the First Malaysia Plan (1971–1975), the country's expenditure on flood mitigation has increased substantially. From a mere USD 4.56 million in this plan, it has shot up to a massive USD 228.2 million for the Sixth Malaysia Plan (1991–1995), a 50-fold increase over a 20 year period. During the 10th Malaysia Plan, the budget allocated for flood management was USD 1.17 billion, a 256-fold increase. Even after discounting inflation, the real increase is still substantial. With the many structural and non-structural measures being implemented for flood control and for flood relief, the country is moving in the right direction towards a comprehensive program of flood mitigation. Yet, there are many areas which can still be improved. While the total number of telemetric stations for rainfall and river flow in the country seems large enough, a closer scrutiny would expose the inadequacies of uneven distribution. Most telemetric stations are located in populated areas while the sparsely populated areas, especially highland watershed areas, do not have enough telemetric stations. The Malaysian Meteorological Department and the Drainage and Irrigation Department have also not utilized remotely sensed rainfall (i.e. using radar and satellite systems) as an input in its forecasting models.

Legislation related to flood control is indirect as there is no flood legislation. Existing legislation is also sector-based and outdated. While there are currently some laws governing the regulation of river use and have some bearing on flood mitigation, they are not sufficiently clear or forceful enough as measures for flood mitigation. These laws were formulated mainly for the purpose of regulating and managing single sectoral water use. More stringent and clear-cut laws must be passed to enable the authorities to have direct control in all aspects of water use which may affect flooding. This includes laws that clearly specify water rights administration, water resource development, flood plain management and all aspects of flood mitigation. Alternatively, the existing laws should be updated with a stronger emphasis on flood mitigation.

Finally, flood hazard management in Malaysia has not kept up in the context of its rapid development. Malaysia is a newly-industrializing country in which the pace of social, economic and political change is fast, as is the pace of physical and environmental change. Other things being equal, these are the contexts in which flood hazards can be magnified and mismanaged. The contexts themselves are also changing, and changing physical systems have given rise to increased risk, exposure and vulnerability to flood hazards. Other contexts, largely structural, such as persistent poverty, low residential and occupational mobility, landlessness, and ethnic culture have also contributed to increased vulnerability to flood hazards amongst specific communities, mainly the poor. Thus, in order to better manage floods and move towards greater flood loss reduction, flood management must be given a higher salience on official agendas. In a country where poverty reduction and income equity amongst all races are targets of policy, the reduction of flood losses appears to be an important vehicle towards achieving those targets. This is because the poor are the most vulnerable to flooding in Malaysia, and any substantial increase in flood protection and flood loss reduction will reduce the income gap between the rich and the poor. The government should also adopt a more pro-active and dynamic approach towards flood management, rather than adhere to a reactive approach.

Finally, the current flood management model lacks a multi-disciplinary approach that should include a well balanced mixture of structural and non-structural measures. In this respect, the employment of legislation to control floodplain encroachment, the development of hill land, and urbanization is vital if Malaysia is to successfully develop at a sustainable pace and yet protect and conserve its environment, and at the same time manage flood hazards effectively. If not, flood hazards will continue to put a tremendous strain on the country's economy, exacerbate poverty and income inequity, and delay its efforts as a newly industrializing country (NIC) by the year 2020 (Chan 2011).

5 Constraints in Post-Flood Disaster Supports

5.1 Politicization of Flood Disasters

Notwithstanding the limitations and weaknesses in the current Malaysian flood disaster management system, there are other constraints which hinder the effectiveness of the system. In Malaysia, almost all facets of life, be it political, social, economic or cultural, are closely linked to politics. Hence, it is not unusual that disaster management is also closely linked to politics. Yusuf (n.d.) calls this linkage "the politicization of disasters." Disaster managers have been cautioned that future disasters will be best depicted as a context for framing and blaming, as politicians with some skill may turn disaster from a threat into an opportunity/political asset (Boin et al. 2009). In the case of Malaysia, politicians are quick to politicize disasters. This is all the more apparent when the Federal Government and State Governments are formed from different political parties. Disaster management research has largely ignored one of the most pressing challenges the ruling government is confronted with in the wake of a disaster, viz. how to cope with what is commonly called the blame game. In order to ensure an effective response to any disaster, political leaders must understand opposition parties' responses in pointing fingers and blaming the ruling government for mishaps in the disaster. It is vital that leaders properly manage the political aspects of disasters and their inquiries. On 12 April 2012, an opposition party leader led some 200 Klang residents to stage a protest in front of the Selangor State Secretariat building, demanding that their flood damage compensation money to be increased to USD 260.8. The group claimed that the USD 163 received from the Selangor government was far too little to compensate for the damage residents suffered in the recent floods. While this claim was beneficial for the flood victims, one cannot hide the fact that previous Selangor State Governments had not previously paid flood victims any compensation at all. This case is in fact a example of the politicization of floods.

In another incident in 2007 when Johor was ravaged by floods, Johor *Mentri Besar* (Chief Minister) Datuk Abdul Ghani Othman had claimed that the devastating floods (18 deaths, USD 0.49 billion damage and 110,000 people evacuated) may have been caused by Singapore's land reclamation at its Pulau Tekong island in a narrow sea lane between Malaysia and Singapore. The *Mentri Besar* blamed Singapore based on its land reclamation at the island which had effectively plugged the mouth of the Sungai Johor, resulting in the river overflowing its banks and inundating the town of Kota Tinggi (The Star 2007). In another incident, Selangor United Malays National Organization (UMNO) deputy chief Datuk Seri Noh Omar has blamed the Selangor State's ruling Pakatan Rakyat's (PR) poor flood mitigation works for the recent spate of flash floods in the state (Chieh 2012). Respondents in the study by Chan (1995) also mentioned that political parties had their own agendas, as they helped only those flood victims (in their constituencies) who supported them. For example, the UMNO Member of Parliament would pay more attention and channel more aid to the Malay majority areas. Similarly, the Malaysian Chinese Association leaders would give priority to help the Chinese victims, and the Malaysian Indian Congress would favor helping the Indians. More recently, floods have triggered further political fallout. The Federal Minister for Housing and Local Government and Alor Setar MP criticized the Kedah State government (led by the opposition Pan-Malaysian Islamic Party (PAS), an opponent of the MP's National Front coalition) for what he considered a slow response to the floods and the government's inexperience (Bernama 2010b; Foong 2010). Deputy Prime Minister Muhyiddin Yassin then claimed the State government had a responsibility to assist victims of the flood (The Star 2010a). In response, Kedah's Chief Minister Azizan argued that his government's response had been "quick" and that 300,000 ringgit in aid had been committed to the affected areas (New Straits Times 2010). Fortunately, Kedah's Sultan Abdul Halim called publicly for politics to be set aside for the purposes of dealing with the floods (The Star 2010b).

5.2 *Mediatization of Flood Disasters*

Another obvious constraint in effective flood disaster management is that of mediatization. In any account, the media are a potent force. This is a factor that significantly affects disaster management. So powerful is the role of the media that they can either help a nation address a disaster or make the country look bad. According to the Thomas Theorem: "If the media define a situation as a disaster or a crisis, be sure that it will indeed be a disaster or a crisis in all its consequences" (Thomas and Thomas 1928). Yusof (n.d.) contends that mediatization would be one of the driving forces in the world of future disasters. The media can either use a disaster for outright sensationalism, or it can self-impose censorship on the event making it "unimportant". The media can also apply pressure on politicians and decision makers to explain and justify the occurrence and impacts of the disaster to the public.

5.3 *Lack of Awareness and Volunteerism*

Lack of awareness towards donating and volunteering to flood disasters is another constraint that impedes advancement of disaster management, especially towards engaging the public and giving the public a more active role. Generally, Malaysians are very private people who have developed the conception that disasters are the responsibility of the government. Few Malaysians would volunteer in social work.

This is a constraint that limits the effectiveness of volunteer groups such as MERCY, and the Red Cross and Red Crescent. Asking Malaysians to donate money or even clothes/food to disaster organizations is a difficult task. Malaysians do not donate towards flood disaster aid simply because they feel that is not their responsibility. They feel that it is the responsibility of the government, be it at the Federal or State level.

5.4 *Erosion of Social Capital*

Aldrich (2010) has found that recovery from disasters is very much dependent on social capital, especially in post-crisis resilience. Hossain and Kuti (2010) similarly highlighted the importance of disaster response, preparedness and coordination through social networks. In the case of flood disasters in Malaysia, social capital as manifested by kinships and family bonds have been found to be a strong factor in helping victims cope with and recover from flood disasters. This factor is all the more important when government aid is not forthcoming to the victims. However, out-migration from families due to the search for jobs in cities has, among other reasons, broken down the extended families. Consequently, families have lost the one thing that protects them from being totally devastated by flood disasters, i.e. the social bonding and self-reliance that has made them resilient in the past. For example, in the 1990s Makcik (Aunty) Mabee never had any problems when her house near the Sungai Pinang in Penang was flooded every month as she could call upon her own children (ten of them) to help her cope with the floods. More than that, she could rely on help from her relatives living in adjacent houses. But now in 2012, she is no longer able to rely on her own children (only two girls have stayed behind) or her relatives as they have all moved out to Kuala Lumpur or other cities looking for jobs.

6 Policy Recommendations: Towards Effective Flood Disaster Risk Management in Malaysia

Disaster preparedness is one aspect of disaster management that clearly needs to be improved, especially in the context of flood disasters. While the NDRM appears to work in the east coast flood-prone areas whereby preparations get under way during the month of October/November just before the monsoon season, residents living on the west coast of the peninsula, in the southern state of Johor and the northern states of Kedah and Perlis are not exposed to this kind of preparedness. That is because in the past the north–east monsoon seldom affected these rain-shadowed areas. In recent years, massive floods are now not affecting the usual east coast states such as Kelatan, Pahang and Terengganu, but have moved south towards

Johor and north towards Kedah and Perlis. The major floods in Johor in 2006–2007 and the massive floods in Kedah and Perlis in 2010 are indications that this trend is happening. Hence, residents in Johor, Kedah and Perlis, or for that matter in Kauala Lumpur (subjected to frequent flash floods) should also be sensitized by exposing them to awareness via flood preparedness campaigns.

Flood Disaster Risk Management in Malaysia has traditionally been over-focused on a top-down government-centric approach. This was workable in the past when population was sparse and the public largely made up of poorly educated citizens, and the role of NGOs and civil society was limited in scope. It is time for a radical change towards a more people-friendly "horizontal" or "bottom-up" approach. People, especially disaster victims, need to be engaged and empowered to be more resilient. If not, they remain highly dependent on government aid and this is not what the Malaysian Government wants. When the public (who are the victims) are actively engaged and involved, their ability to respond to flood or other disasters effectively and appropriately will be enhanced. The general principles of preparedness that should be adopted are as follows: (i) preparedness is a central foundation of disaster/emergency management; (ii) preparedness is not static but a dynamic and continuous process whereby managers and victims learn; (iii) preparedness is an educational activity to increase awareness and understanding; (iv) preparedness is not just about drills but is based on knowledge (which is evolving all the time); and (v) preparedness evokes appropriate actions (from both disaster managers and victims).

Providing disaster services up to international standard should be one of the objectives of disaster managers. The authorities must introduce standards that would serve as the guiding principles for flood disaster managers and other humanitarian workers during disasters. These standards, widely known in the humanitarian sector as the SPHERE Standards, are comprehensive and stress quality as well as quantity in order to achieve the best practice in providing aid during/after a disaster. These standards specify, among others, the minimum amount of uncontaminated water with which a victim should be provided per day (7.5 L), the minimum sizes for shelters, average distances to water distribution points, specifications for toilets, healthcare, etc. in the aftermath of a disaster (www.sphereproject.org, Accessed 15 May 2012).

Other policy recommendations proposed for the Malaysian Government are as follows: (i) Develop disaster/emergency plans which are reviewed and updated regularly. Ensure that early warnings reach and are understood by the most vulnerable people as they need to know what to do, where to go, and how to protect themselves. Hence, the plans must include education and preparedness; (ii) Constantly improve existing flood forecasting and warning systems. Incorporate traditional systems into the official systems so that people can make the adjustment quickly. Employ state-of-the-art technology in such systems; (iii) Provide flood-prone areas/communities with emergency materials such as torch lights, batteries, water purification tablets, stretchers, chain saws, plastic sheeting, first aid supplies, generators, etc.; (iv) Identify and gazette more emergency sites/shelters such as community halls, schools, mosques, etc. and assembly areas such as parks or fields when evacuating people; (v) Construct shelters/houses and infrastructure to withstand future disasters (for example, the Malay stilt house has stood the test of time but this unique flood-proof architectural design is fast disappearing due to changing needs); (vi) Healthcare centers such as hospitals and clinics should be made flood-proof (for example, the ground floor can be used only as a car park or recreational space), roads should be built on the highest ground, water supply mains should be waterproof, and electricity wires should be on high poles; (vii) Relocation should be used as a last resort, considering its negative effects on people. However, if need be, relocation should be carried out and people should be well compensated for it. Alternatively, people should get alternative housing nearby, not in an alien place that is far away from their social networks. During relocation or temporary resettlement, social networks should be preserved; (viii) Government should provide livelihood opportunities, introduce victims to suitable alternatives, and where possible, help people to be responsible for their own reconstruction; (ix) Subsidies in the form of cash or food vouchers can be provided, not as a long term subsidy but as a short-term aid. Cash is a suitable choice as it allows people to purchase their own needs rather than receive items in kind which they might already have; (x) Government must ensure that evacuation centers are always safe and well maintained. A crumbling structure may precipitate another disaster; (xi) Government must consider gender differences when giving out aid and support, as disasters often affect men and women differently.

7 Emerging Threats of Disasters at the National Level

At the national level, many factors impinge on the success or failure of flood disaster management. One of the most influential factors is politicization. In Malaysia, almost everything is political. For example, the issue of water is politically motivated (Chan 2011), river management is politically inclined (Ujang 2010), the business sector has political influence (Chooi 2012) and even education is not free from politics (Tneh 2011). It is therefore no surprise that disasters are also political. The floods in Kedah State in 2010, for example, triggered immediate political fallout. The Federal Minister for Housing and Local Government (National Front Coalition) criticized the Kedah State government (led by the opposition Pan-Malaysian Islamic Party) for what he considered a slow response to the floods and the government's inexperience (Bernama 2010a, b). Deputy Prime Minister Muhyiddin Yassin claimed the State government had a responsibility to assist victims of the flood (The Star 2010a). In reply, Kedah's Chief Minister Azizan argued that his government's response had been "quick" and that 300,000 ringgit in aid had been committed to the affected areas (New Straits Times 2010). Fortunately, the politicization was stopped when Kedah's Sultan Abdul Halim called publicly for politics to be set aside for the purposes of dealing with the floods (The Star 2010b).

Alarmingly, disasters in the modern world are a complex mixture of natural and human-made inputs. Often, when two or more disasters collide, they change into "Compound Disasters" or can evolve into a totally different category of disaster. A good example is when the Asian Tsunami not only flooded the west coast of Penang but also caused contamination of water supplies. This is a challenge that the Malaysian Government needs to be aware of. Related to this is the mutation of disasters, as if disasters were something "alive." Disasters mutate in form in response to population growth and urbanization, economic growth, globalization of commerce, and technological advancement. The challenge is how to contain individual disasters and stop them from evolving and mutating.

Flood disasters continue to impoverish the government coffers. During the 10th Malaysia Plan period (2011–2015), a total of USD 1.17 billion was allocated for flood disaster management. This figure is expected to increase exponentially as it has done so during the last nine Malaysian plans. This is a challenge that the Malaysian Government has to address. Raising tax rates to increase government revenue would not be an acceptable move, given the fact that the citizenry expects the government to foot the bill when it comes to disaster spending. Perhaps a workable alternative would be to involve the private sector and help people become more flood resilient and self reliant. Even so, damaged public structures need to be repaired.

Flood losses are difficult to measure. How much is a life worth indeed? Tangible and intangible losses are complicated by direct and indirect losses. Flood loss profiles are ever changing as a result of population growth, changing needs and changing lifestyles. Technological advancement and the use of sophisticated equipment (for forecasting and warning) may see a drop in the loss of lives, but dense construction may see an increase in property losses and indirect economic losses such as loss of business. These will become major societal vulnerability.

Another major challenge is Malaysia's inability to use new scientific and technological advances to mitigate flood disasters. Currently, the flood forecasting system has just started to use radar and satellite images as inputs in forecasting rains, a necessary input for flood forecasting. Warning systems using short text messages also have problems. Another challenge is that hydro-meteorological hazards are not easily forecastable on an extended time scale, since weather can change abruptly. But today's societies require extended forecasting to increase the time available for evacuation. Sadly, evacuation clearance time has in fact increased due to increased population densities. Hence, road systems need to be markedly improved to ensure swift evacuation.

The pace of engineering advances is not in keeping with their implementation in practice. For example, building codes are not keeping pace with current engineering practice. The Environmentally-friendly Drainage Manual, for instance, is not user-friendly and contractors see it as cumbersome and costly to implement compared to the conventional open drainage system. The challenge here is to educate contractors and house buyers into buying the system.

In the future, floods and other disasters are likely to evolve into new forms yet unheard of. One of the characteristics and conditions of future disasters will be transnationalisation. For example, the original source of flooding may occur in Malaysia, but the immediate and long term impact of the disaster may be spread into neighboring countries such as Thailand or Singapore. It is therefore imperative that Malaysia and its immediate neighbors come to some sort of agreement and establish cooperation in managing disasters, especially those that can cross borders or are transboundary. Regional cooperation is also needed in the light of the effects of globalization on all countries. For example, disasters are said to have a globalization effect when a country affected by a major disaster can no longer export the goods it exports to other countries worldwide. Thus the Kobe earthquake in 1995 affected a large fraction of Japanese shipping, and forced closures of subcontractors' facilities worldwide, including in Malaysia. This affected world trade and many national economies suffered.

8 Conclusion

After more than half a century of flood management, Malaysia is still subject to severe floods. Indeed, Malaysia will never be flood-free. However, what is avoidable is that Malaysians must not forget past disasters. Past disasters present opportunities for us to learn from past mistakes. Just like mistakes from history which we must remember and avoid, disasters are no different. Once we forget them and let our guard down, they will strike us hard. This is attested by the evolution of various safety and emergency laws, acts and regulations since independence. The current NDRM appears rather outdated as it is based on a reactive approach. This machinery needs to be revamped and repackaged, not just with cosmetic changes but with real changes for the better. Institutional arrangements also need to be vastly improved for effective implementation of the national disaster management program. The NSC needs to be revamped to give it a fresh mandate, more funds to operate, and more qualified personnel. Malaysia is constantly revamping ministries and government agencies. This is where the role of the NSC can be better positioned. Putting the NSC under the Prime Minister's Department gives it more clout, but it also marginalizes it as the Prime Minister has other more immediate agendas. Flood management will not feature highly on the Prime Minister's agenda.

Flood Disaster Risk Management in Malaysia has traditionally been overfocused on a top-down government-centric approach. This was workable in the past when population was sparse, the public largely lowly educated, and the role of NGOs and civil society limited in scope. It is time for a radical change towards a more people-friendly "horizontal" or "bottom-up" approach. People, especially disaster victims, need to be engaged and empowered so as to become more resilient. If not, they will remain highly dependent on government aid and this is not what the Malaysian Government wants. When the public (who are the victims) are actively engaged and involved, this will enhance their ability to respond to flood or other disasters effectively and appropriately. The general principles of preparedness that should be adopted are as follows: (i) preparedness is a central foundation of disaster/emergency management; (ii) preparedness is not static but a dynamic and continuous process whereby managers and victims learn; (iii) preparedness is an educational activity to increase awareness and understanding; (iv) preparedness is not just about drills but is based on knowledge (which is evolving all the time); and (v) preparedness evokes appropriate actions (from both disaster managers and victims).

Providing disaster services up to international standard should be one of the objectives of disaster managers. The authorities must introduce standards that would serve as the guiding principles for flood disaster managers and other humanitarian workers during disasters. Malaysia should try its best to adopt the new crisis assistance standards in the country. These standards, widely known in the humanitarian sector as the SPHERE Standards, are comprehensive and stress quality as well as quantity.

The Malaysian flood authorities should not ignoring local leadership, as they have rich experience that can be tapped into. Local leaders such as village heads can provide information and cooperation on the ground. Moreover, these leaders can advise the authorities when distributing relief goods, reconstruction material, or other benefits, especially those which help the poor, women, children, and the elderly. Some things to avoid include rushing in with reconstruction without recycling useful materials from the disaster site, bulldozing over what could be valuable building materials, and rushing in quickly to implement ad-hoc plans. For example, establishing new institutions in short time frames or developing complex and inflexible project designs are not encouraged. The authorities should always use familiar disaster management plans and systems with the local officials/leaders. Another thing to avoid is relocation of people away from their jobs and social contacts. This is useless as they would eventually return. In the case of farmers, care must be taken so that they do not miss the next planting season. Hence, distribution of seeds should be timely. The authorities should also be sensitive, for example not imposing grief counseling where it is found to be inappropriate, especially in the context of multi-ethnic Malaysia with multi-cultural beliefs.

Because Malaysia's main disaster is flooding, the NDRM is largely targeted for handling monsoon flooding. Consequently, this mechanism is less than effective and should be re-modeled into something more pro-active. Stakeholder participation is also seriously lacking, although the authorities have recognized the important role of NGOs, particularly MERCY, the Red Cross, Red Crescent and other specific NGOs. These stakeholders need to be involved during every stage of the disaster cycle. Capacity building is necessary. The disaster management mechanism should also adopt more non-structural measures, and state-of-the-art technology, and cooperate internationally with other countries for addressing transboundary disasters.

In terms of flood warning, there are many areas which can still be improved. While the total number of telemetric stations for rainfall and river flow in the country seems large enough, a closer scrutiny would expose inadequacies in terms of uneven distribution. Most telemetric stations are located in populated areas while the sparsely populated areas, especially highland watershed areas, do not have enough telemetric stations. The Malaysian Meteorological Department and the Drainage and Irrigation Department have also not utilized remotely sensed rainfall (radar and satellite sensed rainfall) as an input in its forecasting models. This could have been deliberately overlooked because of the high cost involved, but real-time flood forecasting cannot be detached from the usage of such techniques, especially in terms of flash flooding.

Legislation related to flood control should also be improved. While there are currently some laws governing the regulation of river use and which have some bearing on flood mitigation, they are not sufficiently clear or forceful as measures of flood mitigation. These laws were formulated mainly for the purpose of regulating and managing single sectoral water use. More stringent and clear-cut laws must be passed to enable the authorities to have direct control in all aspects of water use which may affect flooding. This includes laws that clearly 'specify water rights administration, water resource development, flood plain management and all aspects of flood mitigation. Alternatively, the existing laws should be updated with a stronger emphasis on flood mitigation.

Markets as well as social ties and community could play a role in mitigating hazards. Flood insurance is poorly developed in Malaysia, despite the country been flood-prone. In developed countries, flood insurance is an integral part of overall flood management. The Government should seriously consider introducing an insurance scheme for flood victims to help them get back on their feet after suffering huge losses. In recent years, there have been cases where victims in Johor and Kedah suffered through two major floods and ended up with a total loss twice over. Under a normal scheme to protect properties in Malaysia, insurance companies will not compensate flood victims since it is considered a natural disaster. One could purchase a special flood insurance to protect one's property, but the premium would be very high. Nevertheless, there should be a move by the authorities to introduce an insurance scheme so that the victims can get some compensation.

Another point is the need to create a data management system (i.e. a database), which would display data spatially and temporally, and underpin a more systematic communication system in flood disaster management (Lawal et al. 2006). This disaster data bank could be managed in a geographical information system environment and be put on the NSC website for all disaster organizations to access. Currently, disaster information is often treated as "confidential" and seldom released to the public. This should not be the case as the public has a right to know all the statistics related to disasters. A case in mind is the holding back of the Air Pollution Index (API) during the 1997/1998 haze episodes. The excuse given was that such statistics may "frighten" tourists and drive them away, resulting in the country losing foreign revenue. But surely the health of its own citizens should be given the highest priority. Here again, the confidentiality of disaster statistics is yet another manifestation of politicization. It must be stressed that politics should not mix with disaster management, or else the disaster will just get worse. Politicians must refrain from using disasters as ammunition. All parties must put aside political differences when it comes to disaster management.

Finally, flood hazard management in Malaysia must be viewed in the context of its rapid development. Malaysia is a newly-industrializing country in which the pace of social, economic and political change is fast, as is the pace of physical and environmental change. Other things being equal, these are the contexts in which flood hazards can be magnified and mismanaged. The contexts themselves are also changing, and changing physical systems have given rise to increased risk, exposure and vulnerability to flood hazards. Other contexts, largely structural, such as persistent poverty, low residential and occupational mobility, landlessness, and ethnic culture have also contributed to increased vulnerability to flood hazards amongst specific communities, mainly the poor. Thus, in order to better manage floods and move towards greater flood loss reduction, flood management must be given a higher salience on official agendas. In a country where poverty reduction and income equity amongst all races are targets of policy, the reduction of flood loss appears to be an important vehicle towards achieving those targets. This is because the poor are the most vulnerable to flooding in Malaysia and any substantial increase in flood protection and flood loss reduction will reduce the income gap between the rich and the poor. The government should also adopt a more pro-active and dynamic approach towards flood management, rather than adhere to a reactive approach. Finally, a multi-disciplinary approach encompassing a well balanced mixture of structural and non-structural measures should be adopted. In this respect, the employment of legislation to control floodplain encroachment, the development of hill land, and urbanization is vital if Malaysia is to successfully develop at a sustainable pace and yet protect and conserve its environment, and at the same time manage flood hazards effectively. If not, flood hazards will continue to put a tremendous strain on the country's economy, exacerbate poverty and income inequity, and delay its efforts in becoming a newly industrialising country (NIC) by the year 2020.

Acknowledgements The author gratefully acknowledges funding from the Long Term Research Grant Scheme (LRGS) "Project 5 – Economic Model for Flood Disaster Impact Analysis" and to the Economic Research Institute for ASEAN and East Asia (ERIA) for funding the project "Economic and Welfare Impacts of Disasters in East Asia and Policy Responses".

References

Ab. Ghani, A., Chang, C. K., Leow, C. S., & Zakaria, N. A. (2012). Sungai Pahang digital flood mapping: 2007 flood. *International Journal of River Basin Management*, 1–10.

Ahmad, S., & Hashim, N. M. (2006). Kebakaran Hutan Dan Isu Pencemaran Udara Di Malaysia: Kes Jerebu Pada Ogos 2005. *e-BANGI Jurnal Sains Sosial dan Kemanusiaan, 1*(1), 1–19.

Aldrich, D. P. (2010). Fixing recovery: Social capital in post-crisis resilience. *Journal of Homeland Security*. http://works.bepress.com/daniel_aldrich/7. Accessed 28 June 2012.

Alexander, D. (1993). *Natural disasters*. London: UCL.

Bernama. (2010a). *Floods: Perak sends clean water supply to Kedah, Perlis,* Bernama [online]. 5 November 2010. http://www.bernama.com.my/bernama/v5/newsindex.php?id=541097. Accessed 5 November 2010.

Bernama. (2010b). *Kedah government slow in helping flood victims – Chor*, Bernama [online]. 5 November 2010. http://www.bernama.com/bernama/v5/newsgeneral.php?id=541124. Accessed 5 November 2010.

Bernama. (2010c). *For farmers affected by floods In Kedah, Perlis*, Bernama [online]. 6 November 2010. http://www.bernama.com/bernama/v5/newsindex.php?id=541292. Accessed 6 November 2010.

Blaikie, P., Cannon, T., Davis, I., & Wisner, B. (1994). *At risk: Natural hazards, peoples' vulnerability and disasters*. London: Routledge.

Boin, A., McConnell, A., Hart, P., & Preston, T. (2009). Leadership style, crisis response and blame managment: The case of Hurrican Katrina. *Public Administration, 88*(3), 706–723.

Chan, N. W. (1995). *A Contextual analysis of flood hazard management in Peninsular Malaysia*. UK: Ph.D. Middlesex University.

Chan, N. W. (1996). Risk, exposure and vulnerability to flood hazards in a rapidly developing country: The case of Peninsular Malaysia. *Akademika, 49*, 107–136.

Chan, N. W. (1997a). Increasing flood risk in Malaysia: Causes and solutions. *Disaster Prevention and Management: An International Journal, 6*(2), 72–86.

Chan, N. W. (1997b). Institutional arrangements for flood hazards in Malaysia: An evaluation using the criteria approach. *Disasters, 21*(3), 206–222.

Chan, N. W. (1997c). Warnings in the context of flood hazard management in Malaysia. In J. W. Handmer (Ed.), *Flood warning: Issues and practice in total system design* (pp. 115–132). London: Flood Hazard Research Centre.

Chan, N. W. (1998a). Responding to landslide hazards in rapidly developing Malaysia: A case of economics versus environmental protection. *Disaster Prevention and Management: An International Journal, 7*(1), 14–27.

Chan, N. W. (1998b). Chapter 54 - Flash and monsoon flooding. In S. Sham (Ed.), *The encyclopedia of Malaysia - Volume I environment* (pp. 112–113). Editions Didier Millet: Singapore.

Chan, N. W. (2000). Chapter 29 – Reducing flood hazard exposure and vulnerability in Peninsular Malaysia. In D. J. Parker (Ed.), *Floods volume II* (pp. 19–30). London: Routledge.

Chan, N. W. (2003). Using wetlands as natural forms of flood control. In A. Ali, C. S. Md Rawi, M. Mansor, R. Nakamura, S. Ramakrishna, & T. Mudkur (Eds.), *The Asian wetlands: bringing partnerships into good wetland practices*. Penang: Ministry of Science, Technology and the Environment, Malaysia, Universiti Sains Malaysia, Ramsar Center Japan and Wetlands International Asia Pacific. Penerbit Universiti Sains Malaysia (pp. 909–919), Part VII: Climate change.

Chan, N. W. (2009). *Socio-economic effects of flood losses incurred by residential and commercial properties due to the 2004 Indian Ocean tsunami in Northern Peninsular Malaysia*, Paper presented at the South China Sea Tsunami Workshop 3. Penang: Universiti Sains Malaysia, 3–5 November 2009.

Chan, N. W. (2011). Addressing flood hazards via environmental humanities in Malaysia. *Malaysian Journal of Environmental Management, 12*(2), 11–22.

Chan, N. W., Ibrahim, A. L., Kung, H. T., & Liu, P. S. (2002a). Employing nature to combat floods: Some experiences from Malaysia. In J. B. Ali, A. Rahman, Z. Mohamed, & N. Zainuddin (Eds.), *Disaster management: Strengthening the national security capabilities* (pp. 143–158). Alor Setar: Penerbit Ustara.

Chan, N. W., Ibrahim, A. L., Yusoff, R., & Ismail, N. A. (2002b). The significance of stress and other intangible losses during major flood disasters in Malaysia. In J. Ali, B. A. Rahman, Z. Mohamed, & N. Zainuddin (Eds.), *Disaster management: Strengthening the national security capabilities* (pp. 159–176). Alor Setar: Penerbit Ustara.

Chan, N. W., & Parker, D. J. (1996). Response to dynamic flood hazard factors in Peninsular Malaysia. *The Geographical Journal, 162*(3), 313–325.

Chan, N. W., & Parker, D. J. (1997). Aspek-Aspek Sosio-Ekonomi Berkaitan Dengan Bahaya Dan Bencana Banjir Di Semenanjung Malaysia. In M. R. Agus & F. N. Sidin (Eds.), *Proceedings of*

Persidangan Kebangsaan Kajian Sains Sosial, 29–30 September 1997 (pp. 294–311). Kuala Lumpur: University of Malaya.

Chia, C. W. (2004). *Managing flood problems in Malaysia*. The Ingenieur Bulletin. 22, June-August 2004. Kuala Lumpur: Board of Engineers Malaysia (pp. 38–43). http://www.bem.org.my/publication/juneaug04/F(Flood)(38-43).pdf. Accessed 16 May 2012.

Chieh, Y. H. (2012). *Noh Omar blames Nakatan for Selangor floods*, Malaysian Must Know The Truth Blog Spot [online]. 1 April 2012. http://malaysiansmustknowthetruth.blogspot.com/2012/03/noh-omar-blames-pakatan-for-selangor.html. Accessed 16 May 2012.

Chooi, C. (2012). *Mix of politics with business fuelled economic woes, says Ku li*, Malaysian Insider [online]. 16 February 2012. http://www.themalaysianinsider.com/malaysia/article/mix-of-politics-with-business-fuelled-economic-woes-says-ku-li/. Accessed 16 May 2012.

Drainage and Irrigation Department. (1973). Estimation of design rainstorm, *Hydrological Procedures*. 1, Kuala Lumpur December 1973.

Drainage and Irrigation Department. (1974). Rational method of flood estimation for rural catchments in Peninsular Malaysia, *Hydrological Procedures*. 5, Kuala Lumpur 1974.

Drainage and Irrigation Department. (1976). Flood estimation for urban areas in Peninsular Malaysia, *Hydrological Procedures*. 16, 1976.

Drainage and Irrigation Department. (1988). *Flood forecasting and warning systems in Malaysia*. Unpublished paper of the hydrological section, Drainage and Irrigation Department, Ampang Branch.

Foong, P. Y. (2010). *Double-tracking project worsened flood situation in Kedah – Chor*, The Star [online]. 5 November 2010. http://thestar.com.my/news/story.asp?file=/2010/11/5/nation/20101105123917&sec=nation. Accessed 5 November 2010.

Green, C. H., Parker, D. J., & Emery, P. J. (1983). *The real costs of flooding to households: The intangible costs*, Geography and Planning Paper 12. Middlesex Polytechnic, Enfield.

Green, C. H., Turnstall, S. M., Emery, J. P., & Bossman-Aggrey, P. (1988). *Evaluating the non-monetary impacts of flooding*. Flood Hazard Research Centre, Publication 123, Enfield.

Handmer, J. W., & Parker, D. J. (1991). *British disaster planning and management: An initial assessment*. Flood Hazard Research Centre, Publication 202, Enfield.

Hewitt, K. (Ed.). (1983). *Interpretations of calamity, the risk & hazard series: 1*. London: Allen and Unwin.

Hossain, L., & Kuti, M. (2010). Disaster response preparedness coordination through social networks. *Disasters, 34*(3), 755–786.

Hussaini, Hj. A. (2007). *Flood and drought management in Malaysia*, Speech Given on 21 June 2007. Kuala Lumpur: Ministry of Natural Resources and Environment.

Jamaluddin, M. J. (1985). Flash flood problems and human responses to the flash flood hazard in Kuala Lumpur area. *Akademika, 26*, 45–62.

Japan International Cooperation Agency. (1982). *National water resources study*. Unpublished report to the Government of Malaysia.

Japan International Cooperation Agency. (1989). *Study on flood mitigation of the Klang river basin*. Unpublished report to the Government of Malaysia.

Japan International Cooperation Agency. (1991). *The study of flood mitigation and drainage in Penang Island*. Unpublished Supporting Report, Japan International Cooperation Agency for the Government of Malaysia.

Jones, D. K. C. (1991). Environmental hazards. In R. J. Bennett & R. C. Estall (Eds.), *Global change and challenge* (pp. 27–56). London: Routledge.

Julien, P. Y., Ab, N. A., Ghani, R. A., & Chang, C. K. (2010). Case study: Flood mitigation of the Muda River, Malaysia. *Journal of Hydraulic Engineering, ASCE, 136*(4), 251–261.

Kunii, O., Kanagawa, S., Yajima, I., Hisamatsu, Y., Yamamura, S., Amagai, T., et al. (2002). The 1997 haze disaster in Indonesia: Its air quality and health effects. *Archives of Environmental Health, 57*(1), 16–22.

Lawal, B., Shattri, M., Mahmud, A. R., & Ghazali, A. H. (2006). Comprehensive planning and the role of SDSS in flood disaster management in Malaysia. *Disaster Prevention and Management, 15*(2), 233–240.

Leigh, C., & Low, K. S. (1983). Attitudes and adjustments to flood hazard in a mixed ethnic community in Malacca Town, Peninsular Malaysia. *Singapore Journal of Tropical Geography, 4*(1), 40–51.

Lim, T. K. (1988). *Malaysian rivers and floods*. Paper presented at the Seminar Tebatan Banjir, Organised by the Jabatan Parit dan Tali Air Malaysia and Japan International Cooperation Agency, Kuala Lumpur, 14–17 November.

New Straits Times. (2010). *33,000 in shelters: Flood situation very bad in Kedah*, Precarious in Perlis, New Straits Times [online], 4 November 2010. http://www.nst.com.my/nst/articles/33_000inshelters/Article/. Accessed 5 November 2010.

Parker, D. J. (1992). The mismanagement of hazards. In D. J. Parker & J. W. Handmer (Eds.), *Hazard management and emergency planning: Perspectives on Britain*. London: James and James.

Parker, D. J., Green, C. H., & Thompson, P. M. (1987). *Urban flood protection benefits – A project appraisal guide*. Aldershot: Gower Technical Press.

Parker, D. J., Islam, N., & Chan, N. W. (1997). Chapter 3: Reducing vulnerability following flood disaster: Issues and practices. In A. Awotona (Ed.), *Reconstruction after disaster* (pp. 23–44). London: Avebury.

Pearce, D. W. (1976). *Environmental economics*. London: Longman.

Periasamy, T. (2011). *Slope failure hazards: A spatial and temporal study of the Klang valley region, Peninsular Malaysia*. Ph. D., University of Malaysia, Kuala Lumpur.

Sham, S. (1973). The 1967 flood in Kelantan, West Malaysia. *Akademika, 3*, 1–14.

Syed Muhammad, H., & Binnie Sdn. Bhd. (1988). *Feasibility study on flood mitigation and agricultural development projects in the Krian River Basin*. Unpublished Report to the Malaysian Government.

The Star. (2007). *Singapore: We're not to blame for johor floods*, The Star [online]. 2 February 2007. http://thestar.com.my/news/story.asp?file=/2007/2/2/nation/16758525&sec=nation.

The Star. (2010a). *Do not ignore plight of flood victims, says Muhyiddin*, The Star [online]. 6 November 2010. http://thestar.com.my/news/story.asp?file=/2010/11/6/nation/20101106140013&sec=nation. Accessed 6 November 2010.

The Star. (2010b). *Kedah Sultan sad over flood, urges everyone to work together*, The Star [online]. 6 November 2010. http://thestar.com.my/news/story.asp?file=/2010/11/6/nation/20101106173915&sec=nation. Accessed 6 November 2010.

The Star. (2010c). *Kedah and Perlis scramble to send aid to 19,000 hit by floodwaters*, The Star [online]. 3 November 2010. http://thestar.com.my/news/story.asp?file=/2010/11/3/nation/7352766&sec=nation. Accessed 5 November 2010.

The Star. (2010d). *Alor Setar airport remains closed*, The Star [online]. 4 November 2010. http://thestar.com.my/news/story.asp?file=/2010/11/4/nation/7362218&sec = nation. Accessed 5 November 2010.

The Star. (2011). *Terrible twins' La Nina and monsoon to hit KL and Selangor*, The Star [online]. 6 December 2011. http://thestar.com.my/news/story.asp?file=/2011/12/6/nation/10040911&sec=nation. Accessed March 29, 2012.

Thomas, W. I., & Thomas, D. S. (1928). *The child in America: Behavior problems and programs*. New York: Knopf.

Tneh, D. C. E. (2011). *Education and politics in Malaysia*, Malaysian Insider [online]. 26 April 2011. http://www.themalaysianinsider.com/breakingviews/article/education-and-politics-in-malaysia-david-c.e.-tneh/. Accessed 16 May 2012.

Torry, W. I. (1979). Anthropological studies in hazardous environments: Past trends and new horizons. *Current Anthropology, 20*, 517–540.

Turner, B. A. (1978). *Man-made disasters*. London: Wykeham Publications.

Ujang, Z. (2010). *Water mismanagement? The politics of polluted urban rivers*, Paper Presented at the Merdeka Lecture Series. Penang: Universiti Sains Malaysia, 22 October 2010.

Umar. (2007). *Disaster mitigation support and management in Malaysia*. Malaysian Meteorological Department [Online]. www.met.gov.my/files/ClimateChange2007/session1a/. Accessed 16 May 2012.

Varley, A. (Ed.). (1994). *Disasters, development and environment*. Chichester: Wiley.

Volker, A. (1971). *Flood control (West Malaysia)*. UNESCO Archives, 10–24 March 1971.

Wadell, E. (1983). Coping with frosts, governments and disaster experts: Some reflections based on a new guinea experience and a perusal of the relevant literature. In K. Hewitt (Ed.), *Interpretations of calamity, the risks and hazard series: 1* (pp. 33–43). Winchester: Allen & Unwin Inc.

Winchester, P. (1992). *Power, choice and vulnerability: A case study in disaster mismanagement in South India*. London: James & James Science Publishers Ltd.

Winstedt, R. O. (1927). The great flood 1926. *Journal of the Malayan Branch of the Royal Asiatic Society, V*(II), 295–309.

Chapter 13
Impacts from and State Responses to Natural Disasters in the Philippines

Danilo C. Israel and Roehlano M. Briones

1 Introduction

In Southeast Asia, the Philippines is among the hardest hit by natural disasters, particularly by typhoons, floods and droughts. These natural disasters have negative economic and environmental impacts on the affected areas and the people who live there. Furthermore, the agriculture and natural resources sectors are highly vulnerable because they are directly exposed to natural disasters and their unwelcome consequences.

An analysis of the impacts of typhoons, floods and droughts on agriculture, food security and the natural resources and environment of the Philippines will help bring further to light the nature and extent of these effects. For an economy largely dependent on agriculture and its natural resources and environment, the data and information as well as overall knowledge gained from the study may prove useful in developing strategies to address the ill-effects of natural disasters. Moreover, the results and findings may assist in identifying new studies that can soon be undertaken in relation to natural disasters, an important research concern which still lacks the necessary level of focus in the Philippines.

The main objective of this study is quantitatively and qualitatively analyzing the impacts of typhoons, floods and droughts on agriculture, food security and the natural resources and environment in the Philippines. The specific objectives are to: (a) present an overview of agriculture, natural resources and environment, disaster management, and the occurrences of typhoons, floods and droughts in the country; (b) evaluate the impacts of typhoons, floods and droughts on agriculture at both the national and provincial level; (c) assess the impacts of these disasters on food security; and (d) analyze the effects of these disasters on the natural resources and environment. The ultimate aim for doing so is to recommend measures that can be

D.C. Israel (✉) • R.M. Briones
Philippine Institute for Development Studies (PIDS), Manila, Philippines
e-mail: disrael@pidsnet.pids.gov.ph

D.P. Aldrich et al. (eds.), *Resilience and Recovery in Asian Disasters*, Risk, Governance and Society 18, DOI 10.1007/978-4-431-55022-8_13

undertaken in response to the unwelcome impacts of natural disasters on the agriculture and natural resources and environment sectors and to propose relevant studies that can be undertaken in the future.

2 Methodology

2.1 Framework of Analysis

Theoretically, the impacts of natural disasters on agriculture and the natural resources and environment sectors can be direct or indirect as well as positive or negative. In the case of agriculture, the direct and positive impacts are actually readily identifiable. Typhoons increase the supply of water for agriculture as they usher in rain. Floods improve soil fertility as they deliver nutrients from the uplands to the lowlands. In addition, floods temporarily create a larger water habitat for inland fish and other aquatic animals. Together with other yet-to-be-identified factors, these impacts of typhoons and floods are viewed as positive because, ceteris paribus, they facilitate an increase in agricultural production in the affected areas and help improve the food security situation.

In contrast to the above, there are direct and negative impacts of natural disasters on the agriculture sector as well. Typhoons, floods and droughts have the potential to reduce farm productivity; damage farm inputs, facilities and/or infrastructure, and limit farm planting options. Furthermore, individually, typhoons and floods can damage farm supply routes and cause death or injury to farm workers. As a consequence, these direct and negative factors can further lead to indirect and negative impacts on agriculture and the economy as a whole. Specifically, as a result of typhoons, floods and droughts, the overall cost of agricultural production increases; agricultural production output declines; food supply falls and, as a result, food prices rise. Taken together, the direct and indirect negative impacts on agriculture threaten food security in the affected areas.

As in the case of agriculture, natural disasters impact the natural resources and environment sector. On the positive side, typhoons and floods directly increase the moisture content in the air, resulting in a temporary cooler temperature for the local people to enjoy. Typhoons also clear the air of pollution to the benefit of the population residing in congested urban areas. On the negative side, typhoons, floods and droughts can reduce the impact area's total vegetative cover; typhoons and floods lead to soil erosion, higher coastal tides and storm surges; floods result in siltation and sedimentation, accumulated waste, polluted water and deformed land topography; while droughts reduce rainfall, lower soil fertility and increase saltwater intrusion. Taken together, all of these phenomena indirectly reduce the viability of both land and water ecosystems as suppliers of ecosystem services and endanger human health and safety with the proliferation of natural disaster-related diseases.

In the above framework, while there are both positive and negative impacts on agriculture and the natural resources and environment sectors, it is assumed that the net impact is negative. Also, it should be emphasized that beyond the aforementioned framework, not only do natural disasters affect the natural resources and the environment but the latter influences the former as well (For instance, forests block the force of incoming winds and limit the damage caused by typhoons, while watersheds store rainwater and reduce the incidence of flooding). Although important, these and other reverse relationships are not covered in this study. Thirdly, while it would be interesting to quantitatively measure all the actual impacts of previous natural disasters on agriculture and the natural resources and environment, this would not be possible given the limited data available.

2.2 Econometric Methods

We use the Agricultural Multi-market Model for Policy Evaluation (AMPLE) to quantitatively analyze the impacts of natural disasters, in particular, typhoons, floods and droughts on agriculture. AMPLE is an 18-production sector partial equilibrium model covering crops, livestock, poultry and aquatic products which generates projections of output, area, consumption, imports, exports, and prices. In common with other supply-demand models, AMPLE is suitable for understanding the evolution of underlying economic fundamentals, as opposed to actually predicting market movements. A full description of AMPLE is presented in Briones and Parel (2011) and Briones (2010) and the datasets, variables, and equations of the model are listed in the annexes of these two papers. The model is programmed and solved with the use of the Generalized Algebraic Modelling System (GAMS). Another econometric approach used here in analysing the impacts of natural disasters is regression analysis, the specifics of which are explained in the relevant section below.

2.3 Data and Data Sources

This study used secondary data from institutional sources. Data on the annual occurrence of typhoons at the national, regional and provincial levels were taken from the unpublished records of the PAGASA. There were no data available at the time of writing on the annual occurrence of floods and droughts, but national and regional data for the areas affected by them were available; generated from the unpublished records of the Department of Agriculture (DA). Data on the annual damage by agricultural commodity in terms of production in metric tons, cost of production in million pesos, and area in hectares caused by typhoons, floods and droughts were available only for the national level, except those for rice, which were also available for the regional level. These data were also taken from the unpublished records of the DA. Data on the provincial quantities and prices of paddy rice were generated from the Bureau of Agricultural Statistics (BAS). All the aforementioned data utilized were supplemented by secondary quantitative and qualitative data, as well as information taken from the related literature.

3 Review of the Agriculture and Natural Resources and Environment Sectors of the Philippines

3.1 Agriculture

From 2004 to 2010, agriculture and fisheries contributed an average of 18.4 % to gross domestic product (GDP) and grew at an average rate of 2.6 % annually in the Philippines (National Economic Development Authority 2011). Among the regions, the top contributors to output in 2009 were Region IV-A (CALABARZON) and Region III (Central Luzon). The agriculture sector during this period employed an average of 11.8 million people, which accounted for almost 35.1 % of the total work force of the country. Between 2004 and 2010, the agriculture and fisheries sector exports increased in monetary value from USD 2.5 billion to USD 4.1 billion. The top agricultural exports in terms of value were coconut oil, fresh banana, tuna, pineapple, tobacco, and seaweed. It is worth noting that in 2010 as well as in some years in the past, although the country recorded an overall balance of trade deficit in the agriculture sector, it had positive trade balance in fishery products.

Among the main challenges facing the agriculture sector in the Philippines is its vulnerability to the inherent climate volatility within the region, as well as global climate change. In response to this, an important development goal for the country is an increased resilience to climate change risks of the agriculture sector. With a rapidly increasing population and demand for food, another major development goal is improved food security. To attain these two goals and other objectives within the Philippines' agricultural sector, the strategies promoted by the government are: (a) to raise the productivity and incomes of agriculture and fishery-based households and enterprises; (b) to increase the investment and employment level across an efficient value chain; and c) to transform agrarian reform beneficiaries into viable entrepreneurs.

3.2 Natural Resources and Environment

The natural resources sub-sector of the Philippines includes land, forest and fisheries resources while the natural environment sub-sector refers to the quality of its land, water and air resources. In general, the natural resource and environment sector is facing the twin problems of overexploitation and depletion of natural resources and the deterioration of the overall environmental quality. In recent years, little progress has been made in arresting the worsening pace of these problems even as new challenges have emerged (European Commission 2009).

Similar to agriculture, among the important challenges facing the natural resources and environment sector of the Philippines are natural hazards and disasters. In response, a major development goal in this sector is the enhanced resilience of natural systems and improved adaptive capacities of human communities to cope with natural hazards and disasters including climate-related risks (National Economic Development Authority 2011). To reach this goal, the following strategies are pursued by the government: (a) strengthening the institutional capacities of national and local governments for climate change adaptation and disaster risk reduction and management; (b) enhancement of the resilience of natural systems; and (c) improvement of the adaptive capacities of communities.

4 Results and Analysis

4.1 Occurrence of Typhoons

From 2001 to 2010, the country had a total of 171 typhoons; an average of 17 typhoons per year. The occurrence of typhoons decreased from 2001 to 2002, rose in 2003, fell from 2004 to 2007, increased again in 2008 and 2009, and fell again in 2010. On a yearly basis, the greatest number of typhoons occurred in 2002, and the least in 2011. Regionally, from 2001 to 2010, the highest number of typhoons in the Philippines occurred in Luzon, particularly in the Cagayan Valley, Ilocos Region, Cordillera Administrative Region (CAR), Central Luzon, and the Bicol Region. Luzon was followed by Visayas, including its three regions: Eastern Visayas, Central Visayas, and Western Visayas. Mindanao had the least number of typhoon occurrences with the CARAGA region having the most number.

At the provincial level, from 2001 to 2010 the highest number of typhoons occurred in Cagayan Province in Region II. Some provinces within Mindanao and all the ARMM provinces in particular have not been visited by typhoons at all. Mindanao provinces had fewer occurrences of typhoons compared to Luzon and the Visayas. The World Bank Group (2011) stated that while the trends in the occurrence of typhoons in the Philippines in the future are still a subject of much debate, they are likely to increase in intensity, and with greater consequent damage.

4.1.1 Occurrence of Floods

Flooding occurred yearly in the Philippines from 2007 to 2011. On a regional and annual basis, the region most often visited by floods was Region VI while those with no incidence of floods included CAR, Region I, Region IV-A, and Region VII. The World Bank Group (2011) stated that over time in the Philippines, heavy rainfall associated with typhoons and other weather systems may increase in both intensity and frequency under a changing climate and exacerbate the incidence of flooding in existing flood-prone areas and introduce a risk of flooding to new areas.

4.2 Occurrence of Droughts

During the 2007–2011 period, droughts occurred in the Philippines only in 2007 and 2010. More regions in 2010 were affected by droughts than in 2007. In 2007, all regions in Luzon except Region IV-A and Region VI were affected while no regions in the Visayas and Mindanao were affected. In 2010, on the other hand, most regions in Luzon, Visayas and Mindanao were affected except CAR, Region VII, Region VIII, and CARAGA. The World Bank Group (2011) reported that prolonged droughts are associated with the El Niño phenomenon and that these natural events will likely intensify in the future in the Philippines.

4.3 Impacts of Natural Disasters on Agriculture: Descriptive Analysis

From 2000 to 2010, the national agricultural area affected by typhoons, floods and droughts in the Philippines has been trending upwards. The total area increased from 683,440 ha in 2000 to 977,208 ha in 2010 (Fig. 13.1). The affected area was at its lowest in 2002 at 200,940 ha and at its highest in 2006 at 1,461,608 ha. There are neither available data at the regional nor the provincial levels with respect to the agricultural area affected by typhoons, floods and droughts in the Philippines

There are few available economic studies which have investigated the effects of typhoons, floods and droughts on agriculture in the Philippines. Thus, most of the variables representing both positive and negative impacts of said disasters based on the framework of analysis presented earlier cannot be discussed at length in this paper. Of the available literature, one study (Medina et al. 2009) stated that the flashfloods and mudflows due to heavy torrential rains in November 2004, particularly in the towns of Real, Infanta and General Nakar in Quezon Province, in addition to Dingalan in Aurora Province, resulted in 300,000 ha of prime agricultural land, mainly lowland rice cultivation land, being seriously affected. In another study, Godilano (2004) identified 790,000 ha in the Philippines which are potential sites for natural disasters and asserted that approximately 80 % of these areas fell under the jurisdiction of the agriculture sector.

From 2000 to 2010, the total value of agricultural damage, by commodity, affected by typhoons, floods and droughts in the Philippines amounted to a total

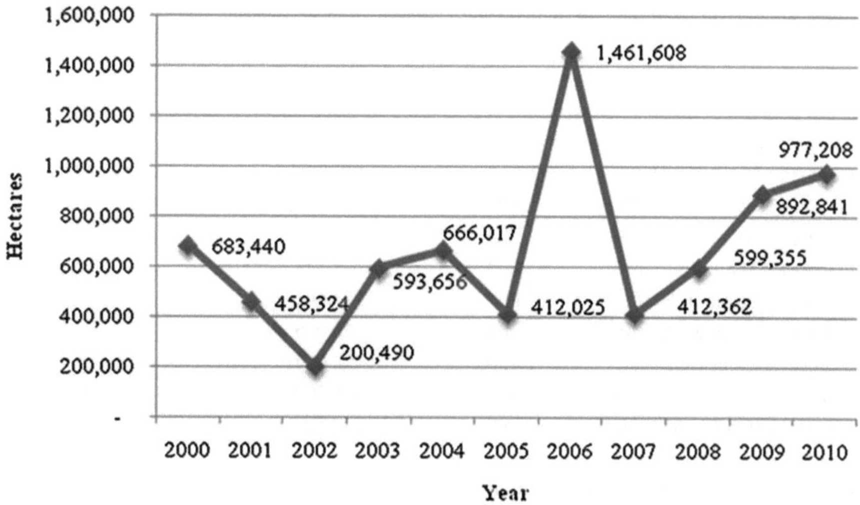

Fig. 13.1 Total agricultural area affected by typhoons, floods and droughts in the Philippines 2000–2010 (hectares). *Source of data*: Author

of USD 2,234.21 million. The crops with the most damage were rice, corn and high value cash crops. Other commodities recording damage included vegetables, coconut, abaca, sugarcane, tobacco, fisheries products, and livestock. While generally increasing, the total damage to agriculture decreased from 2000 to 2002, increased in 2003–2004, fell in 2005, rose in 2006, declined in 2007, increased in 2008 and 2009, and decreased again in 2010. The total damage to agriculture due to typhoons, floods and droughts were lowest in 2002 and highest in 2009.

Aside from agricultural commodities, agricultural facilities and irrigation incurred damage due to typhoons, floods and droughts. Damage incurred from 2000 to 2010 for agricultural facilities was valued at USD 102.39 million while those for irrigation were estimated at USD 203.31 million. The highest level of damage for agricultural facilities occurred in 2008 while that for irrigation occurred in 2009. There was no recorded damage in 2005. There were no regional and provincial data on damage to agricultural facilities and irrigation.

Nationally, National Economic and Development Authority et al. (2008) assessed the direct damage due to natural disasters and found the average cost of direct damage from natural disasters from 1970 to 2006 to be P15 billion at 2000 prices (or USD 339.44 million), including the damage to agricultural crops, public infrastructure and private homes. Government of the Philippines (2009a, b) estimated the impacts of typhoons Ondoy (Ketsana) and Pepeng (Parma) which hit several parts of Philippines within a span of 2 weeks in September and October 2009. The typhoons and the floods they caused created havoc in both the urban and rural parts of northern Luzon, particularly affecting Regions I, CAR, II, III, NCR and IVA. The study estimated that these typhoons resulted in approximately P36.2 billion (or USD 759.87 million) in immediate damage to the agriculture, fisheries, and forestry sectors in the affected areas.

Table 13.1 Average losses as a percent of output or area measure in the Philippines, by Commodity (1995–2010)

Item	Annual average loss	Annual average production/cost of production/area	Loss (%)
Rice (Production in M.T.)	570,531	13,441,901	4.2
Corn (Production in M.T.)	305,690	5,175,980	5.9
HVCC (Cost in million P)	2,801	94,267	3.0
Vegetables (Cost in million P)	202	63,721	0.3
Coconut (Cost in million P)	562	49,473	0.1
Sugarcane (Area in Ha.)	7,097	373,442	1.9
Banana (Cost in Million P)	84	46,066	0.2
Mango (Area in Ha.)	1,750	152,066	1.2
Fisheries (Cost in Million P)	619	47,655,202	0.0
Livestock (Cost in Million P)	90	139,560	0.0

Note: The model specifies the use of peso values
Source of Data: Department of Agriculture

4.4 *Impacts of Natural Disasters on Agriculture: Econometric Analysis*

In this section, the impacts of agricultural damage or losses due to natural disasters by commodity are estimated using AMPLE. As mentioned earlier, this model is capable of simulating changes in quantities of supply, imports, consumption, and exports, together with producer and consumer prices for 18 commodities. The baseline data used in the estimation is a 3-year average for the 2008–2010 period. In this study, AMPLE is used to simulate a counter-factual scenario in which crop losses arising from disasters are avoided at two different levels: (a) complete or 100 % avoidance and (b) 50 % avoidance. The differences between the counter-factual scenario and baseline data are the estimated impacts of natural disasters. Crop losses are measured as a percent of output in volume (metric tons) and, where this was not available, were estimated by cost of production in value (Pesos) or area affected (hectares) based on data availability. The crop loss counter-factual is assumed to cause an exogenous, proportional supply shift, the size of which is stated in Table 13.1.

Since the losses as a proportion of output are small, it is not surprising that changes in quantity of output, imports, exports, and also that of prices, are commensurately minor. There are few large changes in percentage terms, but this is only due to a small base, e.g. cassava output and consumption. Thus, based on these results, it is argued that agricultural damage or losses have insignificant impacts on agricultural production and prices at the national level. The result appears to support the notion that natural disasters have little bearing when the production of the agriculture sector at the national level is taken into consideration.

4.5 Impacts of Natural Disasters on Rice Farming: Descriptive Analysis

From 2007 to 2011, the total monetary value of damage to rice farming due to typhoons in the Philippines amounted to USD1,075.28 million. The damage increased in 2008 and 2009, decreased in 2010 and rose again in 2011. Regionally, during the same period, the highest level of damage occurred in Region III while the lowest was in the CARAGA region. Region XI did not register any damage to rice farming due to typhoons during the period. There are no available data at the provincial level.

From 2007 to 2011, the total value of damage to rice farming due to floods in the Philippines amounted to USD115.32 million. The damage increased in 2008, decreased in 2009, rose in 2010 and fell in 2011. Regionally, the highest level of damage occurred in Region II while the lowest was in Region VII. CAR, Region I and Region IV-A did not register any damage to rice farming due to floods during the period. There are presently no available data at the provincial level.

From 2007 to 2011, the total value of damage to rice farming due to droughts in the Philippines amounted to USD 217.52 million. The damage increased in 2008 and 2009, increased in 2010, and fell again in 2011. Regionally, the highest level of damage occurred in Region II while the lowest was in Region IX. CAR, Region VII, Region VIII and the CARAGA Region did not register any damage to rice farming due to droughts during the 2007–2011 period. There are no available data at the provincial level.

4.6 Impacts of Typhoons on Rice Farming: Econometric Analysis

Data on the occurrence of typhoons at the provincial level in the Philippines between the years 2001 and 2010 are available and together with provincial data on palay (unprocessed rice) production and palay prices, a regression analysis was conducted to assess the impact of typhoons on provincial rice production. The first deterministic equation employed is as follows:

$$QS_{i,t} = \beta_0 + \beta_1 QS_{i,t-1} + \beta_2 p_{i,t-1} + \beta_3 typh_{i,t} + \beta_4 t$$

where i, t are indices for the provinces and years covered, respectively; QS denotes palay output; p denotes palay price; *typh* denotes number of typhoons; t denotes technological change and the β's denote coefficients. Effectively, the aforementioned is a supply equation incorporating response lags for output and price; the t incorporates technological change. Of interest is the coefficient β_4, which shows the effect of typhoons on quantity of provincial palay production. Given the panel

Table 13.2 Results of panel regression on Provincial Palay production in the Philippines

	Random effects		Fixed effects	
	Coefficient	z-value	Coefficient	t-value
Lagged quantity	1.02**	171.7	0.6**	17.6
Lagged price	−3,006.7*	−2.5	−4,224.1**	−2.9
Number of typhoons	−1.111.1*	−1.8	−409.1	0.6
Year	964.1	1.02	4,915**	4.6
Constant	−1,897,108	−1.02	−728,307**	−4.6

Note: *Means t-value or z-value is between 0.01 and 0.05 level of significance and **Means t-value or z-value is below 0.01 level of significance

nature of the data for 2001–2010, both the random and fixed effects regressions were estimated (Table 13.2).

Under the random effects regression, the coefficient for number of typhoons is negative and significant at the 1–5 % level. Each typhoon, on average, controlling for other supply conditions, reduces provincial output by over one thousand tons of palay. Under the fixed effects regression, on the other hand, the coefficient for the number of typhoons is insignificant even at the 1–5 % level. Nonetheless, the results, particularly those based on the assumption of random effects, indicate that at the provincial level, typhoons may have significant and negative impacts on palay production which appears to be consistent with past studies (Loayza et al. 2009; Sivakumar 2005).

Another alternative equation is estimated to take typhoon intensity into account. The deterministic form the equation is as follows:

$$QS_{i,t} = \beta_0 + \beta_1 A_{i,t} + \beta_2 p_{i,t-1} + \beta_3 typh2_{i,t} + \beta_4 typh3i, t + \beta_5 t$$

where A is a control variable for level of production input, p denotes paddy price averaged over the last quarter of the year, *typh2* denotes a dummy variable for incidence of at least one typhoon with an intensity of signal number 2 or more; *typh3* denotes a dummy variable for incidence of at least one typhoon with an intensity of signal number 3 or more and the other variables are defined as before. The dummy variable representation of typhoons specified above places greater emphasis on intensity of typhoons (a higher signal number denoting higher intensity) rather than the simple incidence or number of typhoons hitting a particular province in a particular year. Effectively, the aforementioned is a supply equation incorporating response lags for price, together with a control variable for level of production input (in this case reduced to land). The lagged last quarter price is used based on adaptive expectations, i.e. the farmer uses the previous quarter's price as an estimate of the current cropping season price, as a basis for planting decisions. Of interest is the coefficients β_3 and β_4 which show the effect of typhoons on quantity of provincial palay production. Again, given the panel nature of the data for the period 2001–2010, both random and fixed effects regressions were estimated (Table 13.3).

Table 13.3 Results of panel regression on Provincial Palay production in the Philippines

	Random effects		Fixed effects	
	Coefficient	z-value	Coefficient	t-value
Area	0.0**	2.80	0.0**	3.17
Lagged last quarter price	−3.6**	−5.26	−3.5**	−5.13
Dummy: Signal 2	−8.3*	−2.11	−8.4*	−2.13
Dummy: Signal 3	6.7	1.65	6.6	1.63
Year	7.0**	11.12	6.9**	10.89
Constant	−13,843.5**	−11.02	−3,597.9**	−10.79

Note: *Means t-value or z-value is between 0.01 and 0.05 level of significance and **Means t-value or z-value is below 0.01 level of significance

Under the random effects regression, the coefficient for signal number 2 dummy is negative and significant at the 1–5 % level. This implies that the incidence of at least one typhoon with an intensity of signal number 2 or more, controlling for other supply conditions, reduces provincial output by over 8,000 t of palay. Similar results are obtained under the fixed-effects regression. Somewhat anomalous is the sign of the coefficient for signal number 3 dummy for either regression method although the coefficients are not significant. These results again indicate that, at the provincial level, typhoons may have significant and negative impacts on palay production.

4.7 *Impacts of Natural Disasters on Food Security*

It was indicated in the foregoing analysis that at the national level, typhoons, floods and droughts do not significantly impact agricultural production and prices. Hence, based on food affordability alone, these disasters may have little effect on food security at that level. On the other hand, it was also estimated beforehand that typhoons have a significant and negative effect on rice production at the provincial level. Therefore, based on rice availability alone, typhoons may have diminished food security at that level.

At present, there is a paucity of research actually quantifying the impacts of natural disasters on food security in the Philippines. An exception is the World Food Programme (2009) which conducted a study on typhoons Ondoy (Ketsana) and Pepeng (Parma) including their impacts on food security at the household level. The study found that as a coping strategy to adapt to the effects of Ondoy and Pepeng, the most frequently reported consumption coping mechanism, used by 79 % of the households surveyed, was to rely less on preferred food (Table 13.4). The least used consumption coping strategy, adopted by 5 % of the households, was sending family members outside for food. On the other hand, the most common non-consumption coping mechanism, used by 15.1 % of households, was selling labor in advance, while the least utilized was the selling of household and agricultural assets for food, a mechanism used by just 5.2 % of households.

Table 13.4 Consumption and non-consumption negative coping strategies adopted by households affected by Typhoons Ondoy and Pepeng, 2009 (% of households)

Coping strategies	Northern regions (I, CAR, II)	Region III	NCR	Region IV-A	Overall
Consumption coping strategies					
Eating less preferred food	42	95	94	82	79
Borrowing food from neighbors/friends	44	33	55	34	37
Buying food on credit	53	46	50	54	51
Eating wild/gathered food	45	39	10	21	33
Reducing meal portions	31	34	32	50	39
Reducing number of meals by children	4	10	33	16	12
Reducing number of meals by adults	13	45	46	35	34
Skipping meals for the whole day	7	20	26	13	15
Sending family members outside for food	3	2	15	9	5
Non consumption coping strategies					
Out-migration	5.2	4.3	18.2	15.3	9.1
Selling labour in advance	18.5	2.4	26.3	23.4	15.1
Taking children out of school	2.2	0.5	20.6	10.7	5.7
Selling of household assets for food		1.0	13.3	12.8	5.2
Selling agricultural assets for food	10.4	5.3		2.5	5.2

Source: World Food Programme (2009)

The results of the aforementioned study indicate that, particularly at the household level, natural disasters may have a significant impact on food security. They also show that households differ in their consumption and non-consumption strategies to cope with their difficult food security situation. They further indicate that non-consumption strategies to address their food needs were practiced by households, although not as commonly as consumption strategies.

4.8 *Impacts of Natural Disasters on the Natural Resources and Environment*

Limited available data and information also preclude a quantitative evaluation of the negative impacts of natural disasters on the natural resources and the environment of the Philippines. Thus, a descriptive and generally qualitative assessment is instead conducted below based on past research.

4.8.1 Soil Erosion

The water-related natural factors that influence the rate of soil erosion are rainfall, vegetative cover, slope of the land, and soil erodibility (Asio et al. 2009). Due to its wet tropical climate, the Philippines has a comparatively high average annual rainfall. It also has a rugged and mountainous topography with large sections having a gradient of more than 18 %. These and other natural factors such as wind, and man-made factors such as slash and burn agriculture, all contribute to soil erosion. The little available evidence on the actual impact of natural disasters on soil erosion in the Philippines is site-specific and anecdotal. In particular, Medina et al. (2009) mentioned that in 2004, flashfloods and mudflows resulting from heavy torrential rains induced mountain soil erosion, landslides and the overflowing of river systems in the provinces of Quezon and Aurora in Luzon.

4.8.2 Reduced Rainfall

Typhoons increase rainfall while droughts decrease it, but on the net it has been projected that there will be decreases in the average annual rainfall by the year 2020 in most parts of the Philippines, except in Luzon where either an increase or no change in rainfall is projected (Manila Observatory for the Congressional Commission on Science and Technology and Engineering 2010). It was also foreseen that by 2050, Visayas and Mindanao will be drier than normal, as will most of the western part of Luzon. Clearly then, typhoons may increase rainfall at the times they occur and places they affect, but over time and for the country as a whole, average rainfall is expected to decrease. An important water resources-related negative effect of reduced rainfall is a concomitant reduction in the country's hydropower supply.

4.8.3 Siltation and Sedimentation

Silts and sediments caused by floods tend to clog rivers, lakes, drainage systems, reservoirs, dams, irrigation canals and other inland water bodies. This in turn reduces the viability of these water resources for economic activities such as fishing, aquaculture, water storage, irrigation, water recreation, water transportation and many others. Similarly, siltation and sedimentation of coastal areas damage mangroves, coral reefs, sea grasses, estuaries, beaches and other marine ecosystems, rendering them less viable as providers of ecosystem goods and services for the population.

No study, however, has quantified the impacts of floods in terms of inland and coastal siltation and sedimentation in the Philippines, although the impacts of siltation and sedimentation have been investigated. Government of the Philippines (2009a) mentioned that the existing infrastructure that protects Manila and other populated areas in nearby Laguna Lake has been inadequate and has not been properly maintained. As a result, the siltation and sedimentation and other unwelcome impacts of the floods generated by Ondoy in 2009 had severe consequences for people living near the Marikina River and adjacent areas.

4.8.4 Reduced Tree and Vegetative Cover

Because of the strong winds and water currents they carry, typhoons and floods typically flatten or uproot trees. The siltation and sedimentation produced by floods also cover grasslands and other ground-level and below-water vegetation. In a similar vein, because of the length of time that it is exposed to intense sunlight, ground vegetation withers or dies during droughts. No study has quantitatively measured the effects of typhoons, floods and droughts on trees and other vegetation in the Philippines. Mjoes (2005) mentioned that in 2004, the Philippines experienced two typhoons and two tropical storms which resulted in considerable damage including a significant number of trees being brought down.

4.8.5 Reduced Soil Fertility

Droughts reduce soil fertility because higher temperatures reduce soil moisture, water storage capacity and overall soil quality. No study has quantified the effects of droughts on soil fertility in the Philippines. Mitin (2009) mentioned that Ilocos Norte was one of the provinces worst hit by the drought in Northern Luzon in 2007 along with Ilocos Sur, La Union and Pangasinan. It further explained that before the dry spell hit, Ilocos Norte in particular had high sufficiency levels of rice, corn, garlic, and onions.

4.8.6 Accumulation of Wastes and Water Pollution

Flood water currents carry all sorts of wastes that are then dumped into catchment areas. These wastes in turn pollute surface and ground water, including that used for drinking and sanitation. There is also no available study at present that quantifies the impact of floods on waste accumulation and water pollution in the Philippines. Asian Disaster Preparedness Center (2008) stated that while the riverbanks in Marikina City, Metro Manila used to be a site of religious celebrations in the past the river has been seen only as a site of filth and stench at present. Uncontrolled encroachment on the riverbanks by informal settlers, structures within the river, and the indiscriminate disposal of both domestic and industrial wastes have worsened the impacts of annual flooding from the Marikina River. GOP (201) also mentioned that about 50 % of the wells monitored by the Environmental Management Bureau (EMB) in 2005 were found to be contaminated with fecal coli forms and that

Regions II and Region VI, which were seasonally-arid and drought-prone areas, had the highest number of contaminated sites.

4.8.7 Saltwater Intrusion

Demand for freshwater during periods of drought is higher than normal and this in turn may lead to higher rates of groundwater withdrawal. If the withdrawal rate is faster than the replenishment rate in a coastal area, seawater may be pulled into the freshwater aquifer resulting in the increased salinity of the groundwater. On a more temporary scale, high tides and storm surges caused by typhoons may also cause saltwater intrusion. The World Bank Group (2011) mentioned that during El Niño events, among the significant pressures on the freshwater resources in the coastal areas of the Philippines is saltwater intrusion. Citing past studies, Government of the Philippines (2010) reported that saltwater intrusion in the country was evident in nearly 28 % of coastal municipalities in Luzon, 20 % in the Visayas and 29 % in Mindanao.

4.8.8 Higher Coastal Tides and Storm Surges

Floods and typhoons bring in a lot of rain that may raise coastal tides beyond normal levels, whilst strong winds from typhoons potentially drive huge wave surges into the coastal areas. The effects of rising coastal tides and strong storm surges have been devastating at times to people residing close to the water's edge. The World Bank Group (2011) stated that the Philippines is particularly vulnerable to rises in sea level and storm surges as about 60 % of its municipalities and ten of its largest cities are located along the coasts. Four Philippine cities also ranked among the top ten East Asian cities likely to be affected by sea level rises and storm surges. In particular areas, it has been projected that a 1.0 m rise in sea level will inundate more than 5,000 ha of land in 19 municipalities of Manila, Bulacan and Cavite (Capili et al. 2005). The worst-case scenario of a 2.0 m rise is expected to aggravate riverine flooding in most of the tributaries of Manila Bay, especially the Pampanga and Pasig rivers.

4.8.9 Deformed Land Topography

Below water level, floods deposit silts and sediments, thus raising the elevation of the soil beds and making the affected rivers and water bodies shallower than before. Above ground, floods level land areas and reduce their economic and aesthetic value. Because they deposit so much soil both under water and on land, floods elevate the level of the soil, thus requiring substantial excavation or dredging to bring the area back to its original state. There has been no study conducted in the Philippines that quantitatively evaluates the impacts of floods on the land topography and the subsequent effects on land value.

4.8.10 Reduced Viability of Ecosystems

Typhoons, floods and droughts also constitute a threat to the health and survival of forests and other terrestrial ecosystems. It has been projected, for instance, that if the climate projections showing drier conditions in most regions of the Philippines actually materialize, the size of dry forests will decrease (Manila Observatory for the Congressional Commission on Science and Technology and Engineering 2010). In line with this loss of forest cover will be the loss of existing and possibly yet to be discovered flora and fauna that constitutes the terrestrial biodiversity of the Philippines.

As well as negative aboveground effects, droughts also tend to negatively impact marine ecosystems. Rising temperatures coupled with the rising carbon dioxide levels in the atmosphere cause coral reef bleaching, or the chalky appearance coral takes on when it dies (Manila Observatory for the Congressional Commission on Science and Technology and Engineering 2010). The destruction of coral reefs reduces marine biodiversity which is critically important for the ecological balance and productivity of marine ecosystems. It has been reported that the El Niño episode which occurred in 1997 and 1998 in the Philippines, decreased the coral cover ranging from 46 to 80 % in Bolinao, Pangasinan (Government of the Philippines 2010). Other areas affected included Batangas, other parts of Northern Luzon, West Palawan, and parts of the Visayas. In addition to droughts, floods could inundate mangrove, coral reef and sea grass areas along the coast, making them less viable as important providers of ecosystem goods and services to both the economy and environment.

The total value of the ecosystem goods and services provided by coral reefs, mangroves and seagrass nationally in the Philippines was estimated at about USD116.2 million in 2006. Although the exact level of damage directly caused by previous typhoons, floods and droughts on coastal ecosystems has not been measured as yet, it is clear that the marine resources provide significant economic and social benefits to the country as a whole.

4.8.11 Endangered Human Health and Safety

Overcrowding, inadequate water supply and sanitation, and poor access to health services following the sudden displacement of an affected population after the occurrence of natural disasters increase the risk of communicable transmission of diseases (World Health Organization 2006). These diseases include water borne diseases such as diarrhea, hepatitis, and leptospirosis; diseases associated with overcrowding such as measles, meningitis, and acute respiratory infections; vector-borne diseases such as malaria and dengue fever; and other diseases like tetanus, coccidiomycosis and mental health problems. Other health and safety-related impacts, particularly with respect to typhoons and floods, include injuries or even death due to falling trees and debris, electrical exposure and similar accidents.

It is projected that the displacement of families living in natural disaster-prone areas in the Philippines will be a public health challenge that will become more frequent in the coming years (Manila Observatory for the Congressional Commission on Science and Technology and Engineering 2010). A decline in the volume of groundwater will heighten water-related disputes and increasingly expose the population to water-borne diseases. In addition, health-related facilities and infrastructure could be severely damaged under increased frequency and intensity of severe weather events (Philippine Atmospheric and Astronomical Services Administration 2011). Studying the flood hazards in Metro Manila, Zoleta-Nantes (2000) asserted that the economic losses due to floods escalated through time and health-related risks such as dengue fever, diarrhea-related diseases, unsanitary conditions, and water contamination levels were high.

5 Summary and Conclusion

This study quantitatively and qualitatively analyzed the impacts of typhoons, floods and droughts on agriculture, food security and the natural resources and environment in the Philippines using available secondary data. In general, the study found that: (a) typhoons, floods and droughts have an insignificant impact on overall agricultural production at the national level, yet typhoons may have a significant negative impact on paddy rice production at the provincial level; (b) typhoons, as exemplified by Ondoy and Pepeng in 2009, have a significant negative impact on the food security of the households in the affected areas; (c) households have varying consumption and non-consumption strategies to cope with the impacts of typhoons; and (d) the different impacts of typhoons, floods and droughts on the natural resources and environment have not been quantitatively assessed in detail, however available evidence suggests that these are also substantial.

6 Recommendations

Recent studies undertaken in this field have provided strategies to address the impacts of: climate change on agriculture and the natural resources and environment (The World Bank Group 2011; Manila Observatory for the Congressional Commission on Science and Technology and Engineering 2010); climate change on the coastal natural resources and environment (Capili et al. 2005); natural disasters on overall and sub-national development (National Economic and Development Authority et al. 2008; The World Bank and National Disaster and Coordinating Council n.d.); typhoons on agriculture and the natural resources and environment

(Government of the Philippines 2009a, b); typhoons on food security (World Food Programme 2009); and droughts on agriculture and the natural resources and environment (Government of the Philippines 2010). The recommendations made by these works should be seriously reviewed and considered by the government.

Based on its results and findings, the study recommends the following: (a) As typhoons may have significant negative impacts on rice production at the local level as opposed to the national level, assistance for rice farmers and the agriculture sector as a whole should be made more site-specific, zeroing in on the affected areas that actually need it; (b) Those assisting affected households and areas in overcoming the resulting ill-effects of natural disasters should consider not only consumption strategies, such as the provision of emergency food aid, but also non-consumption strategies, such as the provision of post-disaster emergency employment; and (c) While the available evidence suggests that the natural resources and environment sector is significantly affected by natural disasters, it is currently less considered, as attention is presently focused on agriculture. It may now be high time to provide concrete assistance to this sector, in particular the provision of defensive investments and rehabilitation expenditures to cope with these natural disasters.

7 Areas for Future Research

Based on the results and findings of the study, the potential topics for future economic research on the impacts of natural disasters on agriculture, food security and the environment in the Philippines are as follows: (a) economic analysis of the impacts of natural disasters in disaster-prone local areas such as the identified typhoon belts; (b) economic analysis of the defensive investments and rehabilitation expenditures needed for the natural resources and environment in ecologically sensitive and disaster-prone areas; (c) analysis of the health and other social impacts of natural disasters in disaster-prone local areas; and (d) detailed analysis of the impacts of natural disasters on food security at the household, local and national levels.

References

Asian Disaster Preparedness Center. (2008). *Flood disaster mitigation and river rehabilitation by Marikina city, Philippines, Safer Cities 22,* Case studies on mitigating disasters in Asia and the Pacific, p. 8. http://www.adpc.net/v2007/programs/udrm/promise/INFORMATION%20RESOURCES/Safer%20Cities/Downloads/SaferCities22.pdf. Accessed 14 January 2012.

Asio, V. B., Jahn, R., Perez, F. O., Navarrete, I. A., & Abit, S. M., Jr. (2009). A review of soil degradation in the Philippines. *Annals of Tropical Research, 31*(2), 69–94.

Briones, R. (2010). *Scenarios and options for productivity growth in Philippine agriculture: An application of the AMPLE*, Discussion Paper Series No. 2010-05. Philippine Institute for Development Studies, NEDA sa Makati Bldg., Makati, Metro Manila, p. 46. http://www.eaber.org/sites/default/files/documents/PIDS_Briones_2010.pdf. Accessed 1 February 2012.

Briones, R., & Parel, D. K. (2011). *Scenarios and options for productivity growth in Philippine agriculture: An Application of the Agricultural Multi-Market Model for Policy Evaluation (AMPLE)*, Revised Final Report. Submitted to the productivity growth in Philippine agriculture project, Southeast Asian Regional Center for Graduate Studies and Research in Education, p. 55.
Capili, E. B., Ibay, A. C. S., & Villarin, J. R. T. (2005). Climate Change Impacts and Adaptation on Philippine Coasts. *Proceedings of the International Oceans 2005 Conference*, Washington D. C., 1–8, 19–23 September 2005. Available at: http://info.worldbank.org/etools/docs/library/230308/Session%202/Session%202%20Reading%201.pdf. Accessed February 1, 2012.
National Economic and Development Authority, United Nations Development Programme, & European Commission Humanitarian Aid. (2008). *Mainstreaming disaster risk reduction in subnational development and land use/physical planning in the Philippines*, p. 343. http://www.neda.gov.ph/references/Guidelines/DRR/Guidelines%20on%20Mainstreaming%20DRR%20in%20Subnational%20Development%20Land%20Use%20Planning.pdf. Accessed 1 February 2012.
European Commission. (2009). *Country environmental profile updates Philippines*, p. 24. http://eeas.europa.eu/delegations/philippines/documents/more_info/coop_news/cep_update_09_en.pdf. Accessed 14 January 2012.
Godilano, E. C. (2004). *Geospatial technology in disaster prediction and agriculture and natural resources management*. Philippines: Bureau of Agricultural Research, Department of Agriculture, p. 27. http://www.bar.gov.ph/downloadables/2004/Disaster_Leyte.pdf. Accessed 14 January 2012.
Government of the Philippines. (2009). *Typhoons Ondoy and Pepeng: post disaster needs assessment*. Joint initiative of the Government of the Republic of the Philippines, Representatives of the Private Sector and Civil Society Organizations, Multilateral Development Partners, and Bilateral Development Partners, p. 62. Available at: http://www.pdrf.org/pdf/POPJAVolume1.pdf. Accessed 1 February 2012.
Government of the Philippines. (2009a). *Typhoons Ondoy and Pepeng: Post disaster needs assessment sector reports*. Joint initiative of the Government of the Republic of the Philippines, Representatives of the Private Sector and Civil Society Organizations, Multilateral Development Partners, and Bilateral Development Partners, p. 62. http://siteresources.worldbank.org/INTPHILIPPINES/Resources/PDNAVol2SectorReports.pdf. Accessed 1 February 2012.
Government of the Philippines. (2010). *The updated Philippine national action plan desertification, land degradation and drought FY 2010-2020*. Department of Agriculture, Department of Agrarian Reform, Department of Environment and Natural Resources and Department of Science and Technology, p. 129. http://bswm.da.gov.ph/unccdphilippines/Files/PDFs/The%20Philippine%20NAP%20to%20Combat%20DLDD%20and%20Poverty%202010-2020.pdf. Accessed 1 January 2012.
Loayza, N., Olaberría, E., Rigolini, J., & Christiaensen, L. (2009). *Natural disasters and growth going beyond the averages*, Policy Research Working Paper 4980. The World Bank East Asia and Pacific Social Protection Unit & Development Research Group, p. 40. Available at: http://gfdrr.org/docs/WPS4980.pdf. Accessed 20 February 2012.
Manila Observatory for the Congressional Commission on Science & Technology and Engineering. (2010). *Technical primer on climate change in the Philippines. COMSTE Conference Engineering Resilience, Confronting Risk Beyond Adaptation*. 15 & 16 March 2010, Manila: Sofitel Philippine Plaza. p. 60. http://resilience.comste.gov.ph/files/primer.pdf. Accessed 1 February 2012.
Medina, S. M., Villancio, V. T., Garcia, J. N. M., Natural, Jr, H. G., Vergara, J. R. M., Paningbatan, Jr. L, E. P., & Reguyal, A. A. (2009). Rehabilitation and natural resource management in changed agricultural landscape as a result of disasters. *Journal of ISSAAS*, *15*(2), 70–80. http://www.issaas.org/journal/v15/02/journal-issaas-v15n2-07-medina-et_al.pdf. Accessed 1 February 2012.
Mitin, A. (2009). *Documentation of selected adaptation strategies to climate change in rice cultivation*, East Asia Rice Working Group. Quezon City, p. 41. http://www.eastasiarice.org/Books/Adaptation%20Strategies.pdf. Accessed 14 January 2012.

Mjoes, O. D. (2005). *Draft field report: Philippines flooding/typhoon rapid environmental impact assessment*. Philippines REA Summary Report – 1/19/2005, p. 46. http://pdf.usaid.gov/pdf_docs/PNADD447.pdf. Accessed 14 January 2012.

National Economic Development Authority. (2011). *Philippine development plan 2011-2016*. (p. 411). Available at: http://www.neda.gov.ph/PDP/2011-2016/default.asp. Accessed January 14, 2012.

Philippine Atmospheric, Geophysical, and Astronomical Services Administration. (2011). *Climate change in the Philippines*, February 2011. http://kidlat.pagasa.dost.gov.ph/cab/climate_change/Climate%20change%20in%20the%20Philippines%20-%20August%2025%202011.pdf. Accessed 14 January 2012.

Sivakumar, M. V. K. (2005). Impacts of natural disasters in agriculture, rangeland and forestry: An overview. In M. V. K. Sivakumar, R. P. Motha, & H. P. Das (Eds.), *Natural disasters and extreme events in agriculture* (pp. 1–22). Heidelberg/Berlin/New York: Springer. http://books.google.com.ph/books?id=SquWkdG19o8C&pg=PA1&lpg=PA1&dq=Impacts±of±Natural±Disasters±in±Agriculture,±Rangeland±and±Forestry:±An±Overview&source=bl&ots=255Au3wjwH&sig=CNxQJ2x42gllcle8zjyvG0zKtVQ&hl=tl&sa=X&ei=pz5oT-nlCqu6iAeSsryYCg&ved=0CBwQ6AEwA A#v=onepage&q=Impacts%20of%20Natural%20Disasters%20in%20Agriculture%2C%20Rangeland%20and%20Forestry%3A%20An%20Overview&f=false. Accessed 20 February 2012.

The World Bank and National Disaster and Coordinating Council. (No Date). *Natural disaster risk management in the Philippines: Enhancing poverty alleviation through disaster reduction*, p. 62. http://www-wds.worldbank.org/external/default/WDSContentServer/WDSP/IB/2007/09/28/000020439_20070928092727/Rendered/PDF/338220REPLACEM1aster0Report1combine.pdf. Accessed 20 February 2012.

The World Bank Group. (2011). *Vulnerability, risk reduction, and adaptation to climate change in the Philippines. Climate risk and adaptation country profile*, p. 13. http://sdwebx.worldbank.org/climateportalb/doc/GFDRRCountryProfiles/wb_gfdrr_climate_change_country_profile_for_PHL.pdf . Accessed 20 February 2012.

World Food Programme. (2009). *Philippines Luzon typhoons and floods emergency food security assessment*. In collaboration with the DSWD, Government of Philippines, FAO, UNICEF, Save the Children, OXFAM, World Vision, ADRA, Christian Aid and CFSI, p. 35. http://documents.wfp.org/stellent/groups/public/documents/ena/wfp220033.pdf. Accessed 1 February 2012.

World Health Organization. (2006). *Communicable diseases following natural disasters risk assessment and priority interventions*, Programme on disease control in humanitarian emergencies communicable diseases cluster. Geneva: World Health Organization. http://www.who.int/diseasecontrol_emergencies/guidelines/CD_Disasters_26_06.pdf. Accessed 1 February 2012.

Zoleta-Nantes, D. B. (2000). Flood hazards in Metro Manila: Recognizing commonalities, differences, and courses of action. *Social Science Diliman* (January–June 2000), *1*(1), 60–105. http://www.journals.upd.edu.ph/index.php/socialsciencediliman/article/viewFile/36/7. Accessed 1 February 2012.

Chapter 14
Impacts of Natural Disasters and Disaster Risk Management in China: The Case of China's Experience in the Wenchuan Earthquake

Yi-Ming Wei, Ju-Liang Jin, and Qiong Wang

1 Introduction

Natural disasters are extreme events which cause damage and destruction to human life safety, economic development, the living environment and resources. A natural hazard is a complex system with interactions between natural hazard-inducing factors (natural mutation factors) and the socio-economic system (the person-property-environment-resource composite system) under certain conditions. This complex system has intricate characters of structure, functionality, heterogeneity of spatial and temporal distribution, openness, high dimensionality, and uncertainty (Wei et al. 2002). Natural disasters often affect large numbers of people worldwide. Every 10 years the death tolls reaches 1 million and more millions of people are rendered homeless. Destruction to the global economy caused by natural disasters reached USD40 billion in the 1960s, USD70 billion in the 1970s and USD120 billion in the 1980s (Domeisen 1995).

1.1 Overview

Various frequent natural disasters affect China, which stretches across a vast area and has a significant monsoon climate. Over the past 30 years, along with the

Y.-M. Wei (✉)
Center for Energy and Environmental Policy Research, Beijing Institute of Technology, Beijing, China
e-mail: ymwei@263.net

J.-L. Jin
Hefei University of Technology, Hefei, China

Q. Wang
National University of Singapore, Singapore, Singapore

D.P. Aldrich et al. (eds.), *Resilience and Recovery in Asian Disasters*, Risk, Governance and Society 18, DOI 10.1007/978-4-431-55022-8_14

sustained and rapid development of China's social economy, natural disasters in China created multi-hazard concurrence, mass disaster occurrence and disease outbreaks. Rarely seen in history, there have been serious natural disasters, such as the Wenchuan earthquake, freezing rain and snowy weather in southern areas, extended winter-spring drought, the Yushu earthquake, debris flows and flash floods in Zhouqu. Losses from natural hazards continue to increase. Since the beginning of the twenty-first century, there have been 13 earthquakes above magnitude 8 in the world with two of them in China. China's casualties inflicted by earthquake were the highest in the world. In the twentieth century, there were about 1.2 million deaths caused by earthquakes in the world including 600,000 deaths in China. China, which occupies 70 % of the land, has 20 % of the population, and has 80 % of industrial and agricultural areas and cities in the world, is harshly affected by natural disasters (Zhang et al. 2006).

The most familiar disasters are those caused by meteorological factors, including droughts, floods, freezing rain and snowy weather, hail and sandstorm. In addition, there are continuous geological disasters, such as earthquakes, debris flows, land subsidence, avalanches, landslides and ground fissures. In addition, some natural disasters arise from oceanic occurrences, such as tropical storms, storm surges, sea ice, coastal erosion and red tide. Furthermore, there are environmental disasters like soil erosion, desertification, vegetation degradation, sharp decline of biodiversity, shortage of water and environmental pollution. Among all these natural disasters, meteorological disasters, which account for more than 70 % of all disasters, with great variety and high strength and frequency, pose serious threats to economic and social development and to people's lives and property. Such hazards impede the implementation of a sustainable development strategy.

According to Sun (2009), during 1978–2002, there have been 13 major floods and 12 major droughts. Disasters—primarily floods in the south and drought in the north—happened nearly every year. Since the 1990s, in the context of climate change and global warming, global meteorological disasters have increased significantly, and have affected social and economic development. Mitigating the damage from natural disasters, responding to the threat of climate change and promoting the coordinated development of the economy are important issues in dealing with disasters. Even national economic and social development are critical here, as well as vital parts of national security strategy in the twenty-first century. In future, exploration of the impacts of natural disasters on the social and economic development of China, recognizing the impacts of disasters from the perspectives of science and management, and then minimizing destruction remain crucial research projects.

1.2 Literature Review

There has been a great deal of research into the impacts of natural disasters on social and economic development (Ma and Gao 2010). There is an old saying in China:

"Famine happens every 3 years, epidemic happens every 6 years, and natural hazard happens every 11 years." This is a perfect description of the pattern of natural disasters in China. Take flood and drought disasters as an example, from 1766 BCE to 1937 CE, records show that there have been 1,058 floods, 1,074 droughts. The annual average of floods and droughts is 0.86 a year (Deng 1937). Hirshleifer (1966) analyzed the short-term and long-term impacts of plague outbreaks on the economy of Western Europe in 1348–1350. Yu (1988) and Du (1988) are representative publications of the research into China's hazard economics. According to the records of natural disasters in China, Wang et al. (1994) suggested that China's disaster regions could be divided into western, northern and southern parts, using the Hu Huanyong population line[1] and the 34°N line of latitude as the boundaries.

Along the Hu population line, there may additionally be a transition region, and the time characteristics of the China's natural disasters show droughts from March to October, floods from June to September. The Huang-Huai-Hai area has always been a frequent location for disasters frequently. Zhang and Shen (1995) argue that the opinion that natural disasters would cause negative impacts to economic growth, and based on the Harrod-Domar model, presented a method to calculate the economic losses from natural disasters indirectly.

To do so they quantitatively analyzed the relationship between natural disasters and economic growth. Hu (1996) calculated the statistics and pointed out that, a "hazard cycle" has clearly existed since 1949 with an average cycle length ranging from 3 to 3.5 years. On the impacts on food production, due to spread of the hazard-affected and damage-affected areas in China, while the per unit grain yield increased, grain losses rose, which directly led to fluctuation of food production. Zheng (1998) argued that the substance of disasters was the economic issue, and summed up four basic laws and five principles of the functions of disasters. In his analysis he showed the characteristics of the agricultural hazard economics, the cyclic fluctuations, the differentiation of regions and the orientation of macroeconomic policy. Lu et al. (2002) discussed the direct losses from natural disasters and their indirect economic losses, using input-output tables, and built a quantitative analysis model for disaster loss assessment. They took agriculture as an example to analyze the impacts on the entire economic system of agricultural yield losses caused by natural disasters. He (2002) investigated the theoretical framework and research approach of hazard economic analysis, and made an empirical study of the hazard economy.

In order to draw a definite conclusion regarding the impacts of disasters on economic development, Benson and Clay (1998) analyzed the impacts of disasters on long-term economic development using trans-departmental data of 115 countries' real GDP from 1960 to 1993. The results demonstrated that economic growth rates in a country with frequent disasters is lower than a country with relatively

[1] Professor Hu Huanyong was a forefather of modern Chinese demography and the founder of China's population geography. He drew the "Aihui-Tengchong Line," which was known internationally as the "Hu Line," in 1934; the line marked a striking difference in the distribution of China's population.

fewer disasters. Xie (2003) analyzed the economic losses caused by floods, including reduction of agricultural production, asset ineffectiveness or cessation of industry and mining enterprises, recession of the urban economy, impacts on finance, poverty and famine. Then from the viewpoint of economics, he illuminated the impact of floods both at macro-level and micro-level. Liu et al. (2005) took the view that drought is one of the disasters which affect social economic development mainly in agriculture. Since 1949, China's annual average food loss caused by drought amounts to 5 % for several years and the loss trend is on the rise, especially in the northeast, northwest and north of China.

Kunreuther and Pauly (2006) came to the conclusion that the occurrence of natural disasters would constrain economic growth, in the first place because of the losses caused by disasters, and then because of investment which has to be made in hazard prevention, rescue and recovery which could have been directed to promoting the development of the economy. Yuan and Zhang (2006) pointed out that the establishment of specified standards for disaster statistics, provision for catastrophic disaster statistics, assessment of disaster statistics and quality improvement for statisticians is a "master pathway" to promote China's disaster statistics.

Zhang et al. (2008) argued that in the twentieth century, along with the tremendous changes in China's social economy, the effect of natural hazards presented significant changes over age and differences among phases. Particularly, from 1900 to 1949, China experienced a semi-feudal and a semi-colonial period, and that resulted in no reduction in the frequency of disasters, and in more casualties and famines, which exacerbated the poverty of people and led to social unrest. Later, from 1950 to 1979, following the initial founding of the New China, there were low capacities for disaster reduction, and disasters happened regularly. Therefore, disasters not only caused serious damage, casualties and property losses, but also critically affected the development of the social economy. After 1980, with rapid and sustained economic development in China, the ability to reduce disasters improved. Even as the affected population increased, therefore, the death tolls and famines reduced notably. Moreover, the destructive effects and incidences of natural disasters spread widely.

As well as damage to agriculture, industrial, transportation and other industries were widely affected. Though the direct and indirect losses caused by disasters increased, the relatively losses became smaller and the relationships among disasters, resources and the environment became intertwined, thus impacts on the sustained development of the social economy became profound. The analysis above indicates that the impacts of disasters are not only the result of natural conditions, but are also closely related to the socio-economic background. Economic development, therefore, with improvement in the country's hazard-reduction ability will help to alleviate the hardships arising from natural disasters.

On the basis of the above studies, we use 30 years of recent data from the China Civil Affairs' Statistical Yearbook and the China Statistical Yearbook, and focus on impacts of natural disasters on human life security, agriculture and economic security, in order to provide government policy-makers with an evidence base on disaster prevention and mitigation.

2 Impact Analysis of Natural Disasters on the Social and Economic Development of China

2.1 Impacts of Natural Disasters on the Security of Human Life

The impacts of natural disasters on human life security during the past 30 years were significant in a number of ways.

First, the number of affected individuals was between 209 and 498 million people, accounting for 20–39 % of national population. The annual average affected population reached 358 million people who made up 30 % of the national population. Death tolls and the number of people missing after disasters ranged from 1,528 to 88,928, and the annual average number of dead and missing people arising from disasters was 8,020. Next, 1991, 1994, 1997, 2000, 2005–2010 were the worst of the 30 years, and the affected population was more than 400 million people in the past 10 years, the affected population increased radically. Finally, the numbers of dead and missing people following disasters showed a decreasing trend. However, when struck by devastating earthquakes and other severe natural disasters, the numbers of dead and missing were very high.

2.2 Impacts of Natural Disasters on Agricultural Security

Our analysis shows that the impacts of natural disasters on agricultural security were extensive during the past 30 years. The area of crops affected ranged from 22.3 to 59.8 million ha and the annual average area of affected crops reached 45.1 million ha which accounted for 14.32–39.21 % and 30 % of the total sown area of farm crops (hectare) respectively. The crop damage areas ranged from 13.8 to 37.5 million ha and the annual average damaged area extended to 23.8 million ha which accounted for the proportion of the total sown crops area to 8.86–24.59 % and 16 % respectively.

In 1980, 1988, 1991, 1992, 1994, 1996, 1997, 2000, 2001 and 2003 the areas of crops affected extended to 50 million ha. The area of damaged crops covered more than 20 % of the total sown crop areas in 1980, 1994, 1996, 1997, 2000, 2001 and 2003. For nearly the whole of the 30 years period covered by the statistical record used, crops were brutally affected by disasters.

2.3 Impacts of Natural Disasters on Economic Security

The number of collapsed houses in each year totaled between 0.922 million and 10.977 million rooms, and the annual average number was 3.3954 million rooms. The number of damaged rooms ranged between 3.121 and 26.287 million, and the annual average figure was 9.3225 million rooms. Direct economic losses extended from USD 8.23 billion to USD 212.30 billion, and the annual average direct economic losses caused by natural disasters amounted to USD 39.35 billion, which is ten times the losses suffered by the developed countries like the United States.

The range of direct economic losses caused by natural disasters over 30 years, as a proportion of annual gross domestic product (GDP) was 0.7 to 5.6 %. The annual average direct economic loss was 2.5 % of GDP. As a result, the impacts of natural disasters offset a portion of China's economic achievements. In the past two decades, direct economic losses caused by natural disasters showed an increasing trend. However, once in the event of catastrophic natural disasters, the direct economic losses will come to a huge amount.

Over the past two decades, the percentage of direct economic losses to GDP has declined. However, in the event of catastrophic natural disasters, the direct economic losses will highly account for the proportion of GDP. Direct economic losses and the growth rate of GDP are negatively correlated. One piece of evidence for this is that, while the growth rate of direct economic losses caused by natural disasters reduced from 9.7 % in 2003 to −15 % in 2004, the growth rate of GDP increased from 12.9 % in 2003 to 17.7 % in 2004. Moreover, although the growth rate of direct economic losses caused by natural disasters rose from −15 % in 2004 to 27.4 % in 2005, the growth rate of GDP fell from 17.7 % in 2004 to 14.6 % in 2005.

2.4 *Discussion of Natural Disaster Impact*

The impacts of natural disasters on human life security have been significant over the past 30 years in China. The annual average affected population reached 358 million people who made up 57 % of the world's annual average affected population and 30 % of the national population. The annual average rate of dead and missing people stemming from disasters was 8,020 which amounted for 9.9 % of the world's annual average rate of dead and missing people. While the affected population has risen significantly in the past 10 years, the numbers of dead and missing people have tended to fall. In the event of devastating earthquakes and other severe natural disasters, however, large numbers of people die or become missing. That indicates the high vulnerability of the human life security system to severe natural disasters.

The impacts of natural disasters on China's agricultural security have been substantial. The annual average area of affected crops reached to 45.1 million ha which made up 30 % of the total sown area of farm crops. The annual average damaged area extended to 23.8 million ha, accounting for 16 % of the total area of sown crops. For nearly every one of the 30 year period covered by our data crops were severely affected by disasters, indicating the high vulnerability of the crop production system to natural disasters.

The impacts of natural disasters on China's economic security were notable. The annual average number of collapsed houses reached 3.3954 million rooms, and the annual average figure of damaged rooms was 9.3225 million rooms. The annual average direct economic losses caused by natural disasters amounted to USD39.35 billion, or 2.5 % of GDP and 22 % of the global losses. In the past two decades, while direct economic losses caused by natural disasters showed an increasing trend, the percentage of direct economic losses to GDP has declined. However, once in the event of catastrophic natural disasters, the direct economic losses will come to a huge amount and highly account for the proportion of GDP. Consequently, direct economic losses and the growth rate of GDP are negatively correlated. Natural disasters offset part of China's economic achievements, pose a great threat to national wealth, and constrain economic development. All these factors reveal the high vulnerability of China's economic system to natural disasters.

According to Qin et al. (2005), climate warming in China has been almost synchronized with the global trend, but the range of warming may be greater. By 2020, the national average surface temperature could increase by 1.7 °C, by 2030 2.2 °C and by 2050 2.8 °C. What's more, the extent of climate warming in China would increase from south to north, except for the increased rainfall in the western part of the northwest, while the north and southern part of northeast would be permanently dry. Climate warming would lead more droughts in China, the drought-prone area would continue to expand, and droughts would grow more intense. As a result, heavy rainfall, floods, soil erosion, landslides and other geological disasters would increase dramatically, and further aggravate the vulnerability to natural disasters of the socio-economic development system of China.

In order to effectively deal with the high risk of natural disasters in China, and build a low disaster-risk society, there is an urgent need for transition from disaster reduction to a comprehensive strategy of hazard reduction for sustainable development, and adding integrated hazard risk management throughout the whole process of natural hazard management. Accordingly, capacity-building for comprehensive hazard prevention and reduction must be strengthened and sustainable development alongside hazard risk needs to be achieved, thus reducing the vulnerability of the socio-economic development system to natural disasters.

3 Disaster Risk Management in China

3.1 The Chinese Integrated Disaster Management System

In order to enhance emergency management and implement the governments' function entirely, the national Emergency Management Office of the State Council was established in April 2006. It works as an operational "hinge," taking charge of the daily work of national emergency management, responding to public security events, collecting real-time information and harmonizing the related departments.

Since its establishment in 2006, the State Council Emergency Management Office has carried out some effective work to enhance disaster emergency management: it has helped implement the State Master Plan for Rapid Response to Public Emergencies in China; it has held an emergency management working meeting of the State Council and a management working meeting of enterprise emergency work, to deploy and unify emergency management. It coordinates governments of all levels to enhance emergency construction ability and to prepare for prevention of and dealing with public security emergencies. It has also started a Key Technologies research and design program for emergency platform construction to provide science and technology support for emergency management, and to increase emergency treatment efficiency.

So far, the Chinese disaster risk (public security) management system has established one office and four committees: the establishment of the State Council Emergency Management Office at the national level and corresponding organizations with regard to the four types of public security incidents. These are the National Committee for Disaster Reduction to manage natural disasters, the National Committee for Work Safety to manage industrial accidents, the National Committee for Patriotic Health to manage public health and the National Committee for integrated management to manage public security. The four committees are made up of a vice president or a committeeman of the State Council of China as committee director, a minister or vice minister from the main related ministries as administrative vice director or vice director, and the vice ministers from the corresponding ministries as committee members. At the local levels, there are corresponding disaster risk (public security) management organizations with accordance to the national level. Local emergency management centres and the committees of management for the four public security incidents have been gradually established. The disaster risk management organization system of China can be shown as follows (Fig. 14.1).

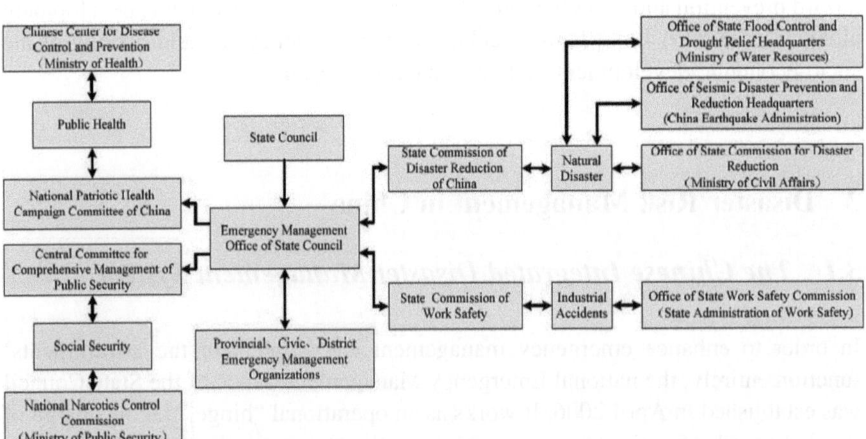

Fig. 14.1 Disaster risk reduction strategy of China ("One office and four committees")

Additionally, in order to enhance the disaster risk management work in these related ministries and commissions, corresponding management centers have been established, such as the Chinese center for disease control and prevention (Ministry of Health), the National Disaster Reduction Center of China (Ministry of Civil Affairs), the Chinese Supervision Center for Work Safety (State Administration of Work Safety), etc. Among these committees, the National Committee for Disaster Reduction (NCDR) is the national counseling and coordination body under the guidance of the State Council for emergency disaster response and relief. NCDR consists of 34 disaster related member agencies.

In conclusion, China has started disaster risk (public security) management work on the basis of traditional disaster management and reduction, and has formed a primary disaster risk management framework involving related professional fields. In addition it is intended to pass emergency laws to enhance the legal basis of disaster risk emergency management. The China Association for Disaster Prevention has also established the first professional organization for risk research, which has been named as the Risk Analysis Specialty Committee. Many Chinese universities and research institutes have also been doing research on natural disasters, engineering hazards, economic risks, crisis management and disaster risk management, and so on. However, compared with the international situation, disaster risk management in China faces not only an austere and significant challenge but also a very good opportunity.

3.2 *Regional Adaptation Strategies for Disaster Risk Reduction: The Disaster Management Cycle*

The Chinese regional integrated disaster risk management philosophy adheres to the principle of "give priority to disaster prevention, and combine disaster prevention with disaster resistance and relief." Namely, before disaster occurrence, it is important to establish and test the monitoring and warning system, to carry out emergency planning, to strengthen the ability to procure emergency materials, to build an ecologically healthy environment, to accelerate regional economy and reduce disaster vulnerability. When a disaster takes place, it is important to improve emergency response ability to emphasize actions oriented toward human welfare, to reduce the casualty rate and the rate of property loss and to provide maximum protection to natural resources and the environment. After a disaster, government and society's relief ability at all levels must be strengthened, especially community self-rescue and self-relief ability. Finally, based on the results of a rapid disaster loss assessment, it's urgent to recover lifeline and product line systems and accelerate the effectiveness and efficiency of reconstruction (Shi, 2005).

At present, governance of natural disaster risk in China is the responsibility of different ministries or bureaus related to the different kinds of natural hazards, e.g. the China Earthquake Administration takes charge of governance in the case of earthquake disasters, and the China Meteorological Administration takes charge of governance following meteorological disasters. Further, the Ministry of Water Resources takes charge of governance in the case of floods and droughts, the Ministry of Land and Resources takes charge of governance following landslides and debris flows, the State Ocean Administration takes charge of governance in the case of ocean disasters, and so on. To enhance governance in the case of some large-scale disaster, the State Council has set up several leading groups for natural disaster governance, such as the State Flood Control and Drought Relief Headquarters and the State Earthquake Relief Headquarters. Correspondingly, each regional and local government has set up relevant departments. There are organizations in local governments at all levels in China. In a word, China has adopted a natural disaster governance system which combines vertical inter-government and inter-regional management modes, where vertical sector management comes before integrated regional management. The existing adaptation planning called the "disaster management cycle."

3.2.1 Monitoring and Warning

During the disaster preparedness period, mitigation and prevention work are the responsibility of the professional technical departments, namely the bars. In recent years, the Chinese government has increased investment in respect of natural disaster monitoring and warning system construction, and has established a natural disaster monitoring, warning and forecasting system, including meteorological disaster monitoring and forecasting, earthquake monitoring and forecasting, hydrological monitoring, forest fire prevention, forest and crop pest monitoring and forecasting, marine environment monitoring, and geological disaster monitoring and early warning. This natural disaster monitoring, warning and forecasting system can monitor a disaster's dynamic development and provide information for disaster emergency decision-making.

3.2.2 Emergency Response

During a disaster period, the emergency management offices and the disaster reduction committees of all levels are in charge of emergency response, together with the Civil Affairs departments, the Public Security departments, the armed forces, etc. The agencies work together quickly and closely to deal with the emergency as soon as it begins. At present, the disaster emergency response system guarantees that rescue taskforces, relief supplies, funds and information are on the ground and in place to address the immediate and real needs of the affected.

According to disaster emergency management, the Chinese government has strengthened the emergency planning system. In the Master State Plan for Rapid Response to Public Emergencies, public security events are divided into four kinds (natural disasters, industrial accidents, public health and social security) according to their causes, characteristics and mechanisms, and into four grades (huge, bigger, big and ordinary grade) according to their degree of severity, their controllability and the area affected. "Huge" and "bigger" grade emergencies must be reported to the State Council within 4 h of the occurrence. Local governments or related departments have to start their related emergency plan promptly and effectively, in the responsibility and power range to control the further development. Additionally, several special plans and department plans for rapid response top emergencies have been drawn up.; and similar plans have also been compiled by national and local governments. This planning makes disaster risk management and disaster reduction more regular and systematic.

In the case of a natural disaster emergency, as prescribed in the "State Emergency Response Planning for Natural Disasters," according to the degree of loss arising from the disaster, the Ministry of Civil Affairs of China adopts a four-grade response system. In other words, different levels of emergencies are to be dealt with by governments of different levels. The more severe the situation it is, the higher level of the government that will respond and make decisions.

3.2.3 Restoration and Reconstruction

During the post-disaster period, the disaster relief and recovery work is controlled by the local disaster reduction committee, which works as a coordinator for the main departments to organize people in disaster area and helps them to recover their normal lives These include the Civil Affairs departments, the Health departments, the Development and Reform Commission, the Finance departments, the Communications departments, the Construction departments, the Railway departments, etc. Namely, the blocks are the main responsibility body. Among these different departments, the Civil Affairs department takes the main responsibility for the disaster victims' life relief, and the insurance companies carry out the compensation for the disaster victims to help them to recover as soon as possible.

In addition, the Chinese government encourages the public social donations and voluntary activities from the whole society, and NGOs are to be an important force in the post-disaster period. This social mobilization mechanism provides a solid material support for disaster management, and helps the people in less-developed areas to recover rapidly after disasters.

3.2.4 Legislation

China has instituted, promulgated and enforced laws and regulations as it moves forward to phase in a legal framework for disaster reduction. The laws and regulations are, however, all about single aspects of disaster risk management, such as the "Law of the People's Republic of China on Protecting Against and Mitigating Earthquake Disasters," the "Flood Control Law of the People's Republic of China," the "Law of the People's Republic of China on Safety in Mines" and so on. There is no systematic and comprehensive series of laws and regulations about disaster reduction, especially in respect of disaster relief, disaster insurance, post-disaster subsidies for reconstruction, tax reduction for the victims, and so on. Moreover, existing laws and regulations are generally aimed at singe disaster types. It is therefore urgent to construct a law in respect of integrated disaster risk management, so as to carry out integrated disaster prevention and reduction. There is currently no explicit legal status for any integration and coordination of sectors.

Since the 1990s, moreover, in the context of climate change with global warming, global meteorological hazards have increased significantly, and are negatively affecting social economic development. Accordingly, capacity-building relating to comprehensive hazard prevention and reduction will be strengthened and sustainable development alongside hazard risk will be achieved, thus reducing the vulnerability of the socio-economic development system of to natural hazards.

4 China's Experience in the Wenchuan Earthquake

4.1 Overview of Earthquake Impact in Affected Areas

The Wenchuan earthquake struck China on May 12, 2008 with a strength of 8.0 on the Richter scale. Its strength and deadly impact made it one of the most disastrous earthquakes in the world (U.S. Geological Survey 2008). The earthquake epicenter was located in Yingxiu in Wenchuan County, Sichuan province. Figure 14.2 shows the location of Sichuan province and the impact zone of the Wenchuan earthquake. The area shaded dark grey is the most intense impact zone, while the semicircular lines surrounding it indicate boundaries between areas of progressively lower intensity.

The Wenchuan earthquake caused destruction across ten provinces in China, and its tremors were felt as far away as Thailand. Strong aftershocks, landslides, mud-rock flows, barrier lakes and other secondary disasters continued to threaten people's lives and property for many weeks, and made the rescue work difficult. Altogether, more than 45.5 million people were affected by the earthquake. By August 25, 2008, 69,226 people were confirmed to have been killed in the disaster, while 17,923 were missing and 374,643 had been injured (U.S. Geological Survey 2008: 4). At least 15 million people were evacuated from their homes following the earthquake. In total, an estimated 5.36 million buildings collapsed and 21 million buildings were damaged (U.S. Geological Survey 2008). The direct economic loss from the earthquake was more than USD125.7 billion, most of it due to loss of infrastructure and buildings (China State Council Information Office 2008). It is estimated that around 1.2 million people had lost their jobs by the end of July 2008 (China Ministry of Human Resources and Social Security 2008).

While large parts of the country can be said to have been affected by the Wenchuan earthquake, efforts were made to delimit the areas that had received

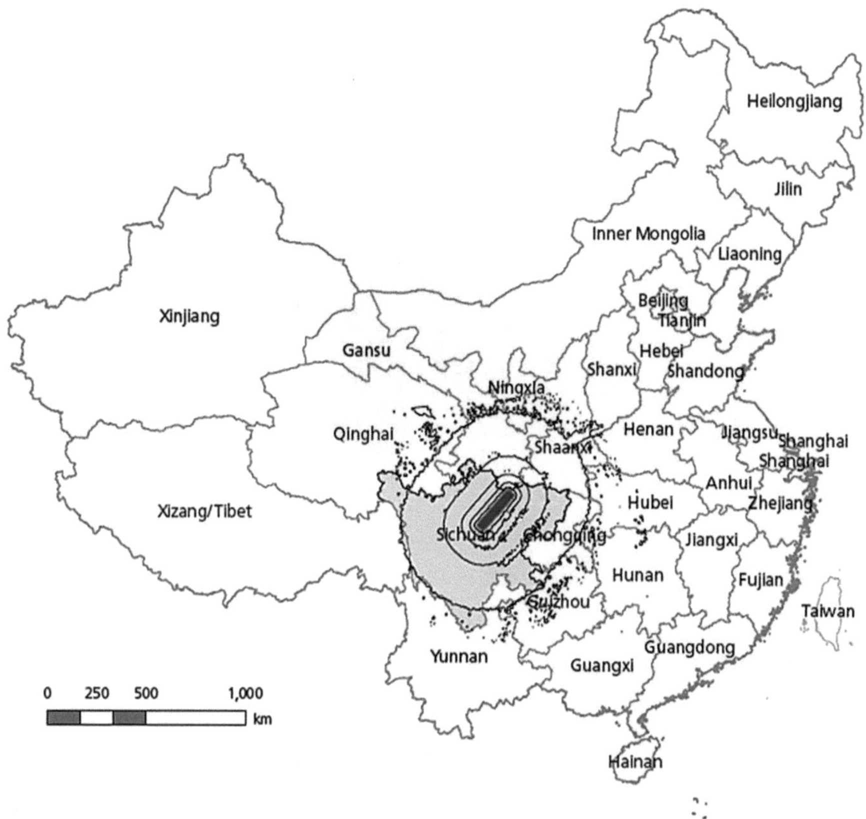

Fig. 14.2 Sichuan and the impact zone of the Wenchuan earthquake

the heaviest direct impact and were thus in most need of help. In what has been the Government's official classification since August 2008, 51 counties were eventually officially defined as "seriously" or "very seriously" affected by the Wenchuan earthquake. Decisions about which counties should be considered "seriously" or "very seriously" affected were political ones based on a review of what was known about the situation in the various counties at the time, rather than on strict scientific criteria. Most of the counties that were "very seriously" affected faced near-complete devastation.

At the time of the earthquake disaster, the total population of the 51 seriously and very seriously affected counties was 19,867 million people,[2] of which approximately four million were living in very seriously affected areas (The State Planning Group of Post-Wenchuan Earthquake Restoration and Reconstruction 2008:

[2] This was the official population count at the end of 2007.

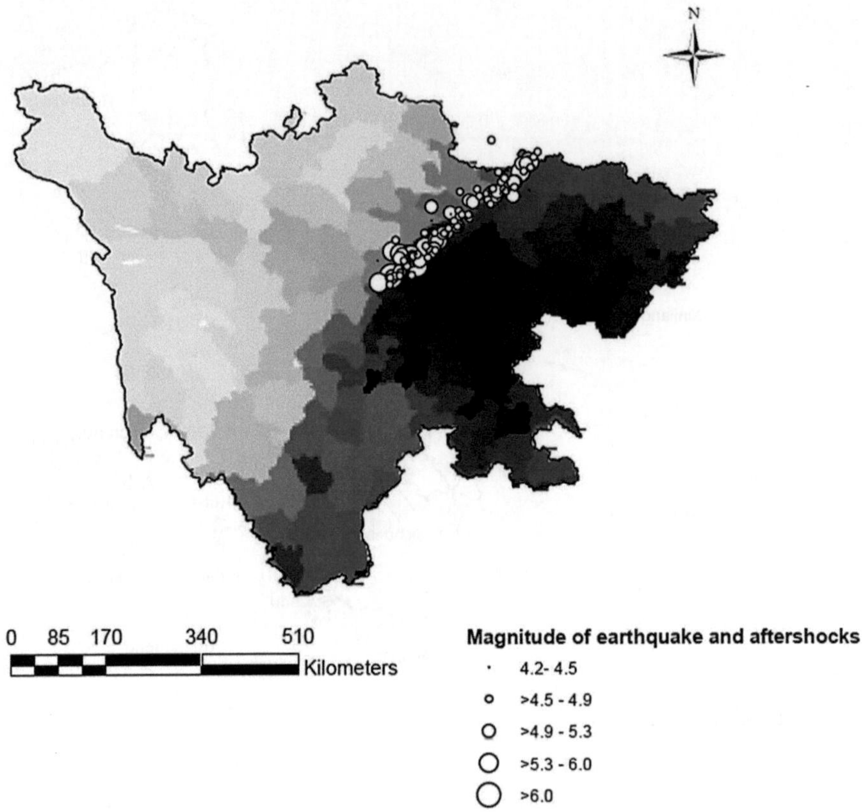

Fig. 14.3 Population density in Sichuan and location of the Wenchuan earthquake (Population Density)

p. 2). Covering an area of more than 130,000 km^2, these counties are spread across Sichuan, Gansu and Shaanxi provinces. Most are located in Sichuan, including all the counties classified as the most seriously affected.

The large majority of people in the earthquake-affected areas were rural residents who were relatively underprivileged compared to those in other parts of China. The Wenchuan earthquake and its aftershocks were centered just north of the most densely populated areas in Sichuan as seen in Fig. 14.3. The North–west part of the impact area is sparsely populated, while the south-east area is densely populated. There are large differences between the North–west and the south–East with regard to resources, ecology and economic development. The plain area in the east, with Sichuan's capital Chengdu at its centre, is a fertile, well-irrigated agricultural region. The area was developed as an industrial base during the Mao era, and its level of industrialization remains comparatively high, including industries in the fields of mechanical equipment, electronics, energy, chemicals, steel and biopharmaceuticals. Many of these local industries were seriously damaged in the earthquake.

By contrast, the mountainous western region is geographically isolated, scarce in resources and population, and home to many of China's ethnic minorities. It is relatively isolated and economically underdeveloped, with a vulnerable ecology and limited industrial development. Most of the heavily-hit zones are located in these western mountains and valleys, which are difficult to access under normal circumstances and were extremely difficult to reach for rescuers facing destroyed or blocked roads as well as secondary disasters (The State Planning Group of Post-Wenchuan Earthquake Restoration and Reconstruction 2008: 2–3).

4.2 Aftershocks

As is often the case for earthquakes on reverse faults, aftershocks are of high intensity and long duration due to a lag in tectonic strain release. According to (Cui et al., 2009), as of 10 a.m. June 5, a sum of 10,254 aftershocks had been detected by the China Earthquake Monitoring Web. Among these aftershocks, the number with a magnitude 4.0 and above was 197, 166 had magnitudes among 4–4.9, 26 had magnitudes among 5.0–5.9, and five aftershocks occurred with magnitudes of 6.0 or greater. The strongest aftershock was of magnitude 6.4.

Within 10 h after the major shock of May 12, there occurred one aftershock of magnitude 6.0, and 12 of >5.0. As time passed, the number decreased, but the magnitude remained high. Two weeks after the major quake, an aftershock of magnitude 6.4 Mw occurred. The aftershocks occurred mainly in the middle and northern portion of the Longmenshan Fault zone. Aftershocks showed a tendency of moving to the northeast along the Longmenshan Fault zone, moving toward Wenxian County in Gansu Province and Ningqiang County in Shaanxi Province.

4.3 Partner Support regarding Wenchuan Earthquake

The "Partner support" program is a system where provinces or cities provide support to a related affected area on a one-to-one basis, under the principle of "one province helps one significantly affected county." With resources reasonably placed based on the economic development level of each area, 19 provinces (cities) support 18 heavily affected counties (cities) as well as seriously damaged areas (seriously affected district) in Gansu and Shaanxi provinces. Table 14.1 displays these inter-city relationships. Provinces (cities) assigned under the program provide assistance for 3 years. Each supporting province (city) is required to allocate 1 % of local financial revenue in the preceding year for goods and work operations every year.

Table 14.1 Partner support regarding the Wenchuan Earthquake in China

Supported areas		Supporting areas
(Sichuan)		
Wenchuan	←	Guangdong
Beichuan	←	Shandong
Qingchuan	←	Zhejiang
Mianzhu	←	Jiangsu
Dujiangyan	←	Shanghai
Shifang	←	Beijing
Jinagyou	←	Henan
Pingwu	←	Hebei
Anxian	←	Liaoning
Pengzhou	←	Fujian
Maoxian	←	Shaanxi
Lixian	←	Hunan
Heishui	←	Jilin
Songpan	←	Anhui
Xiaojin	←	Jiangxi
Hanyuan	←	Hubei
Chongzhou	←	Chongqing
Jiange	←	Heilongjiang
(Gansu)		
Seriously affected district in Gansu province	←	Shenzhen
(Shaanxi)		
Seriously affected district in Shaanxi province	←	Tianjin

Source: United Nations Centre for Regional Development (2009)

4.4 The Government's Recovery Plan

As soon as the immediate post-earthquake emergency had passed, the Government started planning longer-term post-disaster reconstruction. From the beginning, the Government did not merely aim for full recovery. Instead, it aimed for reconstruction to contribute to political processes initiated with the 1999 "Development of the West" policy, and to the Hu Jintao administration's heavily promoted "scientific development" approach, which seeks to pursue a "harmonious society" by addressing inequities that have arisen with China's economic growth.

The General Office of the State Council announced "The State Overall Planning for Post-Wenchuan Earthquake Restoration and Reconstruction" on September 23, 2008 (The State Planning Group of Post-Wenchuan Earthquake Restoration and Reconstruction 2008). The Plan served as a long list of guiding principles for the process of reconstruction. Although the Plan stated that the main priority was to reconstruct residential houses and public facilities within a period of 3 years, it also encouraged local authorities to consider the reconstruction process as a development opportunity, and it explicitly stated that one of the objectives for recovery and future development in Sichuan was to contribute to existing strategies of economic and rural development.

There is a strong focus on rural development, continued economic growth and market reform throughout the policy document. It states that "We shall promptly restore the public facilities and infrastructures, earnestly expand employment, and increase the residents' income..." Urban and rural spatial layout, population distribution, industrial structure and productivity layout were to be readjusted "so as to promote the harmony between man and nature". The Plan calls for using reconstruction to spur development and self-sufficiency, particularly in poverty-stricken and ethnic minority areas. Future development was to be ensured by furthering industrialization and urbanization, as well as by constructing new rural areas. The Plan underlined that such processes should be conducted in an environmentally friendly manner, with strict protection of farmland.

USD 157 billion was allocated in the Plan for restoration work in the 51 counties classified in the Plan as seriously and very seriously affected in the provinces of Sichuan, Gansu and Shanxi. Local governments at all levels were given a predominant role, and the Plan introduces diverse and collaborative funding arrangements including "counterpart assistance" from provinces in other parts of China to designated earthquake counties.

In order to reach the overriding goals, the Plan stipulates six specific objectives which were to be attained by the end of the 3-year reconstruction period:

(1) To complete the restoration and reconstruction of urban and rural residences, making it possible for the disaster-affected population to live in safe, economical, practical and land-saving houses.
(2) To ensure that at least one member in each family has a stable job, and that urban household per capita disposable income and rural household per capita net income surpass the pre-disaster levels.
(3) To ensure that everyone in the disaster-affected population enjoys basic social security and has access to fundamental public services such as compulsory education, public sanitation and basic medical treatment in addition to public culture and sports, social welfare etc.
(4) To completely restore infrastructure functions such as transportation, communications, energy, water conservancy etc. to meet or surpass pre-disaster levels.
(5) To develop the economy, improving and expanding industries with special advantages, optimizing industry structure, and enhancing capacity for scientific development.
(6) To gradually restore ecological functions, improve environmental quality and ensure visible improvement in disaster prevention and mitigation ability.

4.5 Recovering from the Wenchuan Earthquake

The results from the three post-Wenchuan earthquake surveys (Dalen et al. 2012) give grounds for describing the recovery process as successful. Communities in disaster areas were severely disturbed, but in the long term society remained stable. Their report shows that most damage caused by the earthquake was quickly repaired, that households were able to resume economic activities relatively quickly, and that education and healthcare systems continued to function under extraordinarily difficult circumstances, and resumed normal operations well before the end of the recovery period. In material terms, the recovery process did succeed in "building back better" by providing new and improved public facilities, houses and infrastructure.

A fundamental observation is that China's Government efficiently managed and coordinated the disaster response and recovery processes, striking a balance between the commitment of considerable financial, human and organizational resources on the one hand and devolution to local and external agencies on the other.

However, the fact that societies in earthquake-affected areas remained stable also meant that social inequalities and other structural problems that were to some extent mitigated in the period immediately following the disaster were reproduced by the end of the recovery process. Few of these challenges were directly caused by the earthquake disaster; instead, they are related to socio-economic inequities and other problems prevailing in Chinese society in general.

5 Policy Implications

The Integrated Disaster Risk Management Strategies of China are shown as below:

5.1 To Establish the "National Disaster Reduction Planning"

Disaster reduction has been high on the agenda for the central government, which views it as vital to sustainable economic and social development, coordinated development and harmony between economy, natural resources and ecology. The central government has created the State Disaster Reduction Commission (SDRC) to harness the synergy of relevant efforts and initiatives. In 1998, the Disaster Reduction Plan of the People's Republic of China (1998–2010) was designed to identify guidelines, targets, commitments and measures for disaster reduction efforts. With the guidance of the Disaster Reduction Plan, all the local governments, departments, and industries have enhanced their disaster reduction work effectively, and their integrated disaster reduction ability has been improved. During the 12th Five-Year Plan, there is an urgent need to establish a further "National Disaster Reduction Plan".

5.2 *To Accelerate the Creation of a Disaster Reduction Ability*

The Chinese government has paid much attention to creating disaster reduction ability. This can be seen from the disaster risk management research programs. The National Natural Science Foundation of China has sponsored and carried out a large number of risk management research projects, such as "regional disciplines of Chinese natural disaster" and so on. The Ministry of Science and Technology also supports risk management research in the fields of major natural disasters, engineering accidents, public health, and public security, through the Key Technologies R&D Program in every five-year planning period.

During the period of the 12th Five-Year Plan (2011–2015), China will make consistent efforts to improve its ability to prevent and mitigate disasters. The country's disaster reduction ability will be accelerated, by learning from developed and other developing countries, and through all the possible means, to utilize its disaster reduction resources efficiently and effectively.

5.3 *To Improve the Emergency Response Program*

The Master State Program for Emergency Response is the general program for national emergency responses and is the criterion file for the prevention and treatment of public security events, clarifying the classification and framework of incidents, prescribing the organization system and operation mechanism for dealing with a severe emergency. Although the Master State Program is of great importance and guidance, it only pays major attention to the in-disaster integrated response, and overlooks the need for integrated optimization among the in-disaster emergency management, pre-disaster mitigation, and post-disaster recovery and reconstruction. It is therefore necessary to improve the rapid emergency response plans, harmonize all the aspects of integrated disaster reduction, and ensure the emergency response program is political, scientific and feasible.

6 Conclusion

China faces increasingly complex natural situations for disaster management, but has insufficient experience both for creating appropriate institutions and for capacity building. These are therefore a subject of focus for policy makers and bureaucrats in China. China is using a stronger government role to take the leadership in dealing with disasters, together with a multiple approach and more participation from all fields. The chain of governance can lead to improved efficiency, or to the opposite.

China is confident that it can create effective cooperation for disaster management both at home and abroad, while keeping developments in line with the interests of both China and the bordering states. This latter is in the initial stages, and some sensitive issues need to be resolved. In addition, more sub-regional or local cooperation within China should be stressed. Finally, China is improving its abilities in disaster management together with its domestic comprehensive and sustainable growth, including political, social, cultural, economic and conceptual changes. Moreover, China is now focusing on the impact assessment of climate change in relation to disasters, and not simply on the issue of disaster management only.

References

Benson, C., & Clay, E. J. (1998). *The impact of drought on Sub-Saharan African ECONOMIES: A preliminary examination*, World Bank Technical Paper no. 401. Washington D. C.: World Bank. http://water.worldbank.org/publications/impact-drought-sub-saharan-african-economies-preliminary-examination. Accessed 22 December 2011.

China Ministry of Human Resources and Social Security. (2008). *Labour force situation in Sichuan earthquake affected area*. The Central People's Government of the People's Republic of China, 1 August 2008. http://www.gov.cn/jrzg/2008-08/01/content_1061415.htm. Accessed 9 November 2011.

China State Council Information Office. (2008). *Loss in the Sichuan earthquake*, CCTV [online]. 4 September. http://news. cctv.com/china/20080904/102837.shtml. Accessed 9 November 2011.

Cui, P., Chen, X. Q., Zhu, Y. Y., Su, F. H., Wei, F. Q., Han, Y. S., et al. (2011). The Wenchuan earthquake (May 12, 2008), Sichuan province, China, and resulting geohazards. *Natural Hazards*, 56(1), 19–36

Dalen, K., Flatø, H., Jing, L., & Huafeng, Z. (2012). *Recovering from the Wenchuan earthquake. Living conditions and development in disaster areas 2008–2011*, Fafo-report 2012, 39. Oslo: FAFO.

Deng, Y. T. (1937). *History of relief of famines in China*. Beijing: The Commercial.

Domeisen, N. (1995). *Disasters: Threat to social development*, Stop Disasters: the IDNDR magazine no.23 Winter. International Decade for Natural Disaster Reduction, Geneva, Switzerland.

Du, Y. (1988). *Hazards and hazard-economy*. Beijing: China's Urban Economy and Society.

He, A. P. (2002). *Theoretical framework and positive study of disaster economy of China*. Xi'an: Northwest University.

Hirshleifer, J. (1966). DISASTER AND RECOVERY: THE BLACK DEATH IN WESTERN EUROPE. http://www.rand.org/content/dam/rand/pubs/research_memoranda/2005/RM4700.pdf

Hu, A. G. (1996). *Natural hazards and economic development in China*. Hubei: Wuhan Scientific & Technical Publishers.

Kunreuther, H., & Pauly, M. (2006). *Rules rather than discretion: Lessons from Hurricane Katrina*, NBER Working Paper Series, No. 12503. Cambridge: NBER.

Liu, Y. Q., Song, J. J., & Zhang, Q. J. (2005). *Impacts of droughts on the social economy of China*. Beijing: China Water Power.

Lu, Z., Wei, Y. M., Fan, Y., & Xu, X. (2002). Quantitatively analytic model for the impact of natural disaster on national economy. *Journal of Natural Disasters, 11*(3), 15–20.

Ma, Z. J., & Gao, Q. H. (2010). Achievements on Chinese natural disaster research of past sixty years since 1949. China population. *Resources and Environment, 20*(5), 1–5.

Qin, D. H., Ding, Y. H., Su, J. L., Ren, J. W., Wang, S. W., Wu, R. S., et al. (2005). Assessment of climate and environment changes in China (I): Climate and environment changes in China and their projection. *Advances in Climate Change Research, I*(1), 4–9.

Shi, P. J. (2005). Theory and practice on disaster system research in a fourth time. *Journal of Natural Disaster, 14*(6), 1–8.

Sun, Y. N. (2009). *The impacts of major floods and droughts on China's rural economy during the past 30 years*. Harbin: Heilongjiang University.

The State Planning Group of Post-Wenchuan Earthquake Restoration and Reconstruction. (2008). *The state overall planning for the Post-Wenchuan earthquake restoration and reconstruction (public opinion soliciting draft)*. Beijing: Central Government of the People's Republic of China.

U.S. Geological Survey. (2008). *Earthquakes with 1,000 or more deaths since 1900*, U.S. Geological survey earthquake hazards program [online]. http://earthquake.usgs.gov/regional/world/world_deaths_sort.php. Accessed 12 February 2008.

United Nations Centre for Regional Development. (2009). *Report on the 2008 Great Sichuan earthquake*, Project Report. pp. 6–12.

Wang, Z., Peng, T., Wei, G. H., & Liu, X. L. (1994). The statistical characteristics of natural disasters in last 40 years in China. *Journal of Natural Disasters, 3*(2), 16–21. 27.

Wei, Y. M., Jin, J. L., Yang, C. J., Huang, S. F., Fan, Y., & Chen, D. Q. (2002). *Theory of risk management of flood disaster*. Beijing: Science.

Xie, Y. G. (2003). *Water disaster economics*. Beijing: Economic Science.

Yu, G. Y. (1988). *Research on hazard-economics*. Beijing: China Economic Publishing House.

Yuan, Y., & Zhang, L. (2006). Present situation on natural disaster statistics in China and the prospect. *Journal of Catastrophology, 21*(4), 89–93.

Zhang, H. D., Luo, Y., Wang, B. Z., Dong, W. J., & Wang, Z. Q. (2006). Impacts of meteorological disaster and climate change on national security. *Advances in Climate Change Research, 2*(2), 85–88.

Zhang, X. D., & Shen, R. F. (1995). The quantitative study on the relationship between disasters and economic growth. *Journal of Natural Disasters, 4*(4), 20–26. 40.

Zhang, Y. C., Zhang, L. H., Ma, Z. J., & Gao, Q. H. (2008). Age change and phase difference of the influence of natural disaster in China in the 20th century on social economy. *Journal of Catastrophology, 23*(2), 55–58. 70.

Zheng, G. C. (1998). *Hazard economics*. Hunan: People's Publishing House.

Chapter 15
Impact of Disasters and Disaster Risk Management in Singapore: A Case Study of Singapore's Experience in Fighting the SARS Epidemic

Allen Yu-Hung Lai and Seck L. Tan

1 Introduction

Situated in Southeast Asia yet outside the Pacific Rim of Fire, Singapore is fortunate enough to have been spared from major natural disasters such as typhoons, floods, volcanic eruptions, and earthquakes. However, this does not imply that Singapore is safe, or immune from being affected by disasters. Singapore houses a population of 5.2 million, a ranking of the third highest population density in the world. About 80 % of Singapore's population resides in high-rise buildings (Asian Disaster Reduction Center 2005). A major disaster of any sort could inflict mass casualties and extensive destruction to properties in Singapore. Clearly, like its neighboring countries, Singapore is also vulnerable to both natural and man-made disasters alongside its remarkable economic growth. The potential risks may result from its dense population, intricate transportation network, or a transnational communicable disease. Moreover, Singapore can be affected by the situations in surrounding countries. For example, flooding in Thailand and Vietnam may affect the price of rice sold in Singapore.

Indeed, Singapore in her short history of 47 years has experienced a small number of disasters. Chief among these, the Severe Acute Respiratory Syndrome (SARS) epidemic in 2003 was the most devastating. The SARS outbreak brought about far-reaching public health and economic consequences for the country as a whole. Fortunately, the outbreak was eventually contained through a series of risk mitigating measures introduced by the Singapore government and the

A.Y.-H. Lai (✉)
The Institute of Health Economics and Management, ESSEC Business School – Asia Pacific, Singapore, Singapore
e-mail: allen.yuhung@gmail.com

S.L. Tan
Centre on Asia and Globalization, Lee Kuan Yew School of Public Policy, National University of Singapore, Singapore, Singapore

D.P. Aldrich et al. (eds.), *Resilience and Recovery in Asian Disasters*, Risk, Governance and Society 18, DOI 10.1007/978-4-431-55022-8_15

responsiveness of all Singaporeans. It is important to point out that these risk mitigating measures, along with the public's compliance, were swiftly adjusted to address the volatile conditions—such as when more epidemiological cases were uncovered.

In this chapter, we introduce Singapore's all-hazard management framework as well as the insights drawn from Singapore's risk management experience with specific references to the SARS epidemic. To achieve our research objective, we utilized a triangulation strategy of various research methodologies. To understand the principles and practices of Singapore's approach to disaster risk management, we carry out an historical analysis of official documents obtained from the relevant Singapore government agencies as well as international organizations, literature reviews, quantitative analysis of economic impacts, qualitative interviews with key informants (e.g. public health professionals and decision-makers), and email communications with frontline managers from the public sector (e.g. the Singapore Civil Defense Force, the Communicable Disease Centre) and non-governmental organizations. The authors also employed the 'cultural insider' approach by participating in epidemic control procedures against SARS.[1] In particular, we use the method of case study to illuminate Singapore's approach to disaster risk management. The rationale of doing a case study of SARS along with Singapore's all-hazard approach is that the case study can best showcase the contextual differences, those being political, economic, and social. This case study aims to highlight the lessons drawn from past experiences in a specific context and timeframe, through which we are able to focus more on the nature of the risks, and the processes and the impacts of the disaster risk management and policy intervention. We also examined relevant literature on risk mitigating measures against communicable diseases in order to establish our conclusions. We evaluated oral accounts provided by key health policy decision-makers and experts for valuable insights.

This chapter offers empirical evidence on the role of the whole-of-government approach to risk mitigation of the SARS epidemic. Applying the approach to a case study, our research enriches the vocabulary of risk management, adding to the body of knowledge on disaster management specific to the region of Southeast Asia. Indeed, the dominant perspective in this field holds that the state must be able to exercise brute force and impose its will on the population (Lai and Tan 2012). However, as shown in our paper, this dominant perspective is incomplete as the exercise of authority and power from the government is not necessarily sufficient to contain the transmission of transnational communicable diseases. Success in fighting epidemics, as most would agree, is also contingent on a concerted effort of partnership between governmental authorities and the population at large. As discussed in the first section of this volume, community and family ties along with government responses can mitigate disasters.

This chapter has four main sections. Following this introduction, we provide an overview of Singapore's historical disaster profiles. Second, we introduce the

---

[1] One of the authors, Allen Lai, worked on the rescue mission in fighting SARS in 2003.

policy and legal framework, and budgetary allocations for risk mitigation in Singapore. Third, we detail a case study of Singapore's experience in fighting SARS, as well as the impact of SARS on Singapore in its economic, healthcare, and psychosocial aspects. In the fourth section, we discuss the implications for practice and future research in disaster risk management, followed by conclusions.

2 Singapore's Historical Disaster Profile

Singapore has experienced a small number of disasters since it was founded in 1965. In this section, we briefly provide an historical account of Singapore's disaster risk profiles including earthquakes, floods, epidemics, civil emergencies, and haze.

2.1 Risk of Earthquake and Tsunami

Singapore has a low risk of earthquakes and tsunamis. Geographically, Singapore is located in a low seismic-hazard region. However, the high-rise buildings that are built on soft-soil in Singapore are still vulnerable to earthquakes from far afield (Asian Disaster Reduction Center 2005). This is because Singapore is at a distance (nearest) of 600 km from the Sumatran subduction zone and 400 km away from the Sumatra fault both of which have the potential of generating large magnitude earthquakes. This geographic vicinity may produce a resonance like situation within high-rise buildings on soft-soil. Recent tremors from the September 2009 Sumatra offshore earthquake were experienced in 234 buildings located mainly in the central, northern and western parts of Singapore. On the front of potential tsunamis, Singapore has developed a national tsunami response plan which is a multiagency government effort comprising of an early warning system, tsunami mitigation and emergency response plans, and public education.

2.2 Risk of Flooding

Though Singapore does not suffer from flood disasters due to the continuous drainage improvement works by the local authorities, the country has a risk of local flooding in some low-lying parts. The floods take place due to heavy rainfall that aggregates over short periods of time. The worst floods in Singapore's history took place on 2 December 1978. The floods claimed seven lives, forced more than 1,000 people to be evacuated, and the total damages reached SGD10 million (Tan 1978). The swift and sudden floods in 1978 were caused by a combination of factors including torrential monsoon rains, drainage problems, and high incoming tides.

Over the following years, Singapore saw a series of flash floods hit various parts of the city-state. For example, 2006–2007 Southeast Asian floods hit Singapore on 18 December 2006 as a result of 366 mm rainfall in 24 h. From 2010 onwards, Singapore has experienced a series of flash floods due to the higher-than-average rainfall. One severe episode occurred on16 June 2010 that flooded shopping malls and basement car parks in its most famous shopping area—Orchard Road.

2.3 *Risk of Epidemics/Pandemics*

As per the reported historical disaster data from the CRED International Disaster Database, Singapore has suffered only two disaster events caused by epidemics. In 2000, Singapore experienced its largest known outbreak of Hand-Foot-Mouth Disease (HFMD) which affected more than 3,000 young children, causing three deaths. Later in 2003, SARS hit Singapore and it was Singapore's most devastating disaster to date. The SARS virus infected around 8,500 people worldwide and caused around 800 deaths. In Singapore, SARS infected 238 people, 33 of whom died of this contagious communicable disease. In 2009, novel avian influenza H1N1 struck Singapore, which affected 1,348 people with 18 deaths.

2.4 *Risk of Civil Emergencies*

Civil emergencies are defined as sudden incidents involving the loss of lives or damage to property on a large scale. They include (1) civil incidents such as bomb explosions, aircraft hijacks, terrorist hostage-taking, chemical, biological, radiological and explosive (CBRE) agents and the release of radioactive materials by warships, and (2) civil emergencies, for example major fires, structural collapses, air crashes outside the airport boundary, and hazardous material incidents. In Singapore, the Singapore Civil Defense Force (SCDF) is responsible for civil emergencies. Since 1965, Singapore has experienced several episodes of civil emergencies. For example, the Greek tanker Spyros explosion at the Jurong Shipyard in 1978 was Singapore's worst industrial disaster in terms of lives lost (Ministry of Labor, Singapore 1979). In 1986, the six-storey Hotel New World collapse was Singapore's deadliest civil disaster claiming 33 lives. The collapse was due to structural faults. The SCDF, together with other rescue forces, spent 7 days on the whole relief operation. After the collapse, the government introduced more stringent regulations on construction building codes, and the SCDF went through a series of upgrades in training and equipment (Goh 2004).

2.5 Risk of Haze

Singapore experienced its first haze in the period of the end of August to the first week of November 1997 as a result of prevailing winds. The haze in 1997, called the Southeast Asian haze, was caused by slash and burn techniques adopted by farmers in Indonesia. The smoke haze carried particulate matter that caused an increase of acute health effects including increased hospital visits due to respiratory distress such as asthma, pulmonary infection, as well as eye and skin irritation. The haze also severely affected visibility in addition to increasing health problems. As a result, Singapore's health surveillance showed a 30 % increase in outpatient attendance for haze-related conditions (Emmanuel 2000). Apart from healthcare costs, other costs associated with the haze included short-term tourism and production losses. A study by environmental economists of the 1997 Southeast Asian haze indicated a total of USD$74.1 million in economic losses in Singapore alone. Singapore is actively involved in various regional meetings to deal with transboundary smoke haze pollution in order to reduce the risk (Singapore Institute of International Affairs 2006).

3 Disaster Risk Management in Singapore

3.1 Policy Framework for Disaster Risk Mitigation

The Singapore government adopts a cross-ministerial policy framework—a Whole-of-Government Integrated Risk Management (WOG-IRM), for disaster risk mitigation and disaster management (Asia Pacific Economic Cooperation 2011). This is a framework that aims to improve the risk awareness of all government agencies and the public, and helps to identify the full range of risks systematically. In addition, the framework identifies cross-agency risks that may have fallen through gaps in the system. This framework also includes medical response systems during emergencies, mass casualty management, risk reduction legislation for fire safety and hazardous materials, police operations, information and media management during crises and public-private partnerships in emergency preparedness.

The WOG-IRM policy frame work in Singapore functions in peacetime and in times of crisis. It refers to an approach that all relevant agencies work together in an established framework, with seamless communication and coordination to manage the risk (Pereira 2008). In peacetime, the home team comprises of four core agencies at central government level. These four agencies are the Strategic Planning Office, the Home front Crisis Ministerial Committee (HCMC), the National Security Coordination Secretariat, and the Ministry of Finance at the policy layer. Among them, the Strategic Planning Office provides oversight and guidance as the main platform to steer and review the overall progress of the WOG-IRM framework. During peacetime, the Strategic Planning Office convenes meetings quarterly for the permanent secretaries from the various ministries across government. In a crisis, the Home front Crisis Management system provides a "ministerial committee" responsible for all crisis situations in Singapore.

In the WOG-IRM structure, the HCMC is led by the Ministry of Home Affairs (MHA). In peacetime, MHA is the principal policy-making governmental body for safety and security in Singapore. In the event of a national disaster, the MHA leads at the strategic level of incident management. The incident management system in Singapore is known as the Home front Crisis Management System (HCMS). Under the HCMS, the SCDF is appointed as the Incident Manager, taking charge of managing the consequences of disasters and civil emergencies. Reporting to the HCMC is an executive group known as the Home front Crisis Executive Group (HCEG), which is chaired by the Permanent Secretary for MHA. The HCEG is in charge of planning and managing all types of disasters in Singapore. Within the operation allayer, there are various functional inter-agency crisis management groups with specific responsibilities, integrated by the various governmental crisis-management units. At the tactical layer, there are the crisis and incident managers who supervise service delivery and coordination. The Singapore government holds relevant ministries accountable in accordance to the nature and scope of the disaster. Among those ministries and government agencies, the SCDF is the major player in risk mitigation and management for civil emergencies. Now, let us look into the SCDF in more detail.

For civil security and civil incidents, the Singapore Civil Defense Force (SCDF)[2] is Singapore's leading operational authority—the Incident Manager for the management of civil emergencies. The SCDF is responsible for leading and coordinating the multi-agency response under the Home front Crisis Management Committee. The SCDF operates a three-tier command structure, with Headquarters (HQ) SCDF at the apex commanding four Land Divisions. These Divisions are supported by a network of Fire Stations and Fire Posts strategically located around the island. The SCDF also serves the following pivotal functions. The SCDF provides effective 24-h fire fighting, rescue and emergency ambulance services. The SCDF developed the Operations Civil Emergency (Ops CE) Plan—a national contingency plan. When Ops CE is activated, the SCDF is vested with the authority to direct all response forces under a unified command structure, thus enabling all required resources to be pooled. However, the WOG-IRM policy framework only came to existence when Singapore encountered SARS.

The SARS epidemic in 2003 was an institutional watershed for Singapore's approach to risk mitigation and disaster management (Pereira 2008). Prior to the SARS epidemic, Singapore's Executive Group[3] mainly focused on crises or

[2] According to 2006 data, SCDF has a workforce of about 5,100 staff comprising of 1,700 regular uniformed staff, 200 civilian staff and 3,200 full-time National Servicemen. The budget size for SCDF on a national level is about SGD$300 million per annum.

[3] Prior to SARS in 2003, the Executive Group in the Homefront Crisis Management System was the key executive body charged with managing peacetime crises in Singapore.

disasters that were civil defense in nature. These emergencies were merely conceived to be well managed by a solitary incident manager, supported by other relevant agencies. A specific multi-sectoral governance structure was not considered necessary to handle the crisis. The SARS epidemic challenged the prevailing Home front Crisis Management structure as the epidemic transcended just managing civil defense incidents. The policymakers realized the necessity to adopt a comprehensive disaster management framework, an all-hazard approach that includes a mechanism for seamless integration at both the strategic and operational levels among various government agencies. To this end, Singapore revamped its Home front Crisis Management framework to produce the current inter-agency structure.

3.1.1 Legal Framework in Disaster Reduction

The main legislation supporting emergency preparedness and disaster management activities in Singapore are the Civil Defense Act of 1986, the Fire Safety Act of 1993, and the Civil Defense Shelter Act of 1997. The Civil Defense Act provides the legal framework for, amongst other things, the declaration of a state of emergency and the mobilization and deployment of operationally-ready national service rescuers. Provides the legal framework to impose fire safety requirements on commercial and industrial premises, as well as the involvement of the management and owners of such premises in emergency preparedness against fires; and The Civil Defense Shelter Act provides the legal framework for buildings to be provided with civil defense shelters for use by persons to take refuge during a state of emergency. To tackle disease outbreak, Singapore had earlier promulgated the Infectious Disease Act in 1977. This legislation is jointly administered by the MOH and the National Environment Agency (NEA).

3.2 Budgetary Allocations

Unlike most governments that make regular national budgetary provision for potential disaster relief and early recovery purposes, the Government of Singapore makes no annual budgetary allocations for disaster response because the risks of a disaster are low (Global Facility for Disaster Reduction and Recovery 2011, p.24). However, the Singapore government can swiftly activate the budgetary mechanisms or funding lines in the event of a disaster and ensure these lines are sufficiently resourced with adequate financial capacity.

4 Case Study: Singapore's Experience in Fighting SARS Epidemic

To illuminate Singapore's approach to disaster management, we now use a case study of Singapore's fight against SARS to highlight policy learning and lesson-drawing in a specific context and timeframe. This case study has three sections. We first introduce the epidemiology of SARS in Singapore. In the second section, we describe the impact caused by SARS epidemics on Singapore in the economic, healthcare, and psychosocial aspects. In the third section, we demonstrate Singapore's risk mitigating management, and detail the government's risk mitigating measures to contain the epidemic.

4.1 *Epidemiology of SARS in Singapore*

SARS hit Singapore in early 2003. But what began as a few isolated cases swiftly turned into a major public health emergency within a few short weeks. In early March 2003 the first Singaporean to contract SARS was hospitalized upon her return from Hong Kong. As it turned out, she had contracted SARS from a super-carrier while both were staying on the same floor of the M Hotel. That super-carrier—a physician from China—was later identified by the World Health Organization (WHO) to be the primary source of infection for multiple cases of SARS worldwide (Centers for Disease Control and Prevention 2003). Back in Singapore, this first SARS victim quickly infected 21 others. In late July 2003, among all SARS affected countries, Singapore reported 238 probable cases. By the time, Singapore was removed from the WHO advisory list on 31 May 2003, 205 (86 %) had recovered while 33 (14 %) had died. A further breakdown reveals that 8 cases (3 %) were infected while abroad whereas 97 cases (41 %) were healthcare workers.

4.2 *SARS's Impact on Singapore*

4.2.1 Economic Impact

Singapore is a small open economy. External shocks can result in high levels of volatility resonating across the domestic economy. These shocks in turn would bring about higher levels of risk and uncertainty in Singapore. At the beginning of 2003, Singapore's economic outlook was clouded by the Iraq War and its impact on oil prices (Attorney-General's Chambers 2003). The unexpected outbreak of SARS led to greater uncertainty in the Singapore economy. Singapore's financial markets were severely affected due to the loss of public confidence and reduced floor

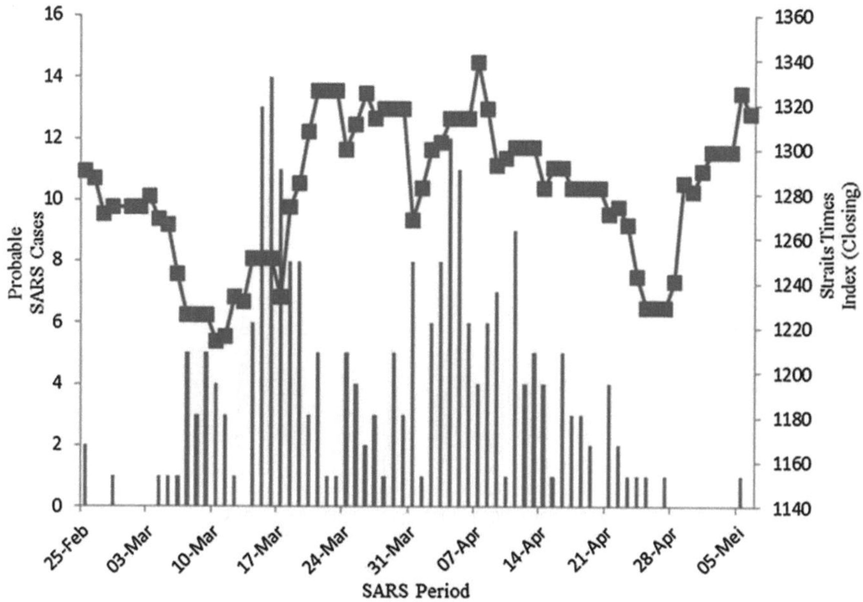

Fig. 15.1 SARS probable cases and straits times index (closing) (25th February to 6th May 2003). *Source*: Straits Times Index available at http://quotes.stocknod.com (Accessed 15 April 2012); Ministry of Health, Singapore (2003a)

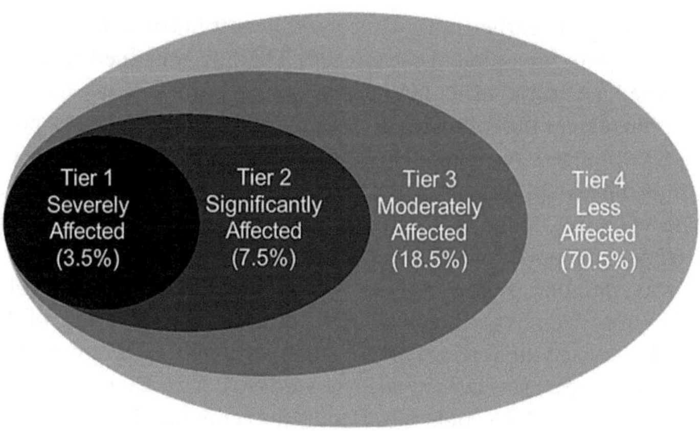

Fig. 15.2 Impact of SARS on Singapore's domestic economy*. *Note*: *MAS internal estimates. *Source*: Monetary Authority Singapore 2003/2004

trading. The impact of SARS on the stock market reflected in the Straits Times Index (STI) (see Fig. 15.1). The market did not react well to the SARS epidemic. In the first fortnight of the epidemic, the STI closed down 76 points. Even though more cases were reported, the STI climbed progressively up 86 points over the next

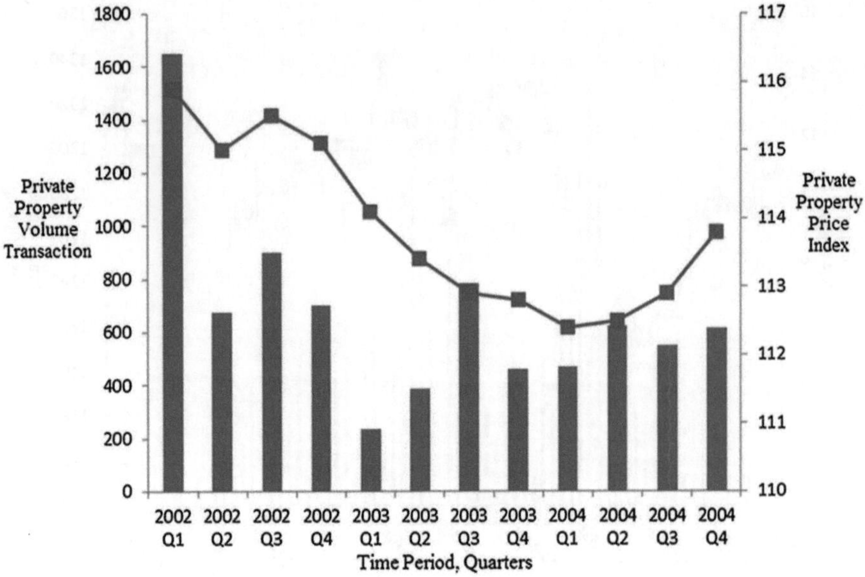

Fig. 15.3 Private property volume transactions (condominiums), private property price index (Quarterly 2002–2004). *Source*: Singapore Real Estate, http://www.singaporerealestate.info/blog/property-tools/spsf-chart-d09-10/ (Accessed 15 April 2012), http://www.h88.com.sg/property_stats/property_price_index.php (Accessed 15 April 2012)

fortnight, eclipsing the earlier falls. This could be attributed to the strict measures which the Singapore government introduced. The STI remained relatively stable over the immediate fortnight as new cases were reported. However, it started a downward plunge over the following fortnight as the number of cases peaked once more. The STI plunged 96 points. However, the resilience of the STI was shown when it climbed back up, surpassing the level reported at the beginning of the SARS period. The volatility of the STI demonstrates the vulnerability of a small open economy from exogenous forces—in this case, the SARS epidemic.

SARS was the one single activity which contributed to the volatility of Singapore's Gross Domestic Product (GDP) in 2003. The Ministry of Trade and Industry (MTI) revised the forecast for Singapore's annual GDP growth down from 3 to 0.5 %. This forecast was later revised upwards to 2.5 %. There were a number of channels by which the SARS epidemic affected the economy. The economic impacts will be discussed from the positions of demand and supply shocks. The main economic impact of the SARS outbreak was on the demand side, as consumption and the demand for services declined (Henderson 2003). The economic consequence caused fear and anxiety among Singaporeans and potential tourists to Singapore. The hardest and most directly hit were the tourism, retail, hospitality and transport-related industries, for example airline, cruise, hotel, restaurant, travel agent, retail and taxi services, and their auxiliary industries (see Fig. 15.3 and Table 15.1). Visitor arrivals fell by one third in March 2003, and two thirds in April 2003.

Table 15.1 Impact of SARS on Singapore's domestic economy

Tier	Industry	Percentage in GDP (%)
1 (Severely)	Hotels, air-transport	3.50
2 (Significantly)	Restaurants, retail trade, land transport	7.50
3 (Moderately)	Real estate, financial services	18.50
4 (Less)	Manufacturing, construction, post and communications, wholesale trade, sea transport, service allied to transport	70.50

Source: Monetary Authority Singapore, Annual Report 2003/2004

This had a direct impact on hotel occupancy rates, which declined sharply to 30 % in late April 2003. Cancellation or postponement of tourism events increased by about 30–40 %. Revenues of restaurants dropped by 50 % while revenues of the travel agents decreased by 70 %. SARS had an uneven impact on various sectors of the economy. A four-tiered framework to assess the impact on the respective sectors showed that Tier 1 industries, such as the tourism and travel-related industries were most severely hit. Tier 1 industries account for 3.5 % of GDP. The Tier 2 industries, such as restaurants, retail and land transport industries were significantly hit, which account for 7.5 % of GDP. The next two tiers were less directly affected by the SARS outbreak. Tier 3 industries include real estate and stock broking, which account for close to 19 % of GDP. The remaining 70 % of the domestic economy in Tier 4 includes manufacturing, construction and communications. These industries were not directly impacted by the outbreak of SARS. All in all, the estimated decline in GDP directly from SARS was 1 %, equaling SGD875 million.

Singapore experienced a significant drop in tourist arrivals where visitors usually stay for up to 3 days and transit onto their next destination. The trend for visitor inflow is that visitor inflows fall sharply. This is especially true in the case of Singapore, when visitor stays tend to be shorter and the high-end visitors stayed away. As a result, tourism and other related industries were nearly crippled due to a significant reduction in both leisure and business travel. For example, tourist arrivals saw a significant drop of 15 % in March 2003. The drop in tourist arrivals was 67 % in April 2003, and 65 % for the month of May 2003 until the first week of June 2003. The outcome was low visitor numbers relative to other months in 2003.

Visitors from around the world cancelled or postponed their trips to Singapore, causing a drastic decrease of total expenditure from visitors. (See Table 15.2) Plummeting visitor arrivals directly impacted hotel occupancy rates, which declined sharply to 30 % in late April (See Table 15.3). The hotel occupancy rate plummeted from 72 to 42 %, compared to the normal level of 70 % or above. The annual averages for hotel occupancy rates were 74.4 % in 2002, 67.3 % in 2003, and 80.6 % in 2004. Singapore's national carrier, Singapore Airlines (SIA), faced a record-breaking low passenger capacity of 29 % in April and May 2003. SIA cancelled approximately 30 % of its weekly schedules (Henderson 2003). SIA laid off 414 employees, of which 129 were ground staff, as a consequence of a USD200 million loss in June 2003.

Table 15.2 Change of expenditure of visitors and incoming flights from 2002 to 2004

Year	Annual total expenditure of visitors (SGD)	Number of incoming flights (per week)	Number of seats on incoming flights (per week)
2002	5,425,800	1,569	417,952
2003	4,315,600	1,490	408,606
2004	6,278,300	1,728	452,221

Source: Singapore Tourism Board, "Annual Report on Tourism Statistics" (2002–2004)

Table 15.3 Hotel statistics, first to fourth quarter 2003

Quarter	Average occupancy rate (%)	Average room rate (SGD)	Hotel room revenue (million SGD)	Food and beverage revenue million SGD)
First	72	121.5	221.7	374.3
Second	42.1	106.7	92.6	284.8
Third	73.6	107.3	191.8	357.7
Fourth	76.9	117.4	220.2	399.6

Source: Singapore Department of Statistics, http://www.singstat.gov.sg/ (Accessed 15 April 2012)

The hospitality industry had to resort to cutting budgets, which led to a steep plunge in the number of employed in the service sector. Out of a total of 12,100 made unemployed, hotels and restaurants went through the biggest cut, that being 5,800 employees. The breakdown of total job losses showed 47 % in the service sector, 28 % in construction, and 25 % in manufacturing. Additionally, transactions in the retail sector were dropped by 50 %.

The private property volume transactions for condominiums and private property price index are also good proxies on the impact of the economy from SARS. Based on quarterly figures between 2002 and 2004, the volume transactions dipped to a low in the first quarter of 2003. Also, there was a corresponding decline in the price index. Transactions recovered steadily by the third quarter boosted by confidence in market sentiments (See Fig. 15.3). The STI and private property price index seemed to display fairly similar trends, albeit with some observed lag. Note also that there is a lagged effect of consumer's deferred purchases after the outbreak of SARS in Singapore.

Demand creates its own supply. Therefore, a fall in demand of goods and services is likely to bring about a fall in the supply of such goods and services. Also, the loss of consumer and business confidence would reduce the level of aggregate demand. These effects were observed as the manufacturing industry experienced supply chain disruptions as the Singaporean economy and employment market continued to weaken. Singapore was taken off the WHO's list of SARS affected countries on 31st May 2003—one of the first countries to be removed from the list. With the "fear-factor" managed, normal daily activities slowly resumed. SARS affected industries and sectors started to show signs of recovery towards the end of the second quarter in 2003. A more comprehensive analysis of the economic costs of SARS will need to consider the direct impact on consumer spending and indirect repercussions of the shock on trade and investment (Asian Development Bank Outlook 2003). The economic costs from a global disease, such as SARS, go beyond the immediate impacts incurred in the affected sectors of disease-inflicted countries. This is not just because the disease spreads quickly across countries through networks related to global travel, but also because any economic shocks to one country spread quickly to other countries through the increased trade and financial linkages associated with globalization. However, just calculating the number of cancelled tourist trips, the declines in retail trade, and some of the factors discussed earlier do not provide a complete picture of the impact of SARS. This is because there are close linkages within economies, across sectors, and across economies in both international trade and international capital flows. Thus, analyzing the tourism sector alone may not be sufficient in analyzing the overall financial impact of SARS. SARS inflicted a heavy toll on businesses and immediately impacted severely the viability of business.

Businesses lost employees for long periods of time due to factors such as illness, the need to care for family members and fear of infection at work, or retrenchment. As the workforce shrunk due to absenteeism, business operations, for example supply chain, flow of goods worldwide and provision of services, were all affected both locally and internationally. In terms of retrenchment, the job prospects of employees in affected companies appeared miserable. A survey performed during the SARS period showed that the jobless rate increased more than 5.5 %, the highest for the last decade in Singapore (Ministry of Manpower, Singapore 2003). In absolute numbers, overall employment diminished by 25,963 in the second quarter of 2003, the largest quarterly decline since the mid-1980s recession. Unlike previous retrenchment that affected mainly blue-collar labor, SARS also affected white-collar employees too. The implementation of workplace SARS control measures added to operational and administrative costs. For example, the policy of temperature taking was implemented at workplaces in the private sector. Numerous private establishments installed thermal-scanners in their entrances from day one. However, such precautionary measures were necessary to contain the disease. This helped to restore business confidence and investment potential (a lower level of investments will lead to slower capital growth). But the reduction in an economy's capacity may linger on for a few quarters before it is restored to pre-SARS levels. The loss of productive working days from quarantine, and implementation costs incurred to monitor movements of employees contributed to the reduction in the aggregate supply front. Some of these economic effects may have worsened the public health situation if strategic planning was not in place.

4.2.2 Healthcare System Impact

SARS reduced levels of service and care in Singapore's healthcare system as the system mobilized its medical resources to deal with the SARS epidemic. The influx of influenza patients to hospitals and clinics crowded out many other patients with less urgent medical problems for treatment. This particularly affected those seeking elective operations that had to be postponed until the epidemic ended in Singapore. SARS also severely impacted Singapore's healthcare manpower. During the peak of SARS from mid-March 2003 to early April 2003, there was a shortage of medical and nursing professionals because (1) the demand for care of influenza patients substantially increased, and (2) the supply of healthcare manpower decreased as some were also affected by the epidemic. Like other business sectors, hospitals, clinics and other public health providers also faced a high staff-absenteeism rate and encountered difficulties in maintaining normal operations. This resulted in a further reduction in the level of service capacity.

4.2.3 Psychosocial Impact

Psychosocial impact from SARS was mainly caused by limited medical knowledge of SARS when it began its insidious spread in Singapore. Such uncertainty of contracting a highly contagious disease actually deteriorated the fear of security breaches, and the panic of overexposure (Tan 2006). Responding to the uncertainty of disease transmission, the Singapore government instituted many draconian public policies, such as social distancing, quarantine and isolation, as risk mitigating measures. All of these control measures created an instinctive withdrawal from society for the general population. This brought about a behavior which resulted in the public avoiding crowds and public places with human interaction. On 24 March 2003, the MOH invoked the Infectious Disease Act (IDA) to isolate all those who had been exposed to SARS patients. After IDA was invoked, on 25 March 2003, schools and non-essential public places were closed. Public events were cancelled to prevent close contact in crowds. Singaporeans with contact history were asked to stay home for a period of time to prevent transmission. Harsh penalties, such as hefty fines of more than USD4,000 or imprisonment, were imposed on those who defied quarantine orders. In a drastic move reminiscent of a police state, closed-circuit cameras were installed in the houses of those ordered to stay home to monitor their compliance with the quarantine order (ABC News Online 2003). At the height of SARS, 12,194 suspected cases were ordered to stay home, all of whom were monitored either by cameras or in less severe cases, by telephone calls. Quarantine, regardless of its effectiveness, received strong criticism from the general public during the outbreak of SARS due to the invasive nature of that measure (Duncanson 2003). Impact of social distancing remains unclear, but WHO has recommended such control measures depending on the severity of the epidemic, risk groups affected and epidemiology of transmission (World Health Organization 2005). Singapore's MOH advocated the practice of social distancing during the outbreak of SARS. The sole intention of social distancing was to limit physical interactions and close contact in public areas to slow the rate of disease transmission. Additionally, social distancing measures in particular have a psychological impact. The practice of social distancing led to a social setback in businesses that suffered economic losses as a result (Duncanson 2003).

The psychological impact of SARS is longer lasting. The most immediate and tragic impact was the loss of loved ones.

4.3 Singapore's Risk Mitigating Measures

In this section, we detail Singapore's command structure, legal framework in fighting SARS, as well as risk mitigating measures in economic, healthcare, and psychosocial perspectives.

4.3.1 Command Structure and Legal Framework

One of the most important lessons the Singapore government learned from the SARS epidemic was the crucial role played by the bureaucracy in disaster management. The bureaucratic structure in place then was severely inadequate in terms of handling a situation that was both fluid and unprecedented; indeed, fighting SARS required more than a medical approach because resources had to be drawn from agencies other than the MOH. Accordingly, a three–tiered national control structure was created in response to SARS—these tiers were individually represented by the Inter-Ministerial Committee (IMC), the Core Executive Group (CEG) and the Inter-Ministry SARS Operations Committee (IMOC) (Tay and Mui 2004). The nine-member IMC was chaired by the Minister of Home Affairs (MHA) and it fulfilled three major functions: (1) to develop strategic decisions, (2) to approve these major decisions, and (3) to implement control measures.[4]

Notably, the IMC also played the role of an interagency coordinator overseeing the activities of other ministries and their subsidiaries. On 7 April 2003 (5 weeks after the first case of SARS was reported), the CEG and a ministerial committee was formed. The CEG was chaired by the Permanent Secretary of Home Affairs and consisted of elements from three other ministries: the MOH, the Ministry of Defense (MOD) and the Ministry of Foreign Affairs (MFA). In particular, the role of the CEG was to manage the SARS epidemic by directing valuable resources to key areas. The IMOC, meanwhile, was seminal in carrying out health control measures issued by the IMC (see Fig. 15.4 below). The MOH, at the operational layer, formed an Operations Group responsible for the planning and coordination of health services, and operation in peacetime. During SARS, it commanded and controlled all medical resources and served as the main operational linkage between the MOH and all the healthcare providers.

[4] Other than Ministries of Home Affairs and Health, the Inter-Ministerial Committee comprised other eight ministries: Foreign Affairs, Defence, Education, National Development, Manpower, Environment, Transport and Information, Communications and the Arts.

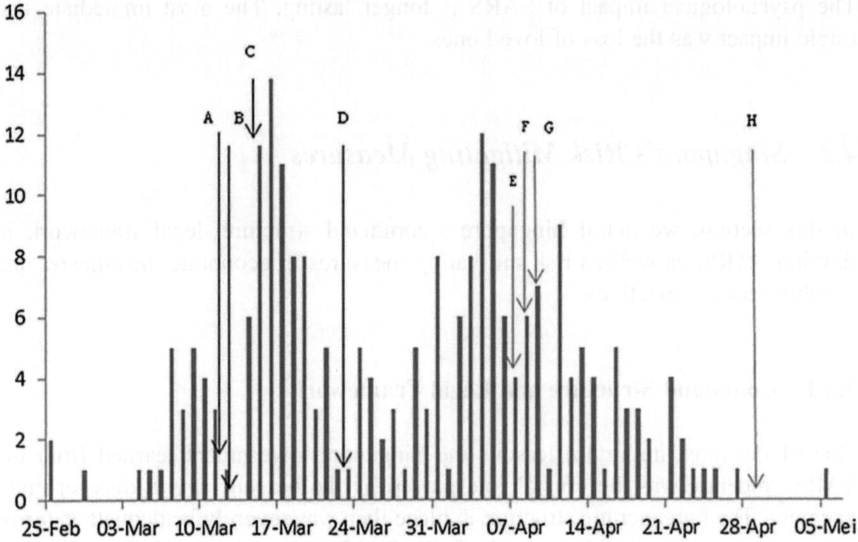

Fig. 15.4 Chronology of Singapore's control measures. *Note: A*: (*13 March*) WHO's global alert on SARS, MOH's directive to isolate all cases of atypical pneumonia; *B*: (*14 March*) MOH advisory to the public to avoid travel to SARS-affected countries; *C*: (*16 March*) triage at Emergency Departments to separate out febrile patients from other types of patients and unprotected staff and members of the public; *D*: (*22 March*) Tan Tock Seng Hospital designated as the SARS hospital. Home quarantine and daily telephone surveillance of contacts with suspected SARS cases; *E*: (*7 April*) formation of the Ministerial Committee on SARS chaired by the Minister for Home Affairs; *F*: (*8 April*) MOH directive under the Private Hospitals and Medical Clinics Act requiring all hospitals and nursing homes to ensure effective implementation of detailed procedures on triage, isolation, use of personal protective equipment and infection control; *G*: (*9 April*) passengers of all inbound flights required to complete a Health Declaration Card. Thermal scanners deployed at airport; *H*: (*30 April*) Mandatory temperature screening of children in schools. *Source*: Tan (2006)

On 15 March 2003, when the epidemiological nature of SARS was still unclear, the MOH initiated a SARS taskforce to look into the mysterious strain. Only 2 days later, after more SARS cases were reported and a better epidemiological understanding of the strain was developed, the Singapore government swiftly declared SARS a notifiable disease under the Infectious Disease Act (IDA) (Ministry of Health, Singapore 2003a). In the case of a broad outbreak, IDA made it legally permissible to enforce mandatory health examination and treatment, exchange of medical information and cooperation between healthcare providers and the MOH, and the quarantine and isolation of SARS patients (Infectious Disease Act 2003). In particular, the government amended the IDA on 24 April 2003 requiring all those who had come into contact with SARS patients to remain indoors or report immediately to designated medical institutions for quarantine (Ministry of Health, Singapore 2003b). Asa legacy of Singapore's British colonial past, the Singapore legislature is unique and well-known for passing laws in a swift and efficient manner. The uniqueness in Singapore's legal framework allows Singapore to swiftly amend the IDA during health crises to suit volatile conditions, for instance when more epidemiological cases were uncovered and the virus was better understood. All in all, the IDA played an adaptive role in terms of facilitating a swift response to the outbreak of this particular epidemic. On 22 March 2003, the CEG designated the restructured public hospital—Tan Tock Seng Hospital (TTSH) as the SARS hospital (James et al. 2006; Tan 2006). That is, once a suspected SARS patient was detected at a local clinic or emergency department, he or she would then be transferred to TTSH immediately for further evaluation and monitoring. The national healthcare system prioritized life-saving resources such as medicine and medical equipment to allocate manpower and protective equipment to the TTSH. To ease the flu-like patient influx into the TTSH, the government diverted non-flu patients away from TTSH so that the sudden surge in the number of flu cases at TTSH did not paralyze its service delivery.

4.3.2 Economic Measures

The full impact of SARS on the economy by and large depended on how quickly SARS was contained, as well as the course of the SARS outbreak in the region and beyond. To mitigate SARS impact on Singapore's economy, the government took every precaution and spared no effort to contain the SARS outbreak in Singapore. Two aspects of SARS warranted government intervention to mitigate economic impact. First, the information that needs to be collected and disseminated to effectively assess SARS displays the characteristics of public good. Second, there are negative externalities related to contagious diseases in the sense that they affect third parties in market transactions. Public good and negative externalities are typical areas where government action is needed (Fan 2003). There are three major factors which can explain why some economies are more vulnerable and susceptible to the effect of SARS than others (Asian Development Bank Outlook 2003). These factors are structural issues (e.g. shares of tourism in GDP and the composition of consumer spending), initial consumer sentiments, and government responses. As the research shows, the Singapore government implemented a USD 132 million (SGD 231 million in 2003) SARS relief package to reduce the costs for tourism operators and its auxiliary services. On the other hand, an economic relief package worth USD 131m (SGD 230m) was created to aid businesses hit by SARS.[5] In addition, the government incurred USD$109m (SGD 192m) in direct operating expenditure related to SARS, and committed another USD 60m (SGD105m) development expenditure of hospitals for additional isolation rooms and medical facilities to treat SARS and other infectious diseases. The government's economic incentives worked when seeking cooperation of other healthcare

[5] Singapore government dispensed a total of SGD 300 m to battle SARS directly and SGD230m to help business, on 1 July 2003.

providers (such as public hospitals and local clinics) so that they would absorb additional cases of non-flu illnesses.

To help SARS affected firms tide over the plight and minimize job losses, Singapore's National Wage Council widely consulted the private sector, and recommended SARS-struck companies adopt temporary cost-cutting measures to save jobs.[6] The measures adopted by the private sector included the implementation of a shorter working-week, temporary lay-offs and the arrangement for workers to take leave or undergo skills training and upgrading provided by the Ministry of Manpower and associated agencies. When these measures failed to preserve jobs, the last resort was temporary wage cuts.

4.3.3 Public Health Control Measures

Surveillance and Reporting

Surveillance and reporting is critical in combating pandemics because it serves to provide early warning and even detection of impending outbreaks. The surveillance process involves looking out for possible virulent strains and disease patterns within a country's borders as well as at major border-crossings (Jebara 2004; Ansell et al. 2010; Narain and Bhatia 2010). When SARS first surfaced, the nature of this virus was largely unknown. As a consequence, health authorities worldwide were mostly unable to detect and monitor suspected cases. Health authorities in Singapore encountered this same problem. But with thc aid of WHO technical advisors, Singapore managed to establish in a timely manner identification and reporting procedures. Furthermore, the MOH also expanded the WHO's definitions for suspected cases of SARS (to include any healthcare workers with fever and/or respiratory symptoms) in order to widen the surveillance net (Goh et al. 2006). As the pace of SARS transmission quickened, the Singapore Parliament amended the IDA on 25 April 2003 requiring all suspected SARS cases to be reported to the MOH within 24 h from the time of diagnosis.

Although these control measures were laudable, SARS also exposed the weaknesses of Singapore's fragmented epidemiological surveillance and reporting systems (Goh et al. 2006). As a major part of lesson-drawing in the post-SARS era, a number of novel surveillance measures were introduced to integrate epidemiological data and to identify the emergence of a new virulent strain faster. One of the most notable was the establishment of an Infectious Disease Alert and Clinical Database system to integrate critical clinical, laboratory and contact tracing information. Today, the surveillance system has four major operational components that

[6] These measures were agreed by the tripartite partners who issued a tripartite statement on 15 April 2003. The tripartite approach reflects the willingness and ability of the three social partners to work together to face the crisis (Source: NWC Recommendations for 2003/2004).

include community surveillance, laboratory surveillance, veterinary surveillance, external surveillance, and hospital surveillance.

Hospital Infection Control

To limit the risk of transmission in healthcare institutions once the SARS epidemic had broken out, the MOH implemented a series of stringent infection-control measures that all healthcare workers (HCWs) and visitors to hospitals visitors had to adhere to. The use of personal protective equipment (PPE)[7] was made compulsory. Visitors to public hospitals were barred from those areas where transmission and contraction were most likely. The movements of HCWs in public hospitals were also heavily proscribed. Unfortunately, except for TTSH, these critical measures were not enforced in all healthcare sectors until 8 April 2003, and this oversight resulted in a number of intra-hospital infections (Goh et al. 2006). In addition, the policy of restricting the movements of HCWs and visitors to hospitals was taken further. More specifically, their movements *between* hospitals were now restricted. Patient movement between hospitals, meanwhile, was strictly restricted to medical transfers. The number of visitors to hospitals was also limited and their particulars recorded during each visit. It is also important to point out that these somewhat draconian control measures required strong public support and cooperation. Indeed, their implementation would not have been successful had these two elements been missing.

Public Education and Communication

Public education and communication are two indispensable components in health crisis management (Reynolds and Seeger 2005; Reddy et al. 2009). Communication difficulties are prone to complicate the challenge, especially when there is no established, high-status organization that can act as a hub for information collation and dissemination. Therefore, it is necessary to disseminate essential information to the targeted population in a transparent manner. During the SARS outbreak, the MOH practiced a high degree of transparency when it shared information with the public. Indeed, the clear and distinct messages from the MOH contributed significantly to lowering the risk of public panic.

The MOH worked closely with the media to provide regular, timely updates and health advisories. This information was communicated to the public through every possible medium. In addition to the media (e.g. TV and radio), information pamphlets were distributed to every household and the MOH website provided constant updates and health advisories to the general public. Notably, a government

[7] Personal protective equipment includes N95 masks, disposable gloves, gowns, and goggles or visors.

information channel dedicated to providing timely updates was created on the same day—13 March 2003—when the WHO issued a global alert. A dedicated TV Channel called the SARS Channel was launched to broadcast information on the symptoms and transmission mechanisms of the virus (James et al. 2006). The importance of social responsibility and personal hygiene was a frequent message heard throughout the SARS epidemic. As an example, when Tan Tock Seng Hospital was designated as the SARS hospital at the peak of SARS epidemics, the government undertook many efforts in public communication and education to seek cooperation and support from other healthcare providers, such as public hospitals and local clinics, so that they would absorb the additional cases of non-flu illnesses. Many organizations displayed prominent signs in front of their building entrances that reminded their staff as well as visitors to be socially responsible. School children were instructed to wash their hands and take their body temperature regularly. The public was told to wear masks and postpone non-essential travel to other countries.

Social Distancing

The MOH advocated the practice of social distancing during the outbreak of SARS. The sole intention of social distancing was of course to limit physical interactions and close contact in public areas thereby slowing the rate of transmission. As a result, all pre-school centers, after-school centers, primary and secondary schools, and junior colleges were closed from 27 March to 6 April 2003. School children who had stricken siblings were advised to stay home for at least 10 days. Moreover, students who showed flu-like symptoms or had travelled to other affected countries were automatically granted a 7-day Leave of Absence and home-based learning program were instituted for those affected. Extracurricular activities were also scaled down to minimize social contact. Meanwhile, the MOH also advised businesses to adopt social distancing measures such as allowing staff to work from home and using split-team arrangements. Those who were most at higher risk of developing complications if stricken were moved and removed from frontline work to other areas where they were less likely to contract the virus. As mentioned earlier, the practice of social distancing also drew strong criticisms from those businesses that suffered economic losses as a result. Apart from providing economic compensation, measures to mitigate psychosocial impacts are also important.

4.3.4 Psychosocial Measures

The government's measures of public health control, as mentioned above, drew strong criticisms from businesses and the public during the outbreak of SARS due to the invasive nature of those actions. Besides these, the economic slowdown affected overall employment and personal income. Some households required financial assistance. In response to the public complaints, authorities in Singapore provided economic assistance to those individuals and businesses who had been affected by home quarantine orders through a "Home Quarantine Order Allowance Scheme" (Tay and Mui 2004; Teo et al. 2005).

At the same time, the MOH worked together with various ministerial authorities to provide essential social services to those affected by the quarantine order. For example, housing was offered to those who were unable to stay in their own homes (because of the presence of family members) during their quarantine, ambulance services were freely provided by the Singapore Civil Defense Force to those undergoing quarantine at home to visit their doctors, as well as high-tech communication gadgets such as webcams, for those undergoing quarantine to stay in touch with relatives and friends. Impacts on social welfare in large part relate to economic outlook, especially in the area of consumption patterns. All these risk mitigating measures were not only effective in containing the epidemic, but also valid for implications in disaster risk management.

5 Implications for Practice and Research

In this section, we draw on the lesson-learning from Singapore's experience in fighting the SARS epidemic, and discuss implications for future practice and research in disaster risk management. The implications are explained in four aspects: *staying vigilant at the community level, remaining flexible in a national command structure, demand for surge capacity,* and *collaborative governance at regional level.*

5.1 Staying Vigilant at the Community Level

It remains questionable that Singapore's draconian health control measures may not be applicable or replicable in other countries, for example setting a camera to monitor the public's compliance during home quarantine. The evidence suggests that draconian government measures, such as quarantine and travel restrictions, are less effective than voluntary measures (such as good personal hygiene and voluntarily wearing of respiratory masks), especially over the long term. However, reminding the public to maintain a high level of vigilance and advocate individual social responsibility can be a persuasion tactic by an authority to influence and pressure, but not to force individuals or groups into complicity with a policy. Therefore, promoting social responsibility is crucial in terms of slowing the pace of infection through good personal hygiene and respiratory etiquette in all settings.

To achieve this goal, public education and risk communication are two indispensable components in health crisis management (Reddy et al. 2009; Reynolds and

Seeger 2005). The community must be aware of the nature and scope of disasters. They have to be educated on the importance of emergency preparedness and involvement in exercises, training and physical preparations. At the community level, institutions and capacities are developed and strengthened which in turn systematically contribute to vigilance against potential risks.

This is best illustrated in the Singapore government's communication strategy to manage public fear and panic during the outbreak of SARS (Menon and Goh 2005). Throughout the epidemic, the Singapore government relentlessly raised the level of vigilance of personal hygiene and awareness of social responsibility. This, in large part, has to rely on public education and risk communication. To effectively disseminate the idea of vigilance across the public, political leaders were seen as doing and initiating a series of countermeasures to reassure the public. By showing the people that government leaders practiced what they preached, the examples served to naturalize and legitimize the public discourse of social responsibility for all Singaporean citizens (Lai 2010).

The need to stay vigilant is never overemphasized, but being vigilant does not equate to a panacea that ensures all government agencies work together. To be well prepared for the unexpected, we need a clear and swift national command structure that can flexibly respond to, and even more promptly than in the case of disease transmission, the changing situation.

5.2 Remaining Flexible in a National Command Structure

All local agencies responding to an emergency must work within a unified national command structure to coordinate multi-agency efforts in emergency response and management of disasters. On top of facilitating close inter-agency coordination, the strength of this flexible structure is in its ability to ensure a swift response to an epidemic outbreak by implementing risk mitigating measures more effectively and efficiently. Structural flexibility involves swift deployment of forces to mitigate the incident at the tactical level, and to provide expert advice at the operational level, in order to minimize damage to lives and property. Among other things, the flexibility endemic to this command structure facilitates the building of trust between the state and its people (Lai 2009). This in turn ensures that government measures are quickly accepted by the general public.

As shown in this chapter, the MOH has been entrusted by the Singapore government and pre-designated to be the Incident Manager for public health emergencies. When a sudden incident involves public health or the loss of lives on a large scale, the MOH is responsible for planning, coordinating and implementing an assortment of disease control programs and activities. During the outbreak of SARS, the Singapore government established a national command and control structure that was able to adapt to rapidly changing circumstances that stemmed from the outbreak.

Specifically, the MOH set up a taskforce within that ministry even when the definition of SARS remained unclear. As more SARS cases were uncovered and better epidemiological information became available, the government quickly created the Inter-Ministerial Committee (IMC) and Core Executive Group (CEG)—both of which were instrumental in the design and implementation of all risk mitigating measures—to coordinate the operation to combat the outbreak (Pereira 2008). While this overarching governance structure is more or less standard worldwide ('t Hart et al. 1993; LaPorte 2007), the case of Singapore is unique in that the city-state was able to overcome bureaucratic inertia and adapt this governance structure.

From Singapore's experiences during the SARS crisis, we have learnt that the strength of a national command structure lies in its flexibility to link relevant ministries on the same platform. These linkages ensure a timely, coordinated response and service delivery. Having a flexible structure was not the only reason behind the successful defeat of SARS. In Singapore's case, we also notice the success of containing an uncertain, high-impact disaster has to rely on surge capacity.

5.3 *The Demand for Surge Capacity*

In the context of this paper, surge capacity refers to the ability to mobilize resources (such as PPEs, vaccines and HCWs) to combat the outbreak of a pandemic. Singapore's response to SARS in 2003 illustrates the importance of being able to increase surge capacity swiftly to deal with an infectious disease outbreak. In the Asia Pacific region, this problem continues to hamper many countries' ability to combat infectious diseases (Putthasri et al. 2009). For many public health organizations in Asia, it is a matter of fact that they are unable to deal with pandemics because the resources to do so are simply absent (Balkhy 2008; Hanvoravongchai et al. 2010; Lai 2012b; Oshitani et al. 2008). Meanwhile, there are evidences which suggest that surge capacity alone is not the full answer. For example, during the SARS outbreak, abundant resources contribute an important but not all-encompassing element in the fight against these pandemics. As it turned out, when different stakeholders brought to the task-at-hand their unique skill sets and resources, they actually complicated the fight due to their lack of synergy. In fact, abundant resources without synergy might even undermine collaborative efforts. Therefore, it is essential that the ability to link up various stakeholders must be complemented by some type of synergy between them. Such ability can be enhanced through close collaboration. This brings us to the third implication for disaster management: collaborative governance at regional level.

5.4 *Collaborative Governance at Regional Level*

The trans-boundary nature of the disasters calls for a planned and coordinated approach towards disaster response for efficient rescue and relief operations (Lai et al. 2009; Lai 2012a). Combating epidemics requires multiple states and government agencies to work together in close (Webby and Webster 2003). Therefore, it is clear that collaborative capacity of various stakeholders is central to the fight against transboundary communicable diseases (Lai 2011; Lai 2012b; Leung and Nicoll 2010; Voo and Capps 2010). While member states that are of advanced economic development typically lead such efforts, the inclusion of other developing countries, non-traditional agencies, and organizations (including non-governmental ones) is necessary and ultimately, inevitable. Indeed, major countermeasures such as border control and surveillance are often made possible with the aid of regional collaboration. Take the Association of Southeast Asian Nations (ASEAN) as an example.

ASEAN countries take regional, national and sub-national approaches to disaster risk management (Lai et al. 2009). The ASEAN Committee on Disaster Risk Management (ACDM) was established in 2003 and tasked with the coordination and implementation of regional activities on disaster management. The Committee has cooperated with United Nations bodies such as the United Nations International Strategy for Disaster Reduction (UNISDR) and the United Nations Office for the Coordination of Humanitarian Affairs (UNOCHA). The ASEAN Agreement on Disaster Management and Emergency Response (AADMER) provides a comprehensive regional framework to strengthen preventive, monitoring and mitigation measures to reduce disaster losses in the region. In recent years, Singapore has been active in providing training and education for disaster managers from neighboring countries. Singapore has an ongoing exchange program with a number of Asia Pacific nations and Europe. For example, to partner with APEC to increase emergency preparedness in the Asia-Pacific region, Singapore's SCDF provides short-term courses on disaster management in the Civil Defense Academy (Asia Pacific Economic Cooperation 2011).

6 Conclusions

The world today is far more inter-connected than ever before. International travel, transnational trade, and cross-border migration have drastically increased as a consequence of globalization. No country is spared from being influenced directly or indirectly by disasters. Singapore is no exception. Singapore is vulnerable to both natural and man-made disasters alongside its remarkable economic growth. In response, the Singapore government adopts an approach of Whole-of-Government Integrated Risk Management, a concerted, coordinated effort based on a total national response.

We have witnessed in the case study Singapore's all-hazard management framework with specific references to the SARS epidemic. In fighting SARS, Singapore's health authority was responsive enough to swing into action when they realized that the existing bureaucratic structure was inadequate in terms of facilitating close cooperation between various key government agencies to tackle the health crisis on hand. Therefore, a command structure was swiftly established. The presence of a flexible command structure, the way and the extent it was utilized, explains how well an epidemic was successfully contained. Flexibility actually enhanced organizational capacities by making organizations more efficient under certain conditions.

Epidemic control measures such as surveillance, social distancing, and quarantine require widespread support from the general public for them to be effective. Singapore's experiences with SARS strongly suggest that risk mitigating measures can be effective only when a range of partners and stakeholders (such as government ministries, non-profit organizations, and grass-roots communities) become adequately involved. This is also critical to disaster risk management. Whether all of these aspects are transferrable elsewhere needs to be assessed in future research. Nonetheless, this unique discipline certainly has helped Singapore come out of public health crises on a regular basis. Singapore's response to the outbreak of SARS offers valuable insights into the kinds approaches needed to combat future pandemics, especially in Southeast Asia.

Acknowledgement The authors would like to thank the Economic Research Institute for ASEAN and East Asia (ERIA) to initiate this meaningful research project, and four commentators—Professor Yasuyuki Sawada (Tokyo University), Professor Chan NgaiWeng (University Sains Malaysia), Dr. Sothea Oum (ERIA), Mr. Zhou Yansheng (SCDF) and all participants in ERIA's two workshops, for their insightful comments for an earlier draft of this chapter.

References

ABC News Online. (2003). *Singapore imposes quarantine to stop SARS spreading*. ABC News [online]. 25 March 2003. http://www.abc.net.au/news/2003-03-25/singapore-imposes-quarantine-to-stop-sars-spreading/1823362. Accessed 29 June 2012.

Ansell, C., Boin, A., & Keller, A. (2010). Managing transboundary crises: Identifying the building blocks of an effective response system. *Journal of Contingencies and Crisis Management, 18* (4), 195–207.

Asia Pacific Economic Cooperation. (2011). *APEC partners with Singapore on disaster management*. Singapore: APEC. http://www.apec.org/Press/News-Releases/2011/0401_disaster.aspx. Accessed 29 June 2012.

Asian Conference on Disaster Reduction. (2010). *HFA implementation review for ACDR 2010*. Kobe, Japan: ADRC [online]. http://www.adrc.asia/acdr/2010kobe/documents/HFA/Singapore.pdf. Accessed 29 June 2012.

Asian Development Bank Outlook. (2003). *Asian development outlook 2003 update*. Manila: ADB. http://www.scribd.com/doc/49451493/Asian-Development-Outlook-2003-Update. Accessed 29 June 2012.

Asian Disaster Reduction Center. (2005). *ADRC country report, 2005*. ADRC [online]. http://www.adrc.asia/countryreport/SGP/2005/english.pdf. Accessed 29 June 2012.

Attorney-General's Chambers. (2003). *Impact of SARS on the economy*, Singapore Government. AGC [online]. http://statutes.agc.gov.sg/aol/search/display/view.w3p;page=0;query=CompId%3A2eff60ec-1a14-4368-a0c5-03d5bf324d02%20ValidTime%3A20120307000000%20TransactionTime%3A20120307000000;rec=0. Accessed 29 June 2012.

Balkhy, H. (2008). Avian influenza: The tip of the iceberg. *Annals of Thoracic Medicine, 3*(4), 154–157.

Centers for Disease Control and Prevention. (2003). Editorial Note to: Y. S. Leo et al., Severe acute respiratory syndrome – Singapore, 2003. *Morbidity and Mortality Weekly Report, 52* (18), 411. http://www.cdc.gov/mmwr/PDF/wk/mm5218.pdf. Accessed 8 May, 2012.

Duncanson, J. (2003). *How Singapore avoided WHO advisory*, Toronto star [online]. 25 April 2003. http://www.singapore-window.org/sw03/030425ts.htm. Accessed 8 May 2012.

Emmanuel, S. C. (2000). Impact to lung health of haze from forest fires: The Singapore experience. *Respirology, 5*(2), 175–182.

Fan, E. X. (2003). *SARS: Economic impacts and implications*, ERD Policy Brief No. 15. Manila: Asia Development Bank.

Global Facility for Disaster Reduction and Recovery. (2011). *Advancing disaster risk financing and insurance in ASEAN countries: Framework and options for implementation, Global facility for disaster reduction and recovery, 2011*. GFDRR [online]. http://www.gfdrr.org/gfdrr/sites/gfdrr.org/files/DRFI_ASEAN_DRFI_draft_report(October%2030,%202011).pdf. Accessed 8 December 2011.

Goh, C. L. (2004). *A new world now after hotel collapse*, The Straits Times. 15 March 2004.

Goh, K. T., Cutter, J., Heng, B. H., Ma, S., Koh, B. K. W., Kwok, C., Toh, C. M., & Chew, S. K. (2006). Epidemiology and control of SARS in Singapore. *Annals of the Academy of Medicine, Singapore, 35*, 301–316.

Hanvoravongchai, P., Adisasmito, W., Pham, N. C., de Conseil, A., de Sa, J., Krumkamp, R., Mounier-Jack, S., Phommasack, B., Putthasri, W., Shih, C. S., Touch, S., & Coker, R. (2010). Pandemic influenza preparedness and health systems challenges in Asia: Results from rapid analyses in 6 Asian countries. *BMC Public Health, 10*, 322.

't Hart, P., Rosenthal, U., & Kouzmin, A. (1993). Crisis decision making: The centralization thesis revisited. *Administration and Society, 25*(1), 12–45.

Henderson, J. (2003). Managing a Health-related Crisis: SARS in Singapore. *Journal of Vacation Marketing, 10*(1), 67–77.

Infectious Disease Act. (2003). *Infectious disease act, chapter 137 (Singapore)*, Singapore Government. AGC [online]. http://statutes.agc.gov.sg. Accessed 23 April 2012.

James, L., Shindo, N., Cutter, J., Ma, S., & Chew, S. K. (2006). Public health measures implemented during the SARS outbreak in Singapore, 2003. *Public Health, 120*, 20–26.

Jebara, K. B. (2004). Surveillance, detection, and response: Managing emerging diseases at national and international levels. *Revue Scientifiqueet Technique (International Office of Epizootics), 23*(2), 709–715.

Lai, A. Y. (2009). Shaping the crisis perception of decision makers and its application of Singapore's voluntary contribution to post-tsunami reconstruction efforts. *Journal of Administration and Governance, 4*(2), 1–12.

Lai, A. Y. (2010). Shaping the crisis perception of decision makers and its application of Singapore's voluntary contribution to post-tsunami reconstruction efforts. *Journal of Administration and Governance, 4*(2), 1–12.

Lai, A. Y. (2011). Organizational collaborative capacities in post disaster society. *Asian Journal of Social Science, 39*(4), 442–464.

Lai, A. Y. (2012a). Organizational collaborative capacity in fighting pandemic crises: A literature review from the public management perspective. *Asia-Pacific Journal of Public Health, 24*(1), 1–14.

Lai, A. Y. (2012b). Toward a collaborative cross-border disaster management: A comparative analysis of voluntary organizations in Taiwan and Singapore. *Journal of Comparative Policy Analysis, 14*(3), 1–18.

Lai, A. Y., He, A. J., Tan, T. B., & Phua, K. H. (2009). A proposed ASEAN disaster response, training and logistic centre: Enhancing regional governance in disaster management. *Transition Studies Reviews, 16*(2), 299–315.

Lai, A. Y., & Tan, T. B. (2012). Combating SARS and H1N1: Insights and lessons from Singapore's public health control measures. *ASEAS - Austrian Journal of South-East Asian Studies, 5*(1), 74–101.

LaPorte, T. R. (2007). Critical infrastructure in the face of a predatory future: Preparing for untoward surprise. *Journal of Contingencies and Crisis Management, 15*(1), 60–64.

Leung, G. M., & Nicoll, A. (2010). Reflections on pandemic (H1N1) 2009 and the international response. *PLoS Medicine, 7*(10), e1000346.

Meier, K. J., & O'Toole, Jr., L. J. (2001). Managerial strategies and behavior in networks: A model with evidence from U.S. public education. *Journal of Public Administration Research and Theory, 11*(July), 271–295.

Menon, K. U., & Goh, K. T. (2005). Transparency and trust: Risk communications and the Singapore experience in managing SARS. *Journal of Communication Management, 9*(4), 375–383.

Ministry of Health, Singapore. (2003a). *Daily distribution of SARS cases statistics*, Singapore Government. http://www.moh.gov.sg/content/moh_web/home/diseases_and_conditions/s/sars.html. Accessed June 29, 2012.

Ministry of Health, Singapore. (2003b). *Chronology of SARS events in Singapore*, Singapore Government. http://www.moh.gov.sg/corp/sars/news/chronology.html. Accessed 29 June 2012.

Ministry of Labor, Singapore. (1979). The explosion and fire on board S.T. Spyros, 12th October 1978: The inquiry report. *Committee of Inquiry into the Explosion and Fire on Board S.T. Spyros (Call no.: RSING 623.83 SIN)*. Inflopedia [online]. http://infopedia.nl.sg/articles/SIP_806_2004-12-30.html. Accessed 29 June 2012.

Ministry of Manpower, Singapore. (2003). *Manpower research and statistics*, Singapore Government. http://www.mom.gov.sg/publish/momportal/en/communities/others/mrsd/statistics/Unemployment.html. Accessed 29 June 2012.

Monetary Authority Singapore. (2003/2004). *Annual report*, Singapore Government. http://www.mas.gov.sg/about_us/annual_reports/annual20032004/pdf/mas_annualReport. Accessed 29 June 2012.

Narain, J., & Bhatia, R. (2010). The challenge of communicable diseases in the WHO South-east Asia region. *Bulletin of the World Health Organization, 88*, 162. http://www.who.int/bulletin/volumes/88/3/09-065169/en/index.html. Accessed 29 June 2012.

Oshitani, H., Kamigaki, T., & Suzuki, A. (2008). Major issues and challenges of influenza pandemic preparedness in developing countries. *Emerging Infectious Diseases, 14*(6), 875–880.

Pereira, D. (2008). *Crisis Management in the Homefront*, Presentation at Network Government and Homeland Security Workshop. Singapore, 7 January 2008.

Putthasri, W., Lertiendumrong, J., Chompook, P., Tangcharoensathien, V., & Coker, R. (2009). Capacity of Thailand to contain an emerging influenza pandemic. *Emerging Infectious Diseases, 15*(3), 423–432.

Reddy, M. C., Paul, S. A., Abraham, J., McNeese, M., DeFitch, C., & Yen, J. (2009). Challenges to effective crisis management: Using information and communication technologies to coordinate emergency medical services and emergency department teams. *International Journal of Medical Informatics, 78*, 259–269.

Reynolds, B., & Seeger, M. W. (2005). Crisis and emergency risk communication as an integrative model. *Journal of Health Communication, 10*, 43–55.

Shalala, D. E. (1998). Collaboration in the fight against infectious diseases. *Emerging Infectious Disease, 4*(3), 355–358.
Singapore Department of Statistics. (2003). *Economic survey of Singapore 2003*, Singapore Government. http://www.singstat.gov.sg/. Accessed 15 April 2012.
Singapore Institute of International Affairs. (2006). *Singapore's efforts in transboundary haze prevention, 2006*. Singapore: SIIA. http://www.siiaonline.org/?q=events/singapores-efforts-transboundary-haze-prevention. Accessed 29 June 2012.
Singapore Real Estate. (2011). *Singapore real estate, and property price*. Available at http://www.singaporerealestate.info/blog/property-tools/spsf-chart-d09-10/, http://www.h88.com.sg/property_stats/property_price_index.php. Accessed 29 June 2012.
Singapore Tourism Board. (2002). *Annual report on tourism statistics*. Singapore Tourism Board, Singapore.
Singapore Tourism Board. (2003). *Annual report on tourism statistics*. Singapore Tourism Board, Singapore.
Singapore Tourism Board. (2004). *Annual report on tourism statistics*. Singapore Tourism Board, Singapore.
Tan, L. Y. (1978). *1978 Singapore floods*, Singapore Inflopedia [online]. http://infopedia.nl.sg/articles/SIP_780_2004-12-30.html. Accessed 29 June 2012.
Tan, C. C. (2006). SARS in Singapore – Key lessons from an epidemic. *Annals of the Academy of Medicine, Singapore, 35*, 345–349.
Tay, C. B., & Mui, W. K. (2004). *An Architecture for Network Centric Operations in Unconventional Crisis: Lessons Learnt from Singapore's SARS Experience*. California: Thesis of Naval Postgraduate School.
Teo, P., Yeoh, B. S. A., & Ong, S. N. (2005). SARS in Singapore: Surveillance strategies in a globalizing city. *Health Policy, 72*(3), 279–291.
Voo, T. C., & Capps, B. (2010). Influenza pandemic and the duties of healthcare professionals. *Singapore Medical Journal, 51*(4), 275–281.
Webby, R. J., & Webster, R. G. (2003). Are we ready for pandemic influenza?'. *Science, 302*(5650), 1519–1522.
World Health Organization. (2005). *WHO guidelines on the use of vaccines and antivirals during influenza pandemics*. Geneva: Word Health Organization, 2004. http://www.who.int/csr/resources/publications/influenza/11_29_01_A.pdf. Accessed 29 June 2012.

Part IV
Conclusion

Chapter 16
Approaches Towards Effective Disaster Risk-Coping Strategies and Regional Cooperation on Disaster Management

Daniel P. Aldrich, Yasuyuki Sawada, and Sothea Oum

1 Introduction

Natural disasters serve as one of the most challenging events for advanced and developing nations alike. This book has focused particularly on the events in East Asia, a region which includes a number of developing nations alongside developed ones. Along with taking lives, destroying homes and businesses, events such as typhoons, earthquakes, and tsunami disrupt livelihoods, interrupt supply chains, and damage important infrastructure. Witness the ongoing effects of the devastating earthquake, tsunami, and nuclear radiation crisis in the Tohoku region of Japan, that has killed tens of thousands of people and resulted in damage of around US$200 to 300 billion (Cabinet Office 2011). Ando (Chap. 6 of this volume) showed the 2011 Great East Japan Earthquake affected Japan's agriculture and food experts. Her research traced how mining and manufacturing indices for disaster-affected areas, such as Iwate, Miyagi, and Fukushima Prefectures, dropped by nearly thirty percent as a result of the catastrophe. Isono and Kumagai (Chap. 8 in this volume) examined another serious natural disaster, flooding, which hit Thailand in 2011. Their numerical analysis reveals that negative long-run impacts of the flood will likely be moderate as many companies' first reaction to the flood was to seek possible relocation of their production sites within Thailand.

Disasters affect not only industrial production and trade but also agricultural production especially in developing countries where that sector plays an important

---

D.P. Aldrich (✉)
Purdue University, West Lafayette, IN, USA
e-mail: daniel.aldrich@gmail.com

Y. Sawada
Faculty of Economics, University of Tokyo, Tokyo, Japan

S. Oum
Economic Research Institute for ASEAN and East Asia, Jakarta, Indonesia

D.P. Aldrich et al. (eds.), *Resilience and Recovery in Asian Disasters*, Risk, Governance and Society 18, DOI 10.1007/978-4-431-55022-8_16

role in facilitating economic growth. Chantarat et al. (Chap. 9 in this volume), for example, looked at rice production in Thailand which has more than 9 million hectares of land set aside for that purpose. Dry spells in Thailand have destroyed whole groups and set back food security for individuals, villages, and regions. Their models suggested a 50 % probability that income consumption for Thai farming households could collapse to zero without government support and disaster insurance. Similarly, Trung (Chap. 4 in this volume) investigated how Typhoon Damrey damaged close to 250,000 ha of rice in Vietnam, resulting in a loss of 60 % to farmers in affected regions. Israel and Briones (Chap. 13 in this volume) looked at the critical issue of food security in the Philippines, demonstrating how typhoons prevented local households from achieving food security. Agricultural disasters sit among a number of other types of crises.

Hundreds of thousands of lives were lost in the 2013 super typhoon Haiyan in the Philippines, the 2004 Indian Ocean tsunami, Hurricane Katrina in 2005, and earthquakes in central Chile, Haiti, the Sichuan province of China, northern Pakistan, and the Hanshin area of Japan in 1995. Casualties, evacuation, business loss, and property damage are not solely a function of nature but also of technological, societal and political choices. The tsunami disaster in Tohoku was accompanied by a serious technological disaster involving Fukushima Dai-ichi nuclear power plant's leaking radioactive matter. This compound disaster has altered the way that civil society interacts with the Japanese central government and also the decision calculus for local "host communities" for controversial energy projects (cf. Aldrich 2013a, b). Around the world, economies are still being suffering from the global financial crisis triggered by the 2008 Lehman Shock. Nations in Africa are still at war and involved in smaller conflicts, and terrorist attacks, and the threat of terrorist attacks are having serious impact even on advanced nations.

Natural and man-made disasters show distinct rising trends across the globe: Natural and technological disasters have been increasing more rapidly in frequency, in terms of the average occurrence of disaster per country per year, than financial crises and violence-related disasters (Cavallo and Noy 2009; Kellenberg and Mobarak 2011; Strömberg 2007). As Aldrich, Oum, and Sawada discussed in Chap. 1, we can categorize disasters into four categories: natural disaster, technological disaster, economic crisis, and war. It is clear that the latter three are man-made disasters. While we provided a special focus on natural disasters in this book, we believe that following discussions and policy recommendations will apply to all types of disasters.

As we continue our efforts to recover from different disasters around the world, we are rediscovering the importance of advance preparations, such as drawing up emergency plans, disseminating and teaching emergency knowledge, conducting evacuation drills, constructing early warning systems, and investing in infrastructure. Moreover, we have begun to realize the importance of risk finance schemes such as individual- and national-level parametric insurance arrangements as an indispensable part of ex ante interventions. Governments, NGOs, and residents alike struggle to understand how we should protect ourselves and the people of the entire world from catastrophe. Chan (Chap. 12 in this volume) stresses the need for

NGOs and other essential actors to participate in the disaster cycle. In this chapter, we will summarize different approaches towards effective disaster risk-coping strategies and regional cooperation on disaster management.

We organize our concluding chapter as follows. In Sect. 2, we set up a conceptual framework of disaster risk management and coping mechanisms/strategies. Section 3 discusses innovative frameworks such as microcredit, microinsurance, and regional insurance pooling scheme to strengthen ex ante risk management capacities. In Sect. 4, we summarize policy implications to enhance effective insurance capacities by encompassing schemes against a variety of natural and man-made disasters.

2 Conceptual Framework

2.1 Household-Level Strategies

In response to the wide variety of shocks caused by natural and manmade disasters, households have developed and employ formal and informal insurance mechanisms. We classify such uses of insurance mechanisms into ex ante risk management and ex post risk-coping behaviors. First, household risk management strategies mitigate risk and reducing income instability before exogenous shocks. These strategies include investments in earthquake-proof housing, an insurance contract subscription, and access to an early-warning system. These ex ante management strategies cost-effectively mitigate losses due to disasters (World Bank and United Nations 2010) mainly because of the significance of the welfare costs of disaster risks. Using the framework of the Arrow-Pratt risk premium, we can capture the negative welfare costs of risks by calculating how much money households would be willing to pay to completely eliminate income variability. Mathematically, such an amount of money is represented by m which satisfies the following relationship: $u(\overline{y} - m) = E[u(\widetilde{y})]$, where $u(\cdot)$ is a well-behaved utility function, $\widetilde{y}$ is a stochastic income, $\overline{y}$ is its mean value, and the variable m represents a standard risk premium.

Using a Taylor expansion we understand that, approximately, the fraction of average income that a household would be willing to give up can be calculated as half of the coefficient of relative risk aversion multiplied by the square of the coefficient of variation of income. Sawada (2007) showed the estimated welfare costs of risks in India and Pakistan. These results indicated that the welfare cost of risks is at least 10 % and can be 30–50 % of household income. As natural and manmade disasters can generate larger income volatilities than these income fluctuations, the welfare costs estimated here may be regarded as lower-bound estimates of the negative welfare impacts of natural or manmade disasters.

These analyses indicate the importance of ex ante risk management mechanisms and strategies in reducing the welfare costs of disasters. However, it is often difficult to popularize such mechanisms and strategies because the disasters are typically characterized by rare events and, even worse, they are often unexpected. Also, disaster risks may be correlated in nature, which could not be diversified away within a region or country. Thus, the aggregated macro welfare cost can be non-negligible. Indeed, Barro (2009) found that macro welfare loss due to disasters can be as large as 20 % of welfare. The significance of potential risk management implies two important issues. First, it is indispensable for government to strengthen national and regional level market and non-market insurance mechanisms against natural disasters. Wei and Jin (Chap. 14 in this volume) suggest that the Chinese central government implement more comprehensive risk reduction strategies to help deal with what have become almost yearly large scale disasters. Second, risk-coping strategies become important because even if households, communities, and governments adopted a variety of risk management strategies, a disaster can happen unexpectedly, causing serious negative impacts on household welfare.

Accordingly, against these unexpected natural disasters, it is indispensable for people to adopt ex post risk-coping strategies which are defined as strategies to reduce consumption fluctuations and to maintain desirable levels of livelihood. In general, the existing literature identifies the following different mechanisms for coping with risk. First, households can employ different market mechanisms, such as credit markets, to reallocate future resources to today's consumption, insurance market transactions to eliminate losses resulting from disasters, and ex post labor market participation to utilize market returns to human capital. Second, people can adopt self-insurance mechanisms such as consumption reallocation by cutting back luxury expenses while maintaining total calorie intakes and dis-saving financial and physical assets, i.e., utilization of precautionary saving.

Finally, households can adopt non-market insurance mechanisms such as public transfers from the government, and informal private aids from networks based on extended family, relatives, and communities. As Aldrich (2012), (see also Chap. 2 in this volume) has demonstrated, cohesive communities are better prepared for shocks, whether natural or technological. Neighborhoods where residents can draw on informal insurance and mutual aid can overcome collective action problems (such as potential looters or the need to work together to clean up affected areas) and increase the likelihood that residents will return to their homes. Against all crises, ex post risk-coping is indispensable. In his chapter on New Zealand's recent disasters, Leyton (in Chap. 7) underscored the "wait and see" problem when local businesses and residents were caught in a Catch-22 situation. Both sides would not commit resources to relocate and restart without information from the other. Research on social networks has shown that trusted sources can overcome this collective action problem and jump start the return process (Chamlee-Wright 2010).

Fig. 16.1 The community, the market, and the state in the economic system. *Source*: Hayami (2009)

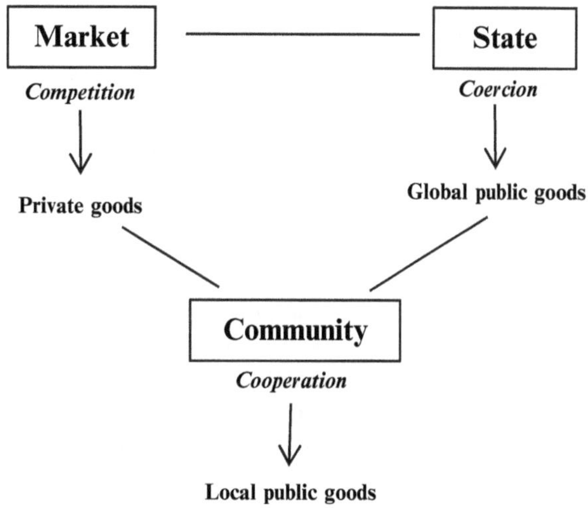

2.2 *The Market, State, and Community Triangle in Disaster Management and Coping*

The general risk management and coping strategies mentioned above imply the divided roles of market, state, and community as elaborated by Hayami (2009). As is shown in Fig. 16.1, the economic system is composed of three domains, i.e., market, state, and community, interacting with each other.

According to Hayami (2009), the market is the mechanism that coordinates profit-seeking individuals and firms through competition using price signals. Naturally, the market has an advantage in matching the demand for and supply of private tradable goods. Ando (in this volume) showed how market forces allowed the production networks in machinery industries to show strong resilience to the various exogenous shocks such as the Thailand floods and the 2011 3/11 disaster. The state, in contrast, is the mechanism that forces people to adjust their resource allocations by command of the government. Typically, the state plays an important role in supplying global or pure public goods. In contrast, the community is the mechanism that guides community members to voluntary cooperation based on intensive social interactions, facilitating supply of the local public goods such as the provision of reciprocal social safety nets, the conservation of commons, and the enforcement of informal transactions.

To address the roles of the market, the state, and the community in facilitating disaster management and coping, it will be useful to classify two different types of risks by the level at which they occur, i.e., idiosyncratic and aggregate risks. Idiosyncratic risks affect specific individuals and/or firms while aggregate shocks affect groups of households, an entire community and region, or a country as a whole. This distinction is important because the geographic level at which risks arise determines the effectiveness of market and non-market institutions in dealing with risk.

On the one hand, a risk that affects a specific individual can be traded with other people in the same insurance network through informal mutual insurance and a well-functioning formal insurance or credit market. In the last two decades, micro-development economists have shown that households have, to some extent, developed formal and informal risk-coping mechanisms against a wide variety of idiosyncratic risks (Townsend 1994). The community-based mutual insurance mechanism can be effective, provided that all the members contribute due informal insurance premiums, according to the principle of reciprocity dictated by customs and norms (Hayami 2009). The community can enforce the collection of due contributions from community members by means of the reputation/opprobrium/ostracism mechanisms. In short, the community can play an important role in weathering losses caused by natural disasters, if such losses are largely idiosyncratic.

Yet, according to the NatCatService data of one of the largest reinsurance companies, Munich Re, the proportion of insured losses of overall losses caused by disasters in the world is quite limited, around 20 % on average.[1] Currently, formal insurance mechanisms combating natural disasters are quite limited. Indeed, studies based on micro-data show the overall ineffectiveness of formal and informal insurance mechanisms in dealing with natural disasters (Kohara et al. 2006; Sawada and Shimizutani 2007, 2008).

On the other hand, a risk that affects an entire region cannot be insured within the region and thus community mechanisms can only function imperfectly. Natural, technological, and manmade disasters are likely to fall into this category of aggregate or covariate risks. As we have seen, efficient risk sharing mechanisms are likely to be absent, especially for a natural disaster as a rare, covariate event. In fact, the extent to which a risk is idiosyncratic or correlated depends considerably on the underlying causes. These risks should be covered by well-designed formal market or similar arrangements backed by the public enforcement mechanisms in which region-specific risks are diversified away across regions. If these mechanisms cannot work properly or are difficult to set, households are forced to insure themselves against shocks by using self-insurance measures. For example, by analyzing a 1998 survey of areas affected by Hurricane Mitch, Morduch (2004) found that for 21 % of households, the main response to the hurricane was not to use savings, nor to borrow money; the main response was a drastic reduction in consumption. This suggests that these households are constrained from borrowing against shocks. By investigating how victims of the Great Hanshin-Awaji (Kobe) earthquake in 1995 coped with their unexpected losses, Sawada and Shimizutani (2005) found that households without borrowing constraints can borrow and/or

[1] In the formal insurance market, the insurers need international reinsurance markets to pool disaster risks. Yet, it is known that reinsurance markets and trades of catastrophe (CAT) bonds are still thin.

dissave to respond to damages caused by the earthquake, while those under a constraint are unable to cope with housing losses effectively.

3 Towards Effective Disaster Risk-Coping and Regional Cooperation on Disaster Management

We draw out insights from previous studies to facilitate more effective disaster management. This can be accomplished by strengthening complementarities among the market functioning under the price signals, state enforcement mechanisms, and community informal insurance mechanisms. According to Kahn (2005), natural disasters occur in advanced and developing nations alike, but when a nation is democratized and has better governance, the number of casualties is drastically reduced. Such societies better communicate and share disaster risk information, develop early warning systems, and set up infrastructure and other risk management mechanisms to prevent or mitigate the impact of disasters. Poaponsakorn and Meethom (Chap. 5 in this volume) demonstrated in their exhaustive study that estimates from the World Bank were incomplete or inaccurate and that, while better data was available, it had yet to be fully utilized in ongoing research.

Because the insurance market for natural disasters is far from complete, the government plays an important role in disaster management and rehabilitation. For example, a report by the World Bank and United Nations (2010) described how Bangladesh, where frequent cyclones have affected several hundred thousand people, has significantly reduced the number of casualties by investing in emergency infrastructure such as improving its early warning system, which operates via radio, and building numerous cyclone shelters. Having noticed this, Yang (2008) used data on the storms around the world of the past 30-plus years to show that the economic damage has been enormous. This tells us that, to prepare ourselves for natural disasters, we should balance emergency information systems and infrastructure that prevent damage to people with market-based insurance systems that prevent economic damage. In a study of the Chuetsu Earthquake, Ichimura et al. (2006) found that earthquake insurance and public transfers had functioned quite well.

3.1 Innovative Ideas

There are a few emerging, innovative ideas which strengthen the complementarities among the market, the state and the community in the context of disaster management and coping. Here, we discuss social cohesion, transfers, microcredit and microinsurance.

3.1.1 Social Cohesion Strengthening Policies

A growing body of literature has emphasized that stronger community ties pre-disaster reduce the negative consequences of disasters and speed up the recovery process. Across disasters, culture, nationality, and time, better connections between individuals within disaster affected communities have made more effective recoveries possible (Nakagawa and Shaw 2004; Stuart-Menteath, Felicity n.d.; Cox and Perry 2011; Meyer 2013; Kage 2013; Tse et al. 2013). Research has underscored that it is possible to create social capital through a variety of deliberate policy instruments. These include moderated focus groups in which groups of residents meet regularly for dialogue and issues. In randomized field experiments scholars have demonstrated that it is possible to increase both specific and generalized levels of trust (Pronyk et al. 2008; Brune and Bossert 2009). Further, a number of other policies, including community currencies, time banking, and local festivals have been shown to deepen bonding and bridging social capital (Aldrich 2012). Societies with high levels of vulnerability and regular exposure to natural hazards should take seriously the role of social connections in mitigating damage and increasing collective efficiency before, during, and after crisis.

3.1.2 Transfers

In this volume Vathana, Oum, Kan, and Chervier looked at the role of ex-ante cash transfer programs that provided critical assistance to the poor in Cambodia, a developing country with a large rural population. They argued that "Cash transfer programs provide direct assistance in the form of cash to the poor. Ex-ante cash transfer programs can play a crucial role in encouraging poor households to invest in business rather than spending on food" (Chap. 3). This result is consistent with a study by De Mel et al. (2008) in which the authors provided randomized cash transfers to microenterprises in Sri Lanka. They found that cash transfers generated average real return to capital of 55–63 % per year, substantially higher than market interest rates. These studies can serve as a pilot program for broader programs across East Asia.

3.1.3 Microcredit

While researchers have long understood that the remarkable performance of microcredit programs is based on community enforcement mechanisms, new studies have identified multiple roles of microcredit. Poor households are not just struggling entrepreneurs using microcredit programs for business facilitation. They are sophisticated households seeking to manage expenses (consumption credit), cope with emergencies (disaster protection), and seize opportunities. Potentially, microcredit programs can play a role in disaster insurance. For example, most micro-finance institutions in Bangladesh introduced a flexible repayment system in 2002, which permits members to reschedule installments during disasters. Also, a Bangladesh microfinance institution, BURO Tangail, initiated a special loan program called "disaster loan" for disaster affected clients in the wake of the disastrous floods of 1998 (Wright and Hossain 2001). Such a loan program can function effectively as an ex post risk-coping instrument for disaster-affected individuals in poor regions.

3.1.4 Microinsurance

Another innovative idea is to use a new microinsurance program called "index insurance" or "parametric insurance contracts" which are written against specific aggregate events such as drought or flood defined and recorded at a regional level (Hazell 2003; Morduch 2004; Skees et al. 2004). This type of insurance pays out on storms that exceed a pre-designated speed, rainfall that falls short of a threshold level, and earthquakes that exceed a certain seismic intensity. It is an excellent system that alleviates the time and costs required by conventional indemnity-based insurance systems to assess damage.

As such, index insurance involves a number of positive aspects; they can cover the aggregate correlated events; they are affordable and accessible even to the poor; they are easy to implement and privately managed; and they are free from the moral hazard, adverse selection, and high transaction costs that have plagued traditional agricultural insurance contracts such as crop insurance schemes. Nakata (Chap. 10 in this volume) suggested that an index insurance scheme undertaken by local governments with ex post payments would be most desirable. The World Bank and other institutions have been piloting weather-based index insurance contracts in Morocco, Mongolia, Peru, Vietnam, Ethiopia, Guatemala, India, Mexico, Nicaragua, Romania, and Tunisia.

Since natural disasters are typically aggregate events, index insurance is thought to be an appropriate instrument to combat them. Yet, there are three major constraints to designing index-type insurance against natural disasters. First, natural disasters are often characterized by a rare event which makes it difficult to design actuarially fair insurance. Since obtaining historical data on the pattern of natural disasters is hard, it is almost impossible to set appropriate premiums for insurance.

Secondly, and related to the first issue, even if appropriate premiums are set, the poor who potentially should demand insurance against natural disasters may find it difficult to recognize the value of index-type insurance against natural disasters. This may be inevitable, because natural disasters are often characterized by unforeseen contingencies by their very nature, and because the poor seem often to be myopic, with high time-discount rates. Indeed, human beings do tend to ignore rare bad events (Camerer and Kunreuther 1989). Moreover, the existence of the "basis risk" with which an individual could incur damage but cannot be compensated sufficiently, will also deter demand for index insurance. This problem has been identified as an inevitable drawback of index insurance because index contracts essentially tradeoff basis risk for transaction costs (Morduch 2004; Hazell 2003).

Nakata et al. (2010) utilized a unique survey dataset collected jointly by the Research Institute of Economy, Trade and Industry (RIETI) of Japan and the Center for Agricultural Policy in Vietnam (CAP), which they call the RIETI-CAP survey. The dataset resurveyed of subsamples of the Vietnam Household Living Standards Survey (VHLSS) 2006 households. They employed hypothetical questions on avian influenza (AI), flood (FL), and drought index insurance in Vietnam. According to their analysis of this unique data set, a past experience dramatically increases the probability assessment of the event (10 and 100 times for AI and FL) and willingness to pay (WTP) for the insurance (30 % and 50 % for AI and FL). A first loss experience tends to have a large impact on the subjective loss probability, and consequently on the willingness to pay for insurance, especially for flooding insurance (both index and indemnity-based insurance). This indicates that it would be less likely for a household with no past loss experience to purchase flooding insurance, even if the insurance premium is actuarially fair in accordance with the loss probability model of the insurance supplier.

They also found that people may not behave in accord with the subjective expected utility framework as far as AI insurance is concerned. In other words, it is not clear that the subjective loss probability drives the behavior of the people concerning AI insurance. This is not very surprising, since AI involves mutations of viruses, and so there are possible unforeseen contingencies. This makes it harder to agree on the terms and conditions of insurance.

3.1.5 Index Insurance as a Mitigation Device in Human-Made Disasters

Miguel et al. (2004) used data from 41 countries in Africa from 1981 to 1999 to find a robust causality between drought, a type of natural disaster, and conflict, a type of human-made disaster. This signifies that preventative action taken against natural disasters could also prevent conflicts. Today, we are capable of issuing early warnings of drought risk based on rainfall measurements and vegetation indices obtained from satellite images. Accordingly, Miguel (2009) proposed a new type of foreign aid-Rapid Conflict Prevention Support (RCPS), which would reduce the risk of conflicts by using this information to estimate droughts and natural disasters, and by transferring aid immediately. Foreign aid provisions would be targeted to drought or other disaster vulnerable countries beforehand. Indeed, Botswana, Africa's economic superstar for the past 40 years, has been implementing a Drought Relief Program (DRP). It can safely be said that the drought insurance played an important role in its success (Miguel 2009).

3.1.6 Regional Index Insurance

Index insurance or parametric insurance can be designed for disaster risk pooling at the regional level. One example is the Caribbean Catastrophe Risk Insurance Facility (CCRIF), which is a parametric, multinational hazard insurance fund for hurricanes and earthquakes that works with the international reinsurance market and was established as the first of its kind in the world. Haiti was a member of the Facility, and after the Haiti Earthquake in January 2010, the government received \$7.75 m in earthquake insurance - around twenty times its premium—as soon as two weeks after the quake. While the amount is not necessarily significant, the Haiti government received insurance payouts very quickly, indicating the importance of preparing a new insurance system such as CCRIF.

Another example is the Pacific Disaster Risk Financing and Insurance Program which builds on the Pacific Catastrophe Risk Assessment and Financing Initiative (PCRAFI) through a joint initiative between the Secretariat of the Pacific Community (SPC/SOPAC) founded in 2007, the World Bank, and the Asian Development Bank, with financial support from the Government of Japan and the Global Facility for Disaster Reduction and Recovery (GFDRR). PCRAFI aims to enhance the disaster risk management and to reduce the financial vulnerability of the Pacific Island Countries (PICs) against natural disasters. It will do this by improving their financial response capacities while protecting their long term fiscal balances.

The PDRFI Program provides the PICs with tailor-made advisory services for disaster risk modeling and assessment tools, financial instruments for national disaster risk financing and insurance strategies, and catastrophe risk insurance market development.[2] There are three project components. The first component is institutional capacity-building for disaster risk financing through setting national disaster risk financing strategies, and technical assistance to design and implement their integrated financial strategy against natural disasters. The second component is Pacific disaster risk insurance market development, aiming to offer technical assistance to improve disaster risk insurance solutions in the Pacific. The final component is the Pacific Disaster Risk Financing and Insurance (PDRFI) Pilot Program which is piloting natural disaster derivatives aimed at serving as support measures for disaster prevention and disaster mitigation through a Public-Private Partnership (PPP). The Pacific Disaster Risk Financing and Insurance Program is the first of a series of applications of PCRAFI to be developed in disaster risk management and urban/infrastructure planning.

As part of Japan's international cooperation in disaster prevention, the Japanese government announced it would "establish an insurance system as natural disaster

[2] Countries receiving technical assistance in disaster risk financing and insurance through the PDRFI Program include Papua New Guinea (PNG), Fiji, the Solomon Islands, Vanuatu, Samoa, the Federal States of Micronesia (FSM), Tonga, Kiribati, the Republic of the Marshal Islands, Palau, the Cook Islands, Tuvalu, Nauru, Niue and Timor-Leste. The Pacific catastrophe risk insurance pilot was launched in November 2012 with Vanuatu, Tonga, the Marshall Islands, the Solomon Islands, and Samoa.

support in Pacific island countries" at the 6th Pacific Islands Leaders Meeting (PALM) held in May 2012. Accordingly, this program was established in collaboration with Pacific island countries (governments), the World Bank and private-sector insurance companies.

Let us also touch upon preparations for economic crises. The Group of 20 nations/regions (G20) and other meetings are discussing the installation of an early warning system that predicts and helps to counter the currency and financial crises that have occurred frequently since 1990. But as Rose and Spiegel (2011) pointed out, current research has not yet developed a sufficiently reliable early warning system. Preparations for economic crises, however, have been enhanced. In 2009, for example, the International Monetary Fund (IMF) established a new prevention facility against economic crises. In the East Asia region, the Chiang Mai Initiative (CMI), a bilateral currency swap agreement to be implemented in times of a currency crisis, expanded to a multilateral framework (CMIM) in 2010.

4 Policy Implications

Advanced nations can deal with a major disaster by managing their own domestic financial resources. But developing nations, which carry diverse risks of major disasters, have weak fiscal groundwork and are less tolerant of such risks. Different disasters tend to come in combination, as was the case with the Great East Japan Earthquake and conflicts in Africa.

First, it is imperative to develop formal mechanisms to diversify aggregate disaster risks at national and regional levels as shown in Fig. 16.2. Trung (Chap. 4 in this volume) stressed how Vietnam—as a developing country—can simultaneously benefit from and contribute to regional development and food security through a broader, regional framework. Noy (Chap. 11 in this volume) argued for a Global Fund for Disaster Risk Reduction which would effectively coordinate and pool resources across nations to create early warning systems and other mechanisms, such as retrofitting essential infrastructure, which would reduce vulnerability to hazard. We may need to elaborate on multi-country risk pooling schemes, i.e., regional funds, to cover sovereign disaster risk. Against natural disasters, regional level index insurance such as CCRIF and PDRFI can function effectively to support the disaster affected country with immediate liquidity in the aftermath of a catastrophic disaster, by using the insurance mechanism. Microcredit and microinsurance schemes can also enhance the disaster resilience of individual households and firms. While the regional index insurance schemes are based on PPP, the microcredit and insurance programs are supported by informal community enforcement mechanisms. Hence, complementarities among the market, the state, and the community will be the keys to success.

In the case of economic disasters, the Chiang Mai Initiative (CMI) has been and will be playing an important role. CMI is a bilateral or multilateral currency swap arrangement pooling foreign exchange reserves, and was designed as an ex post

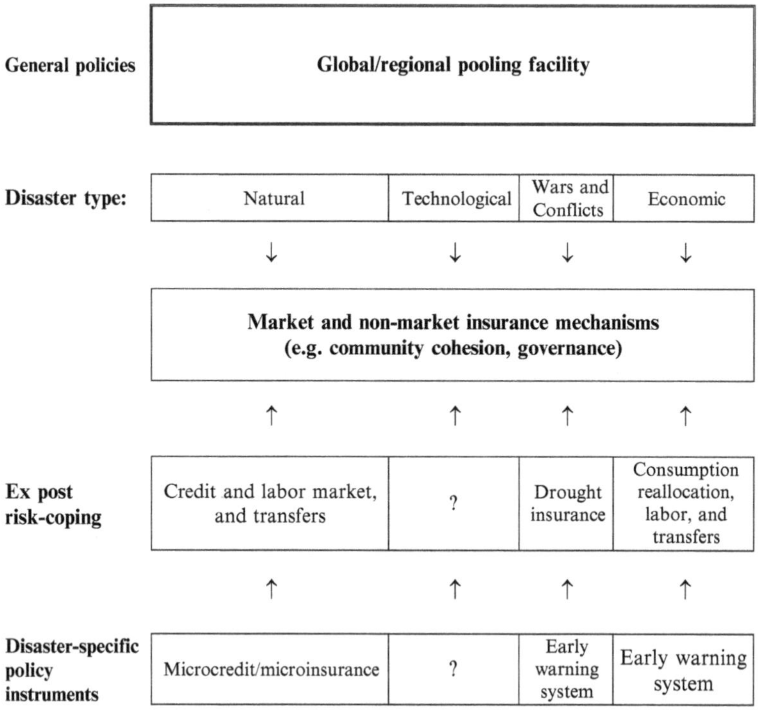

Fig. 16.2 Towards effective disaster risk-coping strategies and regional cooperation

coping mechanism against a financial crisis. Further development of Asian bond markets will also be indispensable because bond markets are composed of a large number of individual bond holders, and idiosyncratic risks can therefore be diversified away effectively. It is generally considered that bond markets form effective risk-sharing mechanisms. In order to diversify the shocks caused by disasters, developed bond markets can potentially play important roles.

To further improve national and regional risk management capabilities, a global system of pooling the risks of the four types of disasters would be effective for both developing and advanced nations needing to diversify the risks of disasters (see Fig. 16.2). In other words, we should also work on the securities and reinsurance markets to develop a global disaster insurance system that would encompass various regional frameworks such as CCRIF, PCRAFI, and CMIM beyond existing disaster types.

When we consider the actual form of such a system, there are numerous issues involved, such as whether it would be an institutionalized system like a disaster fund, or something more flexible such as a coordination forum. Lai and Tan (Chap. 16 in this volume) recommended that governments remain open to innovation and bottom up approaches even at the national level. Yet the Asian region has experienced diverse forms of disasters, including floods, typhoons, earthquakes, epidemics, and the financial crises of the late 1990s. It is worth pursuing reforms that undertake comprehensive preparations against the risks of a variety of risks in Asia and beyond. Changes to policy should strengthen social cohesion, ensure that markets are accessible by the most vulnerable, and improve governance and regulatory oversight. In doing so, policy makers, NGOs, and local residents alike will enhance their capacity to undertake recovery and generate resilience in their communities to disaster.

References

Aldrich, D. P. (2012). *Building resilience: Social capital in post-disaster recovery*. Chicago: University of Chicago Press.

Aldrich, D. P. (2013a). Rethinking civil society-state relations in Japan after the Fukushima incident. *Polity, 45*(2), 249–264.

Aldrich, D. P. (2013b). A normal accident or a sea-change? Nuclear host communities respond to the 3/11 disaster. *Japanese Journal of Political Science, 14*(2), 261–276.

Barro, R. J. (2009). Rare disasters, asset prices, and welfare costs. *American Economic Review, 99* (1), 243–264.

Brune, N., & Bossert, T. (2009). Building social capital in post-conflict communities: Evidence from Nicaragua. *Social Science & Medicine, 68*, 885–893.

Cabinet Office. (2011). *Monthly economic report (in Japanese, Getsurei Keizai Houkoku)*, Cabinet Office, The Government of Japan, March 2011.

Camerer, C. F., & Kunreuther, H. (1989). Decision process for low probability events: Policy implications. *Journal of Policy Analysis and Management, 8*(4), 565–592.

Cavallo, E., & Noy, I. (2009). *The economics of natural disasters - a survey*, Working Paper. Washington, D.C.: Inter-American Development Bank.

Chamlee-Wright, E. (2010). *The cultural and political economy of recovery: Social learning in a post-disaster environment*. London and New York: Routledge.

Cox, R. S., & Perry, K. M. (2011). Like a fish out of water: reconsidering disaster recovery and the role of place and social capital in community disaster resilience. *American Journal of Community Psychology, 48*(3–4), 395–411.

De Mel, S., McKenzie, D., & Woodruff, C. (2008). Returns to capital in microenterprises: Evidence from a field experiment. *Quarterly Journal of Economics, 123*(4), 1329–1372.

Hayami, Y. (2009). Social capital, human capital, and community mechanism: Toward a consensus among economists. *Journal of Development Studies, 45*(1), 96–123.

Hazell, P. (2003). Potential role for insurance in managing catastrophic risk in developing countries. *Proceedings of the World Bank Conference on Financing the Risks of Natural Disasters*, June 2–3, 2003.

Ichimura, H., Sawada, Y., & Shimizutani, S. (2006). Risk sharing against an earthquake: the case of Yamakoshi village. Mimeo, Faculty of Economics, University of Tokyo.

Kage, R. (2013). Social capital and the future of disaster recovery research. *Risk, Hazards, and Crisis in Public Policy, 4*(1), 6–10.

Kahn, M. E. (2005). The death toll from natural disasters: The role of income, geography, and institutions. *Review of Economics and Statistics, 87*(2), 271–284.

Kellenberg, D. K., & Mobarak, A. M. (2011). The economics of natural disasters. *Annual Review of Resource Economics, 3*(1), 297–312.

Kohara, M., Ohtake, F., & Saito, M. (2006). On effects of the Hyogo earthquake on household consumption: A note. *Hitotsubashi Journal of Economics, 47*(2), 219–28.

Meyer, M. (2013). Social capital and collective efficacy for disaster resilience. Unpublished Ph.D. Dissertation submitted to the Colorado State University in Fort Collins, Colorado.

Miguel, E. (2009). *Africa's turn?* Cambridge: MIT.

Miguel, E., Satyanath, S., & Sergenti, E. (2004). Economic shocks and civil conflict: An instrumental variables approach. *Journal of Political Economy, 112*(4), 725–753.

Morduch, J. (2004). Micro-insurance: The next revolution? In A. Banerjee, R. Benabou, & D. Mookherjee (Eds.), *What have we learned about poverty?* Oxford: Oxford University Press.

Nakagawa, Y., & Shaw, R. (2004). Social capital: Missing link to disaster recovery. *International Journal of Mass Emergencies and Disasters, 22*(1), 5–34.

Nakata, H., Sawada, Y., & Tanaka, M. (2010). *Entropy characterisation of insurance demand: Theory and evidence*, RIETI Discussion Paper 10-E-009.

Pronyk, P.M., Harpham, T., Busza, J., Phetla, G., Morison, L.A., Hargreaves, J.R., et al. (2008). Can social capital be intentionally generated? A randomized trial from rural South Africa. *Social Science & Medicine, 67*: 1559–1570.

Rose, A. K., & Spiegel, M. M. (2011). *Cross-country causes and consequences of the crisis: An update*, Federal Reserve Bank of San Francisco Working Paper Series 2011-02. Federal Reserve Bank of San Francisco.

Sawada, Y. (2007). The impact of natural and manmade disasters on household welfare. *Agricultural Economics, 37*(s1), 59–73.

Sawada, Y., & Shimizutani, S. (2005). *Are people insured against natural disasters? Evidence from the Great Hanshin-Awaji (Kobe) earthquake in 1995*', CIRJE DP F-314, University of Tokyo, Faculty of Economics.

Sawada, Y., & Shimizutani, S. (2007). Consumption insurance against natural disasters: Evidence from the Great Hanshin-Awaji (Kobe) earthquake. *Applied Economics Letters, 14*(4), 303–306.

Sawada, Y., & Shimizutani, S. (2008). How do people cope with natural disasters? Evidence from the Great Hanshin-Awaji (Kobe) earthquake in 1995. *Journal of Money, Credit and Banking, 40*(2–3), 463–488.

Skees, J., Varangis, P., Larson, D. F., & Siegel, P. (2004). Can financial markets be tapped to help poor people cope with weather risks? In S. Dercon (Ed.), *Insurance against poverty*. Oxford: Oxford University Press.

Strömberg, D. (2007). Natural disasters, economic development, and humanitarian aid. *Journal of Economic Perspectives, 21*(3), 199–222.

Stuart-Menteath, F. (n.d.). Social capital: A concept for disaster recovery. Unpublished Ph.D. Dissertation for University of Brighton, UK.

Townsend, R. M. (1994). Risk and insurance in village India. *Econometrica, 62*(3), 539–591.

Tse, C., Wei, J., & Wang, Y. (2013). *Social capital and disaster recovery: Evidence from Sichuan Earthquake in 2008*, Working Paper 344. Washington D.C.: Center for Global Development.

World Bank and United Nations. (2010). *Natural hazards, unnatural disasters*. Washington, D.C.: World Bank.

Wright, G. A. N., & Hossain, M. (2001). *BURO, Tangail's approach to product development: A case study, mimeographed*. Kenya: MicroSave Nairobi.

Yang, D. (2008). Coping with disaster: The impact of Hurricanes on international financial flows, 1970-2002. *B. E. Journal of Economic Analysis & Policy, 8*(1), 1–45 (Advances), Article 13.

Index

D.P. Aldrich et al. (eds.), *Resilience and Recovery in Asian Disasters*, Risk, Governance and Society 18, DOI 10.1007/978-4-431-55022-8

W

MIX
Papier aus verantwortungsvollen Quellen
Paper from responsible sources
FSC® C105338

If you have any concerns about our products,
you can contact us on
ProductSafety@springernature.com

In case Publisher is established outside the EU,
the EU authorized representative is:
Springer Nature Customer Service Center GmbH
Europaplatz 3, 69115 Heidelberg, Germany

Printed by Libri Plureos GmbH
in Hamburg, Germany